John Ruskin's Politics and Natural Law

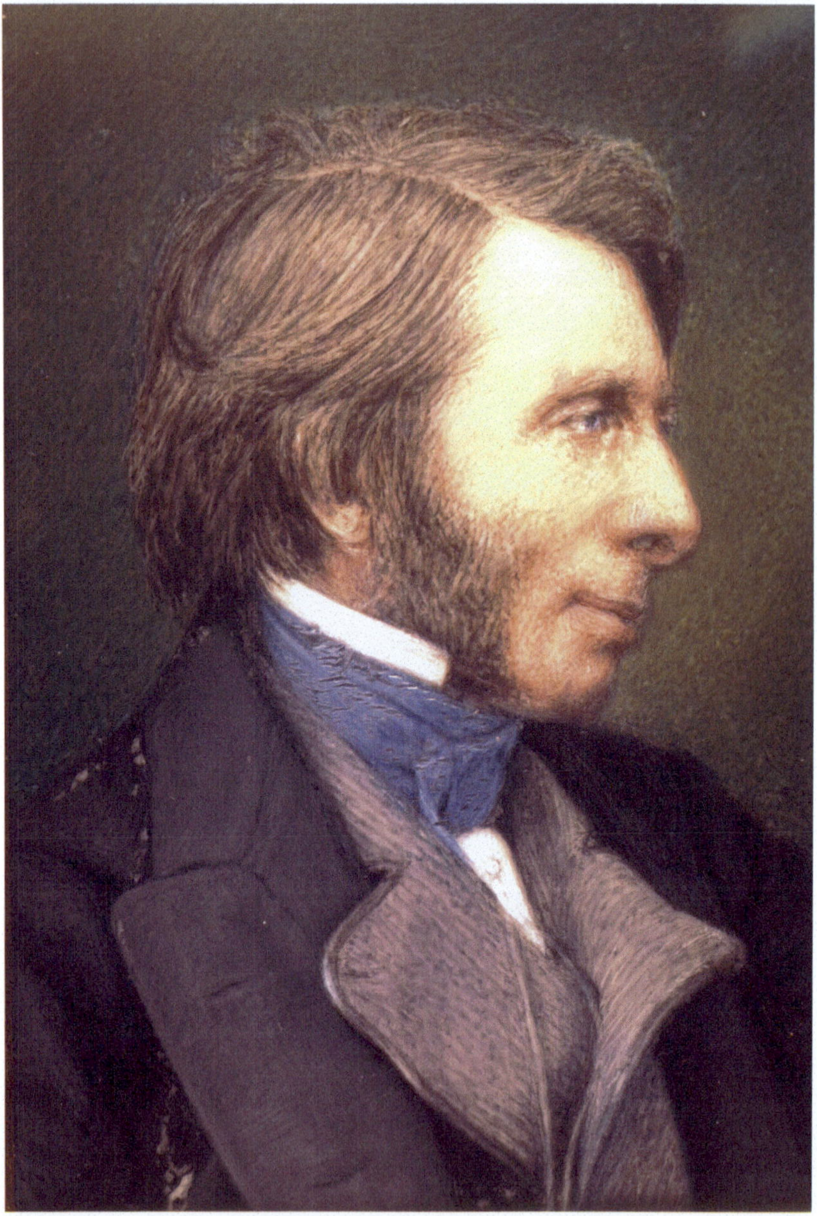

Front Piece. John Ruskin. Miniature on ivory, by J. C. Berry
Credit: Ruskin Foundation (Ruskin Library, Lancaster University)

Graham A. MacDonald

John Ruskin's Politics and Natural Law

An Intellectual Biography

palgrave
macmillan

Graham A. MacDonald
Parksville, BC, Canada

ISBN 978-3-030-10181-7 ISBN 978-3-319-72281-8 (eBook)
https://doi.org/10.1007/978-3-319-72281-8

Cover illustration: PAINTING / Alamy Stock Photo

Printed on acid-free paper

This Palgrave Macmillan imprint is published by Springer Nature
The registered company is Springer International Publishing AG
The registered company address is: Gewerbestrasse 11, 6330 Cham, Switzerland

In Memoriam

William H. McNeill
(1917–2016)

The original version of this book was revised. An erratum to this book can be found at (DOI 10.1007/978-3-319-72281-8_9)

Preface

As many readers of Ruskin know, coming to terms with his discursive style is an important task. His biographers and commentators have wrestled with this difficulty. Even such a warm admirer as young Arnold Toynbee complained to a friend about the abuses of 'word painting' and that 'the worst are those interminable pages of mere word-daubing which even Ruskin is not guiltless of.'[1] One may assume, however, that such wordiness was less frowned upon in Victorian times when there were fewer daily means of appeal for the citizen's undivided attention. For thousands of Victorians and Edwardians it was a forgivable trait and Ruskin was widely read. All later students of his work have come to appreciate that the magnificent edition of his collected works prepared by Edward T. Cook and Alexander Wedderburn, with its extended commentaries, references and biographical segments, represents one of the great sources for Victorian studies. Former Oxford students of Ruskin, they saw through what is by far the most detailed and useful edition of any of the major Victorians. When supplemented by the far-flung archive of a vast number of personal and professional letters, one has at hand a unique corpus as an aid to the understanding of a most unusual and creative life. In styling the present work as an 'intellectual biography' the ambitions are modest, for there are many good formal biographies of Ruskin. The format is used mainly as a support for an effort to trace the unfolding of a specific manner of thinking about things which, I argue, came to inform Ruskin's general outlook. Aspects of his biography are also referenced to shed light on the several unresolved tensions in his thought and life. While I do not pursue at any length the on-going interest in the nature of his mental disorders, these matters are mentioned where appropriate and are important to keep in mind with respect to the late work particularly.

The lines of his political thought I associate with the concept of natural law, an ancient concept but one which started to come under modification in early seventeenth-century Europe, as new fashions of scientific enquiry started to emerge. The word 'law' was much used by Ruskin and its connotation usually retained the classical sense of natural law, with moral implications or with that sense of 'fate' and 'fortuna' so popular in medieval thought and imagery. 'Fortuna' is implied in the title of that most extraordinary of his late works, *Fors Clavagira*. It may be said that the natural law tradition in western societies, in its social applications, has never died out but has rather shared the stage with modern empirical and national versions of law administration. Its effects are far from evident at the national and sub-national level in some countries where arbitrary and shifting rules marked by *Realpolitik* or by pragmatic decisions are all too evident. Its abstract appeal, like that of the word 'democracy', can be much greater than its success in practice. The concept of 'law' Ruskin usually endowed with a meaning in line with pre-Hobbesian versions of natural law, which is to say versions represented in ancient Greek or Roman texts, Biblical texts or medieval Christian works.

The emergence of natural law, as a more formal principle in Ruskin's thought, came about gradually through his shifting views on art, religion and history. It shows early, if reluctantly, in his youthful studies of science, particularly geology and chemistry, where he quickly came to concede that the Bible had great limitations as a source of reliable scientific earth and biological history. It was after his turn to economics and political reform in the 1850s that the pluralistic implications of natural law came to dominate his thinking in league with his revived interest in the works of the ancient Greeks and Romans, the *Apocrypha* and works of the early Church Fathers. This was accompanied by the adoption of a starker kind of non-denominational Christian belief, this resulting from a steady departure from his early upbringing in the ways of evangelical Protestantism.

In his insightful commentary on the history and theory of natural law, A.P. d'Entrèves cautioned students of the topic about adopting easy generalizations about the term or of drawing too rapid a parallel in its use by practitioners widely separated in time. The presumed reasons for the seventeenth- century separation of natural law into distinct scientific and humanistic channels have now become less convincing, the observable world confused once again in the age of Einstein. Previously measurable concepts such as motion, time and space have themselves become unstable. In the humanities, the reign of 'positivism' has come under a cloud with even well-armed opponents of the role of natural law in legal studies coming around to the suggestion that there may be elements of the old classical aspects of 'reasonableness' which need to be acknowledged in modern practice.[2] In considering Ruskin as a practical proponent of natural law, somewhat in the style of Burke, we encounter a man who never entertained the possibility that the 'moral' could ever be usefully separated out from the 'natural' in any sphere of human endeavour, including the scientific.

By invoking the name of Burke, we also invoke a view of history. Elizabeth Helsinger has commented insightfully on the way in which Ruskin, as an historian, has generally been regarded, which is to say, not very favourably.[3] He was, to be sure, a man who made use of history as an argumentative tool and by which to make moral judgements. Natural law, or God's law (or '*Fors*' or 'fate' or 'fortune') is used in his writings like a moral sledge hammer, driving home veritable truths of old. The degree, however, to which Ruskin remained captive to a particularly evangelical version of moral and allegorical history, I believe to be another question entirely. To contend that Ruskin often read history with a view to making practical moral judgements about present circumstances is no doubt true. To see his reading of history as taking only the form of an account of the endless implications of the Biblical 'fall' leaves his other approaches to history to one side.[4] His early mastery of Homer and Scott left lasting imprints, which fostered an appreciation for the grander cycles of history and for displays of cultural pluralism. Richard Titlebaum has appropriately pointed to the parallels between Ruskin and the approach to history of Giambatista Vico.[5] From one of his most admired sources, Walter Scott's novels, Ruskin learned to read history through the portrayal of the full-blooded experience of others, imaginatively conceived by one who made a disciplined use of historical documents.[6] Ruskin's appreciation of the role of 'imagination' in the writer's craft approximates Vico's term '*fantasia*'.[7]

An attempt to come to terms with the legitimacy of different moralities embedded in diverse cultures is a marked feature of the late works, accompanied by the articulation of political principles appropriate to such recognition. While works such as *The Stones of Venice* have usually been the focus for those commenting on his historical views, I have drawn much on his 1873 lectures, *Val D'Arno*, to illustrate his adoption of more rigorous enquiry, designed to answer some specific questions. Here, some of his main statements about natural law occur, along with an openness towards pluralistic cultural thinking, features which no doubt owe much to his contemporary friendship with the Oxford philologist, Fredrich Max

Müller. These lectures have not attracted a great deal of attention from Ruskin commentators. As lectures, they were unusual in being closely written out by hand before presentation. In his attempt to explain the emergence of a Christian style of art in Florence, at a particular time, the lectures drew much on Sismondi and Villani. If Ruskin ever attempted to become a more proper historian, it was probably in this series.

In stressing Ruskin's gathering appreciation for the role of 'cultural pluralism' in politics, it is important to note that he did not solve, nor try to solve, the many shades of difficulty which surround this question, or the more complex question of how such pluralism relates to cultural relativism, a question much in the air in modern scholarship.[8] He did not see a conflict between the universal suggestions implied by natural law and the facts that human societies were, by degree, culture-bound by their times and circumstances. He would have understood the way in which Shirley Letwin outlined the importance of history as an emergent factor in the classical world, as he understood the same principle in the works of Richard Hooker.[9] The stability of the world was something to be accepted in its mystery while the phenomena of the world exhibited on-going change within that larger unity.

The question of the character of Ruskin's political conservatism is also raised. It has been suggested by Robert Hewison that his toryism was of the 'ultra' kind.[10] The argument is well made but I find reasons to qualify the claim on a number of fronts, developed within this volume. His radicalism in politics was of the Red Tory kind but it contained a certain socialist fragment which drew early supporters of the labour movement to him. It was a fragment with few modern welfare state implications, however, and, as such, it remained largely inspirational to his contemporaries. The practical route that Ruskin actually chose, along with his class strictures, was of little interest to them. What did interest Ruskin has since become of greater moment, not just with respect to the garden city movement but also through his back-to-the land approach. In his own mind, a return to the land was not meant to extoll the virtues of getting-away-from-it-all as much as altering the laws of the nation with respect to land management and offering a critique of seemingly endless economic growth. His method was often one of advancing cultural and natural history education. It is notable that the first property given over to the new National Trust in 1895, was a property in Wales, the Cliff of Light (*Dinas Oleu*), at Barmouth, originally given to the Guild of St. George in 1874 by Fanny Talbot. From the perspective of the twenty-first century, the most modern thing about Ruskin is arguably his environmentalism, given his interest in air and water quality and in reducing the 'human footprint' on the land.

Finally, this study considers Ruskin's politics from the standpoint of the ways in which his thought conforms or deviates from that English tradition of politics informed by 'the politics of imperfection'.[11] The origins of that tradition Quinton located in the events of the Tudor period. Ruskin's reading of the formidable Elizabethan theologian, Richard Hooker, played an important role in grounding him in the natural law, one he found useful in thinking about the proper civic route to the fostering of good lives. As a point of view, it contrasted strongly with the dominant philosophical positivism of his day.[12]

Parksville, BC, Canada Graham A. MacDonald

Notes

1. Cited in F.C. Montague, *Arnold Toynbee* (Baltimore: Johns Hopkins University, 1889), 27.
2. See the appendices in A.P. d'Entrèves, *Natural Law: An Introduction to Legal Philosophy.* Rev. ed. Introduction by Cary J. Neederman. (New Brusnwick: Transaction Publishers, 1994).
3. Elizabeth K. Helsinger, *Ruskin and the Art of the Beholder* (Cambridge: Harvard University Press, 1982), Ch. 5.
4. See Judith Stoddart, 'Conjuring the Necromantic Evidence of History' in her *Ruskin's Culture Wars* (Charlottesville: University Press of Virginia, 1998), 108–12.
5. Richard Titlebaum, *Three Victorian View of the Italian Renaissance,* (New York: Garland Publishing, 1987), 20–21.
6. See Stephen Bann, *Romanticism and the Rise of History* (New York: Twayne, 1995), 23–25, 37; Isaiah Berlin, *The Crooked Timber of Humanity* (London: Fontana Press, 1991), 49–69.
7. See Isaiah Berlin, *Against the Current: Essays in the History of Ideas* (London: Pimlico, 1997), 98–9, 104–5.
8. For a lucid exploration of these questions, see Steven Lukes, *Liberals and Cannibals: The Implications of Diversity* (London: Verso, 2017).
9. Shirley Letwin, 'Nature, History and Morality', in R.S. Peters, ed., *Nature and Conduct.* (London: Macmillan, 1975), 229–50.
10. Robert Hewison, 'Notes on the Construction of The Stones of Venice', in Robert Rhodes, and Del Ivan Janik, eds. *Studies in Ruskin: Essays in Honour of Van Akin Burd* (Athens: Ohio State University Press, 1982) 131–52.
11. Anthony Quinton, *The Politics of Imperfection* (London: Faber and Faber, 1978).
12. Noel Annan, *The Curious Strength of Positivism in English Political Thought* (London: Oxford University Press, 1959).

'Let us all share the same lot: if any miss let all bear it.'
—Motto of the Frith Guilds in the time of King Athelstan, c. 930 A.D.

Acknowledgements

On the long road to completion of this book many debts have been incurred, first to my parents, who, as with their own, were unfailingly supportive of education for their children. As an undergraduate at Waterloo Lutheran University (as it then was), I was put onto the scent of political thought, not by a professor but by a fellow student, Barry Bartmann, who went on to a fine teaching and writing career at the University of Prince Edward Island. At the University of Western Ontario, I owe thanks to Professor William H. Stockdale, who first brought Ruskin to my attention as a person of interest. Professor Frederick A. Dreyer, a Burke scholar and a close student of Methodism, advised that a knowledge of the old poor laws would be important with respect to Ruskin. The pleasures and benefits of Wallace K. Ferguson's seminars on the Renaissance and his many writings have been lasting rewards. Graham Murray of the Political Science Department was a regular source of stimulation, as were Robert Sansom, Hugh Henderson, Susan Brooke, Manuel Prutschi, Jerry Mulcahy, William McKerchur and others who gathered at the CPR Hotel tap room. In Winnipeg, among other members of the Aberdeen Club, I owe thanks to Robert Coutts, editor of *Manitoba History* and a fine Orwell scholar, for many conversations on the pitfalls of political thought and the perplexities of heritage conservation. The encouragement of Leslie Marsh at the University of British Columbia has been much appreciated as have the extended conversations at 'Buzzards' in Calgary with many of my past associates in Parks Canada. In England, the staff at the Ruskin Library and Archives of Lancaster University, at the Bodleian Library, Oxford, the Sheffield Museum and at the Brantwood Trust, Lake District, have all been unfailing in their service and courtesy. Thanks to Dr. Stella Panayotova of The Fitzwilliam Museum, Cambridge, for observations on Ruskin's medieval manuscripts. For their kind provision of photos and editorial advice I am indebted to Dr. Cynthia Gamble of London, UK, Tom Stapledon of Liverpool, UK, and Peter Blair of Chamonix Mont Blanc, France. For permission to quote from her translation of Latin passages from the *Tractatus* of Henry Totting of Oyta, I thank Dr. Annabel Brett, University of Cambridge. To my editors at Palgrave Macmillan, Megan Laddusaw and Christine Pardue, I owe special thanks for their encouragement and always helpful guiding hands.

Contents

List of Figures

CHAPTER 1

Introduction

I

In Isobel Colgate's splendid *fin de siècle* novel, *The Shooting Party*, the pastimes of aristocrats in the Oxfordshire countryside of 1913 are portrayed amidst their crumbling conventions and illusions. During the day's hunting episodes, Olivia Lilburn finds herself walking next to Lionel Stephens who is carrying a pocket edition of Ruskin. 'I love Ruskin,' exclaims Olivia, 'Even when I think he is talking nonsense. I love the sound of it.'[1]

The episode well encapsulates Ruskin's great difficulty as a writer in his own time and ours. It is a commonplace of Ruskin commentary that he was a brilliant word painter but that the interspersed 'nonsense' caused critics and readers alike to qualify their admiration. This was true concerning his main writings on art and architecture and also his later social tracts. Writing came easily to Ruskin, too easily perhaps. With parental encouragement, he started to write when very young and it became as habitual as his sketching. A child of privilege, he was soon published through connections with such as the Rev. George Croly and William H. Harrison, but without the benefit of much editorial guidance.[2] The main exception arose from the close-watching eye of his father whose criticisms the son took seriously. As he matured, he usually bent to the occasional censorial wishes of the father out of respect or even agreement. The larger lack of editorial discipline, however, complicated the reception of his writings and often became the source of negative comment. Ruskin himself was often the

G. A. MacDonald, *John Ruskin's Politics and Natural Law*,
https://doi.org/10.1007/978-3-319-72281-8_1

source of such criticism when he brought out new editions of past work. It is only in a few cases, such as the youthful children's tale, *The King of the Golden River*, or his most effective piece of social criticism, *Unto This Last*, that he managed to stick to the point with rigour. After 1870, the writing often took on a stream-of-consciousness aspect which, for many readers, robbed them of coherence, seriousness of purpose or else merely left them confused.[3]

The defects of the late writings were not entirely absent in the earlier ones on art and architecture, but in the early works, the language colour, his worship of nature, the impressive visuals, all served to attract readers such as Olivia Lilburn. His asides and preoccupations with the morality of art were more forgivable than in the later works where his didactic tone and social preaching often gave offence. A man of wealth attacking the conventional wisdom of the prevailing economic order was bound to generate a good deal of heat or accusations of hypocrisy. Even so measured a man as Anthony Trollope became impatient with Ruskin's outbursts in print.[4]

Ruskin's political and economic thought emerged hesitantly and in a fragmentary way, rising out of the more firmly established writings. In their final form, his social proposals were stark but perhaps not as unfinished as has sometimes been suggested. To those contemporaries who paid attention at all, his ideas were usually considered well intended but eccentric or tangential to the main currents of late Victorian political reform. In politics, religion and ethics, he was aware that he was fighting rear-guard actions against certain popular and learned accounts of the tale of progress associated with nineteenth-century thought and the more distant roots of its underlying rationalism which he thought he found first-nourished in the Italian Renaissance. His resistance was not waged against the resultant new sciences, as such, for he was not hostile to science; nor was it waged against the cause of 'enlightenment' as such. His objection concerned what he took to be inappropriate intrusions of one dominant account of science, that associated with late eighteenth-century 'utilitarianism', into other distinct modes of understanding.

There had been earlier manifestations of this recognition of inappropriate category intrusion, associated with his great love of geology, a study he took up early in life. Fully aware of the revolution in that field accomplished by Charles Lyell and his forerunners, and reinforced by conversation with the young Darwin, he did not reject their findings outright. He made use of their conclusions to refine his understanding of the Bible, concluding that, with respect to geological earth history, it was not a credible source. It remained, however, a valuable ethical source, if not the only source, of social wisdom. Before the age of 20, he understood that it was important not to confuse the proper study of geology with the proper study of ethics and religion.

The results were not so clear cut in terms of his general religious outlook. As with many of his contemporaries, such as James A. Froude, Mark Rutherford or Alfred Tennyson, Ruskin became a doubter and underwent many alterations in belief. Unlike the rebellious Froude, who was drummed out of Oxford over his anti-Christian views unveiled in his novel, *The Nemesis of Faith*, Ruskin always wore his scepticism more discretely and found a way to deal with the Christian tradition in more traditional or pragmatic ways. As a social critic, he adopted a comprehensive but less certain view of history than that offered by many of the leading eighteenth- and nineteenth-century lights. He is more easily associated with representatives of what Geoffrey Clive called 'the Romantic Enlightenment', people who made room for the shifting currents of history, for doubt, poetry, art and traditions as important factors in human experience.[5] As an outlook, Clive characterized it as one marked by a tension between two grand sources of anxiety: the possibility of the 'inexistence of God' and that of the possibility of the 'dehumanization' of the autonomous individual.[6] As an antidote to this tension, the romantic looked to the comfort of the arts, poetry, the heroic, the chivalric and the sentimental aspects of history. It was these which provided vectors of social stability. Even if those traditions were partly, or even mainly, illusional, the proof was found in the experience of the tried and true. Such durable illusions provided a flexible retreat for the workings of natural law over the cooler and harder scientific rationalism which informed the minds of many in the eighteenth century who, by degree, furthered their own illusional myths of progress. Similarly, the doubting romantic of the nineteenth century found ways to resist the mounting 'positivism' of his times.

Ruskin's political thought is not easily separated from his views on economics and in this respect it is not exceptional to much literature of the period. Many theorists tended to write in terms of 'political economy'. The incompleteness of his work in this direction is owing partly to the timing of his attempt to take up social criticism in the mid-1850s. Despite some coherent first efforts, after 1863 his emotional and mental difficulties started to complicate his life on a more regular basis and his ability to take large literary projects to completion declined sharply. Despite much creativity in the later years, the contemplated treatise on political economy never appeared, nor did many other promised projects. Since his death, many commentators have pondered the nature of his personal conflicts and their effects upon his work and private life.[7]

He made a mark with *Unto This Last* in 1862, based on four previously published essays in *The Cornhill Magazine*. This work set out the substance of his main critique of those he called the 'orthodox political economists', all of whose works were imbued with what he considered to be the false premises of 'utilitarianism'. Subsequent essays of 1863, later published as *Munera Pulveris*, further refined his economic premises. These were followed by a series of letters of 1866, first exchanged with Thomas Dixon, and published as *Time and Tide*. This work advanced things along political lines, both romantic and conservative. In unveiling his plans for his social experiment, the Guild of St. George, in the public letters known as *Fors Clavigera*, he drew back considerably from *Time and Tide's* essentially statist model of comprehensive reform in favour of the small-scale and the local, what today would be considered 'green' models of enterprise. His agricultural commune and associated institutions were theorized within the context of what was allowable under the British Constitution. In the *Charter* and *Oath*, there was nothing very radical or revolutionary. Its adherents were asked to subscribe to principles sanctioned by an older form of natural law, one with roots in ancient classical, patristic and medieval ethical premises with their attendant visions of the good life.[8]

In the present study, it is argued that an account of natural law informed Ruskin's social and political thought, endorsing a distinctive version of human rights and obligations which contrasted strongly with post-Hobbsian, utilitarian and secular liberal counterparts in which an individual's 'subjective rights' are understood to precede the claims of the general good.[9] This posited modern separation, in Sandel's words came about as follows: 'Only in a universe empty of *telos*, such as seventeenth century philosophy affirmed, is it possible to conceive a subject apart from and prior to its purposes and ends.' Such a world view 'ungoverned by a purposive order' left principles of justice 'open to human construction' and 'conceptions of the human good to individual choice'.[10] The emergence of such views was subsequently resisted by many but it gradually came to exercise a wide influence during the Enlightenment and after. For Ruskin, 'the right and the good' remained closely fused and he denied the validity of attempts to establish the precedence of one over the other by those who resorted to complex metaphysical debate, especially 'German' metaphysical debate.[11] He seldom spoke of 'liberty' or 'rights' without also couching the discussion in terms of parallel obligations, stressing a view of humans as culturally situated personalities in the first instance. Thus in *Val D'Arno* he discussed 'libertas' in its older classical and Christian sense (as opposed to Mill's sense), as 'deliverance from the slavery of passion'. Once having learned 'how to rule our passions' and when 'certain that our conduct is right', it remains only to 'persist in that conduct against all resistance'.[12] Regardless of time and place, then, the first consideration for maintenance of any proper civil association is the fostering of acceptable public conduct in a secure setting, a contention which assumes acceptable norms.[13] Just how well Ruskin managed to balance a conception of society grounded in natural law with his wish to make greater room for social pluralism will be a question of interest in the later stages of this work.[14]

Natural law has a long and dignified history as a term, dating back to ancient Greece. The idea that there was a built-in form of 'reason' animating humankind, guiding all matters and conditions, achieved considerable precision during the middle Roman Empire through the writings of Cicero, among others. Its essence was well captured by Emperor Justinian in his important codification of Roman law undertaken in the sixth century. His approach, says d'Entrèves, was to make 'an appeal to the intrinsic dignity of the law rather than to its power of compulsion'.[15] 'Of all subjects,' says Justinian, 'none is more worthy of study than the authority of Laws, which happily disposes things divine and human, and puts an end to iniquity.'[16]

Natural law went through many iterations in Christian writings of the Middle Ages, reaching an apex in the works of Thomas Aquinas.[17] The universal qualities of natural law were both dignified and sufficiently abstract to provide a suitable mechanism to explain the workings of both the spiritual and tangible worlds of human experience.

This had become problematical in seventeenth-century Europe, many argue, as the term started to split into two streams, one scientific and one social, a gradual response to the important advances made in astronomy since the time of Copernicus. The scientific aspect of natural law purportedly dealt with the underlying determinants of observable things of the world in their inanimate or living developmental sense. The social aspect of natural law continued to be concerned with understanding the rules of human conduct; but now it might be supplemented by a more radical view of human nature, one that thought it more profitably studied through the lens of a scientific-sounding knowledge of behaviourism. Throughout the seventeenth century, the uses of 'reason' were explored but often in the context of a debate between 'ancients and moderns' depending on how much of the 'new learning' was embraced by a given practitioner. Thomas Hobbes increasingly embraced the new scientific position after 1651.[18]

Natural law remained a useful organizing idea throughout the eighteenth century but it had many different connotations. Jeremy Bentham became the strong advocate for the view that natural law had lost its usefulness as a covering term in matters social. The Roman Catholic Church remained the main defender of natural law in all its applications. Bentham's position, however, influenced many in the nineteen century who favoured the dominant value of empirical or 'positive' law in court proceedings. Positivists recognized tangible laws of a statute kind only, originated by a human hand, and not those sanctioned by traditions rooted in the mists of time or by Biblical sanction. The Benthamite position, then, was far removed from early seventeenth-century reformers, such as Grotius, who tried to advance, in more secular terms, the older external basis of natural law.

Grotius and other Dutch thinkers reflected the economic and social changes current in western Europe and they expanded upon the work of sixteenth-century Spanish Catholic theologians who had argued for versions of international law fortified by the older traditions. The New World encounters had stimulated radical thinking among the Canon school of theology at Salamanca about the legal requirements and human status of the indigenous populations of the Caribbean and South America.[19] The thrust of the revived concepts of natural law was that there could be detected in nature overarching principles of a law for all, regardless of the apparent relativism of specified historical social structures, including seemingly primitive ones. These new schools came to employ the idea of reason in the direction of more secularly understood universal natural rights, which were eventually consciously proclaimed during the course of the American and French revolutions, and again in the twentieth century with the United Nations Charter and International Declaration on Human Rights. Such principles were, of course, difficult to implement and the natural law aspects remained fuzzy in practice, as the Nuremberg trials revealed.[20] It may be said, however, that the natural law tradition has never died out but has rather shared the legal stage to a degree with modern empirical national versions of law administration. Its effects are far from evident at the national and sub-national level in many modern countries where arbitrary and shifting rules, justified by *Realpolitik* or by more pragmatic decisions, are all too evident. Its abstract appeal has been much greater than its success in practice.

The concept of 'law' was much with Ruskin and he endowed it with an indistinguishable natural and divine source. Richard Hooker's elaborate hierarchy of law, derived from St. Thomas Aquinas, was put to good use in the second volume of *Modern Painters* (1846). Law informed all visible nature, art, science, religion, economics, history and politics. Natural law is used in his work like a moral sledge hammer, driving home veritable truths. The emergence of natural law as a more formal principle in his thought came about initially through his understandings of science, aesthetics and religion, the three closely associated in his mind. First it came through his early study of science, particularly geology and chemistry, whereby he came to see that the Bible had only limited value as science. Secondly, his reading of Hooker in the mid-1840s, followed by the culmination of the so-called 'Papal aggression' in 1850, involved a review of the separatist issues confronting the Church of England. Finally, well after his turn to economics and political reform in the later 1850s, he gradually came to further appreciate the pluralistic implications of the classics and the work of modern students of religion and mythology such as Frederic Max Müller. This last phase was marked by, in personal terms, the adoption of a much starker kind of non-denominational Christian belief.

In his commentary on the history and theory of natural law, A.P. d'Entrèves cautioned readers about adopting easy generalizations about the term or of drawing too rapid a parallel in its use by practitioners widely separated in time. The presumed reasons for the seventeenth-century separation of natural law into distinct scientific and humanistic channels have now become unreliable, the observable world confused once again in the age of Einstein. Seemingly measurable concepts such as motion, time and space have become unstable. In the humanities, as well, the reign of 'positivism' has come under a cloud with even well-armed opponents of natural law in legal studies coming around to the suggestion that there may be elements of the old classical aspects of 'reasonableness' which need to be acknowledged in modern practice.[21]

In considering Ruskin as a practical proponent of natural law, somewhat in the style of Burke, we shall encounter a man who never entertained the possibility that the 'moral' could ever be usefully separated from the 'natural' in any sphere of human endeavour, including scientific study.[22] While there is much 'God talk' in Ruskin, from start to finish, the quality of such talk rather early takes on a certain character. Most distinctly, it separates itself from the Protestant evangelical certitude embraced by his mother, and generally accommodated (for her sake) by his father.

One is seldom persuaded by Ruskin that he is marked by some innate unworthiness or, on the other hand, embraces any firm belief in some 'futurity' as the outcome of life. Any genuine hope in 'futurity' has been reluctantly abandoned by those who take 'Pascal's Wager' as he had done in 1848. His Christian attachment became social, political and pragmatic. 'My faith is a dark one' he told F.D. Maurice in 1851.[23] Anything so self-assuring about future prospects as 'Justification by faith' had become quite out of the question. His way of Christianity was closer to that elusive kind exemplified by his much admired seventeenth-century poet George Herbert. Herbert's language spoke to the practical demonstration of Christian living and attitude. Ruskin saw the realization of such Christian virtues at work in the life of Louis XIV's renegade Bishop of Cambray, Francois Fénelon.[24] The tangibility of Ruskin's Christianity might be seen as bearing a relationship with the Christian Existentialism of the twentieth-century French philosopher, Gabriel Marcel or the thought of Proust. The latter observed: 'All that can be said is that everything in our life happens as though we entered upon it with a load of obligations contracted in a previous life.'[25]

He remained foremost, if not exclusively, a moralist in the Christian tradition. Unexpectedly perhaps, it was through Gandhi's reading of *Unto This Last* in 1904 and his rapid embrace of the creed embedded in that short book – 'there is no wealth but life' – that a person outside of the immediate English cultural tradition grasped that simplified expression of natural law and transformed it, through his concept of *satyagraha,* into the basis of his reform program for India. That program shared, implicitly at least, much that was in keeping with the ideals of Ruskin's Guild of St. George.[26] When Gandhi was in England in 1931 he remembered his debt to Ruskin and wrote to the Guild's historian, Edith Hope Scott, seeking copies of *Fors Clavigera*.[27]

II

Only a few words need be said by way of summary about Ruskin's well-explored biography. He was born in London of parents of mainly Scottish background in 1819. His father, John James Ruskin (1781–1864), had become well established in the wine trade, following years of apprenticeship in Scotland. In 1818, J. J. Ruskin married Margaret Tweedale Cock, his cousin, after a lengthy courtship, the marriage delayed so that Ruskin could cancel the debts of his deceased father. There were no other children after John's birth, although a niece, Mary Richardson, was raised in the household after 1829.[28] The Presbyterian and evangelical views of the parents were strong and church-going was a regular and increasingly depressing routine according to Ruskin's autobiography, although this did not work against a life-long attention to the Bible and church matters.[29] Ever ambitious to rise socially, the parents gradually eased their way out of Presbyterianism and into the evangelical wing of the Anglican Church.[30]

Ruskin's domestic education, if not as severely constricted in terms of content as that of John Stuart Mill, was just as disciplined, enforced with a minimum of toys, as Ruskin put it (with considerable exaggeration) and with no regular playmates.[31] While Mill had Greek drilled into him from age three, Ruskin was set to memorizing passages from the Bible and was exposed to good literature. The great advantage for Ruskin was the presence of his father's well-stocked library and art collecting proclivities along with a stream of prominent and stimulating visitors into the home. There were also opportunities for domestic and foreign travel in keeping with the business needs of his wine-merchant father. The great disadvantage, as with Mill, were the high expectations for his future instilled by the parents.[32] Assumptions and proposals were regularly advanced by the parents concerning their hopes for his education and path in life. Margaret Ruskin was particularly anxious that he become a man of the cloth of high standing while J.J. Ruskin saw greater possibilities in literature and poetry.

None of the parental ambitions were particularly appealing to Ruskin for he was drawn early to natural history and geology and then to artistic studies. His abilities as a writer, however, did blossom steadily and the parents had the good sense not to force their preferences too strongly. The father was more flexible than the mother and he took pleasure in his son's achievements, although he was never hesitant to reign in projects which he considered premature, such as the budding 1836 defence of the great English painter, J.M.W. Turner (1775–1851).

The long series of extant family letters covering the years between 1821 and 1871 is one of the great records of Victorian family life. The close student of Ruskin's biography, Helen Viljoen, came to the untenable conclusion that Ruskin ended up hating his parents. This was most unlikely, whatever evidence of occasional parental friction may be detected on occasion or in periodic episodes of Ruskin's angst.[33] Periods of friction are facts of life in most families. Contrary to what, over the years, many commentators often identified as a tendency towards 'suppression' of personal feelings in Victorian life, it is the frankness expressed in personal exchanges that is such a notable trait of correspondence and novels of the period, a directness which suggests strong personal confidence, usually couched in terms of mutual respect. It is presumably an important trait of language in an imperial culture. The tendency for Victorians to avoid vulgarity in personal exchanges and discourse should not be confused with an inherent prudery or lack of perception.[34]

As the years passed, Ruskin's religion went through many phases, marked by scepticism and non-denominationalism. Commentators have remarked a good deal on the importance of his moment of 'unconversion' in 1858 at a Turin Chapel. This moment marked more of a self-dramatized culmination of a long process which had commenced in the later 1830s as he came to understand the disturbing theological implications of the new geology. While Ruskin made much reference to Biblical text throughout his life, his usage was not indicative of any strong or lasting commitment to evangelical principles as some have argued.[35] The parental views were resisted by one means or another from an early age. Particularly offensive to him, with the passage of time, was the notion of 'justification by faith', a principle so Protestant in its origins.[36] In his late years, a minor battle for Ruskin's soul was waged between Protestants and Catholics but this battle ended in a stalemate as Ruskin had long ago abandoned denominational religion in favour of a more barebones version of Christian human conduct.[37] He remained friendly with Cardinal Manning after his defection to Rome, but the latter's appeals to him to come to the mother church fell upon deaf ears. His death in 1900 came after a decade-long silence. He benefited from the close care of his cousin, who understood the fragility of his mind and who kept his personal contacts minimal.

III

Ruskin's contributions to political thought did not generate wide comment before his death or in the half century after, considerably less even than did his writings on economics.[38] General commentators have understandably attempted to place him within the context of eighteenth- and nineteenth-century developments, often noticing that he had rather little interest in French, Scottish or German Enlightenment philosophy although much in Romantic letters. In this respect, he differed considerably from Thomas Carlyle, (1795–1881) with whom he is so regularly linked. To Carlyle's regret, the enlightenment had little appeal for Ruskin.[39] A few of the Fabians were interested in him and took him up in the Society

Tracts.[40] In 1919, George Bernard Shaw, contended that 'Ruskin was more misunderstood as a politician than in any other department of his activity.'[41] For Shaw he was a communist of the Bolshevik variety, one who put little stock in democracy: 'thus Ruskin, like Dickens, understood that the reconstruction of society must be the work of an energetic and conscientious minority'.[42] Further, 'If you like to call Bolshevism a combination of the Tory oligarchism of Ruskin and Mr. W. Churchill, with the Tory Communism of Ruskin alone, you may.' Thus 'when we look for a party which could logically claim Ruskin today as one of its prophets we find it in the Bolshevik party'.[43]

The Shaw view did not recommend itself to most other chroniclers of socialist history. Ruskin received no mention in G.D.H. Cole's monumental *History of Socialist Thought.*[44] Cole was certainly not unaware of Ruskin's work: he merely thought it was of a different order.[45] The maintenance of social-class ideals in Ruskin's thought led away from the kinds of parliamentary reform schemes advocated by most post-1880 liberals and socialists who saw increased social and political mobility as important aspects of the solution to the ills of the labouring men and women of Great Britain.[46] Cole's contemporary, James Fuchs, for example, noticed the conservative aspects in Ruskin's political outlook, leading Fuchs to distinguish between 'revolutionary radicals' and 'reactionary radicals', a distinction which has certainly been noted by various chroniclers of political thought.[47] Fuchs understood a radical to be one who saw the key to reform in some uprooting process. The French Revolutionary radical democrat, François-Noel Babeuf, may be taken as an example of the first type, being one who felt that the slate of the past must be wiped clean in any attempt to usher in a new order. Others, believing that social arrangements had merely gone astray, sought to re-establish ancient structures in modified form through radical measures. Fuchs saw strong signs of this second type in Ruskin.[48]

A variation on this theme was provided by writers who identified Ruskin with that 'Tory Radicalism' linked to Southey and the later Wordsworth. The conservative writers of the Lake District, once recovered from earlier infatuations with the French Revolution, promoted much by way of social reform.[49] Previously, in one of the first critical studies of Ruskin's thought, F.W. Roe described the context of such Tory radicalism as one rooted in the aftermath of the Industrial Revolution and the inadequate poor law and factory reform responses.[50] If rather laudatory, Roe's was an insightful study which reinforced the view that Carlyle was a significant influence on Ruskin.

Fuchs's interpretation was later echoed in the work of Adam Ulam, who discussed Ruskin under the head of 'idealist' notions of the state.[51] Ulam viewed the notion of an 'organic' social order, which Ruskin appeared to favour (with other guild socialists), as one essentially incapable of movement. 'It is difficult,' he observed, 'to build a political theory from a purely negative element.' Guild Socialism 'was constructed by people who were quite sure of what they did not like, but who were not equally sure of what they wanted'. He concluded that such advocacy lacked 'the historic appeal of collectivism' and did not 'share in the moral appeal of individualism'.[52] The 'Republics of Carlyle and Ruskin were behind, if not in time, then in influence and importance'.[53] The 'lack of movement' which Ulam identified can be related to 'steady' or 'stationary' state economic arguments. That image has no doubt been a factor in the neutralizing of Ruskin's thought, although such ideas were also important to J.S. Mill who feared uncontrolled economic growth.[54] It may be observed, as discussed later, that this 'stationary state' idea subsequently took on greater import in the twentieth century through the rise of 'green economics' and the 'limits to growth' movement.

More positive elements were recognized in some early commentaries. R. H. Tawney, for example, took a different view of Ruskin's collectivism from other critics. Its 'moral appeal' he took to be the backbone of his social thought. 'If men have been taught,' argued Tawney, 'that the whole meaning of economic activity is to accumulate profits for a private employer' then they are not likely to listen 'when they are told that they ought to show tender solicitude for the interest of the community'. And further, 'if there is no principle which determines what each group should justly get, then it is idle for the public to complain if each group organizes itself to get what it can'. Against such criticisms, he noticed that Ruskin thought that 'there was such a principle' and that 'men should be paid for the service, and service only' and that the trade of the usurer should be abolished outright. He advised men to 'achieve peace not by seeking peace but by seeking to serve a common end, and organizing their industry for the attainment of that end and that alone'.[55] Such political purposes, identified as 'common' ends, were presumably goals of a fairly abstract nature, at the first level, approximating the political 'good' or a condition of social harmony and domestic peace. At a second level, however, they approximated a material condition quite distinct from that which issued from the self-regulating 'harmony of interests' favoured by the utilitarians. People were not to be merely kept in some minimum state of survival if good lives were to be led.

Ruskin's influence on the labour movement after 1880 was certainly a mixed one.[56] The ambiguity of his political position had registered on some of the agricultural men of the Lake District where he spent his declining years. One veteran of the land is reported to have told Ruskin at the end of a casual pathway conversation: 'Well, to my waays o' thinking, for aw your conservative talk and writings and what not, thoo's as radical as t' best on us.'[57] To others in the Lake District in those years, his ideas were not so much ambiguous as difficult to implement, yet worthy of the effort.[58]

After World War I labour politics took on a quite distinct idealogical character in England, one very different from the small scale, conservative proposals of the late Ruskin. Aspects of his work and that of Carlyle came in for critical comment. Recollection of works such as *Time and Tide* and *Hero Worship* gave cause for concern to some in the 1930s who read back contemporary fascist ambitions into mid-Victorian minds.[59] The facts would seem to be that neither man was much read after 1920.

Post-World War II writers have attempted to place Ruskin within wider critical contexts, making room for not just the complications of his biography but acknowledging his wide familiarity with classical, medieval and more modern sources. If he was attracted to Elizabethan and Jacobean literature, he had rather little interest in eighteenth-century Enlightenment works, French, Scottish or German, although there were exceptions such as the works of Jean-François Marmontel (1723–99), which he greatly admired.[60] Of the other main French *philosophes*, only Rousseau held any special interest, owing largely to his qualities as a naturalist and thinker on education.[61] When Ruskin said that 'Rousseau laid the foundations of whatever is just in modern social theories', it was something of a lukewarm compliment, there being, in Ruskin's view, little of value to be *found* in most modern theories.[62] At any rate, Ruskin had little to say about Rousseau's political writings. He was more attached to Romantic letters, not only for their emotional content but for their full-blooded historical characters, a literature largely free of any suggestions that there was some inevitable march of mind advancing towards human perfectibility.[63] Indifferent to party politics, more interested in pre-moderns, Ruskin has frequently been seen as someone little in tune with the political developments of his times.[64]

Gill Cockram has effectively summarized the various reform trends current in late Victorian England, be they in the direction of socialism, the 'New Liberalism' of Hobson, Shaw's Fabianism or the cooperative theories of A.R. Orage. Participants in those movements sometimes acknowledged Ruskinian influence but it is clear that many did not quite know what to make of him. In contrast with William Morris, his lack of interest in democratic reform, his preference for class distinctions and his anti-technological biases all seemed out of keeping with contemporary aspirations more reflective of the changing makeup of an increasingly mobile English urban workforce.[65]

If Morris was interested in Marx, the latter's writings were quite unknown to Ruskin, although both were attracted to a version of the labour theory of value. P.D. Anthony has carefully explored Ruskin's interest in that concept. While there are points of contact at the theoretical level, the great difference concerns the importance that Ruskin attached to the experience of work itself, as a positive social value and as a real or potential component of human happiness.[66] Linda Austin, reviewing the late works, sees this attachment to the value of labour as a negative and takes the view that he was committed to an interpretation of political economy that 'verifies a universe of scarcity' and she sees him in league with Marx in this respect.[67] The view expressed in the current study suggests the opposite, that Ruskin and Mill (as opposed to Marx) were both interested in the possibilities of the stationary state, rather than the growth state. Encouraging a view of limits to growth would help eliminate the production of useless commodities, reduce environmental erosion of many kinds and encourage better forms of work, as experience. Such an approach would redress the imbalances in a world in which scarcity was an appearance, not a reality, being mainly a function of mal-distribution and of demand for useless productions in the first instance. What James Sherburne called 'the ambiguity of abundance' in Ruskin's social thought was to be sorted out through a formulation of sounder rules of political economy.[68] The choices involved better modes of consumption and the control of population by positive policies. It is the attitude towards religion which provides the sharpest divide between the two men. David Craig has stressed the difference in attitude towards religion in the works of both, Marx being well known for his suspicion of its role in society and for a pragmatic desire to redirect such ancient attitudes into secular forms.[69]

The years between 1848 and 1854 were particularly significant in the development of Ruskin's ideas about religion and government. Despite the much discussed 'un-conversion' of 1858 by his biographers, his revolt in a Turin chapel was merely the climax to a long developing disenchantment with evangelical Christianity, one strongly reinforced by what he took to be the too-easy alliance between that outlook and utilitarian economics. His frank letters on religion penned to his father between 1848 and 1852 reveal how far he had gone in his reading of German Biblical criticism, issuing in his making 'Pascal's Wager'. The steady abandonment of evangelical Protestantism and slow advance towards a neo-Thomist version of natural law, first through the works of Richard Hooker and reinforced by his mounting interest in the constitution of old Venice, became important elements in his essentially Red Tory, virtue-oriented politics. Just as important was the gathering influence of Plato as a source of natural law doctrine. In *The Stones of Venice*, he noted connections between traditional Biblical wisdom literature and ideas endorsed by Roman Stoicism and the works of Epictetus.[70]

The argument of this study will, perhaps, be unexpected for those accustomed to seeing Ruskin filling a niche in the origins of late nineteenth-century liberalism or early labour-endorsed socialist thought, both with positivist underpinnings. Those connections were more coincidental than intended. From the standpoint of early twentieth-century politics, his place is more easily found within the ranks of the early founders of social credit, of theorists of steady-state economics, or with back-to-the-land advocates and promoters of an environmental 'green' politics.[71] Late in his life, the main forces of change in England were in the direction of a utilitarian centralizing of government administration and *laissez-faire* economic liberalism. In 1888, England passed the Local Government Act, spelling the beginning of the end for the many and diverse 'quarter sessions' local government procedures first put in place by King Edward III in the fourteenth century.[72] Ruskin's politics had been oriented towards the preservation of this ancient tradition of local politics, shaped by custom, the church and the guidance of the King's law, but not by the long reach of an overarching Parliament-inspired bureaucracy. His late Guild of St. George was anachronistic not because it smacked of medievalism, but because medievalism was finally under assault in its oldest quarter: the world of local county administration staffed by citizens, (often voluntarily), involved itself with a host of fundamental activities, including the military, under the watchful eye of a justice of the peace.[73] The Poor Relief Reform Act of 1834 had been the early shot over the bow, signalling that this older and more organic world was now under attack from the centre by progressive young men inspired by the improving ideas of the Enlightenment project.

Ruskin reacted against the 1834 Act and countered not with better rational ideas but by means of a retreat to a conservative revival of traditions of mixed government. In particular, it was to the version gradually refined by Hooker in response to the Elizabethan Settlement. That world, much-altered by 1850, also required a renewal of the church-state relationship and a renewal of the daily roles of bishops and local clergy. A revival of a sense of social purpose in the nobility, with a view towards their fuller engagement in properly constituted commercial enterprise and the military, he considered essential. These were the principles stressed in works such as *Time and Tide* and in the late 'constitution' of The Guild of St. George.

Notes

1. Isobel Colgate, *The Shooting Party* (Harmondsworth: Penguin, 1982), 35.
2. On Croly, see *Works*, 1: 409, 445; 3: xxxvii, n; 8: 269. After Harrison's death in 1874, Ruskin claimed that he had been an important editorial influence. See *Works*, 34: 93. There is some ambiguity about this claim, according to Michael Wheeler. www.lancaster.ac.uk/fass/ruskin/empi/notes/xhist007.htm
3. For a sampling of critical reaction to Ruskin's main writings, see J.L. Bradley, ed. *Ruskin: The Critical Heritage* (London: Routledge and Kegan Paul, 1984). See also Leslie Stephen, 'Mr. Ruskin's Recent Writings', *Fraser's Magazine*. 9 (June, 1874), 688–701; Dinah Birch, 'Ruskin's Multiple Writing: *Fors Clavigera*', in Dinah Birch, ed., *Ruskin and the Dawn of the Modern* (Oxford: Oxford University Press, 1999), 175–87.
4. Anthony Trollope, 'Review' of *The Crown of Wild Olive*, *Fortnightly Review*, 5: (15 June, 1866), 381–4. Reproduced in Bradley, ed. (1984), 310–15.
5. Geoffrey Clive, *The Romantic Enlightenment: Ambiguity and Paradox in the Western Mind, 1750–1920* (New York: Meridian, 1960).
6. *Ibid.*, 185.
7. See Ch. 6, note 11.
8. On the historical development of the natural law, see Michael B. Crowe, *The Changing Profile of the Natural Law* (The Hague: Martinus Hijhoff, 1977); Shadia B. Drury, *The Concept of Natural Law* (Toronto: York University, Ph.D. Thesis, 1977); A.P. d'Entrèves, *Natural Law: An Introduction to Legal Philosophy*. Rev. ed. Introduction by Cary J. Nederman. (New Brunswick: Transaction Publishers, 1994); Leo Strauss, 'On Natural Law' in *Studies in Platonic Political Philosophy*, Thomas L. Pangle, ed. (Chicago: University of Chicago Press, 1983), 137–46.

9. On the modern debate about the 'right' over the 'good', see Michael J. Sandel, *Liberalism and the Limits of Justice,* 2nd ed. (Cambridge: Cambridge University Press, 1998), 1–14; 184–218; Leo Strauss, *Natural Right and History* (Chicago: University of Chicago Press, 1965), Ch. 5; on the late medieval account and the interconnection of the right and the good, see Brian Tierney, *The Idea of Natural Rights* (Grand Rapids: William B. Eerdman's, 1997), 76–77; Howard P. Kainz, *Natural Law: An Introduction and Re-examination* (Chicago: Open Court, 2004), 17–30.
10. Sandel (1998), 175.
11. See 'German Metaphysics' in *Works,* 5: 424–6. On the fate of the term 'reason' during and after the seventeenth century, see the exposition in Frederick C. Beiser, *The Sovereignty of Reason: The Defence of Rationality in the Early English Enlightenment* (Princeton: Princeton University Press, 1996).
12. *Works,* 23: 116–17.
13. On the importance of the educational development of character and the persisting role of 'telos' in Ruskin's thought, see David M. Craig, *John Ruskin and the Ethics of Consumption* (Charlottesville: University of Virginia Press, 2006), 339–41.
14. For a stimulating discussion of these topics in current scholarship, see Steven Lukes, *Liberals ad Cannibals: The Implications of Diversity* (London: Verso, 2017).
15. A. P. d'Entrèves (1994), 23–4.
16. Cited in d'Entrèves (1994), 24.
17. An informative review of these shifts is to be found in Crowe, (1977), Chaps. 4–6.
18. A valuable discussion on how Hobbes's views emerged from the world of late medieval scholasticism is provided in Michael Oakeshott, 'Introduction' to Hobbes, *Leviathan* (Oxford: Blackwell, 1946).
19. Lewis Hanke, *Aristotle and the American Indians* (Chicago: Henry Regnery, 1959); Anthony Pagden, *European Encounters with the New World: From Renaissance to Romanticism* (New Haven: Yale University Press, 1993), Ch. 4; Victor M Salas Jr., 'Francisco de Vitoria on the *Ius Gentium* and the American *Indios*', *Ave Maria Law Review,* (2) (2012), 332–41.
20. See Hanna Arendt, *Eichmann in Jerusalem* (New York: The Viking Press, 1963).
21. See Appendix C in d'Entrèves (1994), 185–203.
22. See Jesse Norman, *Edmund Burke: The First Conservative* (New York: Basic Books, 2013), 202–3, 259–60.
23. Ruskin to F. D. Maurice, 30 March, 1851 in *Works,* 12: 562.
24. *Works,* 17: 276.

25. Cited in Richard Heyes, 'Introduction', Gabriel Marcel, *Three Plays* (New York: Hill and Wang, 1965), 11.
26. Elizabeth T. McLaughlin, *Ruskin and Gandhi* (Lewisburg: Bucknell University Press, 1974), Ch. 3. Gandhi translated *Unto This Last* into Gujarati in 1908 under the title of *Sarvodaya* (*Welfare of All*). See also Bruce Hanson and Bridie Diamond, *Ruskin and Gandhi* (Bowness: Brantwood Trust, 1996), 7–8.
27. Edith Hope Scott, 'The Autobiography of an Unknown Author' (c. 1935) Typescript, 304. The writer is grateful to Thomas Stapledon for providing access to this unpublished work.
28. *Works*, 35: 71, 131.
29. *Works*, 35, 13, 25; 27: 167, 421.
30. See Helen Gill Vijoen, *Ruskin's Scottish Heritage: A Prelude* (Urbana: University of Illinois Press, 1956), Ch. 6; Tim Hilton, *John Ruskin: The Early Years. 1819–1859* (New Haven: Yale University Press, 1985), 19–20.
31. *Works*, 35: 20–1, 44–5, 57–8; Tim Hilton, *John Ruskin: The Early Years* (New Haven: Yale University Press, 1985), 12–13.
32. Mill's early emotional collapse is suggestive of his greater difficulties as a child. The absence of any mention of his mother in his famous *Autobiography* is telling.
33. See James L. Spates *The Imperfect Round: Helen Gill Viljoen's Life of Ruskin* (Long View: 2005).
34. On this topic, see Claudia Nelson, *Family Ties in Victorian England* (London: Praeger, 2007).
35. The presence of a persisting evangelical imprint is argued by George Landow. See *The Aesthetic and Critical Theories of John Ruskin* (Princeton: Princeton University Press, 1971), Ch. 4; see also Maurice Cowling, *Religion and Public Doctrine in Modern England, II: Assaults* (Cambridge: Cambridge University Press, 1985), Ch. 2.
36. See R.H. Wilenski, *John Ruskin: An Introduction to Further Study of His Life and Work* (London: Faber, 1933), 329–56; A.W.Harrison, *Arminianism* (London: Duckworth, 1937), 20–22.
37. *Works*, 34: 594. See J. Anthony Hilton, 'Ruskin's Influence on English Catholicism', *Recusant History*, 25 (1) (2000), 96–105; Albert A. Isaacs, *The Fountain of Siena: An Episode in the Life of John Ruskin* (London: S.W. Partridge, 1900). See also Appendix 1 of the present work.
38. See Ernest Barker, *Political Thought in England: 1848–1914*, 2nd ed. (London: Oxford University Press, 1959), 167–75; Patrick Geddes, 'John Ruskin: Economist', *Proceedings of the Royal Society of Edinburgh* (Edinburgh: Brown, 1884); J. A. Hobson, *John Ruskin: Social Reformer*, 2nd ed. (London: James Nisbit and Co, 1899); William Smart, *John Ruskin: His Life and Work* (Glasgow: 1880).

39. Carlyle to Ruskin, 15 July, 1874, in George Allen Cate, ed. *The Correspondence of Thomas Carlyle and John Ruskin* (Stanford, 1982), 204; Ralph Jessop, *Carlyle and Scottish Thought* (London: Palgrave Macmillan, 1997), 196–202, and C. F. Harrold, *Carlyle and German Thought:1819–1834* (New Haven: AMS Press, 1934).
40. Edith J. Morley, *John Ruskin and Social Ethics.* Fabian Tract No. 179 (London: Fabian Society, 1912–1919).
41. George Bernard Shaw, *Ruskin's Politics* (Oxford, 1921), 7.
42. Ibid., 25.
43. Ibid., 30.
44. G.D.H. Cole, *A History of Socialist Thought.* (New York: Macmillan, 1953–58), 5 Vol.
45. G.D.H. Cole and Raymond Postgate, *The Common People, 1746–1946*, 4th ed. (London: Methuen, 1981), 452.
46. G.D.H. Cole, 'Ruskin', *Encyclopedia of the Social Sciences* (New York: Macmillan, 1934), 13: 471.
47. See J.L. Talmon, *The Origins of Totalitarian Democracy* (London: W.W. Norton, 1970), 6–8; Isaiah Berlin, *Freedom and Its Betrayal:Six Enemies of Human Liberty* (Princeton: Princeton University Press, 2002).
48. James Fuchs, 'Introduction', *Ruskin's Views of Social Justice* (New York, 1926), 11.
49. See Jonathan Mendilow, *The Romantic Tradition in British Political Thought* (London: Croom Helm, 1986), Chapters 1 and 2.
50. F.W. Roe, *The Social Philosophy of Carlyle and Ruskin* (New York: Harcourt, Brace and Co., 1921), Ch. 1.
51. A.B. Ulam, *Philosophic Foundations of English Socialism* (Cambridge, 1951), 93.
52. Ibid.
53. Ibid., 51.
54. J.S. Mill, *Principles of Political Economy.* Books IV and V (London: Penguin, 1985), 111–17. And see Mendilow, (1986), 190–91.
55. R.H. Tawney, *The Radical Tradition,* Rita Hinden, ed. (Harmondsworth: Penguin, 1966), 46.
56. See Lawrence Goldman, 'Ruskin, Oxford and the British Labour Movement, 1880–1914' in Dinah Birch, ed., *Ruskin and the dawn of the Modern* (Oxford: Oxford University Press, 1999), 57–86.
57. Conventional local dialect as rendered by H.D. Rawnsley in his *Ruskin and the English Lakes* (Glasgow, 1902), 71.
58. Vicky Albritton and Fredrik A. Jonsson, *Green Victorians: The Simple Life in John Ruskin's Lake District* (Chicago: University of Chicago Press, 2015), Ch. 5.

59. John D. Rosenberg, *Carlyle and the Burden of History* (Cambridge: Harvard University Press, 1985), 115; Benjamin E. Lippincott, *Victorian Critics of Democracy* (Minneapolis, 1938), 4.
60. *Works*, 18: lxi, 47.
61. On Ruskin and Rousseau, see *Works*, 18: xxxviii–lxii; Ruskin to J. J. Ruskin, June 21 1862, *Works*, 18: lxii; and *Praeterita*, in *Works*, 35: 321, 440. See also E. T. Cook, *The Life of John Ruskin* (London, 1915) I: 144; II: 548–9.
62. *Works*, 21: 131.
63. The works of Scott were of continual interest to Ruskin in this sense. On his early education and reading, see Derek Leon, *Ruskin: The Great Victorian* (London, 1949), Chapters 2 and 3; Tim Hilton, *John Ruskin: The Early Years* (New Haven, 1985), 13–14; Joan Abse, *John Ruskin: The Passionate Moralist* (New York, 1981), 20–39.
64. See Stephen (1874); and Barker (1959), 171–73.
65. On these themes, see Gill Cockram, *Ruskin and Social Reform* (London: Tauris Academic Studies, 2007); and see Charles Wilson, 'Economy and Society in late Victorian Britain' in *Economic History and the Historian: Collected Essays* (London: Weidenfeld and Nicolson, 1969), 178–200.
66. See P.D. Anthony, *John Ruskin's Labour: A study of Ruskin's social theory* (Cambridge: Cambridge University Press, 1983).
67. Linda M. Austin, *The Practical Ruskin: Economics and Audience in the Late Work* (Baltimore: Johns Hopkins University Press, 1991), 16.
68. See James C. Sherburne, *John Ruskin and the Ambiguities of Abundance: A Study in Social and Economic Criticism* (Cambridge, MA: Harvard University Press, 1972).
69. See David M. Craig, *John Ruskin and the Ethics of Consumption* (Charlottesville: University of Virginia Press, 2006), 158–61.
70. On Epictetus, see *Works*, 5: 383n; 17: 522; 34: 585. On Ruskin's views on Plato, Cicero and their relationship with Christian doctrine in 1853, see *Works*, 10: 369–71.
71. See Jonsson, (2016); Kenneth E. Boulding, 'The Shadow of the Stationary State', *Daedelus*, 102 (4) (1973), 89–101.
72. Just how many were these traditional procedures may be noticed in W. E. Tate, *The Parish Chest: A Study of the Records of Parochial Administration in England*, 3rd ed. (Cambridge: Cambridge University Press, 1969); and Francis and Joseph Gies, *Life in a Medieval Village* (New York: Harper and Row, 1990).
73. On the long role of the Justice of the Peace in English history, see Esther Moir, *The Justice of the Peace* (Harmondsworth: Penguin, 1969).
74. Footnote references to Ruskin's writings (unless otherwise stated) are cited as *Works*, and refer to Ruskin, John (1903–12), below.

BIBLIOGRAPHY[74]

Abse, Joan. 1981. *John Ruskin: The Passionate Moralist.* New York: Alfred A. Knopf.

Albritton, Vicky, and Fredrik A. Jonsson. 2015. *Green Victorians: The Simple Life in John Ruskin's Lake District.* Chicago: University of Chicago Press.

Anthony, P.D. 1983. *John Ruskin's Labour: A study of Ruskin's Social Theory.* Cambridge: Cambridge University Press.

Arendt, Hanna. 1963. *Eichmann in Jerusalem.* New York: The Viking Press.

Austin, Linda M. 1991. *The Practical Ruskin: Economics and Audience in the Late Work.* Baltimore: Johns Hopkins University Press.

Barker, Ernest. 1959. *Political Thought in England: 1848–1914.* 2nd ed. London: Oxford University Press.

Beiser, Frederick C. 1996. *The Sovereignty of Reason: The Defence of Rationality in the Early English Enlightenment.* Princeton: Princeton University Press.

Berlin, Isaiah. 2002. *Freedom and Its Betrayal: Six Enemies of Human Liberty.* Princeton: Princeton University Press.

Birch, Dinah. 1999a. Ruskin's Multiple Writing: *Fors Clavigera.* In Birch, ed., 175–187.

———, ed. 1999b. *Ruskin and the Dawn of the Modern.* Oxford: Oxford University Press.

Boulding, Kenneth E. 1973. The Shadow of the Stationary State. *Daedelus* 102 (4): 89–101.

Bradley, J.L., ed. 1984. *Ruskin: The Critical Heritage.* London: Routledge and Kegan Paul.

Cate, George Allen, ed. 1982. *The Correspondence of Thomas Carlyle and John Ruskin.* Stanford: Stanford University Press.

Clive, Geoffrey. 1960. *The Romantic Enlightenment: Ambiguity and Paradox in the Western Mind, 1750–1920.* New York: Meridian.

Cockram, Gill. 2007. *Ruskin and Social Reform.* London: Tauris Academic Studies.

Cole, G.D.H. 1934. Ruskin. In *Encyclopedia of the Social Sciences,* vol. 13, 471. New York: Macmillan.

———. 1953–1958. *A History of Socialist Thought.* New York: Macmillan.

Cole, G.D.H., and Raymond Postgate. 1981. *The Common People, 1746–1946.* 4th ed. London: Methuen.

Colgate, Isobel. 1982. *The Shooting Party.* Harmondsworth: Penguin.

Cook, E.T. 1915. *The Life of John Ruskin.* Vol. 2. London: George Allen.

Cowling, Maurice. 1985. *Religion and Public Doctrine in Modern England, II: Assaults.* Cambridge: Cambridge University Press.

Craig, David M. 2006. *John Ruskin and the Ethics of Consumption.* Charlottesville: University of Virginia Press.

Crowe, Michael B. 1977. *The Changing Profile of the Natural Law*. The Hague: Martinus Hijhoff.
d'Entrèves, A.P. 1994. *Natural Law: An Introduction to Legal Philosophy*, Introduction by Cary J. Nederman. Rev. ed. New Brunswick: Transaction Publishers.
Drury, Shadia B. 1977. *The Concept of Natural Law.* Ph.D. Thesis. Toronto: York University.
Fuchs, James. 1926. Introduction. In *Ruskin's Views of Social Justice*. New York: Vanguard Press.
Geddes, Patrick. 1884. John Ruskin: Economist. In *Proceedings of the Royal Society of Edinburgh*. Edinburgh: Brown.
Gies, Francis, and Joseph Gies. 1990. *Life in a Medieval Village*. New York: Harper and Row.
Goldman, Lawrence. 1999. Ruskin, Oxford and the British Labour Movement, 1880–1914. In Birch, ed., 57–86.
Hanke, Lewis. 1959. *Aristotle and the American Indians.* Chicago: Henry Regnery.
Hanson, Bruce, and Bridie Diamond. 1996. *Ruskin and Gandhi*. Bowness: Brantwood Trust.
Harrold, C.F. 1934. *Carlyle and German Thought: 1819–1834.* New Haven: Yale University Press.
Heyes, Richard. 1965. Introduction. In *Three Plays*, ed. Gabriel Marcel. New York: Hill and Wang.
Hilton, Tim. 1985. *John Ruskin: The Early Years. 1819–1859.* New Haven: Yale University Press.
Hilton, J. Anthony. 2000. Ruskin's Influence on English Catholicism. *Recusant History* 25 (1): 96–105.
Hobson, John A. 1899. *John Ruskin: Social Reformer.* 2nd ed. London: James Nisbit and Co. Longview. N.P.
Isaacs, Albert A. 1900. *The Fountain of Siena: An Episode in the Life of John Ruskin.* London: S.W. Partridge.
Jessop, Ralph. 1997. *Carlyle and Scottish Thought.* London: Macmillan.
Kainz, Howard P. 2004. *Natural Law: An Introduction and Re-examination.* Chicago: Open Court.
Landow, George P. 1971. *The Aesthetic and Critical Theories of John Ruskin.* Princeton: Princeton University Press.
Leon, Derek. 1949. *Ruskin: The Great Victorian.* London: Routledge and Kegan Paul.
Lippincott, Benjamin E. 1938. *Victorian Critics of Democracy.* Minneapolis: University of Minnesota Press.
Lukes, Steven. 2017. *Liberals and Cannibals: The Implications of Diversity.* London: Verso.

McLaughlin, Elizabeth T. 1974. *Ruskin and Gandhi*. Lewisburg: Bucknell University Press.
Mendilow, Jonathan. 1986. *The Romantic Tradition in British Political Thought*. London: Croom Helm.
Mill, J.S. 1985. *Principles of Political Economy. Books IV and V*. London: Penguin.
Moir, Esther. 1969. *The Justice of the Peace*. Harmondsworth: Penguin.
Morley, Edith J. 1912–1919. *John Ruskin and Social Ethics*, Fabian Tract No. 179. London: Fabian Society.
Norman, Jesse. 2013. *Edmund Burke: The First Conservative*. New York: Basic Books.
Oakeshott, Michael. 1946. Introduction. In *Leviathan*, ed. Thomas Hobbes. Oxford: Blackwell.
Pagden, Anthony. 1993. *European Encounters with the New World: From Renaissance to Romanticism*. New Haven: Yale University Press.
Rawnsley, H.D. 1902. *Ruskin and the English Lakes*. Glasgow: James MacLehose.
Roe, F.W. 1921. *The Social Philosophy of Carlyle and Ruskin*. New York: Harcourt, Brace.
Rosenberg, John D. 1985. *Carlyle and the Burden of History*. Cambridge: Harvard University Press.
Ruskin, John. 1903–1912. In *The Collected Works of John Ruskin*, ed. E.T. Cook and Alexander Wedderburn, vol. 39. London: George Allen.
Salas, Victor M., Jr. 2012. Francisco de Vitoria on the Ius Gentium and the American Indios. *Ave Maria Law Review* 2: 332–341.
Sandel, Michael J. 1998. *Liberalism and the Limits of Justice*. 2nd ed. Cambridge: Cambridge University Press.
Shaw, George Bernard. 1921. *Ruskin's Politics*. Oxford: Oxford University Press.
Sherburne, James C. 1972. *John Ruskin and the Ambiguities of Abundance: A Study in Social and Economic Criticism*. Cambridge: Harvard University Press.
Smart, William. 1880. *John Ruskin: His Life and Work*. Glasgow: Wilson and McCormick.
Spates, James L. 2005. *The Imperfect Round: Helen Gill Viljoen's Life of Ruskin*. Long View. N.P.
Stephen, Leslie. 1874. Mr. Ruskin's Recent Writings. *Fraser's Magazine* 9: 688–701.
Strauss, Leo. 1971. *Natural Right and History*. Chicago: University of Chicago Press.
———. 1983. On Natural Law. In *Studies in Platonic Political Philosophy*, ed. Thomas L. Pangle, 137–146. Chicago: University of Chicago Press.
Talmon, J.L. 1970. *The Origins of Totalitarian Democracy*. London: W.W. Norton.
Tate, W.E. 1969. *The Parish Chest: A Study of the Records of Parochial Administration in England*. 3rd ed. Cambridge: Cambridge University Press.

Tawney, R.H. 1966. In *The Radical Tradition*, ed. Rita Hinden. Harmondsworth: Penguin.

Tierney, Brian. 1997. *The Idea of Natural Rights.* Grand Rapids: William B. Eerdman's.

Trollope, Anthony. 1866. 'Review' of *The Crown of Wild Olive*, *Fortnightly Review* 5: 381–384. Reproduced in Bradley, ed. (1984), 310–315.

Ulam, Adam B. 1951. *Philosophical Foundations of English Socialism.* Cambridge: Harvard University Press.

Viljoen, Helen Gill. 1956. *Ruskin's Scottish Heritage: A Prelude.* Urbana: University of Illinois Press.

Wilenski, R.H. 1933. *John Ruskin: An Introduction to Further Study of His Life and Work.* London: Faber.

Wilson, Charles. 1969. *Economic History and the Historian: Collected Essays.* London: Weidenfeld and Nicolson.

CHAPTER 2

The Wine Merchant's Son: Ruskin's Discovery of the World

Much has been learned about Ruskin's unusual upbringing, his Scottish background and the circumstances of his relatives and their economic prospects. His early exposures to literature, especially the Bible, included the works of Homer, Shakespeare, Scott, Wordsworth and, more surprisingly, Byron. This steady exposure came about under careful parental guidance.[1] His steady encounters with important exponents of the heroic and of a nature-oriented romanticism certainly imprinted heavily upon his imagination and provided a counterweight to the regular and disciplined study of holy scripture imposed by his mother. Another liberalizing element was provided by the early opportunities for travel provided by his father's wealth and need to consult with his wine business colleagues through regular domestic trips and vacations to the continent. The bucolic life of England's more isolated districts in the 1830s made a great impression on the young man. He would return to his favourite, the Lake District, to spend his later years. At age 11, Ruskin maintained a substantial *Journal* of a family trip through the Lake District followed by another more poetic version for the 1833 family tour of the Continent.[2] Exposure to localities of more common social and industrial conditions or to those of the poor were clearly limited as the elder Ruskin's associates tended to be among the gentry or the urban well-to-do.

John James Ruskin's interest in literature, public affairs, and particularly his patronage of the work of the artist J.M.W. Turner, were some of the more telling long-term influences upon the son. Many productions in

G. A. MacDonald, *John Ruskin's Politics and Natural Law*,
https://doi.org/10.1007/978-3-319-72281-8_2

prose and poetry issued from the pen of the young Ruskin, such as the unfinished play, *Marcolini* (1836), a tragedy conceived along Shakespearian lines. His precocious 'Essay on Literature', in the same year, was the sign of a rapidly developing independent mind. In 1893 this essay was discovered, along with letters written by Ruskin to the Rev. Thomas Dale, a poet and his early Tutor. In Ruskin's late autobiography, *Praeterita*, Dale was described as his 'severest and chiefly antagonist master'.[3] In 1833, Dale had replaced Edward Andrews as Ruskin's tutor and for the next few years Ruskin attended Dale's school at Camberwell, not far from the family residence. In late December 1836, Ruskin wrote to his father giving him an account of the recent school examinations and also of the 'very longitudinal essay' he had submitted to Dale. The students had been asked to address the question: 'Does the perusal of works of fiction act favourably or unfavourably on the moral character?' There was a larger context to this assignment for in that same year Dale had helped bring out a new edition of *The Student's Guide*, by the American divine John Todd. In this guide the works of Scott, Bulwer and Byron were condemned as immoral, a view to which Dale apparently subscribed.[4] Young Ruskin must surely have been aware of this but, clearly not in awe of his teacher, proceeded to defend these very authors in his long 'Essay on Literature'. If Ruskin retained a somewhat jaundiced view of his early tutor, there was also an element of real friendship between them, revealed in Ruskin's letters sent to him from the Continent in 1840 and 1841. At that time, the Ruskin family was touring warmer climes in order to try to ward off a most serious threat of tuberculosis to John's health. The letters are filled with interesting social and geological observations but do not disguise the darkness of mind which had already started to close in around the young author. 'Since my last blood I have not studied at all. Doctors and my own feelings agree in one point – that hard mental labour of any kind hurts me instantly.'[5] The letters also reveal the first hints of Ruskin's reluctance to find his future as a man of the cloth, for he says things to Dale which he would have been more reluctant to say to his parents.[6] Dale, for his part, was not offended by Ruskin's courage in taking him on in his 'Essay' and later communicated to J.J. Ruskin his admiration for the talents of his son. This was a view shared by Sydney Smith, with whom Dale taught at King's College, London.[7] The 'Essay' reveals the early emergence of a contrarian trait in Ruskin, characteristic of a man seldom reluctant to pick an intellectual fight where certain principles were at stake. We shall see that the seeds of his first famous public dispute, that concerning the merits of Turner's art, were also sown in the year of 1836.

Meanwhile, under the pen name of *Kata Pusin*, he published several essays in criticism in 1838 as *The Poetry of Architecture*. The sub-title given this early work is instructive with respect to later interests: 'The Architecture of the Nations of Europe considered in its Association with Natural Scenery and National Character'. This particular characterization foreshadowed much of his later social criticism as the arguments were frequently rendered with a strong appreciation for historical contexts and social forces. If the title of this preliminary essay was rather grandiose, the execution was quite limited, consisting largely of a comparison of vernacular cottage and villa styles as the author had witnessed them during family travels through parts of Europe and England. Only years later, in a famous chapter in *The Stones of Venice*—'The Nature of Gothic'—did he attempt to outline, in moral and economic terms, the connection between architecture and society as a whole.

His attraction to the art of Turner commenced in 1836 when he prepared a response to what he took to be ill-considered remarks in *Blackwood's Magazine* concerning that artist's importance. A detailed defence of Turner's reputation was hardly necessary given the artist's well-established fame. The impassioned draft was censored by both Turner and his father. The paper, nevertheless, took on new life in the project that became his first major work, volume one of *Modern Painters* (1843). In recognition of this achievement, on New Year's Day, 1844, J. J. Ruskin presented his son with Turner's remarkable painting, 'The Slave Ship'.[8]

In addition to art, another counter-weight to the all too frequent evangelical routines of his youth was provided through his outdoor rambling and love of natural history. In nature, he found art's most appropriate subject matter. The habit of sketching all before him set in early as one of his life-long ways of taking notes and of relaxation.[9] Foremost, geology interested him in the years before he went up to Oxford. This interest was not that of a mere amateur for, well before he was 20, he had been frequenting prestigious geological gatherings. Since the appearance of the geological works of the Scottish geologist, James Hutton (1726–97), in the later eighteenth century, the results had been inducing difficult questions for conventional believers in the Bible's historical chronology.[10] By 1830, Charles Lyell had synthesized much of the gathering evidence into a masterpiece which no interested party could ignore.[11] Lyell's resignation from King's College only increased the tension for young Ruskin, who had read his work and heard him speak.[12] No longer could a person dismiss fossils as random, as the mere 'little sporting miracles of nature'.[13] Some of Ruskin's earliest published pieces were on geological themes and by 1837 he had certainly absorbed Lyell's revolutionary *Principles of Geology* and had, after an Oxford conference, talked long into the evening with the young Darwin, just returned from one of his scientific travels.[14] He was also well acquainted with the work of Horace-Bénédict de Saussure (1740–99) the Swiss alpinist, scientist and geologist who held progressive ideas.[15]

For various reasons one cannot imagine that a life in the church was really seriously being contemplated, for Ruskin's inclination to study geology as a profession was strong. He opted for the safer middle ground of the liberal arts, but did not leave his ambitions in science entirely to one side. He balanced the always stimulating geological exercises of the Rev. William Buckland, (with their congenial emphasis on outdoor field work), with the usual pressures from home to contemplate a career in the church or in literature. The eccentric and engaging Buckland managed to keep in the air the balls of theology, geology and teaching, including breakfasts for his more favoured students.[16] As the writer of one of the theologically conservative *Bridgewater Treatises*, Buckland resisted the more troubling implications of the work of Lyell and Darwin. Ruskin could not, however, even if he warped the obvious conclusions in many subsequent public utterances. He remained fond of Buckland but it was Lyell and Darwin that he understood, even if darkly.[17]

Buckland was not alone in attempting to mount rear-guard actions against the new geology. Other well-regarded geologists and scientists such as Adam Sedgwick and William Whewell may be mentioned. In 1844 Robert Chambers published *Vestiges of the Natural History of Creation*, an effort to put forth a theory of evolution that would accord with the facts of the new geology while retaining arguments from design. It proved to be well wide of the mark in its arguments, but the very attempt greatly upset Sedgwick, who was desperately trying to keep the humpty-dumpty of the 'Great Chain of Being' from falling off the wall. His published protest was, as Charles Gillispie put it, 'a cry from the heart of a scientist upon whom had suddenly flashed the full implications of his own endeavours, and who refused to understand them'.[18] This was not Ruskin's way of response. Lyell's revelations about extinct species, such as the Mastodon, he accepted. The notion that some fossilized form of early pre-human might eventually come to light was theologically disturbing, but also grasped as a possibility, as he told Edward Clayton.[19]

It was in the relatively relaxed correspondence with his 'college friend' Clayton that we may see just how seriously and early Ruskin absorbed the new learning.[20] In 1840, he took time to pen a sophisticated essay for him entitled 'Was there death before Adam fell, in other parts of Creation?'[21] The essay reveals that he had not only a good command of geology but also of chemistry. Any suggestion that the Garden of Eden and its contents, animal, vegetable or mineral, existed in some ecological set of circumstances distinct from those generally known in the present, was held to be sheer nonsense on chemical grounds.[22] By the end of his Oxford undergraduate years then, the general conclusion he had reached was that the 6000-year Biblical timescale of world history endorsed by the Primate of Ireland, Bishop James Ussher (1588–1656) and by subsequent Bible Christians, was clearly in a shambles. Whatever great value the Bible might have in ethical and social terms, it was poor environmental and biological history. Indeed, even without Lyell and Darwin, the question of species extinctions was entering into the popular imagination by other routes. Buckland, himself, had been the first to publish on dinosaur bones in England.[23]

The disturbing element of the revamped geological timescale remained that it provided fuel for speculations on animate evolution such that the long-standing and cherished idea of the immutability of species came into question. What also came into question, therefore, was the utility of the comfortable and hoary notion of the 'Great Chain of Being', long embraced by adherents of a comprehensive natural law, confirming that the physical and spiritual worlds were reconcilable.[24] If the telescope had expanded the universe and the general sense of mystery about it, the equally mysterious world seen to be unfolding inward, through nineteenth century microscopic inspections of glass slides, did not excite Ruskin as much as it frightened him, and would continue to do so into old age.[25]

It is evident that the young Ruskin at Oxford was remarkably busy in several directions. His studies were comprehensive but, by his own inclinations, towards science and art. His father having encouraged his efforts in poetry, it appears that Ruskin, soon after his arrival at Oxford, determined to win the Newdigate Prize. In 1839, he was successful and it was of particular moment to him when the prize was awarded by none other than the aged William Wordsworth.

The effort expended in preparing for the poetry competition, combined with the end of an attachment, (one that existed only in his own mind), initiated the onset of one of many bouts of mental depression in 1840. It did much to reinforce his general state of ill-health, which, as mentioned, had taken the family to the continent on tour. Nervous and physical exhaustion in the aftermath of completion of a major work or emotional disappointment became a pattern throughout his entire creative life.[26] All this busyness assured that he did not make a large number of friends at Oxford, but he at least made a few good and lasting ones. He was by no means unsocial and enjoyed 'a wine' on occasion, as well as that kind of energetic informal gathering which tended towards serious discussion of the issues of the day. Indeed, his knowledge of a good vintage and a certain inner confidence in his own interests appears to have gotten Ruskin through the Oxford common rooms without too much of the bullying that might have been directed at one so sheltered. He spoke well in the Oxford Union.[27]

His life at Oxford remained focused on his selected studies until his graduation in 1842, but any assumed future course was in doubt. Partially as a result of his father's personal relationship with Turner and ability to purchase Turner paintings, Ruskin had been thinking about art for at least six years. Having met the great artist in 1840, and with the encouraging attention of Henry Liddell, Ruskin was put in mind to pursue his first great project. He became preoccupied with the deeper meaning of art and its relation to literature, history and morals. The upshot was that shortly after his graduation he was ready to publish his first important statement in art history and criticism, the initial volume of *Modern Painters* (1843). The success of this work 'by an Oxford graduate' suggested that the mother's hopes for a bishopric for her son were unlikely to be fulfilled. When Ruskin had sufficiently recovered from the characteristic mental let down which followed upon completion of this first volume, he quickly turned to the many tasks associated with a sequel. His first effort had arrived to mixed but generally favourable reviews.[28]

Despite Ruskin's obvious preoccupation with art, Osborne Gordon had doubts about whether he should continue along the path of art criticism. Gordon and others in the Oxford teaching fraternity were well aware of the domestic circumstances and the rigorous directional hands continually laid upon the young author. The evangelical routines of the parents were of concern to them and they sought to moderate Ruskin's views. The Rev. Walter Brown gave him Isaac Taylor's *Natural History of Enthusiasm* (1829), a work of broad Anglican views and of anti-evangelical tendency, a book Ruskin still consulted in old age.[29] This was helpful reading but it was becoming clear that a secular future was in the offing. In 1844, Gordon, who was Ruskin's best-loved and most influential tutor, (the closest person, perhaps, Ruskin ever had to a brother), listened to his young charge outline, with much good humour, six reasons why he was not suited to be a clergyman, the sixth being that he 'likes solitude better than company and stones better than sermons'.[30]

Gordon soon accepted the inevitable fact of Ruskin's determination to focus on a literary career. Yet, in 1845 he encouraged Ruskin to venture into serious theological material and to take up John Keble's new edition of *The Laws of Ecclesiastical Polity* by the Elizabethan theologian, Richard Hooker (1556–1600). He recalled being instructed to read it 'both for its arguments and its English'.[31] This he did, and the work had a considerable influence on his writing style as well as his thought. It provided a further expansion of his outlook, supplementing that provided by his travels, which had helped drive home how little he actually knew about the grander scope of European art. He recognized that his initial work on Turner lacked proper context. Gordon remained an important restraining influence on Ruskin, the sense of it caught in a 'Memoir' of Gordon where it was recalled that he 'was constantly bringing his old pupil's theories to the test of experience'.[32]

Ruskin had first been to Venice in 1835 where the seed was sown for his long interest in the art and architecture of that remarkable city. In 1845, finally on his own as a traveller on the continent, he sent expansive messages home from Lucca and elsewhere. The mounting appeal of the more primitive Italian medieval artists and of the grand Gothic architecture of France suggests the beginnings of a greater openness towards Catholicism and the details of social life in the Middle Ages.[33] This tendency was encouraged in 1843 by his sympathetic reading of Alexis Rio's recent work on early Christian art.[34] Such studies helped ignite Ruskin's suspicion of Renaissance values, by which he gradually came to identify overweening pride and individualism as developing historical tendencies in European society. The *'vita activa'* of Renaissance urban commercial life was an important factor in fostering a sense of personal pride that moved Europe towards an ethos in which confidence in private judgements were elevated to a political virtue.[35] The Reformation was another source of such prideful tendencies, taking on greater critical importance in his work as he withdrew from evangelical influences.[36] As early as 1845, he had written to his father that 'as for Munich, Dresden, etc, they are utterly valueless to me'.[37] Northern Renaissance art and architecture was, if for somewhat different reasons, as suspect as the southern varieties. This same trip also stimulated him to consider his views on the history of political constitutions. In Brevano, he summarized for his father a concise version of many of the ideas that would persist in his political outlook, particularly concerning republicanism and its shortcomings.[38] Nearly 30 years later, he reinforced this reading of republicanism in *Val D'Arno*.[39]

His broadening view of European art provided him with new ways to focus his thoughts while preparing volume two of *Modern Painters*. With Hooker in hand, it seemed necessary to reconsider the historical merits of the ecclesiastical experiments of the Elizabethan period, so unique in shaping later English society. In Hooker he recognized a bold historical imagination engaged in an effort to contain the forces of particularist theological divisions and 'enthusiasm', a writer possessed of a wish to restore some semblance of the older, more organic Catholic order that had been so radically altered at the hands of Henry VIII.[40]

Ruskin's reading of Hooker was, at the same time, instrumental in furthering his efforts to fashion a more respectable aesthetic theory in support of his views on art. What emerged was a theory that owed much to Hooker's embrace of the existence of four levels of Natural Law as developed earlier by Thomas Aquinas.[41] What Ruskin called the 'Christian *theoria*' was complex enough and not always clear to nineteenth-century readers, but it suited well enough to advance the notion that art was first moral in its impulses and, when executed properly, capable of revealing nature as the handiwork of God.

The '*theoria*' operated somewhat along these lines. Human capacity to appreciate beauty was akin to the workings of raw nature. Perfection was not within human reach, only intimations of that vast perfection, which is God's nature, and can be dimly perceived.[42] Hence, the 'Christian *Theoria* seeks not, though it accepts and touches with its own purity what the Epicurean sought.' But the 'Christian *Theoria*' is rather more easily satisfied than the Epicurean sensibility, for it 'finds its food and the objects of its love everywhere, in what is harsh and fearful as well as in what is kind, nay, even in all that seems coarse and common-place'. The truly open mind will take delight 'more sometimes at finding the table spread in strange places and in the presence of its enemies' and it will recognize the 'honey coming out of the rock' rather than insisting that all be 'harmonized into a less wondrous pleasure'.[43] For Ruskin, it appears the glass is half-full rather than half-empty. He then goes further in his effort to distinguish the 'imaginative' from the 'theoretic faculty'[44]:

> Both agree in this, that they reject nothing, and are thankful for all; but the Theoretic faculty takes out of everything that which is beautiful while the Imaginative faculty takes hold of the very imperfections which the Theoretic rejects, and by means of these angles and roughness, it joins and bolts the separate stones into a mighty temple, wherein the Theoretic faculty in its turn, does deepest homage.

Malcolm Ross suggested that one of Ruskin's tasks in the second volume of *Modern Painters* was 'to delineate a human as distinct from animal mode of perception'. This he achieved through recognition that there is a human need to 'make discrimination and to direct the swirling traffic of the senses'.[45] As far as Ruskin could tell, one distinguishing feature of the human world, as opposed to the animal, was the capacity to experience beauty. He concluded that it is 'necessary to the existence of an idea of beauty that the sensual pleasure which may be its basis, should be accompanied first with joy, then with the love of the object, then with the perception of kindness in a superior intelligence, finally with thankfulness and veneration towards that intelligence itself'.[46]

Such passages are rather cumbersome to the modern ear, but one can understand clearly enough what he was getting at: it is the artist who is the master of the imaginative, and the artist who brings a unique and distinct vision to all the assembled phenomena before him. Artists are not commonly encountered creatures.[47]

It was not, however, just a view of art and natural law which Ruskin extracted from Hooker but also insights on human nature, insights which helped him to retreat further from the Calvinist account embedded in the religion of his parents. In volume two, he says: 'we come at last…to set ourselves face to face with ourselves' expecting that in 'creatures made after the image of God, we are to find comeliness and completion more exquisite than in the fowls of the air'. Further inspection, however, suggests that we must instead 'behold now a sudden change from all former experience. No longer among the individuals of the race is there equality, a likeness, a distributed fairness and fixed type visible to each'. Instead, there is only 'evil and diversity' and 'terrible stamp of various degradation'. Upon even closer scrutiny, it becomes clear that there was little in humankind's general appearance and condition to recommend it. It is quite possible to observe[48]:

> features seamed by sickness, dimmed by sensuality, convulsed by passion, pinched by poverty, shadowed with sloth, broken down by labour, tortured by disease, dishonoured in foul uses; intellects without power, hearts without hope, minds earthly and devilish; our bones full of the sin of our youth.

Harbouring such sentiments, it is perhaps not surprising that Ruskin eventually developed a high regard for some of Rousseau's writings. In light of such dismal and Dickensian observations, he can only ask whether it would not be well for us 'if after beholding this our natural face in a glass, we desire not straightaway to forget what manner of men we be?' But if not, then in what sense is it possible 'to restore to the body, the grace and power which inherited disease has destroyed; to restore to the spirit the purity, and to the intellect the grasp, that they had in paradise?'[49] What, in short, can humanity accomplish in its fallen state in order to better its lot?

This passage has, on occasion, been interpreted as a sign of Ruskin's lasting embrace of an evangelical attachment to the 'innate depravity' of human nature and the inheritance of 'the fall'. However, there is little compelling evidence for this, certainly not based on any presumed attachment to the sermons of Henry Melvill or J.C. Ryle.[50] He had already come to terms, intellectually at least, with the limitations of the Bible as history. The book was not the word of God directly but of interpreting human minds and hands. The human condition, past or present, is not the result of a fixed and depraved human nature, but of changing social conditions and perhaps even of changes in the creatures themselves, although he never wanted to say that more loudly than he had done to Clayton. His conclusion was that any improvements in the human condition would not be based 'on a work of imagination'. Instead, the 'little good by which we are to redeem ourselves is to be got out of the old wreck, beaten about and full of sand though it be' and 'out of such uninjured and bright vestiges of the old seal as we can find and set together'. Humanity was mind hopelessly compromised by naturally aging matter; but being higher than the lowest, it was 'not necessary to share the degradation of the brute' just because 'we share its mortality'.[51] That which distinguishes humans from the animal world was not just the capacity for the appreciation of beauty but the capacity for judgement and wisdom, what Ruskin, following the Greeks, eventually preferred to call 'sophia'.[52] The upshot of his view of human nature appears to be one hostile to any kind of Calvinist-inspired sense of innate depravity, predestinarian limitations or inevitability. Social arrangements could be improved through wise leadership, law-making and proper education. He was wary of other suggestions about overly complex or reductionist accounts of human nature. Metaphysics and logical theory were never Ruskin's strong points, as he found when struggling with Aristotle at Oxford.[53] He remained hostile to any preoccupation with 'system', particularly the German variety.[54] There remained many gaps in his aesthetic arguments but an idealist strain of philosophy was evident in his extended review of Lord Lindsay's *Sketches of the History of Christian Art* (1847). Although it was a work he generally admired, he yet chastised Lindsay for his dividing up of human nature into artificial logical categories.[55]

Natural law impulses arose from slightly different and more comprehensible quarters after 1845. It was not just the ancient classics, romantics and Elizabethans who he read with attention but also a good number of writers of the early seventeenth century. As an undergraduate he praised George Herbert for his piety and straightforward demonstration of the Christian life, contrasting him favourably with more austere Puritan examples.[56] In Italy, he discovered a copy of *From Grace Abounding* in his luggage and he asked his mother: 'What made you put that funny book of John Bunyan's in my bag?' He then recounted the shortcomings of this narrow and determined Puritan advocate.[57] The charges were repeated a week later: Bunyan was 'always looking to his own interests & his own state – loving or fearing or doubting, just as he happened to fancy God was dealing with him'.[58] He was reading Herbert to much better effect, an author who remained one of Ruskin's great templates for the 'situated' Christian life, an important underpinning for his political conservatism.[59] It was through Herbert, that Ruskin first absorbed something of the broader and more tolerant Arminian outlook, so disruptive in Netherlands society in the early seventeenth century.[60] While Ruskin makes no mention of Herbert's philosopher brother, Edward (Lord Herbert of Cherbury), the latter's connection with Cambridge Platonism and his coining of the term 'Deism' were no doubt important influences on George Herbert's outlook and certainly on that of Grotius.[61]

Ruskin's reading was broad from the start. In late 1836, he astonished his tutor Thomas Dale in revealing its extent. He knew not just the romantics but many of the ancient classics and something of Grotius, probably *The Truth of the Christian Religion* (1624).[62] It was not Ruskin's way to ever delve too deeply into early seventeenth-century theological controversies and tracts. He seems to have known little of the Cambridge Platonists proper, reading only Nathaniel Culverwell's *An Elegant and*

Learned Discourse of the Light of Nature later in the 1860s.[63] Ruskin reported to Lady Trevelyan his view of Culverwell that 'It's great nonsense but a nice enough nonsense book.'[64]

Culverwell and others aside, before 1850 Ruskin had absorbed elements of the new Cambridge Platonic learning more indirectly via his appreciation, not just of George Herbert, but also Edmund Spenser and some of the metaphysical poets, readings which meshed well with the moderating views of Hooker. It was in that world, still on the edge of modern science and in which the 'great chain of being' could still be embraced as a cosmological principle, that he could take refuge. Says one modern writer: 'In the gravity and reasonableness of Hooker and Cornelius Agrippa there is manifested a feeling of close intimacy between man and the universe.'[65] Through such influences, Arminian ideas of tolerance as well as a tendency towards theological breadth came to reinforce Ruskin's already well-advanced retreat from the darker ingrained predestinarian outlook of his parents.

Thus, on the eve of his rather unexpected marriage in 1848 to Effie Gray, Ruskin had achieved much but he was starting to question aspects of his inherited faith and to reflect upon the proper requirements of social organization. Hints of this budding interest in public affairs appeared in both his correspondence and published writings. While in Italy in 1845, for instance, he read an account in the press of serious corruption in a workhouse in the Andover Union and he asked his father if 'anything has been done about it?'[66] By this time, he knew some of Southey and of his interest in reforming modes of industry and communities for the poor.[67] Added to this is the striking passage in the second volume of *Modern Painters* indicating that Ruskin was interested in the effects of the Poor Law reforms of 1834 and had started to consider questions of political economy. He identified Benthamite principles of utilitarianism as corrosive of public policy and morality[68]:

> And yet, people speak… as if houses and lands, and food and raiment were alone useful, and as if Sight, Thought and Admiration were all profitless, so that men insolently call themselves Utilitarians who would turn, if they had their way, themselves and their race into vegetables.

It is not surprising perhaps, that utilitarianism, for all its machine-like coolness on paper, bred its own form of excitement in its adherents. It had its own kind of enthusiastic emotional appeal, evident in many of its devotees. For some adherents 'utilitarianism' was an article of faith every much as firm as the ones embraced by the evangelical believer in the tenets of Christian duty. 'When I was twenty-five,' recalled Nassau Senior, 'I resolved to reform the English Poor Laws.'[69] It would be Benthamite thinking that foremost characterized the minds of those who drove the new and carefully researched Poor Law Amendment Act through Parliament, a bill which when first tabled was offered as 'a measure for agricultural relief'.

If the Napoleonic years had distracted men from the poor law, the kinds of knowledge which would allow men to draw a picture of the society was steadily being compiled. The quest for a rational knowledge of what English social conditions were all about can probably be pushed back to 1777 when, as a result of the efforts of John Howard and Sir George Onesiphorus Paul in Gloucestershire, the courts received reports on the state of the poor.[70] The trend towards factual compilation continued with some important results from various official reports. The reformers who brought in the new Poor Law of 1834 had long been associated with this growing tradition of applied statistics. The 1801 *British Census* had, indeed, been conducted by the Poor Law Commissioners.[71] It was appropriate perhaps, that 1834 was also the year of the founding of the London Statistical Society. Four years later, the first issue of its official journal provided practitioners of the new empiricism with a creed[72]:

> It is indeed truly said that the spirit of the present age has an evident tendency to confront the figures of speech with the figures of arithmetic; it being impossible not to observe a growing distrust of mere hypothetical theory and *a priori* assumption, and the appearance of a general conviction that, in the business of social science, principles are valid for application only in as much as they are legitimate inductions from fact, accurately observed and methodically classified.

Despite the many preconceived notions which can creep into the interpretation of 'facts' and which often show up in legislation as a result, the statistical point of view must be taken as one of the major theoretical developments of the first third of the nineteenth century. The rise of new statistical methods had found positive reinforcement in its origins from a somewhat unexpected quarter: promoters of the literary romantic sensibility of the late eighteenth century. This outlook had, among other things, rediscovered childhood and noted the apparent abuse of children, as well as adults, in the rapidly developing industrial urban milieu. Its effects were quite visible to those of romantic sensibility such as William Blake and Charles Lamb. In 1785, the latter penned one of the most caustic criticisms of landlord and industrial irresponsibility in his *Sentimental History of Chimney Sweepers.* 'There may be some who roast their children for food but they certainly kill them first; they are not tortured with fire and soot, hunger and thirst, cold and nakedness.' When Carlyle came to address the 'condition of England' question in his essay 'Chartism' of 1839, he had much to say about statistics, pro and con.[73] The pre-1848 writings of Carlyle, would soon recommend themselves to Ruskin.

Notes

1. See Helen Gill Viljoen, *Ruskin's Scottish Heritage: A Prelude* (Urbana: University of Illinois Press, 1956). The extent of the Ruskin family library and his own later holdings are listed and annotated in James S. Dearden, *The Library of John Ruskin* (Oxford: Oxford Bibliographical Society, 2012).
2. See James Dearden, ed. *A Tour to the Lakes in Cumberland: John Ruskin's Diary for 1830.* (London: Scolar Press, 1990); 'An Account of a Tour of the Continent', *Works*, 2: 340–87.
3. See Helen P. Dale, ed. *Three Letters and an Essay* (London: George Allen, 1893), vii–xv. These materials were also republished in *Works*, 1: 355–98.
4. Van Akin Burd, ed., *The Ruskin Family Letters* (Ithica: Cornell University Press, 1973), I: 390, n. 1.
5. Ruskin to Dale, 9 June 1841, in Dale, ed. (1893), 75.
6. Ibid., 78–9.
7. Editor's Preface, Dale, ed. (1893), xv.
8. *Works*, 3: lv. On the later sale of this painting, see Nancy Scott, 'America's First Public Turner' *British Art Journal*, 10 (3): (2010), 69–77.
9. The recognition of Ruskin as a talented artist in his own right has gained momentum. See Robert Hewison et al., *Ruskin, Turner and the Pre-Raphaelites* (London: Tate Gallery Publishing, 2000), and Christopher Newall, *John Ruskin: Artist and Observer* (Ottawa: National Art Gallery of Canada, 2014).
10. For Hutton and his works, see Jack Repcheck, *The Man Who Found Time* (Cambridge, MA: Perseus, 2003).
11. See Joan Abse, *John Ruskin: The Passionate Moralist* (New York: Alfred A. Knopf, 1981), 42–3; Roy S. Porter, 'Charles Lyell and the Principles of the History of Geology', *The British Journal for the History of Science,* 32 (2): (1976), 91–103.
12. Ruskin to J. J. Ruskin, 10 Jan. 1837 in Burd, ed., *Family Letters*, I: 141; Ruskin to J.J. Ruskin, 22 April, 1837, in *Works*, 36: 14.

13. W. N. Edwards, *The Early History of Paleontology* (London: British Museum, 1967), 8–9.
14. See Ruskin to J.J. Ruskin, 10 Jan. 1837, *Works*, 36: 9; Ruskin to J.J. Ruskin, 22 April 1837, *Works*, 36: 14.
15. *Works*, 35:162; 3:169; 6: 476.
16. See Van Akin Burd, 'Ruskin and his "Good Master" William Buckland', *Victorian Literature and Culture*, 36 (2008), 299–315.
17. *Works,* 19: xliv–v, 358 n.
18. Charles C. Gillispie, *Genesis and Geology: The Impact of Scientific Discoveries Upon Religious Beliefs in the Decades Before Darwin* (New York: Harper and Rowe, 1959), 149–51.
19. Ruskin to Clayton, 8 Jan. 1843, *Works*, 1: 478; *Works*, 35: 198.
20. Ruskin to Clayton, 31 July 1840, *Works*, 1: 414–5.
21. Ruskin to Clayton, 8 Jan. 1843, *Works*, 1: 475–87. Ruskin's essay is appended.
22. Ruskin to Clayton, 8 Jan. 1843, *Works*, 1: 475–87. At this time Ruskin was familiar with Edward Turner's *Elements of Chemistry* (London: Taylor and Watson, 1840), 3 Vol. See *Works*, 4: 235 and James S. Dearden, *The Library of John Ruskin* (Oxford: Oxford Bibliographical Society, 2012), 345; see also Mark Frost, *The Lost Companions and John Ruskin's Guild of St George: A Revisionary History* (London: Anthem Press, 2014), 32–35.
23. See William Buckland, 'Notice on the Megalosaurus or great Fossil Lizard of Stonesfield'. *Transactions of the Geological Society of London*, 1 (2): (1824), 390–396.
24. This long tradition owed much to Aristotle. See Arthur O. Lovejoy, *The Great Chain of Being* (Cambridge: Harvard University Press, 1964), 58–60.
25. *Works,* 25: 56–7; 34: 586; and 'What Mr. Ruskin Says on Darwinism', *Pall Mall Gazette*, May 25, 1886.
26. See the work-illness correlation charts in R.H. Wilenski, *John Ruskin: An Introduction to Further Study of His Life and Work* (London: Faber, 1933).
27. Burd has reviewed details of Ruskin's relationships with his fellows at Oxford. Burd (2008).
28. See Lester Dolk 'The Reception of Modern Painters', *Modern Language Notes*, 57 (8): (1942), 621–626.
29. *Works*, 35: 291–2.
30. Cited in Cynthia Gamble, *John Ruskin, Henry James and the Shropshire Lads* (London: New European Publications, 2008), 46–7.
31. *Works*, 35: 414; See also Michael Wheeler, *Ruskin's God* (Cambridge: Cambridge University Press, 1999), 54–58, and Malcolm Mackenzie Ross, 'Ruskin, Hooker and "the Christian Theoria"', in Millar MacLure and F.W. Watt, eds., *Essays in English Literature from the Renaissance to the Victorian Age, Presented to A.S.P. Woodhouse* (Toronto: University of Toronto Press, 1964), 283–303.

32. George Marshall, ed. *Osborne Gordon: A Memoir with a Selection of His Writings* (London: Parker and Co. 1885), 18.
33. See Harold I. Shapiro, ed. *Ruskin in Italy: Letters to his Parents, 1845* (Oxford: Clarendon Press, 1972), 58; Stephen Wildman and Cynthia Gamble, *'A Perpetual Paradise': Ruskin's Northern France* (Lancaster: The Ruskin Library, 2002), 4, 10–11.
34. On his reading of Alexis Rio's *De la Poésie chrétiene dans son principe, dans sa matière et dans ses forms* (Paris: 1836), see *Diary*, 20 November, 1843 in Joan Evans and J.H. Whitehouse, eds., *The Diaries of John Ruskin* (Oxford: Oxford University Press, 1956), I: 249. See also *Works*, 4: xxiii; 35: 340–41; Alexander Bradley, *Ruskin and Italy* (Ann Arbor: UMI Research Press, 1987), 19; Aidan Nichols, *All Great Art is Praise* (Washington, DC: Catholic University of America Press, 2016), 8.
35. See Richard Titlebaum, *Three Victorian Views of the Italian Renaissance* (New York: Garland Publishing, 1987), 32–4.
36. See Wilenski (1933), Ch. 4.
37. Ruskin to J. J. Ruskin, 11 Sept 1845, in Harold I. Shapiro, ed., *Ruskin in Italy: Letters to his Parents, 1845* (Oxford: Clarendon Press, 1972), 199.
38. Ruskin to J.J. Ruskin, 24 Aug 1845, *Works*, 36: 55–57. See Appendix II for an abridged version of the letter.
39. *Works*, 23: 152–59. Cf. Wallace K. Ferguson, *Europe in Transition, 1300–1520* (Boston: Houghton, Mifflin, 1962), 146–71. See also Appendix 1.
40. *Works*, 33: 375.
41. See Ross (1964), 283–303; Michael Oakeshott, 'Richard Hooker' in *What is History and Other Essays*. Luke O'Sullivan, ed. (Exeter: Imprint Academic, 2004), 207–18. See also the observations in H.F. Kearney, 'Richard Hooker: A Reconstruction' *The Cambridge Journal*, 5 (2): (1952), 300–311, and the observations on Hooker's natural law ideas in Beiser, (1996), Ch. 2.
42. *Works*, 4: 48 f. See also Anthony O'Hear, 'Ruskin and the distinction between Aesthesis and Theoria. The Meaning of Ruskin's Theoretic Faculty'. http://fortnightlyreview.co.uk/2011/04/ruskin-crown/
43. *Works*, 4: 50.
44. *Works*, 4: 241.
45. Ross (1964), 292.
46. *Works*, 4: 48.
47. Iris Murdoch, in her grandly argued counter-attack against post-1900 'ordinary language' English utilitarian ethics and French existentialist choice ethics, embraces a rather Ruskinian view of the importance of art as an indicator of the moral sensibility of individuals in their respective historical situations. Unlike Ruskin, however, she does not posit the need for a vision of God or an external reference point as an ultimate source of morals. See Iris Murdoch, *The Sovereignty of Good* (London: Routledge, 1970), 22–23, 27, 64–5, 83.

48. *Works*, 4: 175–7.
49. *Ibid.*
50. See particularly, Landow (1971) Ch. 4; C. Stephen Finley, *Nature's Covenant: Figures in a Landscape in Ruskin* (University Park: University of Pennsylvania Press, 1992), Ch. 6; John D. Rosenberg, *The Darkening Glass: A Portrait of Ruskin's Genius* (New York: Columbia University Press, 1961), 23.
51. *Ibid.*
52. Ruskin developed this term for wisdom particularly in *The Eagle's Nest. Works*, 22: 123–44.
53. See Katherine Gilbert, 'Ruskin's Relation to Aristotle' *Philosophical Review*, 49 (1): (1940), 52–62.
54. See 'German Metaphysics' in *Works*, 5: 424–26.
55. *Works*, 12: 176–81. R.G. Collingwood, the philosopher and son of Ruskin's secretary, noticed the presence of idealist content in Ruskin. See his *Ruskin's Philosophy* (Kendal: Titus and Wilson, 1921).
56. *Works*, 1: 409.
57. Ruskin to Margaret Ruskin, 13 April 1845, in Harold I. Shapiro, ed. *Ruskin in Italy: Letters to his Parents, 1845* (Oxford: Clarendon Press, 1972), 17.
58. Ruskin to Margaret Ruskin, 20 April 1845, in Ibid., 33.
59. *Works*, 1: 409. See also John L. Idol Jr. 'George Herbert and John Ruskin', *George Herbert Journal*, 4 (1): (1980), 11–28.
60. See A.W. Harrison, *Arminianism* (London: Duckworth, 1937), 142–46.
61. Basil Willey, *The Seventeenth Century Background* (1953), 127–37. Edward Herbert's main work, *De Veritate,* was published first in Paris in 1624 on the recommendation of Grotius. See *The Life of Edward Lord Herbert of Cherbury, Written by Himself* (1764) and www.iep.utm.edu/herbert/. See also Ernst Cassirer, *The Platonic Renaissance in England* (Austin: University of Texas Press, 1953), 52–3.
62. Ruskin to J. J. Ruskin, 24 Dec. 1836, in Van Akin Bird, ed. *The Ruskin Family Letters* (Ithica: Cornell University Press, 1973), I, 386–7; Dearden (2012), 145.
63. Dr. George Brown, his good friend in Edinburgh, had sent Ruskin a copy of George Brown Sr.'s recently edited version of Culverwell.
64. Ruskin to Lady Trevelyan, 8 Aug. 1863, in Virginia Surtees, ed., *Reflections of a Friendship: John Ruskin's Letters to Pauline Trevelyan, 1848–1866* (London: George Allen and Unwin, 1979), 216.
65. Hardin Craig, *The Enchanted Glass: The Renaissance Mind in English Literature* (Oxford: Basil Blackwell, 1966), 30.
66. Ruskin to J.J. Ruskin, 23 Sept. 1845, in Shapiro, ed. (1972), 211.
67. Ruskin, *Diary*, (4 Dec. 1843), cited in *Works*, 3: 653n.

68. *Works*, 4: 29.
69. Cited in Archibald Grove, ed. *The New Review*, (8): (1893), 221.
70. On the achievements of Paul, see E.A.L. Moir, 'George Onesiphorus Paul' in H.P.R. Finberg, ed., *Gloucestershire Studies* (Leicester: Leicestershire University Press, 1957), 195–224.
71. Nathan Glazer, 'The Rise of Social Research in Europe' in D. Lerner, ed. *The Human Meaning of the Social Sciences* (Cleveland: World, 1959), 52.
72. Ibid., 50.
73. See Kirstie M. McClure, 'Optics Ordinary and Extraordinary: Carlyle, Statistics, and "the Condition of England Question"' Paper prepared for the 2012 meeting of the Western Political Science Association (Portland, Oregon). https://wpsa.research.pdx.edu

Bibliography

Abse, Joan. 1981. *John Ruskin: The Passionate Moralist.* New York: Alfred A. Knopf.

Anon. 1886. What Mr. Ruskin Says on Darwinism. *Pall Mall Gazette*, May 25.

Beiser, Frederick C. 1996. *The Sovereignty of Reason: The Defence of Rationality in the Early English Enlightenment.* Princeton: Princeton University Press.

Bradley, Alexander. 1987. *Ruskin and Italy.* Ann Arbor: UMI Research Press.

Buckland, William. 1824. Notice on the Megalosaurus or Great Fossil Lizard of Stonesfield. *Transactions of the Geological Society of London* 1 (2): 390–396.

Burd, Van Akin, ed. 1973. *The Ruskin Family Letters.* Vol. 2. Ithica: Cornell University Press.

———. 2008. Ruskin and His "Good Master" William Buckland. *Victorian Literature and Culture* 36: 299–315.

Cassirer, Ernst. 1953. *The Platonic Renaissance in England.* Austin: University of Texas Press.

Collingwood, R.G. 1921. *Ruskin's Philosophy.* Kendal: Titus Wilson.

Craig, Hardin. 1966. *The Enchanted Glass: The Renaissance Mind in English Literature.* Oxford: Basil Blackwell.

Dale, Helen P., ed. 1893. *Three Letters and an Essay.* London: George Allen.

Dearden, James S., ed. 1990. *A Tour to the Lakes in Cumberland: John Ruskin's Diary for 1830.* Aldershot: Scolar Press.

———. 2012. *The Library of John Ruskin.* Oxford: Oxford Bibliographical Society.

Dolk, Lester. 1942. The Reception of Modern Painters. *Modern Language Notes* 57 (8): 621–626.

Edwards, W.N. 1967. *The Early History of Paleontology.* London: British Museum.

Evans, Joan, and J.H. Whitehouse, eds. 1956. *The Diaries of John Ruskin.* Vol. 3. Oxford: Oxford University Press.

Finberg, H.P.R., ed. 1957. *Gloucestershire Studies.* Leicester: Leicestershire University Press.

Finley, C. Stephen. 1992. *Nature's Covenant: Figures in a Landscape in Ruskin.* University Park: University of Pennsylvania Press.

Frost, Mark. 2014. *The Lost Companions and John Ruskin's Guild of St. George: A Revisionary History.* London: Anthem Press.

Gamble, Cynthia. 2008. *John Ruskin, Henry James and the Shropshire Lads.* London: New European Publications.

Gilbert, Katherine. 1940. Ruskin's Relation to Aristotle. *Philosophical Review* 49 (1): 52–62.

Gillispie, Charles C. 1959. *Genesis and Geology: The Impact of Scientific Discoveries Upon Religious Beliefs in the Decades Before Darwin.* New York: Harper and Rowe.

Grove, Archibald, ed. 1893. *The New Review*, 221. Vol. 8.

Harrison, A.W. 1937. *Arminianism.* London: Duckworth.

Herbert, Edward. 1764. *The Life of Edward Lord Herbert of Cherbury, Written by Himself.*

Hewison, Robert, et al. 2000. *Ruskin, Turner and the Pre-Raphaelites.* London: Tate Gallery Publishing.

Idol, John L., Jr. 1980. George Herbert and John Ruskin. *George Herbert Journal* 4 (1): 11–28.

Kearney, H.F. 1952. Richard Hooker: A Reconstruction. *The Cambridge Journal* 5 (2): 300–311.

Landow, George P. 1971. *The Aesthetic and Critical Theories of John Ruskin.* Princeton: Princeton University Press.

Lerner, D., ed. 1959. *The Human Meaning of the Social Sciences.* Cleveland: World.

Lovejoy, Arthur O. 1964. *The Great Chain of Being.* Cambridge: Harvard University Press.

Marshall, George, ed. 1885. *Osborne Gordon: A Memoir with a Selection of His Writings.* London: Parker and Co.

McClure, Kirstie M. 2012. *Optics Ordinary and Extraordinary: Carlyle, Statistics, and "the Condition of England Question"*. Paper Prepared for the 2012 Meeting of the Western Political Science Association, Portland. https://wpsa.research.pdx.edu

Murdoch, Iris. 1970. *The Sovereignty of Good.* London: Routledge.

Newall, Christopher. 2014. *John Ruskin: Artist and Observer.* Ottawa: National Art Gallery of Canada.

Nichols, Aidan. 2016. *All Great Art Is Praise.* Washington, DC: Catholic University of America Press.

O'Hear, Anthony. Ruskin and the Distinction Between Aesthesis and Theoria. The Meaning of Ruskin's Theoretic Faculty. http://fortnightlyreview.co.uk/2011/04/ruskin-crown/

Oakeshott, Michael. 2004. Richard Hooker. In *What Is History and Other Essays*, ed. Luke O'Sullivan, 207–218. Exeter: Imprint Academic.

Porter, Roy S. 1976. Charles Lyell and the Principles of the History of Geology. *The British Journal for the History of Science*. 32 (2): 91–103.

Repcheck, Jack. 2003. *The Man Who Found Time*. Cambridge: Perseus.

Rosenberg, John D. 1961. *The Darkening Glass: A Portrait of Ruskin's Genius*. New York: Columbia University Press.

Ross, Malcolm M. 1964. Ruskin, Hooker and "the Christian Theoria". In *Essays in English Literature from the Renaissance to the Victorian Age, Presented to A.S.P. Woodhouse*, ed. Millar MacLure and F.W. Watt, 283–303. Toronto: University of Toronto Press.

Scott, Nancy. 2010. America's First Public Turner. *British Art Journal* 10 (3): 69–77.

Shapiro, Harold I., ed. 1972. *Ruskin in Italy: Letters to His Parents, 1845*. Oxford: Clarendon Press.

Surtees, Virginia, ed. 1979. *Reflections of a Friendship: John Ruskin's Letters to Pauline Trevelyan, 1848–1866*. London: George Allen and Unwin.

Titlebaum, Richard. 1987. *Three Victorian Views of the Italian Renaissance*. New York: Garland Publishing.

Viljoen, Helen Gill. 1956. *Ruskin's Scottish Heritage: A Prelude*. Urbana: University of Illinois Press.

Wheeler, Michael. 1999. *Ruskin's God*. Cambridge: Cambridge University Press.

Wildman, Stephen, and Cynthia Gamble. 2002. *'A Perpetual Paradise': Ruskin's Northern France*. Lancaster: The Ruskin Library.

Wilenski, R.H. 1933. *John Ruskin: An Introduction to Further Study of His Life and Work*. London: Faber.

Willey, Basil. 1953. *The Seventeenth Century Background*. Garden City: Doubleday.

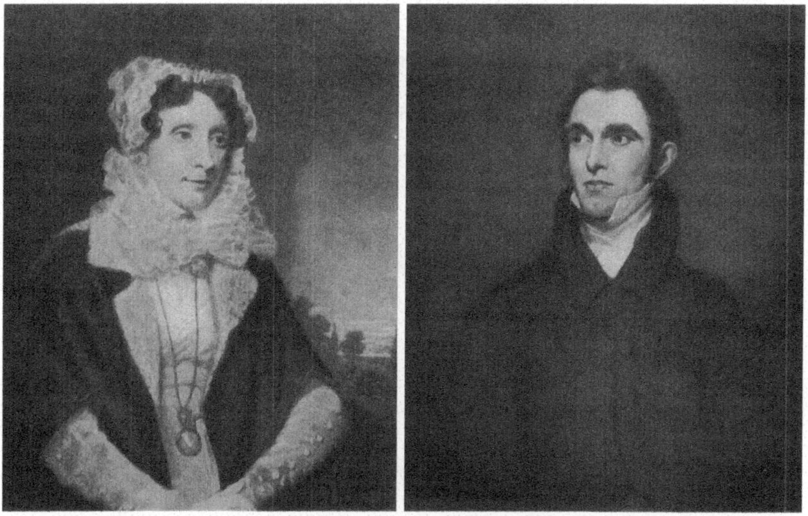

Fig. 2.1 John James Ruskin (1785–1864) and Margaret Ruskin (1781–1871). The relationship between John Ruskin and his generous but stern and religious parents has been the subject of much enquiry. The wealth of J.J. Ruskin allowed the son wide opportunity for travel, private study and art collecting. His mother's early insistence on daily Bible reading turned Ruskin into one of the best informed students of Biblical texts in nineteenth century England. Credit: *Cook and Wedderburn, Ruskin's Collected Works*

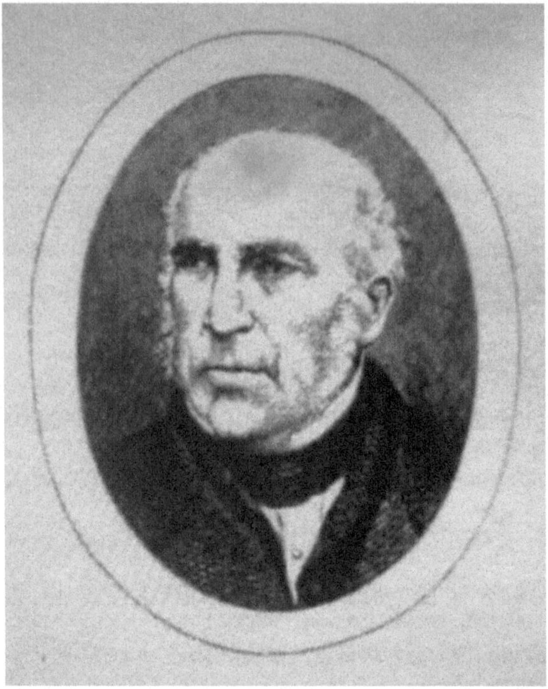

Fig. 2.2 Rev. George Croly (1780–1860). A frequent and engaging guest at the Ruskin family table and a man of 'Ultra-Tory' views, he assisted Ruskin with his first poetry publications. His two-volume study of Burke (1840) was probably known to Ruskin as were his other publications. Ruskin had mixed opinions about Croly's writings. Credit: R.F. Herring, A few Personal Recollections of The Rev. George Croly. London: 1861

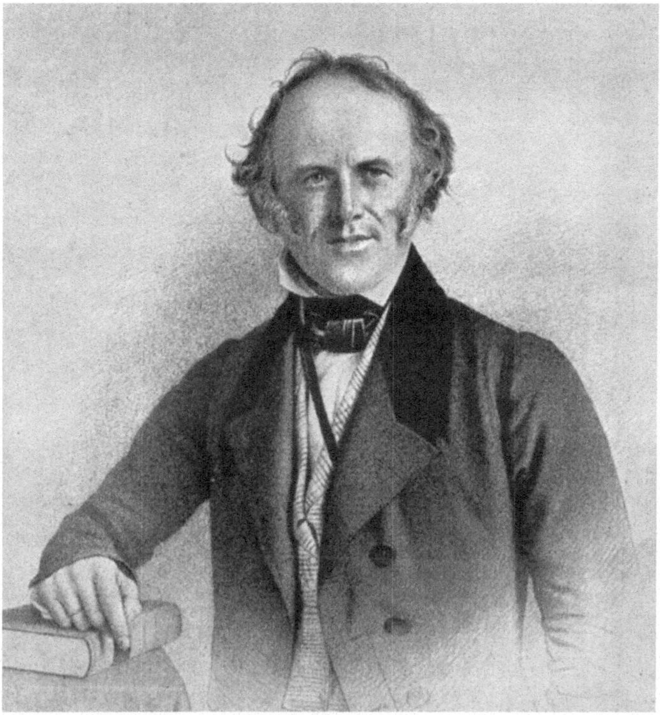

Fig. 2.3 Sir Charles Lyell (1797–1875). This Scottish geologist and lawyer published his important *Principles of Geology* in 1830. The work synthesized much past work by geologists such as James Hutton and established many of the categories used in the greatly expanded geological timescale. Ruskin read his work while still an undergraduate at Oxford and met him at Geological Society conferences. Credit: T.G. Bonney, Charles Lyell and Modern Geology. London: Cassell and Co. 1901

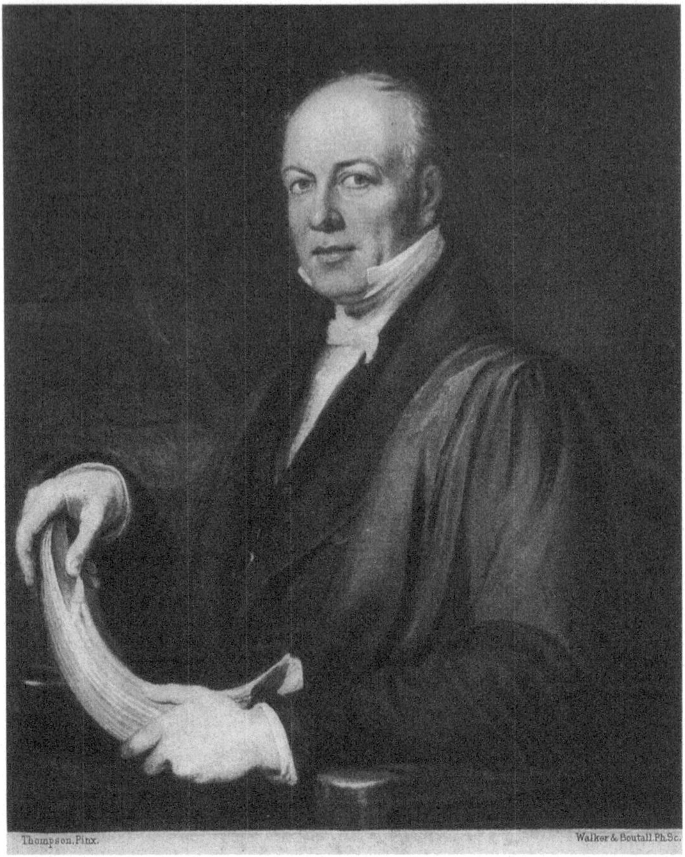

Fig. 2.4 William Buckland (1784–1856). A field-oriented Professor of geology at Oxford, he was a favourite among Ruskin's teachers. He sought to reconcile the new geology of Hutton and Lyle with the Biblical account by means of a theory of catastrophism. The author of one of the theologically conservative 'Bridgewater Treatises', he was also instrumental in establishing the Geological Survey of Great Britain. Credit: Elizabeth Oke Gordon, ed. The Life and Correspondence of William Buckland. London: John Murray, 1894

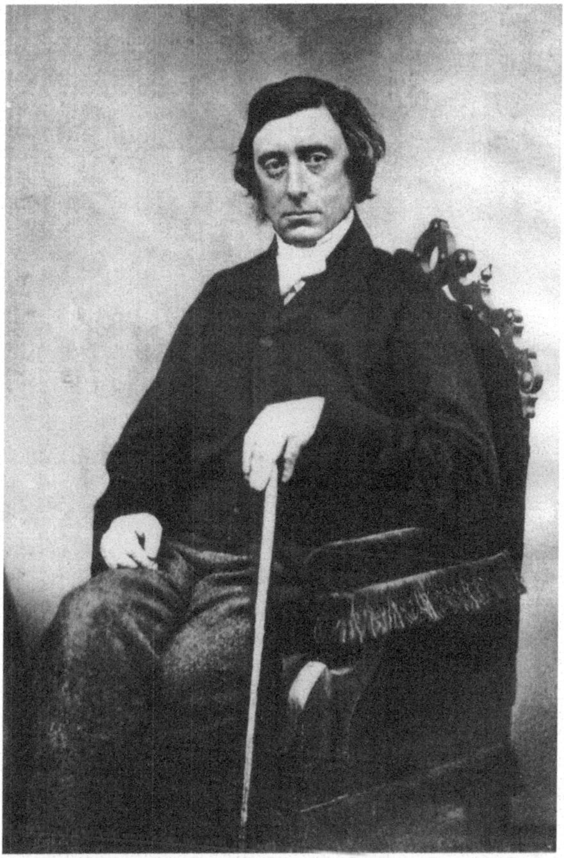

Fig. 2.5 Osborne Gordon (1813–83). A theologian and classicist, he served as Ruskin's most important tutor at Oxford and remained a life-long friend. Through his influence, Ruskin first read the works of Richard Hooker. Ruskin wrote the epitaph for Gordon's memorial plaque in the church of St. Michael and St. Mary Magdalene, Easthampstead, west of London, near Bracknell, where Gordon was the rector. Credit: Courtesy Cynthia Gamble, London, UK

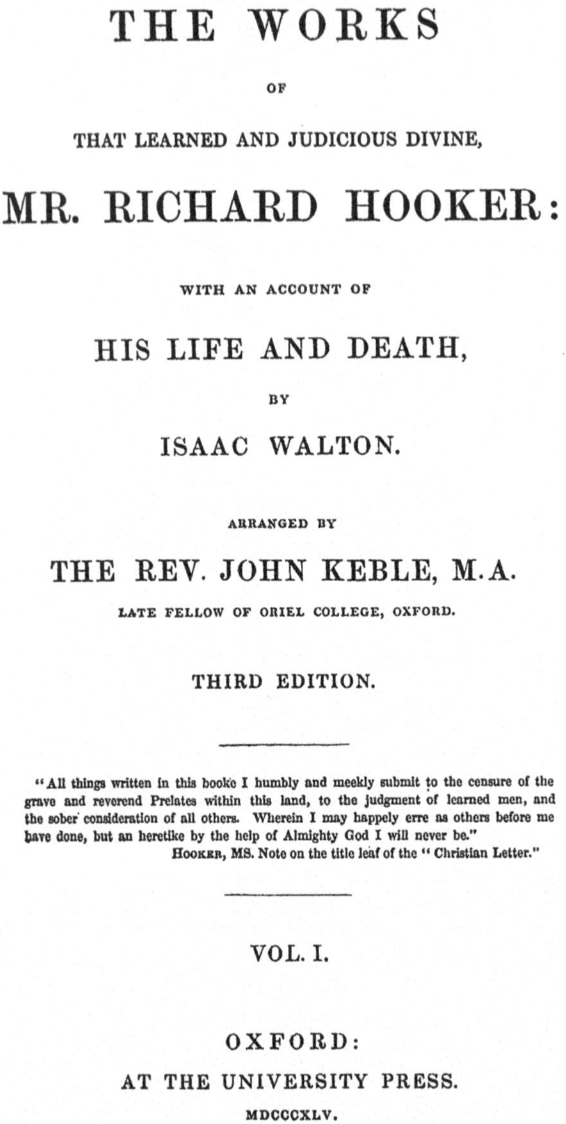

THE WORKS

OF

THAT LEARNED AND JUDICIOUS DIVINE,

MR. RICHARD HOOKER:

WITH AN ACCOUNT OF

HIS LIFE AND DEATH,

BY

ISAAC WALTON.

ARRANGED BY

THE REV. JOHN KEBLE, M.A.

LATE FELLOW OF ORIEL COLLEGE, OXFORD.

THIRD EDITION.

"All things written in this booke I humbly and meekly submit to the censure of the grave and reverend Prelates within this land, to the judgment of learned men, and the sober consideration of all others. Wherein I may happely erre as others before me have done, but an heretike by the help of Almighty God I will never be."

HOOKER, MS. Note on the title leaf of the "Christian Letter."

VOL. I.

OXFORD:

AT THE UNIVERSITY PRESS.

MDCCCXLV.

Fig. 2.6 Title Page of John Keble's new edition of Richard Hooker's *Laws of Ecclesiastical Polity*. The original eight books published intermittently between 1596 and 1662. The work influenced Ruskin's writing style, his thinking about church-state relations and his views on natural law and history. Credit: Laws of Ecclesiastical Polity, Keble edition. London: 1845

CHAPTER 3

Art, Morality and the Fate of Nations: 1848–53

In the context of practical politics, Ruskin was a child of 1848, that remarkable year in European history.[1] A.J.P. Taylor contended it was momentous because the steady movement of population to cities indicated movement towards a collapse of the old landed aristocratic order.[2] Whatever the surface trappings of the post-1815 conservative revival in the wake of the defeat of Napoleon, the *ancienne regime* was under assault or in process of being radically modified in the major heartlands of Europe.[3] The impulse towards urban democratic revolution and industrialization symbolized by 1848 was resisted in Russia, which had land to spare, an un-progressive nobility and little by way of urban industrialization. It was also resisted in Great Britain, already long accustomed to the effects of the industrial revolution and with its own safety-valve for excess population through its colonies or in America.[4] There were, however, difficulties in England after the 'Peterloo' disturbances of 1819.[5] The wheels of reform moved slowly in the 1830s, but gradually achieved something of significance in the two years after the death of George IV in 1830.[6] The generally peaceful 'Chartism' movement gradually came to the fore, its leaders seeking, by petition, to introduce voting and parliamentary reforms.[7] Restrained or not, by 1848 fears were again widespread in England that 'Chartism' might become absorbed by the revolutionary tide mounting in Europe.[8]

In that momentous year, Ruskin, in some apparent confusion, married his cousin, Euphemia Gray, of Perth, Scotland.[9] During the young couple's travels in England and in France, Ruskin could not avoid pondering

G. A. MacDonald, *John Ruskin's Politics and Natural Law*,
https://doi.org/10.1007/978-3-319-72281-8_3

the harder realities of his age. Aware of the demonstrations at home, he and Effie now witnessed first-hand some of the violence of the disturbances in France. In correspondence to W.H. Harrison, he reflected upon the frustration of the workers in Paris and Rouen and the unrelieved threat of continuing violence for the 'the only door of escape seems to be the darkest – that which grapeshot opens.'[10] A letter to his father begins on a similar note but turns quickly to his long-festering doubts about religious belief. He frankly confesses to his father that he has been considering carefully the merits of 'Pascal's Wager'[11]

Such high seriousness provided at least some distraction from the unhappy honeymoon. The state of the unconsummated marriage did not improve when the couple returned home and took up residence in a house not far from the senior Ruskins. Frictions between Effie and her new parents-in-law were compounded by various crises at her own family home in Perth. In early 1849, she returned to Perth in order to look to the needs of her own parents. Ruskin, almost unaccountably, made plans to tour the Alps with his parents instead of with his wife. Nobody in either family circle seemed yet aware of the difficulties in the marriage, thus leaving disguised the true range of the misunderstandings. After his parents returned to England, Ruskin had much of the summer and autumn to himself in the Alps and he put the time to good purpose, gathering information for use in later volumes of *Modern Painters.*

When back in England, efforts were made by husband and wife to repair the damage of the last half year. In this spirit, Effie proposed that they both relocate to Venice where she would assist him as she could in his work while also doing her best to learn about Venice and its people. It was a dutiful offer, quite acceptable to Ruskin, but it ultimately proved to be only a temporary reprieve for an impossible marriage.[12]

The threats posed by the 1848 revolutions to the historic fabric of old Europe in places such as Venice had, meantime, served to turn Ruskin from his work on *Modern Painters* towards architectural studies.[13] The danger to Venice was all too real, for since the Napoleonic Wars the city had become a pawn in European politics, trapped between the ambitions of France and Austria and now complicated by nascent impulses towards democracy and the unification of Italy.[14] The threats of bombardment of the ancient city in 1849 were genuine, if haphazard.[15] Taking up residence in Venice was no mere tourist adventure for the couple. They persevered, however, and the first important literary result was publication of the *Seven Lamps of Architecture* in 1849, followed by the three-volume study, *The Stones of Venice*, completed in 1853.

The social and historical lessons portrayed in these works were not, in fact, the only factors which had turned Ruskin towards sustained social commentary. The impulses were as much theological. The Ruskin family was acutely aware of the various long-festering conflicts over the established church unleashed by the passage of several acts in the late 1820s, by the Reform Bill of 1832 and the Maynooth Grant to Ireland of 1845.[16] Repeal of the Test and Corporation Acts, along with the Catholic Emancipation Bill of 1829, did much to relieve tension in the Catholic and Dissenting communities, but these bills also fostered rising expectations among critics of the Church of England that its days might be numbered. Those sympathetic to the church told its representatives to get the old house in order.[17] In 1838, Gladstone, still essentially Tory, attempted to renew interest in the church-state issue, but his effort fell upon largely indifferent ears, although Macaulay took time to tear it to pieces.[18]

Now came further controversies shaking the foundations of the Church of England. These were manifest through the emergence of the Oxford Movement and specific episodes such as the 'Gorham affair' of 1847.[19] Unresolved questions concerning national church unity and the baptism controversy surrounding Gorham, prompted Ruskin to write two papers: *Notes on the Construction of Sheepfolds*, published in 1851 and an essay on baptism which remained unpublished in his lifetime.[20] The *Notes* proved to be the vehicle by which Ruskin was brought into contact with Frederic Denison Maurice through an exchange of letters facilitated by Frederic J. Furnivall. All three men would end up working together at Maurice's Working Men's College in central London after 1854, but at this juncture Maurice was alarmed by much of what the *Notes* argued. His remarks became rather heated concerning Ruskin's ideas for excommunicating church members for radically improper conduct.[21] Maurice had no reason to doubt Ruskin's statement that 'My faith is a dark one.'[22] To be sure, Ruskin was talking only about temporary excommunication until the transgressor had confessed to error and given positive evidence of a mending of ways. Hooker had taken a broad view of who was admissible to the Church, drawing the line at such 'imps and limbs of Satan' as 'Saracens, Jews and infidels'.[23] Ruskin, as with many others in his time, saw membership for such persons in the Church of England as rather inconsistent but hardly to be proscribed. This was the difference between late Elizabethan times and Victorian times, for the cause of dissent had meanwhile become largely enfolded into what Stefan Collini called the 'National Trust model' of English heritage, which is to say, a civic consciousness acting as 'a repository of treasures which all members of a united nation can enjoy' as part of the shared patrimony.[24] Ruskin was not much interested in outward personal labels or in restricting general participation in civil society.

The continuing refinement of Christianity by means of greater attention to 'reason' in the eighteenth century was an aspect to which Ruskin was not immune, even if he resisted those calls towards rationality made famous by many of the *philosophes*. He was more open to its characteristic English manifestations. Deism took flight in the work of Lord Herbert of Cherbury and it influenced the Cambridge Platonists of the mid-seventeeth century as it did many eighteenth-century English writers, including Burke, whose views on church and state were not significantly different from Ruskin's.[25] Still, deism was a word seldom used by Ruskin. He much preferred the more medieval and lively virtue language of Sidney, Spenser and George Herbert, or the later cooler language of Pope, whom he nevertheless admired.

Notes on the Construction of Sheepfolds explored the presumed utility of a church established at the 'national trust' level. His arguments were consistent with those made by Whitgift and Hooker, that members of a national church were essentially the same as the citizens of the nation.[26] A church conceived broadly, capable of ignoring 'things indifferent' should be capable of carrying out a unifying civil as well as moral function. What was not needed in Victorian England were renewed ambiguities about church authority fostered by *ultra-montane* initiatives from Rome.

If Henry VIII had removed England from the sphere of Roman Papal authority, in doing so he had also 'destroyed the English Church' with his assault on the monasteries and his lean towards Erastian policies aimed at controlling church properties and local jurisdictions.[27] His church revolution having been consolidated, however, Ruskin conceded the importance of adhering to the established relations of church and state in England. Despite the disruptions of the Republican period, these principles still remained much in line with the Elizabethan Settlement of 1559. He was generally supportive of the fruits of Elizabethan pragmatism and not inclined to hear the special pleading of subsequent sectarians, Catholic, Puritan or otherwise.[28] Whatever the errors made by Henry VIII, the 'via media' promoted under Elizabeth had become valuable with respect to social cohesion and the cause of peace, Ireland excepted.[29] Indeed, the memory of the Wars of the Roses were never far below the surface. The importance of law and order were stressed in the *Homilies*, one on obedience (1547) and one on rebellion (1571), set sermons 'ordered to be read in churches' on a regular basis.[30]

Hooker had been the first to provide a durable rationale for this position by which a national church, free of direct Roman influence, prevailed in England. At its crudest, his task had been to justify the Crown of England as a theocratic office along with a corresponding statutory elimination of the Pope as a source of formal national influence. In doing so, however, he had not willingly sought to dissolve the idea of a universal church. The spiritual unity of a nation was held to be of the essence as a policy concern so that projects of schism, whatever their source, had to be resisted in the interests of good government.[31] If the renewed Tudor church was no longer to dominate the monarch in certain particulars, neither was the monarch to neglect the legitimate role of the church in spiritual affairs.[32] Ruskin stressed in his *Notes* the view that the Crown was not to be ruled by the church.[33] The place of 'episcopacy' in the church was subject to historical interpretation relevant to the particular time and case and not just by a resort to scripture. In a *Diary* entry for 1849 he considered this question, as set out in Book Seven of the *Laws of Ecclesiastical Polity*, giving much weight to the values of the traditions supporting episcopacy's long institutional presence in England.[34]

Hooker's logic of defence for the new church was far from airtight but it had the virtue of breadth. G.R. Elton stated that Hooker's role was a moderating one. 'This revival of natural law marked a conservative reaction against the makers of Henry's Reformation' setting the tone for much which lay ahead in church-state relations.[35] The new requirements were those of theological flexibility coupled with a need to define a somewhat distinct character for the reformed national church when measured against on-going practices at the local level. It was in this sense that a twentieth-century historian framed the question as it arose after the Elizabethan Settlement: 'Would it not be better to entrust this task of restraint to a corporate conscience which will take cognizance of all the inclinations of its members; – a church paid to know good and evil, and so to direct the government that it shall eschew evil and pursue good in the performance of its tasks?'[36] This proved to be a delicate undertaking, the results of which were wearing thin by the end of the reign of James I. The dissenting Puritan elements in England were determined to remake the national church in a Presbyterian mould. The violent results are well known. Only in 1648, on the eve of the execution of King Charles I, were Books VI and VIII of Hooker's large work published (Book VII not yet found). In 1662, the complete work was finally published and the general program of the Church of England's 'via media' taken up again.

Even after 1660, following the restoration of the Monarchy, the future of the church was by no means certain.[37] Religious dissent and disabilities were still causes of political instability. By 1718, however, the way seemed to be much clearer, assisted by the cooler forces of deism and its compatibility with the dawning of the eighteenth-century pursuit of reason. If later in that century George III still disliked low church 'latitudinarianism', the society around him had long come to be dominated at many levels by an increasing outlook of reasonableness or mere indifference, not least among the country clergy. 'The way to success was in discretion and man pleasing' observed J.H. Plumb, while 'the worldly virtues became heavenly ones'.[38] This was a reality which crossed class lines and was expressed in many ways. 'Reasonableness' was certainly manifest in the writings of theologians and philosophers of a number of persuasions.[39] As the industrial revolution continued to rearrange town life in the British Isles, the slower ways of the countryside were left behind with an accompanying decline in religious adherence.[40] A close student of English social history stated that during the first three quarters of the eighteenth century 'the Christianity of the upper as of the lower classes in England' was in the main 'both low and cold' and 'nominal to a deplorable degree'.[41] The reaction came with the rise of Methodism, a clear response to the decayed spiritual conditions in the new towns and to the various legal plights of the poor and neglected, a response which owed much to the Moravian evangelical revival in Germany and its influence on John Wesley.[42] The Wesleyan movement soon induced a parallel response within the Anglican Church that led to the appearance of an evangelical wing, one which remained quite distinct in its aspirations when compared with the Wesleyan initiative.[43]

By the 1830s, there was a further appearance of division within the Anglican Church brought on by the so-called 'Papal aggression' that had commenced in 1829 with Catholic Emancipation in England. This 'aggression' was symbolically concluded when John Newman, from within the ranks of the theologically conservative Oxford Movement, defected to Rome in 1845, followed by Henry Manning in 1851. Unlike late Elizabethan times, church unity was threatened less by Puritan-like evangelicalism than by a perceived *ultramontane* resurgence of Roman Catholicism into English affairs.[44] To be sure, gains had been made by both dissenters and Roman Catholics in England since 1829, but the idea of allowing revival of a Roman Catholic diocesan structure in England was viewed with suspicion by many, as it was in the Ruskin family circle.[45] There was, it seems, room for just one official church and perhaps not even one.

Some prominent politicians, particularly Gladstone, had already tested the waters about the feasibility of carrying on with the 'Confessional State' as a suitable model for industrializing England. By 1845, many politicians had come up empty and put the topic behind them as a political risk.[46]

If politicians were cautious, many citizens still thought the cause of church unity an important issue. In the wake of his encounters with working-class revolt on the continent in 1848, Ruskin started to work out his own views on specific matters relevant to the Church of England. In preparing his *Sheepfolds* tract on church unity, he returned to Keble's edition of Hooker's *Laws of Ecclesiastical Polity*, upon which he made notes.[47] In the tract, Ruskin asserted that 'the idea of the separation of Church and State was both vain and impious' but, at the same time, there remained a need to 'limit the sense in which' the word 'church' should be understood. Of the proper relations between church and state, he says, that of the two, the secular arm should dominate. Why should this be so? Ruskin looked to history, where he found two main reasons. The first concerned the fact that evil men will, to some extent, always be found in institutions, and 'it is usually the wicked clergyman who covets civil authority' rather than the converse. Secondly, he believed that even if the wielders of power are both Christians, 'enthusiasm' is nevertheless a 'dangerous concept' in politics. Indeed, to contemplate the history of that idea is to turn over some of 'the most melancholy pages in human records'.[48]

The thrust of Ruskin's argument about the organized church was in line with Hooker's argument that official churchmen were not distinct from the lay membership in anything but degree of learning and leadership capacity and that it was the natural law of reason, not just scripture, which gave shape to the many diverse and legitimate traditions of church organization.[49] There were two equally invalid special claims regularly issuing from Rome or from the dissenting churches: on the one hand, the infallibility and 'Vicarianism' claimed by the Papacy; on the other hand, the belief in a capacity for personal insight into God's workings, accessed through the untrammelled conscience of the 'schismatic' dissenter. In both situations, the 'messengers rarely deliver their message faithfully, and sometimes have declared, as from the King, messages of their own invention'.[50] While an important aspect of being a proper Christian was to become a member of the visible church, more important was it to be a member of the invisible church, the existential reality being that 'a man becomes a member of his church only by believing in Christ with all his heart'.[51]

Such reflections reveal the gathering influence, from several directions, of Ruskin's advance towards a natural law perspective. He had not read deeply into the works of the great Scholastics, such as Albert the Great or Thomas Aquinas, but he had read much Aristotle; and Hooker was a man much influenced by Aristotle and Aquinas.[52] Through Hooker, Ruskin absorbed the importance of the manner in which Aquinas had effected his synthesis of Aristotle and reason with Christian doctrine. 'But how marvellous, yes & beyond all marvel, is it to find Hooker [calling] the Operation of the Spirit of God on mens minds; and that light for which they daily pray, mere Reason. A most pertinent passage this.'[53] While Hooker had been influenced by Calvin to some degree, as were most English Protestants of his day, it was the inclusiveness and organic outlook of medieval times that Hooker sought to revive as the proper way to contain the sectarian extremes which marked the Tudor Church revolution, thereby imparting to the rationale for the new national church a broad coherence, undistracted by 'things indifferent'.[54]

Consider a passage from Book V of the *Laws of Ecclesiastical Polity*: 'Least therefore the name of tradition should be offensive to any' let them consider how far it has been abused by some parties: 'wee meane by traditions ordinances made in the prime of Christian religion, established with the authoritie which Christ hath left to his church for matters indifferent' and in so doing they are considered 'requisite to be observed till like authoritie see just and reasonable cause to alter them'.[55] In any particular individual's comprehension of scripture (now encouraged by the Reformation), he is to give credit and obedience to that which 'scripture doth plainelie deliver' and also to those things he can determine by the use of his reason. Where there is dispute, however, he must yield to that which 'the Church by her ecclesiastical authoritie that probablie thinke and define to be true and good' and allow it to 'overrule all other inferior judgments whatsoever'.[56] Hence, Ruskin's comments above about the importance of retaining the King's role as the head of the National Church in matters more than those merely 'indifferent'.

It may be remarked that this quest for a recapture of the more 'organic' qualities of the Middle Ages via the English Reformation was partially illusory, for it has been well argued that the decline of the papacy and the rise of the mendicant orders was much related to the need to suppress various heresies afoot in late Medieval Europe. With steady urbanization, the outcome was to favour the rise of local monarchies capable of resisting, in some cases, the efforts of the papacy to re-establish its authority, so badly eroded during its 'Babylonian captivity' at Avignon. The erosion of Catholic authority was significant by 1517 in Germany and now further extended by Henry VIII's Reformation in England. The renewed sense of 'organic unity' was justified by Hooker at this stage as a regional one only and tenuous at best, but the larger point was that England was now one of several parts of Europe in open revolt against the authority of Rome.[57]

II

Taken together, Ruskin's commentaries on church affairs from this period reveal much about his developing views on politics and about his growing disparities with the views of his father and some of the 'Ultra-Tories' gathered at the Ruskin table.[58] When Lord Derby took over as Prime Minister in 1852, Disraeli was elevated to Chancellor of the Exchequer. Unlike his father, Ruskin held Disraeli in low esteem. He took a break from his normal routines of architectural documentation in Venice and composed three letters on political matters intended for *The Times* but, as was his habit, sent them first to his father for review. The first concerned 'Taxation, and Especially the Bread-Tax'. The second concerned 'Elections' and the third was about education. They were all suppressed by the father although the third found its way into an appendix in volume three of *The Stones of Venice* (1853). Ruskin took the censorship well enough for at the time he was more interested in just having his views on record for future reference.[59]

The letter on 'Elections' is of interest for indicating that Ruskin favoured universal suffrage in voting but along the lines of so-called 'fancy franchises', which would weigh individual voters according to their general positions in the country and their wealth. While short on details of how this weighting would be assigned, it actually put him in rare agreement with John Stuart Mill, whose views also leaned in this direction.[60]

The letter on taxation was significant for its general departure from the views of his father and his circle. Ruskin advocated free trade and was supportive of the recent repeal of the Corn Laws. His differences with Disraeli, among several, involved the direction of the new Chancellor's remarks of 1850 intimating that continuing agricultural distress in Ireland was caused by the recent establishment of free trade.[61] This Ruskin thought great nonsense and his dissent here provides a way into his views on Ireland.

In many respects Ruskin found himself in agreement with the positions (if not necessarily the methods) of Daniel O'Connell—'the great liberator'—who had argued long and hard for land reform, Catholic emancipation and for repeal of the Union Bills of 1800. The Union Bills had suspended the Irish Parliament but provided Irish MPs to the British House of Commons.[62] Unlike the Ultra-Tories, Ruskin favoured cancellation of the Union for he felt Irish Catholic culture and British Protestant culture were just too distinct to huddle under one political roof. The main support for this contention comes from Ruskin's references to words from an 1839 article by his father in an Appendix to the third volume of *The Stones of Venice*.[63] One must assume that Ruskin and his father were in agreement on the negative qualities of the Irish Union. In a supplementary lecture to *Sesame and Lilies*, given in 1868 in Dublin, he spoke diplomatically about Irish questions generally, criticizing much in past English policy.[64] In 1880, without endorsing Irish revolution, he told an Irish audience: 'But don't you know then, that I am entirely with you in this Irish misery and have been so this thirty years?'[65] His statement here concerned the land question and that absentee landlords were an all too common feature in Ireland. To this situation, he attributed much of the difficulties of Irish agriculture. He agreed with earlier land reform proposals for Ireland including those which J.S. Mill had urged in parliament.[66] Ruskin's views on free trade, which often resembled those of Adam Smith, did not conform well with those of the protectionist Ultra-Tories who supported the Protestant ascendency in Ireland and a continuing role for the Episcopal Church.[67] Indeed, the senior Ruskin was the beneficiary of free trade in terms of his importation into England of the fine Spanish wines and sherries produced by his own firm, Ruskin, Telford and Domecq.[68] Whatever the general inclinations of the Ultra-Tories, then, there were a number of particular points upon which the Ruskin's departed.

The suppressed taxation letter argued for introduction of a graduated income tax which would draw greater public revenue from the wealthy and landed classes.[69] A further departure from the Royalist norms of Ultra-Toryism may be noticed in a letter to his father where he made criticisms of James II. While supportive of monarchy in general, he regarded James II as suspect owing to his lack of respect for the law. He discussed 'loyalty' in *The Seven Lamps of Architecture* and determined that the etymology of the word concerned 'respect for *loy* or law'. One should therefore be loyal to the King 'as long as he observes and represents law; and not merely of established laws at a particular time, but of the principles of law and obedience in general'.[70] This statement has the real ring of natural law principles and James II had come up short in his understanding. Ruskin, however, said nothing about any Lockian 'right of revolution'. His later charter for the Guild of St. George would deny the advisability of claiming such a right. The subsequent 'Glorious Revolution' of 1689–90, on the other hand, had been conducted with a strong constitutional rationale behind it. It was not a fantasy with respect to the normal rules of succession. Ruskin had little to say about the transfer of the crown in that instance, but his customary remarks, in line with those of Carlyle, were that who wore the crown in England was of lesser interest then that some authoritative crown, in fact, be worn.[71]

III

Other shifts going on in Ruskin's mind in 1848 concerned his attitude towards religious belief. A fall letter to his father revealed the extent of his on-going enquiries into recent modern Biblical criticism and of his wavering faith. Characteristically, he attempted to soften the darker implications of his drift away from evangelical belief by structuring the letter somewhat as a dialogue and one in which it may be implied that the father's views were decidedly different from those of Margaret Ruskin[72]:

> I believe that you, as well as I, are in the same condition, are you not father? Neither of us can believe, read what we may of reasoning or proof:
>
> and I tell you also frankly that the more I investigate and reason over the Bible as I should over any other history or statement, the more difficulties I find, and the less ground of belief; and this I say after six years of very patient work of this kind, at least in those hours set apart for such study.

The same letter demonstrated that on the question of belief he had gone so far as to make 'Pascal's Wager': that it was just as prudent to believe as not to believe. This was likely inspired by knowledge of Bishop Butler's version of 'probability' on matters spiritual and philosophical. Unlike some of his fellow eighteenth-century deist writers, Butler pointed to the less satisfying aspects involved in efforts to identify the truth of scripture with the truth of nature, in as much as both were baffling.[73] The same message, says Ladd, could as easily have been derived by Ruskin from his reading of Hooker, although Butler was certainly standard reading for Keble's candidates for the ministry.[74] Doubt arose on all sides, however. It was his long-festering geological knowledge that provides an additional clue to his anxiety at this time. Correspondence with Henry Acland in 1851 indicates that he had not come to terms with the sound 'of those terrible hammers' of the geologists that were so steadily eroding the traditional basis of Biblical history. While understanding the logic behind modern earth science and chemistry, Ruskin maintained a certain reticence towards the implications of this scientific knowledge and did so throughout his life. As Robert Hewison observed, he adopted 'a science of the aspect of things'.[75] A man famous for extolling the virtues of 'seeing correctly' and of using the eye, rather oddly avoided the lessons of the microscope. This reluctance to look at 'the creature within' remained a permanent part of his disposition and is explained in part by what Quentin Bell justifiably implied was a domestically conditioned 'fear of the flesh', a trait well recognized in his art criticism.[76]

This preoccupation with belief in the early 1850s coincided with his first meetings with Carlyle. Although he had not been initially impressed with the 'bombast' of Carlyle's writings, he had been reading him since at least 1841 and signs of this reading started to jell in 1849. His head having been turned towards the larger world, there now seemed to be good reasons to meet the author of *Past and Present*. Ruskin and Effie set about arranging to visit the Carlyles in 1850.

Both men had sympathy for the impulses behind Chartism and the current revolutionary impulses abroad, but were in opposition to arguments that pitted class against class in mere protracted violence. Ruskin admired *Past and Present* throughout his life but there is little reason to think he had much new to learn from it. At many points it merely reinforced his own already well-developed appreciation for the pre-Reformation Christian culture of Europe. He did come to share with 'the sage of Chelsea' a belief that social issues could not be repaired from below. The looming task in Victorian England was not the mere documentation of facts about the abysmal condition of the poor (although this had to be done) or the mere exercise of public and parliamentary debate on means for redress. This, too, had to be done, but both shared a sense that some larger, more fundamental issues were at stake. They endorsed a call for English moral renewal through work, particularly within the upper classes, as a first order of business.

This was not considered by many as a very original or satisfactory reform platform. By1850, Carlyle was becoming ever more bloody minded, his recent writings now rejected by old radical associates such as J.S. Mill.[77] Ruskin was still on the edge of social reform, much of his best artistic and architectural writing still ahead of him. At the outset, their relationship proved a most unusual pairing of sympathies and was viewed as such by Carlyle. He thought Ruskin to be a delightful but dilettantish 'beautiful bottle of soda water'.[78]

At the time of their first meeting, Ruskin's completed works owed much to his on-going discovery of the deeper merits of the art and architecture of old Catholic Europe, first made in the course of his travels of the 1840s.[79] His works still retained a good deal of what later he called Protestant prejudice. His early anti-Catholic asides were served up as much for the reassurance of his parents or as brickbats tossed at the architect, Augustus Pugin, as from real conviction.[80]

Notes on the Construction of Sheepfolds, with its appeal for church renewal and the limiting of sectarian confusion, did not displease his father. Its impulse, however, owed less to the Orange-tinted 'Ultra-Tories' than to his Oxford tutors, Osborne Gordon and Walter Brown, who, we have seen, had led him in different directions in his reading. The works of Hooker and Isaac Taylor moved him towards the sunnier ways of an incarnational Christianity.[81] Increasing contact with F.D. Maurice and Benjamin Jowett took him further down this path.[82] It was, indeed, an exchange of letters over some of the doctrinal issues raised in the *Sheepfolds* tract that first put Ruskin and the heterodox theologian, Frederic Denison Maurice, in touch.[83]

A growing element of Pelagianism is revealed in his lively and somewhat heated correspondence with Maurice. This ancient free-will tendency, so much opposed by St. Augustine, reinforced his hostility towards certain Protestant tenets, particularly the notion of 'justification by faith'. In the unpublished 'Essay on Baptism' of the same period, Ruskin, like Pelagius's disciple Celestius, denied the importance of ritual infant baptism. Of salvation or predestination we could know nothing, thought Ruskin: only proper daily conduct could be attempted, in line with the precepts of current conventional wisdom. If he and Maurice did not agree on certain aspects of doctrine, they nevertheless agreed upon one point: that the better part of religion concerned personal conduct and not doctrine.

Such intimations of Pelagian and anti-atonement tendencies came early in Ruskin's life. 'People be good!' blurted the child from an improvised parlour pulpit.[84] This earliest of his public moralisms revealed a near instinctive attachment to what he later called this 'essentially British heresy', that of the Pelagian variety. This heresy, he thought, by and large, to be a practical and healthy one.[85] In late Roman times, the claim that individuals could 'save themselves by the exertion of their own will' was imputed to Pelagius and strongly opposed by St. Augustine of Hippo.[86] In the event, Pelagius was just as impatient with Augustine and even quoted him in support on his own views on free will.[87]

In the suppressed letter on education from 1851, Ruskin's free-will inclinations helped inform his views on political reform: 'We *can*, if we will but shake off this lethargy and dreaming that is upon us, and take the pains to think and act like men, we can I say make kingdoms to be like well-governed house-holds.'[88] His instincts in religion were, from an early age, inclined towards the latitudinarian and non-denominational.[89] He came by these instincts honestly enough, for his socially mobile parents were themselves not above adopting a broader Anglicanism, despite their mutual upbringings in the Presbyterian Church.[90]

IV

Having disposed of certain theological and political issues for the moment, Ruskin returned to the completion of *The Stones of Venice*. The motives behind the first volume were practical, containing the fruit of his laborious measurements and descriptions of buildings, an early example, perhaps, of that kind of building inventory which has come to represent aspects of the planning of the 'heritage district' in more recent times. These researches, it will be recalled, were first undertaken in the aftermath of the warfare associated with the failed revolutions of 1848. They continued now, undertaken in the fear of rampant restoration and development work as modern tourism started to make increasing demands on the facilities of the old city.[91]

The second volume took him in the direction of historical sociology. Here, as with previous comments in *The Poetry of Architecture*, can be noted his belief in the idea of social conditioning at work in the production of personality, culture and architecture. In a famous chapter, 'The Nature of Gothic', he emphasized that what people were asked to do in their day-to-day lives should not just be seen as a measure of personal preference and conscious contractual consent, but also as a measure of the organizational values of that society in which such personal decisions were taken. As in *The Poetry of Architecture*, he stressed the meaning of buildings in terms of what they indicated about the character of the work force as a whole, considering them to be an 'index' of the society that produced them. 'On the

Nature of Gothic' has often been singled out as a memorable contribution to Victorian thought, particularly by William Morris and Kenneth Clark. The latter considered it one of the 'noblest things written in the nineteenth century' even if the second half of the chapter contained 'paragraphs of nonsense'.[92] Part of that 'nonsense' has been discussed in some detail by students of the history of architecture with particular reference to Ruskin's limited grasp of medieval building techniques and the actual skills required of masons. Ruskin's views come off distinctly at variance with the historical reality.[93] In the empirically oriented *Stones of Venice*, the chapter on the Nature of Gothic just 'does not fit', contended Garrigan, for Ruskin 'must establish the rude imperfection of Gothic, however dubiously, in order to prove something much more important to him'.[94] The pleasing ideal of the unskilled but creative workman replaced the higher and grimmer realities and standards actually enforced by local guilds.[95]

This being said, there was yet an empirical and comparative side to Ruskin's studies of historical architecture of a less controversial nature which gains our admiration and speaks to his keen interest in environmental factors in history. Consider his description in *The Stones of Venice* of a relatively obscure topic, the details of cornices and so-called 'drip stones'. Cynthia Gamble draws our attention to Ruskin's detailed drawings of drip stones at the medieval ruins of Wenlock Abbey which he made in 1850 and how these differ in shape from similar ones in Venice.[96] The Wenlock craftsmen have taken account of the great amount of rain in the northerly terrain of England and shaped the curvature of the drip stones accordingly. The ones in Venice are more appropriate to a dryer climate.[97] This is the kind of subtle observation which made Ruskin's analysis of architecture and paintings so informative.

In the chapter on Gothic, Ruskin began to explore one of the main points underlying the particular version of a labour theory of value he later articulated concerning the question of the happiness of the workers while at their stations and not merely the justness of their deserts. In doing so, he would provide a strong contrast with other classical labour theories of value, particularly that made famous by Marx. Behind the 'Nature of Gothic' lurked a distinct conception of the 'spirit of the age' different in character from that which supposedly animated people of Renaissance times, the eighteenth century or his own times. Patrick Conner understood Ruskin to have lamented the loss of this 'spirit' for Ruskin distinguished 'between the change in formal elements, from Gothic to classical' and what Ruskin therefore saw as a change in approach and building methods leading to increasing social 'demands for perfection'.[98] Gone is that fancied free-play of the mind of the medieval worker with his rougher instinctive ways; waiting in the wings was the predictability of machine technology and time-motion studies. Embodied in this shift were the seeds of a trend towards the liberal and free-thinking writers of the Enlightenment who argued for the cause of individual political liberty in ever more certain and philosophically abstract ways.

Volume three of *The Stones of Venice* took Ruskin in firmer historical directions, but ones conceived in highly psychological terms. The rationalist errors of the Enlightenment are found to have origins in the Italian Renaissance. A Renaissance period concept was not, in Ruskin's day, yet a firm one, although its traits had come to be intimated in the writings of Michelet and a good number of others.[99] Ruskin's views on the Renaissance were narrow and highly subjective when compared with the greater precision achieved by Jacob Burkhardt, Walter Pater or John Addington Symonds.[100] If Burkardt and Ruskin both saw the emergence of ego-driven 'personality' as a basic trait of Renaissance societies, each placed quite different judgements on the meaning of such flowering of individuality. Ruskin rushed to moral judgement about the negative implications of self-conscious individuality, relating it to the resulting disorder of the Italian city states. His views lacked the high historical and moral objectivity of the 'detached vision' of Burkhardt.[101]

Despite many pages of questionable historical interpretation, *The Stones of Venice* became one of his best-regarded works.[102] Not all, of course, were in accord. Ruskin and the philosopher Herbert Spencer held each other in mutual disregard. Spencer had enjoyed aspects of *Modern Painters* but *The Stones of Venice* turned him away from the writer owing to Ruskin's didacticism and 'barbaric' interests.[103] For his part, Ruskin saw Spencer as one of those spinners of systems, his works representing extreme examples of the very worst of utilitarian political economy and modern philosophy.[104]

One of the stated motives of *The Stones of Venice* was plainly to instruct the English about the fates of past sea-based empires by making connections between their historical destinies and the state of their public morals at critical times. The conclusions made were rather procrustean. Making regular use of the exhaustive researches of Rawdon Brown and the works of Pierre Daru, he yet drew his own distinct conclusions, often to the frustration of Brown. He held that, roughly, the year 1410 marked the onset of the decline of the Venetian Republic, occurring when authorities sought to systematically exclude the Roman Church from participating in the Republic's guiding councils.[105] This was certainly difficult to square with the actual sectarian religious history of Venice and its mixed population. Its many places of worship reflected the early growth of a civic pragmatism appropriate to an international trading city state, faiths being hosted from all quarters of the western and eastern empires, including Jews and Moslems. Its success was built on the strength of ships which combined both trade and warfare functions, long produced in a massive public shipyard known as the 'Arsenal'.[106] In its medieval phases, Venetian fleets did much to police the Adriatic against piracy on behalf of various imperial authorities although their own commercial practices on the high seas often resembled nothing less than well-organized piracy. Such flexible policies were quite capable of sanctioning high symbolic gestures, such as bringing home alleged relics of the apostle St. Mark. Such trophies became central ornaments of the republic.[107] To the extent that the Roman Catholic Church had a special place in Venice, up until the early thirteenth century it was a highly symbolic one, but by no means an exclusive one in the minds of Venetian leaders. Their well-toned sense of diplomacy dictated otherwise.[108] Such international latitudinarianism was good for business. In the early thirteenth century, there was no obvious decline in Venice's position until Vasco da Gama's opening of a new trade route around Africa in 1498 had significant, although not fatal, effects on Venice's long geographic trade advantage as 'the hinge of Europe'. Ruskin's attempt to play down the importance of this new naval achievement out of Western Europe was rather unconvincing.[109] His arguments for the precision of cause and effect within the complexity of Venetian history have made it difficult for more recent historians to give much credence to *The Stones of Venice* as history.[110] Later historians have seen the Renaissance as a period of transition in history rather than as the rather sharp moral and economic divide favoured by Ruskin.[111]

More puzzling, perhaps, were Ruskin's attempts to characterize the Italian Renaissance, in its humanist aspects, as inherently pagan, while he simultaneously displayed a high regard for ancient classical writers or those of the English Renaissance. The Elizabethans, despite significant Reformation influences, owed a great debt to similar forces which marked the recovery of learning in the Italian city states.[112] Had not Patristic writers, such as St. Jerome, whom Ruskin admired, recovered and revised old texts? Yet, with his new American friend, Charles Eliot Norton, he came to agree that Petrarch should be neglected and Dante studied, the latter as the culmination of the medieval outlook. The *Divina Commedia*, said Norton, 'is not only the crown of the religious achievement of Italy, – but its close' for it opened the way to scepticism, after which Petrarch came 'sentimentally dawdling, and Boccaccio jesting, down the road, with the whole tribe of unbelievers behind them'.[113] The painter Raphael, with his interest in perspective, was identified by Ruskin as the great harbinger of a decline in European painting in as much as he allegedly foreshadowed the rise of scientific rationalism and its concomitant, atheism.[114] Michelangelo was 'a grand fellow but the ruin of art'.[115] This great artist, it was alleged, had been caught up in events and became a source of much of the mischief.[116] Such artists were not personally responsible but were children of their times and their times were corrupt.[117] These kinds of judgements did not then or now stand up well to inspection, for the entire question of 'ancients and moderns' implied in much of Ruskin's discussion of the Renaissance is a complicated one.[118] His complaints, however, were not uncharacteristic of many Romantic period writers and their successors, who mistook the interest in pagan writings exhibited by Italian humanists, including Petrarch, as a sign of Christian impiety.[119]

Such confusion notwithstanding, Richard Titlebaum has observed that Ruskin's historical method, considered more broadly, shared a good deal with the approach of Vasari, and by implication with Vico, displaying a sensitivity to the cultural importance of legal elements and to the supposed cyclic features of specific national histories.[120] When he came to write *Val d'Arno*, for example, his discussion of Florentine history included reference to the alliance of Frederick II of Germany with the famed Ghibellines of Florence, the internecine warfare with the Guelphs and victory over them. It was, says Ruskin, 'the first interference of the Germans in Florentine affairs which belongs to the real cycles of modern history.'[121]

His studies in the history of art and architecture taught him to measure the fates of societies by means of moral yardsticks and these he applied to the study of contemporary English art and society. The spiritual authority that eluded Carlyle, Ruskin located in mythic and historical evidence indicative of the relative success or failure of various experiments in civil association. The distinct merits of each could be assessed through a reading of the remains of their tangible arts, architecture and literature.

At Oxford in the 1870s, he took seriously the task of cautioning young Victorians about the pitfalls of running an empire, a task much associated with Oxford.[122] In his lectures, he regularly threw out challenges to his students. Such exhortations were acknowledged, even if not heard directly, by such as Cecil Rhodes.[123]

There were reasons additional to his grand historical comparisons between England and Venice as to why *The Stones of Venice* appealed to a continuing readership. These included its value as a well-informed kind of travel literature.[124] Aspects are associated with his concrete suggestions about the range of things being lost in the midst of modern industrial enterprise, things intangible but relevant to the values of an allegedly more organic European past[125]:

> We have much studied and much perfected, of late, the great civilized invention of the division of labour; only we give it a false name. It is not, truly speaking, the labour that it divided; but the men: – Divided into mere segments of men – broken into small fragments and crumbs of life.

And so 'the great cry that rises from our manufacturing cities' is a response to the condition 'that we manufacture everything there except men'.[126] Such were some of the lessons offered in the chapter on 'The Nature of Gothic' indicative of his gradual shift towards political economy. He had detected an ethic of cooperative individualism at work in the medieval world which he thought worth recapturing in the modern.

V

Buried in an appendix to the third volume of *The Stones of Venice* was the suppressed essay on education. In it are found not just his nascent political inclinations favouring revival of a more holistic or collective view of social relations, but also of the state as an instrumental facilitator of broad substantive purposes. The 'first duty of a state is to see that every child born therein shall be well housed, clothed, fed and educated, till it attain years of discretion'. Somewhat ominously, he added that 'to the effecting of this, the government must have an authority over the people of which we now do not as much as dream…'.[127] Reading such disturbing words,

Ruskin's father thought he had good reasons for censoring the original letter. He told his son that these letters, unlike his other works, were 'slum buildings'.[128]

These letters might be appropriately identified as a measure of the economic interpretation of history surfacing in Ruskin's view of the world. It implied that a main political-economic virtue of medieval society concerned the artisan's position of not being required (ideally) to be a slave to some master designer who had the power to sub-divide his labour into ever more specialized, tedious and repetitive routines. Each person had a birth right, limited though it might be, and each person had a legal stake in the fuller range of the community, including that of its economic benefits. He contended that, in a general way, medieval society recognized 'in small things as well as great, the individual value of every soul'.[129] Perfection of performance was not required from every person, only sincere and faithful performance. Such attitudes and expectations as these had helped produce the great cathedrals of the twelfth through fourteenth centuries.[130] His negative views of much Renaissance achievement stemmed less from the fact of the blossoming of virtuoso genius as from evidence presumably promoting an undisciplined and irreligious individuality as the basis of a new social ethos. There, he thought, lay the road to anarchy. Such tendencies led to the degeneration of the arts into what he took to be procedures of mere imitation, encouraged by the demands of the market place. It was the different quality of the moral condition implied to be required by virtuosity as against craftsmanship that was at stake: the medieval work-a-day world had left room for the random play of an important element: imagination.

The mounting influences of Dante and Plato on his thought reinforced an inclination to investigate older sources of European religion and the deeper origins of Christian ethics. These two powerful figures contributed substantially to the amalgam which came to underlie his political program, much of it served up in forms owing something to the historical romanticism of Sir Walter Scott's novels and to the lost image of the gentleman-knight as portrayed in Kenelm Digby's *Broad Stone of Honour* (1823).[131]

Notes

1. See Priscilla Robinson, *Revolutions of 1848: A Social History* (New York: Harper and Row, 1960).
2. A.J.P. Taylor, *Europe: Grandeur and Decline* (Harmondsworth: Penguin, 1967), Ch. 5. For England and the slower unfolding of this collapse, see

F.M.L. Thompson, *English Landed Society in the Nineteenth Century* (London: Routledge and Kegan Paul, 1963), Ch. 10.
3. Ibid., 47–49; and see Mark Jarrett, *The Congress of Vienna and Its Legacy* (London: I.B. Tauris. 2014), Ch. 8.
4. Disbanded British soldiers from the Napoleonic Wars had been offered lands in the military settlements of Upper Canada as early as 1815. See George F. Playter, *An Account of the Founding of Three Military Settlements in Eastern Ontario: Perth, Lanark and Richmond, 1815–20* (Toronto: Ontario Historical Society Papers and Records, Vol. 20, 1923); on emigration from Britain to the Unites States in the first half of the nineteenth century, see *Statistical Abstract of the United States, 1926.* (Washington, DC: US Government Printing Office, 1927), 89.
5. On the events leading up to Peterloo and immediately thereafter see John W. Osborne, *John Cartwright* (Cambridge: Cambridge University Press, 1972), Chapters 6–8.
6. Antonia Fraser, *Perilous Question:Reform or Revolution? Britain on the Brink, 1832* (New York: Public Affairs, 2013).
7. Geoffrey Finlayson, *England in the Eighteen Thirties: Decade of Reform.* (London: Edward Arnold, 1969), 90–100.
8. See Norman Gash, *Reaction and Reconstruction in English Politics, 1832–1852* (Oxford: Clarendon Press, 1965), 129–32; Asa Briggs, *Chartism* (Phoenix Mill: Sutton Publishing, 1998).
9. The literature on this ill-fated marriage is now large. See especially, Mary Lutyens, *The Ruskins and the Grays* (London: John Murray, 1972); Suzanne F. Cooper, *Effie: The Passionate Lives of Effie Gray, John Ruskin and John Everett Millais* (London: St. Martin's Press, 2011).
10. Ruskin to W.H. Harrison, 24 Oct. 1848, *Works,* 8: xxxii–xxxiii.
11. Ruskin to J.J. Ruskin, 24 Aug. 1848, *Works*: 36: 90.
12. See *Works,* 8: xxviii; 12: xxxvi f.; Cooper, (2011), Chapters 4–6; Mary Lutyens, *Young Mrs. Ruskin in Venice* (London: John Murray, 1965), 38–40.
13. Jeanne Clegg, *Ruskin and Venice* (London: Junction Books, 1981), 72–74.
14. See. J.P. Trevelyan, *A Short History of the Italian People*, 4th ed. (London: George Allen and Unwin, 1956), Chapters 25–28; Robinson (1960), Ch. 19.
15. G.M. Trevelyan, *Manin and the Venetian Revolution of 1848* (Longmans, Green and Co., 1923).
16. Much would have been heard of these matters around the family table. See Hewison, 'Notes on the Construction of the Stones of Venice' in Robin E. Rhodes and Del I. Jenik, eds., *Studies in Ruskin: Essays in Honour of Van Akin Burd* (Athens: Ohio University Press, 1982), 139–40.

17. See Gash, (1965), Ch. 3. See also his *Aristocracy and People: Britain 1815–1865* (Cambridge, 1979), 176–79; Desmond Bowen, *The Idea of the Victorian Church* (Montreal: McGill University Press, 1968), 84–90, 96–111.
18. See W.E. Gladstone, *The State in Its Relations with the Church* (London: John Murray, 1839); T.B. Macaulay, 'Gladstone on Church and State' in A.J. Grieve, ed. *Critical and Historical Essays* (London: Everyman's Library. 1937), II: 237–89. On Gladstone's shifting position on matters of church and state, see J.D. Lorenzo, 'Gladstone, Religious Freedom and Practical Reasoning', *History of Political Thought*, XXVI, (2005), 90–119.
19. On this controversy, see *Gorham v. Bishop of Exeter:* The *Judgement of the Judicial Committee of Privy Council. Delivered March 8, 1850, reversing the decision of Sir. H.J. Fust* (London: MacIntosh, 1850).
20. Both are printed in *Works*, 12: 509–58.
21. For the letters between Ruskin, Maurice and Furnivall see *Works*, 12: 561–72.
22. Ruskin to F.D. Maurice, 30 March 1851 in *Works*, 12: 562.
23. Hooker, *Laws*, Bk. III, Sec. 7. Keble, ed. (1845), 1: 341–2.
24. Stefan Collini, *Public Moralists: Political Thought and Intellectual Life in Britain, 1850–1930* (Oxford: Clarendon Press, 1991), 345–6.
25. On these moderating influences, see J.M. Creed and J.S. Boys-Smith, eds. *Religious Thought in the Eighteenth Century* (Cambridge: Cambridge University Press, 1934), xi–xl, 285–90.
26. Book VIII of Hooker was strong on this contention. See H.F. Kearney 'Richard Hooker: A Reconstruction', *Cambridge Journal*, 5 (1951–1952), 306. Ruskin and Maurice, whatever else their differences, were at least agreed on this point.
27. So stated Ruskin in his late years. He approved of the interpretation of the Tudor revolution given by William Cobbett in his *History of the Protestant Reformation* (1826). See Albert C. Isaacs, *The Fountain of Sienna: An Episode in the Life of John Ruskin* (London: S.W. Partridge, 1900), 9–12.
28. *Works*, 33: 111.
29. Nicholas Canny, *The Elizabethan Conquest of Ireland* (Dublin: Branchline, 1976); James O'Neill, *The Nine Years War, 1593–1603: O'Neill, Mountjoy and the military revolution* (Dublin: Four Courts Press, 2017).
30. Christopher Morris, *Political Thought in England: Tyndale to Hooker* (London: Oxford University Press, 1953), 72–3.
31. H.R. Trevor-Roper, 'Richard Hooker and the Church of England' in his *Renaissance Essays* (Chicago: University of Chicago Press, 1985), 103–20.
32. On the Monarch's role in the new dispensation, see the papers in A.S. McGrade, ed., *Hooker and the Construction of Christian Community*

(Tempe: Medieval and Renaissance Texts and Studies, 1997); and H.C. Porter, 'Hooker, The Tudor Constitution and the *Via Media*' in W. Speed Hill, ed. (1972), 77–116.

33. *Works*, 12: 548–50.
34. Ruskin's *Diary*, 18 March 1849, in *Works*, 12: lxxiii.
35. G.R. Elton, *England Under the Tudors* (London: Methuen, 1969), 401–2.
36. H.R. Trevor-Roper, *Archbishop Laud* (London: Phoenix Press, 1962), 18.
37. On the drawn-out publication history of Hooker's *Laws*, see W. Speed Hill, 'The Evolution of Hooker's *Laws of Ecclesiastical Polity*' in W. Speed Hill, ed. (1972), 117–58. See also Robert S. Bosher, *The Making of the Restoration Settlement: The Influence of the Laudians, 1649–1662* (London: Dacre Press, 1957), 231–33.
38. J.H. Plumb, *England in the Eighteenth Century*. Rev. ed. (Harmondsworth: Penguin, 1968), 44.
39. See Creed and Smith (1934).
40. Plumb (1968), 44–5.
41. William Connor Sydney, *England and the English in the Eighteenth Century*, 2d ed. (Edinburgh: John Grant, c. 1892), 2: 328.
42. Ibid., 350 f. See also Frederick A. Dreyer, *The Genesis of Methodism* (Bethlehem: Lehigh University Press, 1999).
43. See G.R. Balleine, *A History of the Evangelical Party in the Church of England* (London: Longmans Green, 1933), Ch. 4.
44. On anti-papal sentiment, see E.R. Norman, *Anti-Catholicism in Victorian England* (London: George Allen and Unwin, 1968).
45. See Hewison (1982), 138–40.
46. On the tangible difficulties between church and state in England between 1829 and 1852, see Gash (1965), Chapters 3 and 4.
47. 'Ruskin's Notes on Hooker', Lancaster University Archives. Mss. M5c and M10a.
48. *Works*, 12: 555.
49. See the insightful discussion in Alexander S. Rosenthal, *Crown Under Law: Richard Hooker, John Locke and the Ascent of Modern Constitutionalism* (Plymouth: Lexington Press, 2008), 61–73.
50. *Works*, 12: 548, 550.
51. *Ibid.*, 12: 528.
52. See Kearney (1952), 304–7; W.D.J. Carghill Thompson, 'The Philosopher of the Politic Society', in W. Speed Hill, ed., (1972), 7–12; W. David Newlands, 'Hooker on Reason, Scripture and Tradition' in McGrade, ed. (1997), 75–94.
53. Ruskin's Notes on Hooker. Lancaster University Archives. Ms 5c (174).

54. On Hooker and 'things indifferent', see Thompson, ed. (1972), 15–17. On Hooker and Calvin, see Richard Tuck, *Philosophy and Government, 1572–1651* (Cambridge: Cambridge University Press, 1993), 150–51; Lee W. Gibbs, 'Richard Hooker's *Via Media* Doctrine of Scripture and Tradition' *Harvard Theological Review*, 95 (2): (2002), 233–34; Hooker, *Of the Laws of Ecclesiastical Polity*, Book II. Ch. 4: Sec. 5, John Keble, ed. (London: Oxford University Press, 1845) 1: 297.
55. Hooker, Book V: 65.2, cited in W. David Neelands, 'Hooker on Scripture, Reason and Tradition' in A.S. McGrade, ed. (1997), 90.
56. Hooker, Book V. 8: 2, cited in Neelands, ibid.
57. See Gordon Leff, 'Heresy and the Decline of the Medieval Church', *Past and Present*, 20 (Nov. 1961), 36–51.
58. See Hewison (1982), 138–40.
59. *Works*, 12: lxxxi.
60. See J.S. Mill, 'Considerations on Representative Government' (1861), in J.A. Robson, ed. *Collected Works* (Toronto: University of Toronto Press, 1977), 19*: 474–79;* 'Representation of the People', Speech to Parliament: 31 May 1866, in *Collected Works,* (1988) 28: 83–5.
61. *Works*, 12: lxxxi, n. 1.
62. See J.H. Whyte, 'Daniel O'Connell and the Repeal Party', *Irish Historical Studies*, 11 (44): (1959), 297–316.
63. See *Works*, 11: 258–63.
64. *Works*, 18: 173–4.
65. *Works*, 34: 544.
66. *Works*, 17: 444 n. On Mill's engagement with Irish issues, see Bruce L. Kinzer, *England's Disgrace?: J.S. Mill and the Irish Question* (Toronto: University of Toronto Press, 2001).
67. On the Ultra-Tories, see Hewison (1982) and Douglas G. Simes, *The Ultra Tories in British. Politics 1824–1834* (Oxford D. Phil., I974).
68. Tim Hilton, *John Ruskin: The Early Years* (New Haven: Yale University Press, 1985), 6, 12.
69. 'Taxation and Principally Bread Tax' (1852), *Works*, 12: 593–99.
70. Ruskin to J.J. Ruskin, March 29, 1852, in *Works*, 12: lxxxii; see also Quinton (1978), 21.
71. *Works*, 25: 295, 308.
72. Ruskin to J.J. Ruskin, Aug. 24, 1848, *Works*, 36: 90.
73. Basil Willey, *The Eighteenth Century Background* (Harmondsworth: Penguin, 1967), 79.
74. Henry Ladd, *The Victorian Morality of Art* (New York: Ray Long and Richard R. Smith, 1932), 156–57; Georgina Battiscombe, *John Keble: A Study in Limitations* (New York: Alfred A. Knopf, 1964), 54.

75. Robert Hewison, 'Paradise Lost: Ruskin and Science' in Michael Wheeler, ed. *Time and Tide: Ruskin and Science* (London: Pilkington Press, 1996), 33–4. See also Patricia Ball, *The Science of Aspects* (London: Athlone Press, 1971).
76. See Quentin Bell, *Ruskin* (New York: George Braziller, 1978), 78–80; George P. Landow, *The Aesthetic and Critical Theories of John Ruskin* (Princeton: Princeton University Press, 1971), 169–71, 254.
77. J.S. Mill 'The Negro Question' *Fraser's Magazine*, 41 (Jan. 1850), 25–31. Reproduced in *Collected Works*, 21: 87–95.
78. Carlyle to John Carlyle, Nov. 27, 1855. Cited in Cate, ed. (1982), 15–16.
79. On Ruskin's discovery of older European art traditions, see Wallace K. Ferguson, *The Renaissance in Historial Thought* (Cambridge: Houghton Mifflin, 1948), 141–44.
80. See Appendix 12 of *The Stones of Venice*, I, in *Works*, 9: 437–9. See also Rosemary Hill, *God's Architect: Pugin and the Building of Romantic Britain* (Toronto: Allen Lane, 2007).
81. *Works*, 28: 342. On Ruskin's retreat from evangelical views, see Van Akin Burd, ed. *The Winnington Letters* (Cambridge: Harvard University Press, 1969), 62–75; Wilenski (1933), Ch. 4.
82. Hilton (1986), 288–93; 298–304; 337; Wheeler (1999), 116–17, 211, 260.
83. For the correspondence, see *Works*, 12: 561–72. See also Ch. 3 below.
84. *Works*, 28: 298; 35: 25–6.
85. *Works*, 33: 210, 428. Since 1900, more measured views of the extent of Pelgius's free-will views have been established. See B.R. Rees, *Pelagius: Life and Letters* (Woodbridge: The Boydell Press, 1998); Theodore De Bruyn, Trans. *Pelagius's Commentary on St. Paul's Epistle to the Romans* (Oxford: Clarendon Press, 1993).
86. Peter Brown, *Augustine of Hippo: A Biography* (London: Faber and Faber, 1988), 345, 354–58, 363.
87. Ibid., 148, 177.
88. *Works*, 11: 261.
89. John Idol sees Ruskin's early attachment to the poetry of George Herbert as a first impulse towards an embrace of the non-denominational in religion. Idol (1980), 12.
90. On the religious background, see Helen Gill Viljoen *Ruskin's Scottish Heritage: A Prelude* (Urbana: University of Illinois Press, 1956), Chapters 6 and 13.
91. *Works*, 8: 3; and See Jean Clegg, *Ruskin and Venice* (London: Junction Books, 1981), 56, 72–3; Robert Hewison, *Ruskin on Venice* (New Haven: Yale University Press, 2009), 138–9.

92. Kenneth Clark, *The Gothic Revival*, Introduction by J. Mordaunt Crook (London: John Murray, 1995), 202.
93. See John Unrau 'Ruskin, the Workman and the Savageness of Gothic', in Hewison, ed. (1981), 33–50; Douglas Knoop and G.P. Jones, *The Medieval Mason* (Manchester: Manchester University Press, 1967), Chapters 3–6.
94. Kristen O. Garrigan, *Ruskin on Architecture: His Thought and Influence* (Madison: University of Wisconsin Press, 1973), 102.
95. Unrau (1981), 39–40.
96. Cynthia Gamble, *Wenlock Abbey, 1857–1919* (Much Wenlock: Ellingham Press, 2015), 17–19.
97. *Works*, 9: 9, 321.
98. Patrick Conner, *Savage Ruskin* (Detroit: Wayne State University Press, 1979), 103.
99. See Ferguson, (1948), 173–77.
100. See Richard Titlebaum, *Three Victorian Views of the Renaissance* (New York: Garland Publications, 1987; Conner (1973), 100–104; John R. Hinde, *Jacob Burkhardt and the Crisis of Modernity* (Montreal: McGill-Queen's University Press, 2000), 4–8.
101. See Michael Oakeshott, 'The Detached Vision: The Letters of Jacob Burkhardt' *Encounter* (June, 1954), 69–73.
102. One modern edition is radically abridged. See Ruskin, *The Stones of Venice*. Edited with an Introduction by Jan Morris (London: Folio Society, 2001).
103. For Spencer, see *Autobiography* (London: William Norgate, 1904) I: 351.
104. See Ruskin in the *Contemporary Review* (May, 1873), in *Works*, 17: 556–58. He was here referencing Spencer's *Study of Sociology*.
105. *Works*, 9: 29, 419–20.
106. See Frederic C. Lane, *Venice: A Maritime Republic* (Baltimore: The Johns Hopkins Press, 1973), Chapters 2–4, 8–9, 25; *Venice and History: Collected Papers of Frederic C. Lane* (Baltimore: The Johns Hopkins Press, 1966), Ch. 10.
107. See Lane (1973), 12 and Ch. 3; William H. McNeill, *Venice: The Hinge of Europe, 1081–1797* (Chicago: University of Chicago Press, 1974), 8–9.
108. Garrett Mattingly, *Renaissance Diplomacy* (London: Jonathan Cape, 1962), 58–59, 77–82; Sabastian Giustiniani, 'Introduction' *Four Years at the Court of Henry VIII*. Rawdon Brown, trans. (1854) 2 v. (Cambridge: Cambridge University Press, 2013), 1: ix–xxvii.
109. *Works*, 10: xlviii; 24: 235; 34: 528; see the entries on the fluctuating economic place of Venice after 1498 detailed in Nigel Cliff, *The Last Crusade: The Epic Voyages of Vasco Da Gama* (New York: Harper, 2011).

110. See J.B. Bullen, 'Ruskin and the Tradition of Renaissance Historiography' in Michael Wheeler, ed., *The Lamp of Memory: Ruskin, Tradition and Architecture* (Manchester: Manchester University Press, 1992), 57; J.D. Rosenberg, *The Darkening Glass: A Portrait of Ruskin's Genius* (New York: Columbia University Press, 1961), 54–55.
111. See Wallace K. Ferguson, *Europe in Transition: 1300–1520* (Boston: Houghton Mifflin, 1962); Douglas Bush, *The Renaissance and English Humanism* (Toronto: University of Toronto Press, 1939), 34–35.
112. See Leicester Bradner, 'From Petrarch to Shakespeare' in Metropolitan Museum of Art, *The Renaissance: Six Essays* (New York: Harper and Row, 1962), 97–119; Bush (1939), 69–73; Arthur B. Ferguson, *The Articulate Citizen and the English Renaissance* (Durham: Duke University Press, 1965), Ch. 6.
113. Norton to Ruskin, 29 Dec. 1872, in Bradley, ed. *The Correspondence of John Ruskin and Charles Eliot Norton* (Cambridge: Cambridge University Press, 1987), 272; and see *Works*, 11: 130–32.
114. *Works*, 3: 276; 5: 77–82; 11: 70; 12: 134–40, 148–50.
115. *Works*, 4: xxxii.
116. *Works*, 11: 18, 70–71.
117. *Works*, 11: 16, 46.
118. See the reviews, presumably by George Merideth, which appeared in 1853, in Bradley, ed. *The Critical Heritage*, 143–76; see also Hans Baron, 'The Querelle of the Ancients and the Moderns as a problem for Renaissance scholarship' in Paul O. Kristeller and Philip Wiener, eds. *Renaissance Essays* (New York: Harper and Row, 1968), 96–114.
119. See Ferguson (1962), 292–301.
120. Titlebaum (1987), 20, 36–37.
121. *Works*, 23: 60.
122. See Ronald Robinson, 'Oxford in Imperial Historiography' in Frederick Madden and D.K. Fieldhouse, eds. *Oxford and the Idea of Commonwealth* (London: Croom Helm, 1982), 30–48.
123. Basil Williams, *Cecil Rhodes* (London: Constable, 1921), 41–2, 50; Robert I. Rotberg, *The Founder: Cecil Rhodes and the Pursuit of Power* (Oxford: Oxford University Press, 1988), 85, 89.
124. See Elizabeth K. Helsinger, *Ruskin and the Eye of the Beholder* (Cambridge: Harvard University Press, 1982), Ch. 5.
125. *Works*, 10: 196.
126. Ibid.
127. *Works*, 11: 263.
128. J.J. Ruskin to Ruskin, March 30, 1852, *Works*, 12: lxxxiv.
129. *Works*, 10: 189–90.

130. A much more plausible account of the realities of cathedral building is given in Douglas Knoop and G.P. Jones, *The Medieval Mason* (Manchester: Manchester University Press, 1967), Chapters 3–6.
131. Scott was read closely by Ruskin. He collected materials towards a projected biography, one of many uncompleted projects. On his reading of Digby see *Works*, 7: 361; 27: 545. See also Mark Girouard, *The Return to Camelot: Chivalry and the English Gentleman* (New Haven: Yale University Press, 1981), 199–200, 220–24.
132. Footnote references to Ruskin's writings (unless otherwise stated) are cited as *Works,* and refer to Cook, Edward T. and Wedderburn, Alexander, eds. *The Collected Works of John Ruskin.* London: 1903–1912. 39 v.

Bibliography[132]

Balleine, G.R. 1933. *A History of the Evangelical Party in the Church of England.* London: Longmans Green.

Battiscombe, Georgina. 1964. *John Keble: A Study in Limitations.* New York: Alfred A. Knopf.

Bell, Quentin. 1978. *Ruskin.* New York: George Braziller.

Bosher, Robert S. 1957. *The Making of the Restoration Settlement: The Influence of the Laudians, 1649–1662.* London: Dacre Press.

Bowen, Desmond. 1968. *The Idea of the Victorian Church.* Montreal: McGill University Press.

Bradley, J.L., ed. 1984. *Ruskin: The Critical Heritage.* London: Routledge and Kegan Paul.

Bradley, J.L., and Ian Ousby, eds. 1987. *The Correspondence of John Ruskin and Charles Eliot Norton.* Cambridge: Cambridge University Press.

Briggs, Asa. 1998. *Chartism.* Phoenix Mill: Sutton Publishing.

Brown, Peter. 1988. *Augustine of Hippo: A Biography.* London: Faber and Faber.

Brown, Rawdon, Trans. 2013. *Four Years at the Court of Henry VIII.* (1854). Vol. 2. Cambridge: Cambridge University Press.

Burd, Van Akin, ed. 1969. *The Winnington Letters.* Cambridge: Harvard University Press.

Bush, Douglas. 1939. *The Renaissance and English Humanism.* Toronto: University of Toronto Press.

Canny, Nicholas. 1976. *The Elizabethan Conquest of Ireland.* Dublin: Branchline.

Clark, Kenneth. 1995. *The Gothic Revival.* London: John Murray.

Clegg, Jeanne. 1981. *Ruskin and Venice.* London: Junction Books.

Collini, Stefan. 1991. *Public Moralists: Political Thought and Intellectual Life in Britain, 1850–1930.* Oxford: Clarendon Press.

Conner, Patrick. 1979. *Savage Ruskin.* Detroit: Wayne State University Press.

Cooper, Suzanne F. 2011. *Effie: The Passionate Lives of Effie Gray, John Ruskin and John Everett Millais*. London: St. Martin's Press.

Creed, J.M., and J.S. Boys-Smith, eds. 1934. *Religious Thought in the Eighteenth Century*. Cambridge: Cambridge University Press.

De Bruyn, Theodore, Trans. 1993. *Pelagius's Commentary on St. Paul's Epistle to the Romans*. Oxford: Clarendon Press.

Dreyer, Frederick A. 1999. *The Genesis of Methodism*. Bethlehem: Lehigh University Press.

Elton, G.R. 1969. *England Under the Tudors*. London: Methuen.

Ferguson, Wallace K. 1948. *The Renaissance in Historical Thought: Five Centuries of Inter-pretation*. Boston: Houghton Mifflin.

———. 1962. *Europe in Transition: 1300–1520*. Boston: Houghton Mifflin.

Finlayson, Geoffrey. 1969. *England in the Eighteen Thirties: Decade of Reform*. London: Edward Arnold.

Fraser, Antonia. 2013. *Perilous Question: Reform or Revolution? Britain on the Brink, 1832*. New York: Public Affairs.

Gamble, Cynthia. 2015. *Wenlock Abbey, 1857–1919*. Much Wenlock: Ellingham Press.

Garrigan, Kristen O. 1973. *Ruskin on Architecture: His Thought and Influence*. Madison: University of Wisconsin Press.

Gash, Nomran. 1965. *Reaction and Reconstruction in English Politics, 1832–1852*. Oxford: Clarendon Press.

———. 1979. *Aristocracy and People: Britain 1815–1865*. Cambridge.

Gibbs, Lee W. 2002. Richard Hooker's *Via Media* Doctrine of Scripture and Tradition. *Harvard Theological Review* 95 (2): 227–235.

Girouard, Mark. 1981. *The Return to Camelot: Chivalry and the English Gentleman*. New Haven: Yale University Press.

Gladstone, W.E. 1839. *The State in Its Relations with the Church*. London: John Murray.

Gorham v. Bishop of Exeter: The Judgement of the Judicial Committee of Privy Council. Delivered March 8, 1850, reversing the decision of Sir. H.J. Fust. 1850. London: MacIntosh.

Grieve, A.J., ed. 1937. *Critical and Historical Essays*. London: Everyman's Library.

Helsinger, Elizabeth K. 1982. *Ruskin and the Eye of the Beholder*. Cambridge: Harvard University Press.

Hewison, Robert, ed. 1981. *New Approaches to Ruskin: Thirteen Essays*. London: Routledge and Kegan Paul.

———. 2009. *Ruskin on Venice*. New Haven: Yale University Press.

Hill, W. Speed, ed. 1972. *Studies in Richard Hooker: Essays Preliminary to an Edition of His Works*. Cleveland: Case Western Reserve University.

Hill, Rosemary. 2007. *God's Architect: Pugin and the Building of Romantic Britain*. Toronto: Allen Lane.

Hilton, Tim. 1985. *John Ruskin: The Early Years*. New Haven: Yale University Press.

Hilton, Boyd. 1986. *The Age of Atonement: The Influence of Evangelicalism on Social and Economic Thought, 1785–1865*. Oxford: Clarendon Press.

Hinde, John R. 2000. *Jacob Burkhardt and the Crisis of Modernity*. Montreal: McGill-Queen's University Press.

Hooker, Richard. 1845. In *Of the Laws of Ecclesiastical Polity*, ed. John Keble. Oxford: Oxford University Press. 3 v.

Idol, John L., Jr. 1980. George Herbert and John Ruskin. *George Herbert Journal* 4 (1): 11–28.

Isaacs, Albert C. 1900. *The Fountain of Sienna: An Episode in the Life of John Ruskin*. London: S.W. Partridge.

Jarrett, Mark. 2014. *The Congress of Vienna and Its Legacy*. London: I.B. Tauris.

Kearney, H.F. 1951–1952. Richard Hooker: A Reconstruction. *Cambridge Journal* 5: 300–311.

Knoop, Douglas, and G.P. Jones. 1967. *The Medieval Mason*. Manchester: Manchester University Press.

Kristeller, Paul O., and Philip Wiener, eds. 1968. *Renaissance Essays*. New York: Harper and Row.

Ladd, Henry. 1932. *The Victorian Morality of Art*. New York: Ray Long and Richard R. Smith.

Landow, George P. 1971. *The Aesthetic and Critical Theories of John Ruskin*. Princeton: Princeton University Press.

Lane, Frederic C. 1966. *Venice and History: Collected Papers of Frederic C. Lane*. Baltimore: The Johns Hopkins Press.

———. 1973. *Venice: A Maritime Republic*. Baltimore: The Johns Hopkins Press.

Leff, Gordon. 1961. Heresy and the Decline of the Medieval Church. *Past and Present* 20 (1): 35–61.

Lorenzo, J.D. 2005. Gladstone, Religious Freedom and Practical Reasoning. *History of Political Thought* 26 (1): 90–119.

Lutyens, Mary. 1965. *Young Mrs. Ruskin in Venice*. London: John Murray.

———. 1972. *The Ruskins and the Grays*. London: John Murray.

Madden, Frederick, and D.K. Fieldhouse, eds. 1982. *Oxford and the Idea of Commonwealth*. London: Croom Helm.

Mattingly, Garrett. 1962. *Renaissance Diplomacy*. London: Jonathan Cape.

McGrade, A.S., ed. 1997. *Hooker and the Construction of Christian Community*. Tempe: Medieval and Renaissance Texts and Studies.

McNeill, William H. 1974. *Venice: The Hinge of Europe, 1081–1797*. Chicago: University of Chicago Press.

Metropolitan Museum of Art. 1962. *The Renaissance: Six Essays*. New York: Harper and Row.

Mill, J.S. 1850. The Negro Question. *Fraser's Magazine* 41: 25–31.

———. 1963–1991. *Collected Works*. Toronto: University of Toronto Press.
Morris, Christopher. 1953. *Political Thought in England: Tyndale to Hooker*. London: Oxford University Press.
Norman, E.R. 1968. *Anti-Catholicism in Victorian England*. London: George Allen and Unwin.
Oakeshott, Michael. 1954. The Detached Vision: The Letters of Jacob Burkhardt. *Encounter*, June, pp. 69–73.
Osborne, John W. 1972. *John Cartwright*. Cambridge: Cambridge University Press.
Playter, George F. 1923. *An Account of Three Military Settlements in Eastern Ontario: Perth, Lanark and Richmond, 1815–20*. Vol. 20. Toronto: Ontario Historical Society Papers and Records.
Plumb, J.H. 1968. *England in the Eighteenth Century*. Rev. ed. Harmondsworth: Penguin.
Rees, B.R. 1998. *Pelagius: Life and Letters*. Woodbridge: The Boydell Press.
Rhodes, Robin E., and Del I. Jenik, eds. 1982. *Studies in Ruskin: Essays in Honour of Van Akin Burd*. Athens: Ohio University Press.
Robinson, Priscilla. 1960. *Revolutions of 1848: A Social History*. New York: Harper and Row.
Rosenberg, J.D. 1961. *The Darkening Glass: A Portrait of Ruskin's Genius*. New York: Columbia University Press.
Rosenthal, Alexander S. 2008. *Crown Under Law: Richard Hooker, John Locke and the Ascent of Modern Constitutionalism*. Plymouth: Lexington Press.
Rotberg, Robert I. 1988. *The Founder: Cecil Rhodes and the Pursuit of Power*. Oxford: Oxford University Press.
Ruskin, John. *Ruskin's Notes on Hooker*. Lancaster University Archives. Mss. M5c and M10a.
Statistical Abstract of the United States, 1926. 1927. Washington, DC: U.S. Government Printing Office.
Sydney, William C. 1892. *England and the English in the Eighteenth Century*. 2nd ed. Edinburgh: John Grant.
Taylor, A.J.P. 1967. *Europe: Grandeur and Decline*. Harmondsworth: Penguin.
Thompson, F.M.L. 1963. *English Landed Society in the Nineteenth Century*. London: Routledge and Kegan Paul.
Titlebaum, Richard. 1987. *Three Victorian Views of the Italian Renaissance*. New York: Garland Publishing.
Trevelyan, G.M. 1923. *Manin and the Venetian Revolution of 1848*. Longmans: Green and Co..
Trevelyan, J.P. 1956. *A Short History of the Italian People*. 4th ed. London: George Allen and Unwin.
Trevor-Roper, H.R. 1962. *Archbishop Laud*. London: Phoenix Press.
———. 1985. *Renaissance Essays*. Chicago: University of Chicago Press.

Tuck, Richard. 1993. *Philosophy and Government, 1572–1651*. Cambridge: Cambridge University Press.

Viljoen, Helen Gill. 1956. *Ruskin's Scottish Heritage: A Prelude*. Urbana: University of Illinois Press.

Wheeler, Michael, ed. 1992. *The Lamp of Memory: Ruskin, Tradition and Architecture*. Manchester: Manchester University Press.

———, ed. 1996. *Time and Tide: Ruskin and Science*. London: Pilkington Press.

———. 1999. *Ruskin's God*. Cambridge: Cambridge University Press.

Whyte, J.H. 1959. Daniel O'Connell and the Repeal Party. *Irish Historical Studies* 11 (44): 297–316.

Wilenski, R.H. 1933. *John Ruskin: An Introduction to Further Study of His Life and Work*. London: Faber.

Willey, Basil. 1967. *The Eighteenth Century Background*. Harmondsworth: Penguin.

Williams, Basil. 1921. *Cecil Rhodes*. London: Constable.

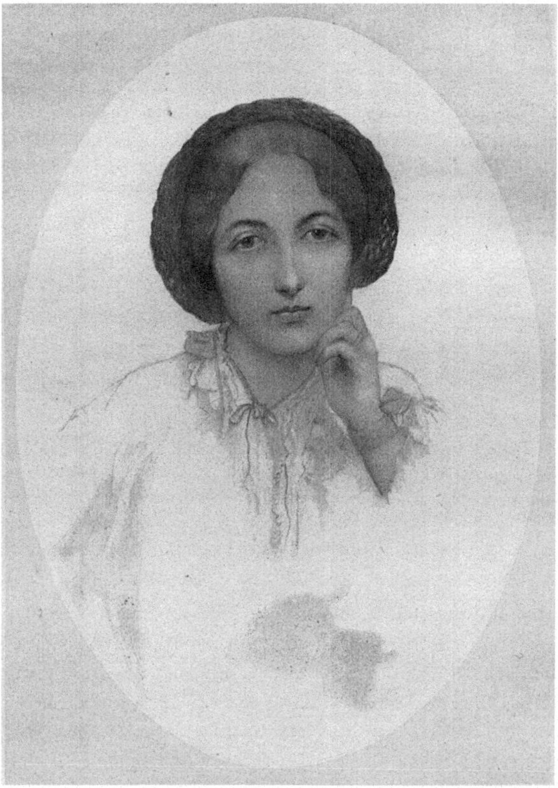

Fig. 3.1 Euphemia Gray Ruskin (1828–97). Ruskin married his cousin 'Effie' from Perth, Scotland, in 1848. The marriage was annulled in 1854. A year later, she married the Pre-Raphaelite painter, John Everett Millais. This pencil drawing by J.F. Watts, shows her at age 18. Credit: Pencil sketch by J.F. Watts. 1846. The Life and Letters of Sir John Everett Millais. J.G. Millais, ed. 2nd ed. London: Methuen. 1900, Vol. 2

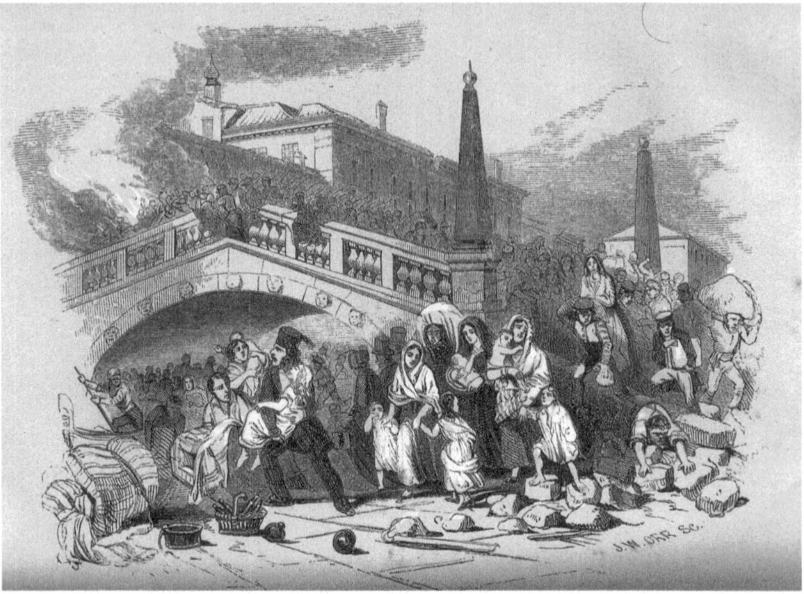

Fig. 3.2 Siege and Bombardment of Venice, 1848. Since 1815, conflicts between Austria, France and groups seeking to guide an Italian 'risorgimento' had been frequent, particularly for control of Venice and other northern parts of Italy. After Patriots declared a new Venetian Republic on 22 March 1848, the Austrians attacked the city. Credit: Edmund Flagg, Venice: The City of the Sea. New York: Charles Scribner, 1853, Vol.2

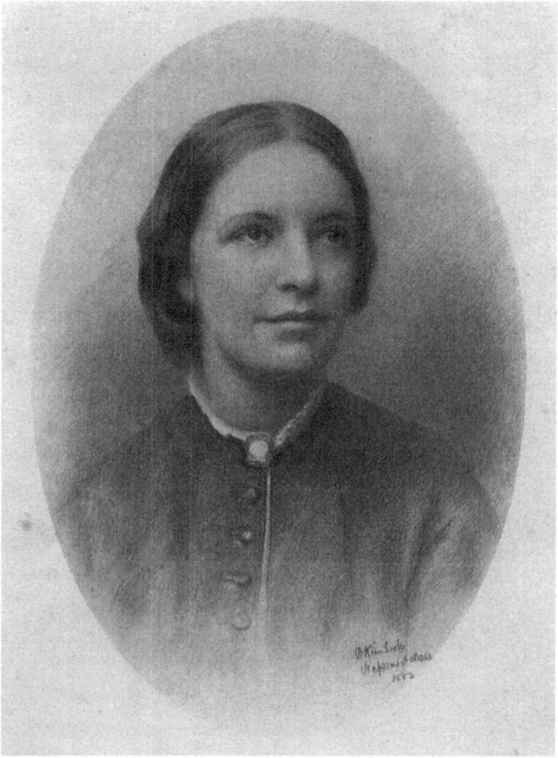

Fig. 3.3 Octavia Hill (1838–1912) from a photograph, 1882. Art student and eventual housing reformer, she met Ruskin in 1855 when she and her mother were also involved with F.M. Maurice's Working Men's College. After 1864, Ruskin supported her efforts to provide better homes for the urban poor. Her practical views on administration led to friction between them. Both figured in the development of the National Trust. Credit: Edmund Maurice, ed. Life of Octavia Hill as Told in Her Letters. London: Macmillan and Co. 1913

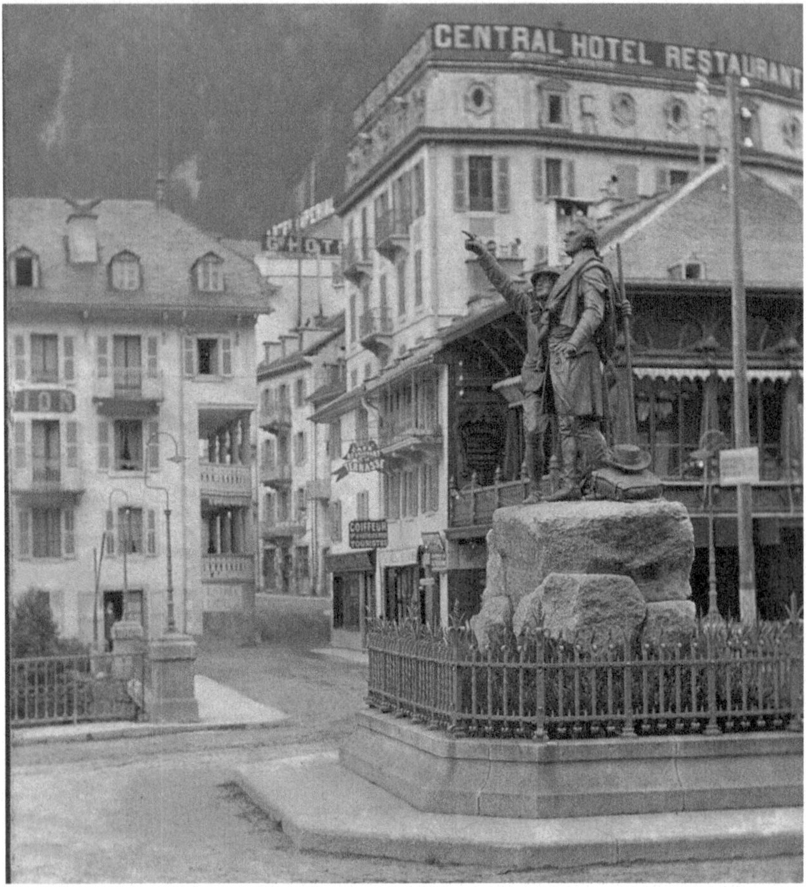

Fig. 3.4 The Union Hotel at Chamonix, France, c. 1910. It was in this hotel, in 1860, that Ruskin penned four essays on political economy for the Cornhill Magazine. These were republished as *Unto This Last* in 1862. The bronze statues date from 1887 and commemorate Alpinists Horace-Bénédicte de Saussure and Auguste Balmat. Credit: Courtesy: Peter Blair, Chamonix Mont Blanc, France

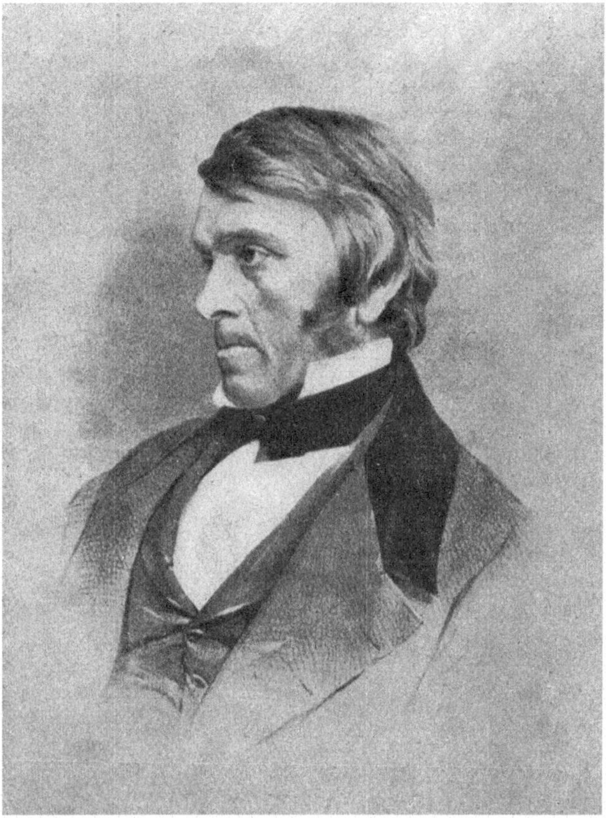

Fig. 3.5 Thomas Carlyle (1795–1881). Portrayed here in 1848, the Scottish writer and social critic made an impression on Ruskin and their personal relationship became close after 1850. While often linked in terms of political attitudes, they each drew on very different sources. Credit: Jane Welsh Carlyle: Letters to Her Family, 1839–1863. Leonard Huxley, ed. Garden City: Doubleday, 1924

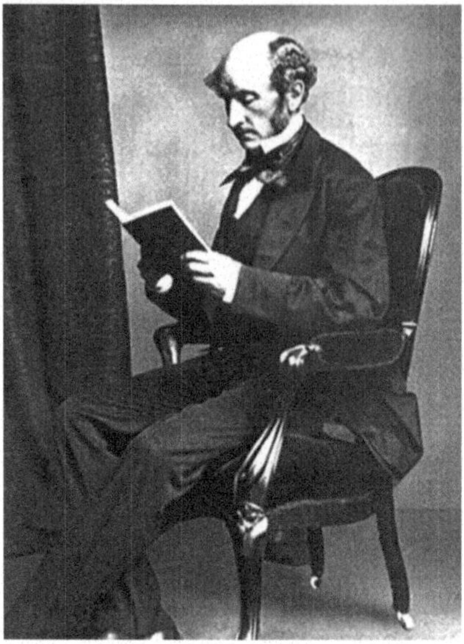

Fig. 3.6 John Stuart Mill (1809–73). The foremost exponent of Victorian liberal political economy, personal liberty and a modified utilitarian ethics, Mill was regularly castigated by Ruskin for his views. Ruskin shared more with Mill than he normally admitted and on certain occasions, even praised his work. The two men never met. Credit: Alamy Collection. New York

CHAPTER 4

On the Moral Disorder of Victorian England: From Art to Political Economy: 1853–63

But if it be not safe to touch the abstract question of man's right in a social state to help himself even in the last extremity, may we not still contend for the duty of a christian government, standing in loco parentis towards all its subjects, to make such effectual provision, that no one shall be in danger of perishing, either through the neglect or harshness of its legislation?
—William Wordsworth
Essay on the Poor Law Amendment Act (1835)

I

The Venetian work finally completed, John and Effie Ruskin returned home to England in the spring of 1852. Among other tasks, Ruskin made a commitment to give lectures on art in Edinburgh in November, an obligation that provided an opportunity for the couple to take some extended vacation time in Scotland, accompanied by the Pre-Raphaelite painter John Millais, his brother William and others. The initially relaxed summer trip became the occasion for Millais to complete a famous portrait of Ruskin, set at Glenfinlas.[1] Others joined the party on occasion, including Thomas Acland of Oxford. Effie had accorded herself well since her marriage in 1848, despite its difficulties and her husband's obsession with his work.[2] The marital road was not easy, however, for friction between the closely related Gray and Ruskin families had mounted over the years and were again aggravated by circumstances after the return of the couple

G. A. MacDonald, *John Ruskin's Politics and Natural Law*,
https://doi.org/10.1007/978-3-319-72281-8_4

from France. The extended trip to Scotland away from the senior Ruskins was, in principle, a good idea for the couple, but other difficulties arose.[3]

By the time of this trip, Effie had already posed for Millais at the Ruskin home in London as a model for the soldier's wife in his notable painting, *The Order of Release*. En route to Scotland, the party visited the Trevelyans at Wallington. It had become obvious to William Bell Scott that Effie and John Millais had fallen in love. The hosts agreed with Scott and cautioned Ruskin, but he would not hear any of it.[4] It all proved quite true and Effie eventually brought an uncontested suit against Ruskin. By the summer of 1854, the marriage had been annulled and a year later, Effie married John Millais.[5]

His life in disarray, Ruskin paused to reconsider the larger social scene. He decided to act on an earlier confession to his father, that he had not yet done anything 'to serve the poor'. F.J. Furnivall had earlier sent a copy of Ruskin's *Notes on the Construction of Sheepfolds* to the rather heterodox church reformer and educator, Frederick Denison Maurice.[6] This gesture served to initiate a not too smooth exchange of letters between Maurice and Ruskin but one that would eventually bear fruit by involving the latter with working people on a more or less regular basis. The lingering sense of a 'debt-owing' was mixed in with mounting religious doubt. A growing friendship with Maurice pushed him to test that active form of the social gospel later called 'Christian Socialism'.[7] In 1854, Ruskin acceded to Maurice's request that he spend some time teaching art at his Working Men's College in central London where he then taught intermittently until 1867.[8]

Related to this commitment to the college was the day in December, 1853 when Ruskin made one of his most fortuitous connections, probably through the suggestion of Furnivall. He visited the Ladies Guild under the direction of Caroline Southwood Hill. This enterprise, sponsored by the Christian Socialists, focused on useful artistic productions. Ruskin met one of the daughters, 15-year old Octavia, who helped run the guild and who was already a close follower of Maurice and his theology. The meeting was a happy one for it took place just as Ruskin was trying to come to terms with the disaster of his failed marriage. Octavia, mature beyond her years, carried convictions and held to moral purposes every bit as strong as those of Ruskin's. She radiated a gentle confidence and provided a strong contrast with Effie, whom he never understood nor made much effort to engage. Here was a young woman who understood him all too well and who was not to be cowed. Over the next decade, he employed her as a copyist and taught her much about art. In return, she taught as much to the teacher about the living conditions of the poor. In 1864 she would put in place, with his financial help, a pioneering and successful housing experiment in London, managed along the theoretical lines later espoused by Ruskin for his Guild of St. George.[9]

His direct encounters with the practical men at the Working Men's College were exhilarating and led to new friendships and a few longstanding working relationships.[10] The college provided a welcome change from his more predictable domestic society or those encountered in his customary travels and social engagements. About these years at the college, said Graham Wallas, Ruskin 'had learnt to loathe the easy social arithmetic which made the "pain" of the week's toil exactly balance the "pleasure" of the week's wages.'[11]

This volunteer commitment fit in well with his other ambitions. Having worked on Venetian architecture for several years, he now responded to the usual pressures from home to complete the last volumes of *Modern Painters.* Since publishing volume two in 1846, his views had been altering in some profusion. Suffice to say he now worked energetically on the next two volumes, drawing much from his notes of 1849 and his now broader knowledge of European art. These later volumes were, indeed, as he wrote to Jane Carlyle, 'of many things' and they appeared in relatively quick succession in 1856.[12] He also found himself increasingly in demand as a public lecturer after 1854, a role to which he quickly warmed, for it catered to that same yearning for more meaningful direct involvement with the public. By the later 1850s, he had certainly established himself as a public arbiter of taste, if not to everybody's liking.[13]

II

The themes of art and its relationship with work provided the focus for his first systematic essays on social policy beyond that of church-state relations. These came about in the form of two lectures delivered in Manchester in 1857 as *The Political Economy of Art.* The talks rehearsed the general economic role of the arts and the training needs of the aspiring artist. Considerations of public taste were introduced into the discussion, helping provide the context for what he understood to be the ideal conditions for the production and distribution of art. Rather bluntly, he informed his audience that his entry into the field of political economy was unencumbered by any knowledge of what other economists have written, except for

Adam Smith, who he had read 'twenty years ago'.[14] The statement, no doubt exaggerated for effect, was made with some inclination to jolt his audience, the well-heeled of Manchester, the urban fountainhead of contemporary *laissez-faire* economic doctrines. The letter to Jane Carlyle, previously mentioned, indicated that he had delved more deeply into political economy than he wished to let on for his audience. A few years earlier, for example, he had set Effie to work in Venice, reading Sismondi's *History of the Italian Republics* with a view to extracting his ideas on economics.[15] It is also a little startling to recall Margaret Ruskin's letter to her husband in March, 1829, in which she describes her regular after-breakfast readings to young John of passages drawn from Adam Smith's *Theory of Moral Sentiments*.[16] In his *Essay on Literature* of 1836, Ruskin commented on this work as one which 'gives only the mechanics of feeling'.[17] It was in this work that Smith first unveiled his notion of an 'invisible hand' guiding economic events, a device more often identified with *The Wealth of Nations*.[18]

By the mid-1850s, Ruskin had absorbed more of Carlyle as well as Wordsworth's *Essay on the Poor Law Amendment Bill* (1835), the latter approvingly cited in the published version of the Manchester lectures. Wordsworth's general question, cited at the beginning of this chapter, was in line with Hooker's contention that a Christian society must be structured so that the general values of its main religion are maintained in close alliance with state procedures and responsibilities.[19]

The lectures addressed first, 'The Discovery and Application of Art', and second, 'The Accumulation and Distribution of Art'. He developed practical proposals on how these two themes could be applied in contemporary England but his larger intent was to rehearse ideas on economics and politics in general. The audience was told that he could not spell out all the details of government organization at the moment but he urged them to try to see with him 'that the notion of Discipline and Interference lies at the very root of all human progress or power'.[20] It is the principle of the 'paternal' that has generally been lacking in past political organization where the emphasis on law giving 'has hitherto been only judicial'. He suggested that 'as we advance in our social knowledge we shall endeavour to make our government paternal as well as judicial'. Knowing that many in his Manchester audience would object to this suggestion, he softened the message with Christian overtones: he endowed 'Paternal government' with a sense of the 'executive fulfillment, by formal human methods, of the will of the Father of Mankind respecting his children'. While notions of paternal guidance can easily enough be related to the needs of artists in training, Ruskin's larger sense of the principle, as applied to general social relations, led to one of his memorable passages: good government 'shall repress dishonesty as now it punishes theft' and 'shall show how the discipline of the masses may be brought to aid the toils of peace, as discipline of the masses has hitherto knit the sinews of battle'. What is wanted is 'a government which shall have its soldiers of the ploughshare as well as of the sword'.[21]

Following upon this somewhat Spartan and rather totalitarian-sounding political creed, he sought to draw his audience's attention toward a proper understanding of the term 'wealth'. He applauded the contemporary 'just and wholesome contempt for poverty' held by most English citizens along with the apparent decline in the influence of 'apostles of the virtue of poverty'. Both the ancient Greeks and Romans, he contended, as well as many medieval folk, all looked down on poverty, but they did so quite tolerantly. These earlier peoples also had a healthy contempt for conspicuous wealth. While he had, himself, a great respect for 'true wealth', his audience was asked to distinguish between 'true' and 'false' wealth, a theme he would expand upon later in *Unto This Last*.[22] He held that in the economy at large, as in the requirements of art production and distribution, there are principles to be recognized. We have 'warped the word "economy" in our English language into a meaning which it has no business to bear'. Political economy is not about 'saving' or 'spending' but about 'administration' or 'stewardship'. First, true political economy is about applying labour rationally; and second, about preserving its produce carefully; and third, about distributing its produce seasonably.[23] He cited Dante on the idea of usury, a negative concept which Ruskin gradually came to see as enshrined in the modern rules of political economy. In the mid-1860s, however, he still distinguished 'usury' only by degree from more justified charges of interest.[24] In the published version of these lectures, he added notes pointing to the grim international results of a bank failure in the United States during the autumn of 1857. These notes reinforced his ideas about the role of unwarranted interest rates and persuaded him further that market gluts can and do happen, contrary to the longstanding conventional wisdom that natural economic laws worked in favour of a harmonization of interests.[25] The *Political Economy of Art*, as an economic text, pointed in a sustained way to a gap separating the ethics of daily English economic practices from the ethics associated with the nation's publicly embraced creed of Christianity. Echoing Hooker, Ruskin stated that 'The moment government ceases to be the practical enforcement of Divine Law, it is tyranny.'[26]

The drift of these lectures was towards a consideration of the importance of the virtues in personal and civic behaviour. He provided a brief analysis of the great frescoes in the *Sala della Pace* of the *Palazzo Pubblico* in Siena, completed by Ambrogio Lorenzetti in the fourteenth century. The main Classical and Christian virtues are featured in that artist's extensive illustrations of 'Good Civic Government'.[27] Ruskin urges readers to 'observe what work is given to each of these virtues' surrounding the crowned head of government. They are not present 'in mere compliance with the common and heraldic laws of precedence among Virtues, such as we moderns observe habitually' but they are there with a particular purpose. Faith, for example, is not merely a symbol of religious faith, for it means also the 'faith which enables work to be carried out steadily, in spite of adverse appearances and experiences'. The faith appropriate to the good ruler is one which acknowledges 'evidence of things unseen'.[28] And so he continues with the other conventional virtues, understood as social qualities to be related to the dictates of that greater hidden natural law.[29]

III

With the Manchester lectures behind him, he looked once more to the completion of *Modern Painters* in order to satisfy his aging father who complained to him that his time was growing short. Ruskin fell into line and returned to the task and to Turner. There were difficulties, however, about which Ruskin could say little, owing to reticence. By 1859, he had completed the large task of arranging the Turner bequest for the National Gallery, a demanding task which he had faithfully executed. In the course of this work, he discovered that his great hero had a darker side which he considered pornographic. He had painted people as sexual beings, just as he might paint anything else of interest. Years later, that late Victorian wag, Frank Harris, set it about that Ruskin had burned many of the offending items, but this has proven unlikely.[30] The discovery, however, caused not just an emotional, but an aesthetic problem for Ruskin. He solved it indirectly by means of his commentary on Titian, Veronese and others in his 'Notes on the Turin Gallery', prepared following his so-called 'unconversion' in a local chapel in that city.[31] In withdrawing from his earlier reluctance to praise the earthier aspects of human art, he now proclaimed that what was wanted in the great artist was 'a good, stout, self-commanding, magnificent animality'.[32]

In the final volume of *Modern Painters*, Ruskin avoided such troubling issues in favour of discussion of the more pleasing ways by which Turner illustrated the details of the natural world and their dependence on natural law. In the chapter called 'The Angel of the Sea', we are back with clouds, that great *leitmotif* of Turner's work, and the way by which storm-clouds seemed to him to be 'messengers of fate', as they would become for Ruskin in the 1880s.[33] Discussion then turned towards the significant interplay of the law of Sinai and of Lebanon in one of Turner's paintings and then to the *Psalms* of David where Ruskin drew yet closer to his eventual fusion of Biblical law with natural law: 'it is always the Law which is spoken of with chief joy'.[34] In telling his readers about where he has taken them in his multi-volume 'investigation of the beauty of the visible world', he denied that he had sought to lead them only into 'fields of fond imagination'. Rather, they may have been surprised to find that 'the following of beauty brought him always under a sterner dominion of mysterious law; that brightness was continually based upon obedience, and all majesty only another form of submission'. It was a confession, in keeping with Ruskin's moralization of the world at large. 'The thing to be shown' the reader 'was not a pleasure to be snatched but a law to be learned'.[35] In such vein did he go on to conclude *Modern Painters* in time for the his father's reading of it and with a good deal of attention paid to ideas his father could approve. The concluding chapters, however, indicate where his interests were actually taking him. It was in the direction revealed in those suppressed letters of 1852 and in *The Political Economy of Art*. Indeed, while finishing *Modern Painters* he had found time to periodically make notes on his new interest. His *Diary* for 1859 contains jottings on the 'Beginnings of Political Economy'.[36]

By late spring of 1860, the recent work had left Ruskin typically exhausted. Leaving the proofs in his father's care, he departed in May for a vacation in the French Alps. 'On the strength of this piece of filial duty I am cruel enough to go away to St. Martin's again, by myself, to meditate on what is to be done next. Thence, I go up to Chamouni – where a new epoch of life and death begins.'[37] Typically, Ruskin viewed his vacation largely as an opportunity to plan new work. Upon receiving a bound copy of the final volume, he commented that he found the event anti-climactic for 'in the valley of Chamouni I gave up my art-work'. At the old Union Inn, he had already 'written a little book' which he considered to be 'the beginning of the days of reprobation'.[38] The 'little book' became one of his most famous, *Unto This Last*. It consisted of four essays first submitted to George Smith's recently established *Cornhill Magazine* under the editorship of Thackeray. This shift in attention, while dramatic in execution, was, we have noticed, long in gestation.

It will be recalled that 15 years earlier a disparaging paragraph about utilitarian economists found its way into the second volume of *Modern Painters*. The new essays were designed to counter the main ideas of that positivist school of political economy so strongly inspired by such as James Mill, Jeremy Bentham, David Ricardo and, more recently, John Stuart Mill.[39] The propositions of the Benthamite reformers who had ushered in the 1834 *Poor Law Amendment Act* were in accord with an atomistic view of society in which it was assumed that people were largely self-correcting mechanisms, responsive to behavioural principles. For example, the promotion of so-called 'less eligible' conditions for tenure in the workhouses would ideally compel men and women to seek those alternative work opportunities which, in the view of the reformers, actually existed outside of the workhouses.[40] Richard Altick described the intent of the 'less eligible' mechanism: 'The most hated feature of the new system was the proposed total abolition of outdoor relief – the dole – and the substitution of workhouses where the conditions of life and labour were deliberately made so wretched as to deter every man and woman, whether able-bodied or unemployable from being poor.'[41] The actual on-the-ground workings of the 1834 proposals were very mixed over the next ten years, reflecting the different regional conditions of the country and the pragmatic requirements of local political patronage and traditional welfare sentiment. Many local authorities carried on as though the act of 1834 did not exist.[42] This was a reflection, says Gash, of 'the difference between the theory of the law and its practical enforcement'.[43]

The utilitarian reformers of the old poor law were, to be sure, inspired by an appreciation of conditions that today are described as symptomatic of 'structural unemployment' but coupled in those times with the view that such conditions were best adjusted through the 'natural harmony of selfish interests'. In short, the longstanding economic disruptions brought on by land enclosures, soldier demobilization and the urbanizing trends of the industrial revolution, were correctable only by allowing for the free play of certain natural laws of economics, unassisted by government policies of interference.[44]

Opinions on the validity of this view polarized around two positions. The first was a somewhat Luddite one which was conservative of countryside values and established procedures, and perhaps even shared by some of the radical 'machine breakers' themselves, although the motives for such activity were varied.[45] The second pole gathered together those of a contrary position who saw industrialization and urbanism as the road to general prosperity.[46] Carlyle's 'Chartism' (1839) posed the question of 'what is to be done' about the 'condition of England' while his *Past and Present*, written in the aftermath of the great Manchester disturbances of 1842, shows him particularly exercised over the way the post-1815 protective Corn Laws played into this larger scenario of social disruption. He saved his best vitriol for the landed gentry, whose members he took to be the parasitic beneficiaries of these laws. He demonstrated, statistically, that the reformed poor law was a sham in terms of the objective of keeping people off the dole.[47]

Ruskin had read *Past and Present* in the mid-1840s but the little work now took on renewed significance as he became more engaged in political economy. Re-reading Carlyle's assault on the 'Corn Laws' no doubt brought back to memory his own letter of 1852 on the 'Bread Tax'. He wrote to Carlyle in late 1859 to express admiration for his work.[48] What Ruskin admired in *Past and Present* was just as much the image of his own work which he saw reflected in it. Their friendship grew into a mutual admiration society but there was, as Cate cautions, only so much for Ruskin to learn from Carlyle, whose views had hardened into ever more reactionary pamphleteering.[49]

Ruskin's new inclinations towards economic enquiry had other sources and were foreshadowed in his recent art criticism. Long supportive of the Pre-Raphaelite Brotherhood of painters, he gave high praise in 1858 to 'The Stone Breaker' by Henry Wallis (1830–1916), calling it 'the picture of the year'.[50] The painting depicted a man at dusk, collapsed at his work. The labourer is not merely exhausted at his station: he is, in fact, dead. In testimony given before the Public Institutions Committee in 1860, Ruskin said very directly to Sir Robert Peel the Younger: 'I want to have our labour regulated so that it shall be impossible for men to be so entirely crushed in mind and body, as they are by the system of competition.'[51] A worker expired at his post revealed a lamentable lack of moral sensibility among industrial masters as well as a want of government interference in public policy.

Such issues provide background to the new essays for the *Cornhill Magazine* with their vigorous onslaught on utilitarian ideas and highlighting of social indifference to many in the workforce. By the end of 1860, the series had been published in London and by *Harper's Magazine* in

New York. Having returned to England from Europe in the fall of 1860, Ruskin had little idea of the critical storm that was about to break upon his head. The *Cornhill* essays had been indicted for the archaic nature of their arguments.

IV

Whatever difficulties there may be with the way Ruskin characterized the Italian Renaissance and its moral shortcomings as an historical period, he had much greater familiarity with the literature and art of later medieval times, particularly with Dante whose work he started to read in the early 1850s. This familiarity became the basis of a great friendship with the American scholar, Charles Eliot Norton.[52] In thinking about Ruskin and Dante, Norton noticed that if the intellectual connection between them was not readily apparent, yet as personalities they were 'morally of a type closely akin'. Some of Dante's appeal for Ruskin was connected with landscape feeling. The great poet also provided a dignified role model in terms of personal behaviour, although Norton observed that 'in spite of the lessons of life' to be found in Dante, Ruskin never learned 'to control the waywardness of his temperament'.[53]

There were broader reasons for Ruskin's embrace of Dante, both personal and professional. On the first count may be noticed a preoccupation with the 'Inferno' section of *The Divine Comedy*. It reflected his more-or-less permanent need to recognize the importance that the notion of hell played in the personal lives of people far removed in time. Both men, for example, came to share the burden of a vanished love, snatched away in the prime of life. Ruskin, 'unstable as water' from an early age, never did achieve a satisfactory integration of his sexuality and he easily identified with the restless, soul-searching Dante. As time went on, Ruskin resorted to Dante with increasing regularity. Cary's edition of *The Divine Comedy* he kept close at hand 'as an antidote to pestilent things and thoughts in general'.[54] As his own relationship with the unreachable Rose La Touche faltered, followed by her early death, a sense of incomprehensible loss took an ever-increasing toll on his mental health.[55]

On the historical level, Ruskin recognized Dante as a man who lived in severely anarchistic times. Devoted to his native city of Florence, Dante had entered the political fray only to be banished in 1302, to his great personal anguish. Reflecting upon the rampant inter-city strife of his times, he developed somewhat cloudy notions of some kind of Italian nationhood and a belief in a need for a strong imperial revival in order to contain not only the widespread secular strife but also the ambitions of the Papacy. In exploring these themes, he had penned first the *Convivio* and then the more polished *De Monarchia*. The latter had been written at roughly the time when Henry VII of Luxemburg descended upon Italy in 1310 with a view to restoring the Holy Roman Empire and curbing papal ambition. Henry's death shortly thereafter, however, assured that Dante remained an exile for the rest of his years.[56] Ruskin knew something of both of these political works of Dante, but just how much he absorbed of them is not certain.[57]

Dante's final political views derive essentially from work appearing after 1312, particularly as outlined in his letter to the Italian Cardinals (1314) and in *The Divine Comedy*. The poet had come to favour some kind of governing authority in which the claims of the state and of the church were mutually respected, within a framework of Christian natural law, conceived as a response to the forces of anarchy afoot in the Italian peninsula. J. Caird, in his notes, prepared for Ruskin on the great frescoe of Simon Memmi (but no longer attributed to Memmi), 'the Strait Gait', drew attention to three heretics seated at the feet of St. Thomas Aquinas, as represented by Sabellius, Arrius and Averroes.[58] These frescoes in the Spanish Chapel of Florence well reflect Dante's ideal and ordered world.

Many of Ruskin's observations on Dante concern the specifics of moral conduct as illustrated by the poet's description of day-to-day civic life and behaviour. The vigour and precision with which Dante isolated various shades of social and economic sin and then assigned appropriate torments for transgressors quite impressed Ruskin. Once a reader recognizes that the virtues and vices described in the *Inferno*, *Purgatorio* and *Paradiso* persist across time, place and circumstance, it then becomes easier to see how these qualities pertain to contemporary life. Ruskin found himself generally in agreement with Dante's outline of the hierarchy of wrong and right doing. In the fourth essay of *Unto This Last*, Ruskin drew upon Canto Seven of the *Inferno* to make a point:

> The Plutus of Dante, who (to show the influence of riches in destroying the reason) is the only one of the powers of the Inferno who cannot speak intelligibly; and also the cowardliest; he is not merely quelled or restrained, but literally 'collapses' at a word.

Plutus was the Greek God of Wealth, says John Ciardi, and was the ideal entity to act as Inferno overseer, administrating eternal fates to the miserly and the prodigal.[59] Ruskin noted that the 'eighth or lowest pit of hell' is given over to 'Treachery' and 'Fraud', represented by an 'Hesperian dragon' also equated with Plutus, 'the demon of all evil passions connected with covetousness'. The deepest pits of hell in *The Divine Comedy* approximated the economic hell of Victorian England.

The early fourteenth century was, then, relevant for its social lessons.[60] The reformed Poor Law of 1834 raised questions for him about related practices which had their genesis well back in Tudor times and earlier. The quest for answers led him towards both a personal and theoretical interest in the work of St. Francis of Assisi.[61] In the thirteenth century, the claims of the poor and the ideal of poverty became subjects of papal enquiry, particularly with respect to the role of the oath of poverty taken within the Franciscan order.[62] The details of this internal church dispute over community of goods and terms of ownership need not detain us, but it had considerable influence on nascent secular trends of enquiry concerning the idea of subjective human rights as they emerged within the work of William of Ockham.[63] The gradual refinement of notions of 'rights of the person' went in many directions thereafter.[64] It ran eventually into ever more abstract channels in Europe after the New World discoveries and eventually aspired to take on universal pretensions during the eighteenth century with well known, but hardly successful, outcomes in the United States and France.

In England a greater attachment to the importance of recognizing the inevitability of persons being first 'situated' in a specific society before they could have any rights whatsoever, did much to preserve inherited class lines, privileges and respect for the role of the church and institutions.[65] According to these more concrete and conservative lights, careful refinement of the historical legal clams of the individual was the proper road to improved human rights for all. In both streams, understandings of natural law underwent parallel modifications, its character being refashioned in keeping with either more or less liberal claims, or, as in the case of Bentham, eliminated altogether as a basis of legislation.[66]

The version of natural law favoured by radical utilitarians embraced a behaviourist psychology of society, one largely free of time-worn altruistic ethical ideals and based instead on a rather crude calculus of pleasure and pain.[67] This allegedly scientific version of behaviour informed utilitarian political economy.[68] The first essay of *Unto This Last*, 'The Roots of

Honour', attacked these scientific pretensions on two main counts. The first was that they claimed as the basis of scientific natural law, a psychology of human behaviour that was false on account of its incomplete consideration of the 'human affections'. He would have agreed with William Hazlitt that Bentham had 'carried this view of the subject too far' and that he had 'not allowed for the wind'.[69] Secondly, in so doing, they endorsed a consequentialist ethics which could only benefit a minority, rather than members of society as a whole, despite claims to the contrary. The attempt to justify the program according to automatic behaviour by which individuals opted for their self-interest by maximizing pleasure over pain, was inadequate and misleading. Such an account lodged at the heart of the contemporary political economy had, he contended, helped produce a general social condition of moral disorder, marked by an erosion of the rights of the person as previously endorsed by Christian social tradition, broadly conceived.[70]

In the second essay, 'The Veins of Wealth', Ruskin made a distinction between accumulated personal wealth and true national wealth, as a store. As in art, he contended that the real value of so-called wealth 'depends on the moral sign attached to it' and that the question surrounding the advantage of national wealth 'resolves itself finally into one of abstract justice'.

The third essay, *Qui Judicatis Terram*, outlined the importance of just dealings with workers in terms of wages and working conditions. The title was borrowed from Dante and in full the quotation reads: *Diligite justitiam qui judicatis terram*—'Ye who judge the earth give diligent love to justice', words taken in turn from the *Wisdom of Solomon* in the Apocrypha. The essay deals mainly with considerations of the terms of the just wage and fair practices towards labour, but the manner of sound national arrangements is also raised.

In the final essay, 'Ad Valorem', Ruskin provides an analysis of the notion of value as used by many economists. His main contention against these accounts is that some scope must be provided for calculations of the 'intrinsic' value of items and actions, and not just for calculations of 'exchange value' in the market place. The validity of this complaint appealed to certain later economists interested in the consumption side of economics and in the developing idea of 'marginal utility'.[71] There were elements of the critique which also appealed to under-consumption theorists, such as J.A Orage, who helped formulate social credit principles. Steady-state economists and environmentalists in the twentieth century have also found suggestive ideas in this essay.[72]

One essential point of *Unto This Last* was that the main economic doctrines of nineteenth- century England reflected an abandonment of attitudes and practices familiar since pre-Tudor times when church law played a more central role with respect to poor relief.[73] Much tinkering with reform of the Elizabethan poor laws had taken place throughout the seventeenth and eighteenth centuries. Such efforts were responses to the structural unemployment associated with land enclosures, increased worker mobility, industrialization and periodic soldier disbandments. Often the adjustments to the poor laws were of a penny-pinching and punitive nature. Occasional humane measures, such as the late eighteenth-century 'Speenhamland' reforms, did not disguise the fact that poor law administration under local Justices of the Peace more frequently had about it the sound of 'tinkling cymbals' and lacked that spirit of 'charity' which had informed medieval policies for the poor administered by the church.[74] In 1820, Sydney Smith satirized frequent popular efforts to deal with the poor[75]:

> A pamphlet on the Poor Laws generally contains some little piece of favourite nonsense, by which we are told this enormous evil may be perfectly cured. The first gentlemen recommends little gardens; the second, cows; the third village shops; the fourth a spade; the fifth, Dr. Bell, and so forth. Every man rushes to the press with his small morsel of imbecility, and is not easy till he sees his impertinence stitched in blue covers.

V

Unto This Last demonstrated an impatience with the attempts of the economists to establish equivalents for labour as a standard of value.[76] Ruskin tried to develop his own labour theory of value but did not get much further than contending that labour was, in fact, a standard of value with several ingredients. Labour was not to be seen as the only standard, however, for just as a person had a right to exchange his or her labour for an equivalent amount of productivity in the market place, so also should commodities and work activities themselves be recognized according to principles of intrinsic value or moral worth. Thus, while Ruskin was a free trader, he qualified his position with respect to the kinds of goods and services which should be encouraged as practices or as items for trade or consumption. The marketplace was not to be conceived as the setting for a utilitarian free-for-all. The term 'utility', properly understood, implied a 'green' sensitivity, in the modern sense, including the validity of quality control and protective environmental measures in law. It has been observed that Ruskin's stress on the importance of quality control in products was also a tribute to the example of his father's enterprise.[77] Just how all such factors might be made to work together in order to come up with a generalized labour theory of value Ruskin never made clear, but something of his argument ran as follows.

To begin, he feels that wages should not be assigned according to some strict theory of supply and demand, but rather with some reference to 'the hardship of the work and the time spent on it'. He provides three 'just principles' with respect to wages. First, a person 'should in justice be paid for two hours work, twice as much as for one hour's work if the effort be similar and continuous.' Second, wages should be higher for 'difficult or dangerous work'. Third, 'If a man does a given quantity of labour for me, I am bound in justice to do, or procure to be done, a precisely equal quantity of work for him; and just trade in labour is the exchange of equivalent quantities of labour of different kinds.'[78] These considerations were dealt with more systematically in the fourth essay of *Unto This Last*.[79]

In assigning an important role to the act of work itself as a qualitative measure of sound economic life, he separates himself from many of his contemporaries. Work was the instrument through which personality developed, at least in part, and it was to be rewarded in a monetary way. Work was not merely something which could be measured on the time clock. Its character was also important and revealed something of the generalized moral worth of the host culture. It concerned matters of taste.[80]

> Labour is of a higher or lower order, as it includes more or fewer of the elements of life: and labour of good quality in any kind, includes always as much intellect and feeling as will fully and harmoniously regulate the physical force...

Ruskin and Marx would have agreed that workers should benefit according to the amount of labour they have expanded, but they are not agreed about the humanistic values of the act of labour itself. Both hold that labour is necessary for survival. Ruskin naturally finds Biblical sanction for the contention that those who do not work will not eat. Marx preferred the more secular version that all must work and each should receive according to his needs. In his early writings, however, Marx set forth a rather alien view of the character of work[81]:

> ...Labour is external to the worker. i.e. It does not belong to his essential being; that in his work, therefore, he does not affirm himself but denies himself, does not feel content but unhappy, does not develop freely his physical and mental energy, but mortifies his body and ruins his mind. The worker therefore only feels himself outside of his work, and his work feels outside of himself. He is at home when he is not working, and when he is working he is not at home... Its alien character emerges clearly in the fact that as soon as no physical or other compulsion exists, labour is shunned like the plague.

Thus, the utilitarian accounts of human motivation received a strong qualification from Marx who was prepared to say that the act of labour itself represents an episode of pain, unrelieved by pleasure. Ruskin's version is not totally devoid of the Marxian idea: 'But labour is the suffering in effort', the human price of production, and 'that quantity of our toil which we die in'.[82] Yet work, except for the most degrading kinds, is redeemable as a satisfying, even happy experience, to the extent that it allows for that spontaneous Gothic quality and to the extent that such work 'avails towards life'.[83] The matrix for the fulfilment of human personality was not the unfettered egoism which Ruskin and Burkhardt recognized to have progressively gained a foothold in Italian Renaissance society, but rather a more co-operative social method by which policy cautiously assimilates the past to the present: 'nearly every great and intellectual race of the world has produced at every period of its career, an art with some peculiar and precious character about it, wholly unattainable by any other race at any other time'.[84] That passage from *The Political Economy of Art* of 1857 reveals Ruskin to be a bit of an historicist, and it will remain to be seen how that fact is made to mesh with his views on natural law.

Ruskin knew nothing of Marx, but the pretensions of formulating political economy as a science to be pursued in isolation of localized ethical and historical considerations he dismissed as a logical impossibility, owing to what was omitted on the side of the 'human affections'. He did not 'doubt the conclusions of such science, if its terms are accepted' but he was 'simply uninterested in them, as I should be in those of a science of gymnastics which assumed that men had no skeletons'.[85] In Mill's school he discerned a pervasive covetous view, bordering on a dangerous orthodoxy. Modern political economy worked against harmonious social development by approaching humans as abstract individuals, neglecting those other factors which helped promote good lives.[86]

VI

Upon his return home to England in late 1860, Ruskin learned more directly of the largely negative response to the *Cornhill* essays and the suspension of their further publication by the editor, Thackeray. After licking his wounds and spending some none too successful time on the lecture circuit, he repaired to the Alps once more for an extended rest. The mounting nature of his own existential religious crisis eventually took his reading back to ancient and medieval classics, particularly, Xenophon, Plato and Dante, ever more fruitful sources for his political economy.[87] If Thackeray had been a disappointment, he still had the continuing support of Carlyle's friend and future biographer, James A. Froude, now editor at *Fraser's Magazine*. He encouraged Ruskin to continue with his economic reflections.[88] Therefore, the *Cornhill* essays were prepared for republication in book form as a prelude to other new pieces. Upon returning home for Christmas, he busied himself with preparation of a Preface for *Unto This Last*. The proofs were then left in the care of his friend John Simon, the public health reformer, who saw the book through publication.[89]

Having reassured Froude that he would send new essays, he returned to the continent in mid-May 1862, accompanied by his good friends, the Pre-Raphaelite painter Edward Burne-Jones and his wife, Georgiana. At Milan the couple departed, leaving Ruskin to his own devices. The first of the 'Essays on Political Economy' appeared in June 1862 and concerned mainly definitions deemed necessary as a result of the directions taken in *Unto This Last*.[90] Discussion unfolded under four heads: 'Maintenance of Life', 'Work and its Reward', 'Value and Valuable Things', and 'Money and Riches'.[91]

The second appeared in the September issue. Here, he sought 'to expand and illustrate' the definitions given in the first, under the heads of: 'Nature of Wealth', 'Variations of Value', 'The National Store', 'Nature of Labour', 'Value and Price', and finally, 'The Currency'.[92]

Relocating to the Geneva area in August, Ruskin took rooms for what he now described to his parents as his 'hermitage'.[93] Removing to Mornex, he took a cottage formerly belonging to the Empress of Russia and there completed over the winter the remainder of his essays. The third appeared in December and the fourth in April 1863.[94] The fourth would be the last to appear, not because Froude had lost editorial interest, but because the publisher now had second thoughts. Ruskin wryly observed that the readers of *Fraser's* 'as those of the *Cornhill*, were protected for that time from further disturbance on my part'.[95]

The reason was in part Ruskin's fault, as he himself admitted, owing to the density of the pieces. They were not easy going and even his father complained they were 'a bit dry'.[96] Deeply into an agnostic phase and stimulated by a renewed exploration of the ancients, Ruskin had not been able to resist garnishing his pieces with abundant references to his recent readings. Whereas *Unto This Last* had been relatively free of literary digressions, the discursive nature of these new tracts made the train of his thought more difficult to follow.

The essays were recast in book form only in 1872, under the typically obscure title *Munera Pulveris*, a play upon lines from Horace. The meaning of the title refers to the futility of that kind of labour which does little more than count sand.[97] Attentive readers, however, recognized the close connection of these essays with *Unto This Last* and the main slogan of that work, that there is 'no wealth but life'. *Munera Pulveris* declared once again that 'the whole matter is the choice between the wealth which makes for life, and that which makes for death'.[98]

The failure of these essays may also be in part attributable to Ruskin's depressed condition. One of his Geneva friends at this time was one Dr. Louis-André Gosse, a distinguished psychologist and public health and prison reformer.[99] During diagnosis for Ruskin's emotional problems in 1862, Gosse put the idea into his head of moving to the Alps, suggesting that he should try and live 'in the gentian zone' as much as possible.[100] In the early months of 1863, Ruskin was certainly not in a good frame of mind, distressed again about the mistress of his mind, Rose La Touche.[101] In November he apologized to Gosse for not being able to properly host Mrs. Gosse and their son when they called upon him earlier in the year. 'That day – & some days before – I had been in real sorrow of a somewhat acute kind – and could hardly speak to anyone.'[102]

Despite these personal difficulties, his last two *Fraser* essays had taken Ruskin along more tangible paths where he discussed principles of 'Commerce', 'Government' and 'Mastership'.[103] Under the last two of these heads, he moved towards a firmer embrace of natural law but certainly not the type that has been distinguished as modern natural law. His version remained one of a pre-Hobbesian kind, steeped in the traditions of Classical Greece, Rome and the later Middle Ages.[104] He had advanced beyond the *Notes on the Construction of Sheepfolds* by focusing on elements which more explicitly revealed as a debt to Hooker's absorption of Thomist natural law and the idea of reason which so strongly influenced seventeenth-century political thought in England. Positive regulatory law was subsumed, by Ruskin, under recognition of a higher divine organizing law.[105]

In a rather Burkean tone, he stated that law concerns 'the definitions and bonds of customs, or what the nation desired should become custom'. Laws may be divided into three types: *archic*, *meristic* and *critic*. The first two kinds are laws of statute while the third are laws of judgement.[106] *Archic* law defines those which give direction, establishing what is and is not to be done. In these kinds of cases, the judge must consider each on its merits.[107] Objecting to the poverty of educational philosophy noticeable in this sector of British law, he stated: 'we think no man's liberty should be interfered with till he has done irrevocable wrong' but it is 'then just too late for the only gracious and kingly interference which is to hinder him from doing it'. Such shortcomings in policy were particularly detrimental to the young: nations should make their 'educational law strict' so that their 'criminal ones may be gentle.'[108]

In turning to *meristic law*, he promoted legislation concerned with division, distribution and tenure of property.[109] Property is of two major divisions: that which produces the objects of life and that which produces life itself. The idea of 'intrinsic value' is of particular importance here, and he recalls five broad categories of valuable property previously discussed in *The Political Economy of Art*[110]: These 'green' categories defined the types of activity or product in which true wealth was to be found as opposed to false wealth, or 'illth'. The provision of such genuine wealth, he also described in terms of 'productive and unproductive labour'.[111]

Private and public property both have a significant bearing on the quality of life and Ruskin insists upon the 'provisory function' of *meristic law* in addition to its securing power. This provisory function 'determines what every man should possess and puts it within his reach' on the basis of 'due conditions'. It also 'puts out of his reach' that which he should not possess. Indeed, 'in certain conditions of a nation's progress, laws limiting accumulation of property may be found expedient'.[112] In this discussion, Ruskin has outlined a preliminary version of a system of distributive justice.

Ruskin's third kind of law—*critic law*—is law which determines 'questions of injury and assigns due rewards and punishments to conduct'. The sense of injury here involves the 'refusal or violation of any man's right or claim upon his fellows'. This claim 'under the term of "right" is mainly resolvable into two branches'. These concern first, 'a man's claim not be hindered from doing what he should' and second, 'his claim to be hindered from doing what he should not'. Here, Ruskin enters upon a consideration of application of such law with reference to the previous conduct and capacities of the individual. It is in 'this higher and perfect function of critic law, enabling instead of disabling' that law 'becomes truly Kingly instead of Draconic'.[113]

The central argument of *Unto This Last* and *Munera Pulveris* was that an ethical system of political economy should help promote full employment and that in order to facilitate such conditions, government should be free to act. David Craig has appropriately identified this organic tendency in Ruskin with his interest in medieval social forms.[114] One legal practitioner has noticed this humanizing aspect when his ideas are analysed with respect to the operation of modern legal systems with their more rigid emphasis on rules.[115]

This second series of essays, like those of *Unto This Last*, must be counted a failure in terms of immediate effect. Froude, however, had liked them and when in late 1863 economist John Elliot Cairnes (1823–75) published a commentary on these offerings, Froude provided Ruskin space to respond. He did so, submitting 'Gold: A Dialogue'. Opposition now appeared from a different quarter: his father again. By this time, the elder Ruskin was usually willing to let pass much of what his son said on the errors of modern political economy and had even helped get *Unto This Last* into book form.[116] On this occasion, however, he remained too much the orthodox businessman to accept these latest heresies on currency. Ruskin was still prepared to accept domestic censorship. In the end, *Gold: A Dialogue* did not appear in print until 1891 in a small limited edition for private distribution.[117]

Being in Switzerland when he heard about the *Fraser* suspension, Ruskin sought solace through one of his perpetual interests, geology. He completed work on the 'Stratified Alps of the Savoy' that had been promised to the Royal Institution.[118] This redirection of attention introduces another point of crisis that had been festering for years. Friction with the narrower views of his parents had remained largely submerged, seldom interfering with that outward civility which had usually been the standard of family conduct. The father's impatience with some of his son's economic views and the mother's concern over his religious heresies certainly registered keenly enough with him, but rather than confront his parents with unkind words, he generally preferred to absent himself or bite his tongue.[119] Not one to wash dirty family linen in public, Ruskin had yet revealed some of this to his good friend in the U.S., Charles Eliot Norton, after completion of the *Cornhill* essays. In a general mood of despair while finishing the essays the previous summer, he had contemplated moving to Paris or Venice and 'breaking away from all modern society and opinion'. He felt scorn for his past achievements 'and of other people's doings and thinkings, especially in religion'. He spoke of his 'perception of colossal power in Titian and of weakness in purism' and now of the 'almost unendurable solitude in my own home, only made more painful to me by parental love which did not and never could help me, and which was cruelly hurtful without knowing it'.[120]

There is little doubt that Ruskin's emotional difficulties were compounded over the next two years, for we have already noticed that by 1863 accounts were heard of Winnington Hall, a school for girls in northern England. This place-name eventually became symbolic of his undoing at the hands of the troubled child-bride of his dreams, Rose La Touche. His immediate plan, after taking some brief respite at the Winnington School, was to remove himself from England, preferably to Savoy. During this visit to Winnington, he had been joined by Edward and Georgina Burne-Jones. The couple later recorded that Ruskin 'dismayed us, however, by speaking of a plan that had taken shape in his mind for building a house near Bonneville and going to live there'.[121]

He returned to France in September of 1863, accompanied by Osborne Gordon, with a view to gaining the latter's opinions on his intended purchase of property in the Savoy Mountains. The project had advanced to the point of a land survey and negotiations, but came to nothing when the town of Bonneville escalated the price steeply, its officers suspecting that all of Ruskin's local geologizing indicated a concealed discovery of rich mineral ores. Even though there was nothing to this, he returned to England upon the advice of his friends, including Gordon, who had personally inspected the proposed real estate purchase and advised against it. Gordon's real purpose, in league with the parents, had been to talk Ruskin out of his purchase and bring him home.[122]

He was back in England in November of 1863 and did finally confront his parents with the long built-up resentments which he attributed, at least in part, to their strict mode of his up-bringing.[123] While twentieth-century scholar, Helen Viljoen, was convinced that a life-long, suppressed hostility had surfaced during Ruskin's period in the Alps, caution is required in making such judgements, given the extensive, almost clockwork-like correspondence between Ruskin and his parents over the years.[124] That he had periodic difficulties with his parents hardly makes for a unique situation among Victorians or among people of most other generations. What is unusual is to have such a large extant correspondence with which to gauge daily family events, joys and moments of strife. That a deep hatred for the parents by Ruskin would have also sustained such a long, frequent and normally warm correspondence, seems unlikely.[125] Hard-hitting words and personal judgements did not always signify a lack of affection among the Victorians.[126] Such frankness was held to be a considerable virtue and is constantly on display in the Ruskin family papers and in the papers of many other families. Frederic Harrison left a more objective outsider's account of just how the Ruskins behaved at home, reflecting the typical Victorian love of good- natured, but highly serious, intellectual banter.[127]

The impulsive nature of the Savoy project had certainly concerned those closest to Ruskin. Sending Gordon was an appropriate gesture on the part of the parents for he was the closest thing Ruskin had to a brother. To such interested parties, Ruskin's sudden desire to become a hermit in the mountains was seen for what it was: an act of desperation by a solitary soul. The recent episode with Dr. Gosse and his family suggests that Ruskin was, if not suicidal, at least acutely depressed. Consider a contemporary letter to Edward Burne-Jones which contains one of Ruskin's most Rilkean passages: 'I dare say love is very nice when it doesn't always mean leaving people – as it always does with me, somehow; and if you can find this dream of yours with its walled garden, I don't think I should want to leave it, when I got in.'[128]

Notes

1. See the Introduction to *Works*, 12: xviii–xxxvii; and Mary Lutyens, *Millais and the Ruskins* (New York: Vanguard Press, 1968), 52–104.
2. Mary Lutyens, *Young Mrs. Ruskin in Venice: Her Picture of Society and Life with John Ruskin, 1849–1852* (New York: Vanguard Press, 1965), 63–89.
3. On Effie's relations with Ruskin's parents, see Suzanne F. Cooper, *Effie: The Passionate Lives of Effie Gray, John Ruskin and John Everett Millais* (New York: St. Martin's Press, 2010), Chapters 4–8; Lutyens (1968) 24–32; (1972) Ch. 14.
4. William Bell Scott, 'Autobiographical Notes', cited in Lutyens, (1968), 54, 276–77.
5. See Cooper (2012), Lutyens (1968), 127–37, 229–43, 259–69.
6. *Works*, 12: 561.
7. On Maurice's role in this movement, see Edward Norman, *The Victorian Christian Socialists* (Cambridge: Cambridge University Press, 1987), Ch. 1; N.C. Masterman, *John Malcolm Ludlow: The Builder of Christian Socialism* (Cambridge: Cambridge University Press, 1963), 55.
8. See Derrek Leon, *Ruskin: The Great Victorian* (London: Routledge and Kegan Paul, 1949), 226–31; and Philip N. Backstrom, Jr. 'The Practical

Side of Christian Socialism in Victorian England', *Victorian Studies,* 6 (4): (June, 1963), 305–24. See also *Works*, 5: xxxvi; 12: 98n; 16: 435; 27: 389; 35: 488; 36:18, 212.

9. William Thomson Hill, *Octavia Hill: Pioneer of the National Trust and Housing Reformer* (London: Hutchinson, 1956), Chapters 4–6; Peter Clayton, *Octavia Hill* (Wisbech: Wisbech Society and Heritage Trust, 1993), 9–15.
10. See William C. Ward, ed., *John Ruskin's Letters to William Ward* (Boston: Marshall Jones, 1922).
11. Graham Wallas, *Men and Ideas* (London: George Allan and Unwin, 1940), 76–77.
12. Ruskin to Jane Carlyle (1855), in *Works*, 5: xlix–l.
13. J.D. Jump, 'Ruskin's Reputation in the Eighteen–Fifties: The Evidence of the Three Principal Weeklies' *Publications of the Modern Language Association of America* 6: 2 (1948), 678–85; J.L. Bradley, ed., *Ruskin: The Critical Heritage* (London: Routledge and Kegan Paul, 1984), 211–72.
14. *Works*, 16: 10.
15. *Works*, 4: xx, xxix; Cooper (2012), 58.
16. Burd, ed., *The Ruskin Family Letters* (Ithaca: Cornell University Press, 1973), 1: 186.
17. *Works*, 1: 370.
18. Adam Smith, *The Theory of Moral Sentiments* (Indianapolis: Liberty Fund, 1976), 304. See also D.D. Raphael, *Adam Smith* (Oxford: Oxford University Press, 1985), 70–73.
19. Wordsworth's 'Essay' appeared as an appendix to his late poem cycle, *Yarrow Revisited*. For twentieth-century views of the distinctly pragmatic aspects of Hooker's large work, and its relationship with late medieval thought, see W.D.J. Cargill Thompson, 'The Philosopher of the Politic Society', in W. Speed Hill, ed. (1972), 7–12.
20. *Works*, 16: 26.
21. *Works*, 16: 25–6.
22. *Works*, 16: 15–16.
23. *Works*, 16: 19.
24. *Works*, 16: 17; 17: 220, n. 2; see C.E. Collet, 'Development of Ruskin's Views on Interest', *Economic Journal Supplement,* 1: (Jan. 1946), 23–33.
25. *Works*, 16: 137.
26. *Works*, 16: 25; and see Alexander S. Rosenthal, *Crown Under Law: Richard Hooker, John Locke and the Ascent of Modern Constitutionalism* (Plymouth: Lexington Press, 2008) 121–23.
27. For detailed illustrations of the frescoes, see Randolph Starn, *Ambrogio Lorenzetti: The Palazzo Publico, Siena* (New York: George Braziller, 1994).

28. *Works*, 16: 54.
29. *Ibid*., 54–56.
30. See Ian Morrell, 'Exploring the Dark Side: Ruskin and the problem of Turner's erotica', *The British Art Journal*, 4 (1): (2003), 5–46.
31. This 'unconversion' moment has been discussed by many Ruskin commentators. See Wilenski (1933), 66, 340–41, Hilton (1985), 254; Landow (1971), Ch. 4; Francis O'Gorman, 'Religion' in Francis O'Gorman, ed. *The Cambridge Companion to John Ruskin* (Cambridge: Cambridge University Press, 2015), 148–9.
32. *Works*, 7: xl.
33. *Works*, 7: 189; and see Ruskin, 'The Storm Cloud of the Nineteenth Century', *Works*, 34: 1–80.
34. *Works*, 7: 192–3.
35. *Works*, 7: 193.
36. *Works*, 17: xxv, n. 2.,
37. *Works*, 17: xxi.
38. *Works*, 13: 497; 17: xxi.
39. For background on the emergence of the Utilitarians, see Elie Halévy, *The Growth of Philosophic Radicalism* (New York: Augustus M. Kelley, 1949); John Plamenatz, *The English Utilitarians* (Oxford: Basil Blackwell, 1966).
40. See E.C. Black, ed., *British Politics in the Nineteenth Century* (New York: Harper and Row, 1969), 96 f.; S. and B. Webb, *English Poor Law History*, Pt. 2. in *English Local Government* (London: F. Cass, 1929), Vol. 8: 58, 63, 114–16; *Report of the Poor Law Commissioners* (London: Poor Law Commission Office. 1840), 45.
41. Richard D. Altick, ed. 'Introduction', Thomas Carlyle, *Past and Present* (New York: New York University Press, 1965), vi.
42. Norman Gash, *Aristocracy and People: Britain, 1815–1865* (Cambridge, MA: Harvard University Press, 1979), 195–99.
43. Ibid., 198.
44. See Plamenatz (1966), 110–14.
45. E. J. Hobsbawm, 'The Machine Breakers', *Past Present* (1952) 1 (1): 67.
46. For the range of arguments on this question developed in the nineteenth century, see Maxine Berg, ed., *Technology and Toil in Nineteenth Century Britain* (Atlantic Highlands: Humanities Press, 1979); for a discussion of the general issues, see Gash (1979), Ch. 7.
47. Altick, ed. (1965), viii–x; 7.
48. Ruskin to Carlyle (December, 1859) in George Allen Cate, ed. *The Correspondence of Thomas Carlyle and John Ruskin* (Standford: Stanford University Press, 1982), 83–4.
49. See George Cate, 'Ruskin's Discipleship to Carlyle: A Revaluation' in John Clubbe, ed. *Carlyle and His Contemporaries* (Durham: Duke

University Press, 1976), 227–56; John Neff, *Carlyle and Mill*, 2nd ed. (New York: Octagon, 1974) 36–53; Michael Goldberg, 'A Universal "howl of execration": Carlyle's Latter Day Pamphlets and Their Critical Reception', in Clubbe, ed. (1976), 129–47.

50. *Works*, 13:, 170.
51. *Works*, 16: 480.
52. See J.L. Bradley and Ian Ousby, eds., *The Correspondence of John Ruskin and Charles Elliot Norton* (Cambridge: Cambridge University Press, 1987).
53. Charles Eliot Norton, 'Introduction' to George P. Huntington, ed. *Comments of John Ruskin on the Divina Commedia* (Boston: Houghton, Mifflin, 1903), x–xi.
54. *Works*, 26: 224.
55. See Van Akin Burd, 'Introduction' to *John Ruskin and Rose La Touche: Her unpublished diaries of 1861 and 1867* (Oxford: Clarendon Press, 1979).
56. For a brief summary of these events and Dante, see A.P. d'Entrèves, *Dante as a Political Thinker* (Oxford: Clarendon Press, 1952), 10–25.
57. J. Caird, prepared notes on these works of Dante for use in *Mornings in Florence* (1877). *Works*, 23: 441–2. The holdings of Dante in the family library were substantial. See Dearden (2012), 87–89.
58. *Works*, 23: 378.
59. John Ciardi, trans. *The Divine Comedy* (New York: New American Library, 2003), 65 n. 2.
60. *Works,* 19: 462–3; 23: 47–49; on Ruskin's use of Dante, see Huntington, comp. (1903).
61. See *Works*, 23: 229, 339; 34: 547; see also Ruskin's letters to Carlyle from Assisi in the summer of 1874, in Cate, ed. (1982), 191–201.
62. See Brian Tierney, *The Idea of Natural Rights* (Grand Rapids: William B. Eerdmans, 1997), Ch. 4; Hans Baron, 'Franciscan Poverty and Civic Wealth as Factors in the Rise of Humanistic Thought', *Speculum,* 13 (1): (1938), 1–5.
63. Tierney (1997), 97–103.
64. See Annabel S. Brett, *Liberty, Right and Nature: Individual Rights in Later Scholastic Thought* (Cambridge: Cambridge University Press, 1997).
65. Burke has been singled out as the high water mark of this attitude. See Peter J. Stanlis, *Edmund Burke and the Natural Law* (Ann Arbor: Michigan State University Press, 1965).
66. See Carl J. Friedrich, *The Philosophy of Law in Historical Perspective* (Chicago: University of Chicago Press, 1963), 91–98.
67. Anthony Quinton, *Utilitarian Ethics* (New York: St. Martin's Press, 1973), Ch. 2.

68. See Halévy (1949), 316–72.
69. William Hazlitt, *The Spirt of the Age* (London: Oxford University Press, 1966), 6.
70. *Works*, 16: 76; *Works*, 33: 112.
71. See the later works of Ruskin's early advocate, William Smart, *An Introduction to the Theory of Value on the Lines of Menger, Wieser, and Böhm-Bawerk* (London: Macmillan, 1910); *Second Thoughts of an Economist* (London: Macmillan, 1916), xxx.
72. Kenneth E. Boulding, 'The Shadow of the Stationary State', *Daedalus*, 102, (4): (1973), 89–101; Graham A. MacDonald, 'The Politics of the Golden River: Ruskin on Environment and the Stationary State', *Environment and History*, 18 (2012), 125–150; Fredrik A. Jonsson, 'Political Economy' in Mark Bevir, ed., *Historicism and the Human Sciences in Victorian Britain* (Cambridge: Cambridge University Press, 2017), 186–210.
73. See Brian Tierney, *Medieval Poor Law: A Sketch of Canonical Theory and Its Application in England* (Berkeley: University of California Press, 1959).
74. See Tierney (1959). On the history of post-Elizabethan reforms, see J.R. Poynter *Society and Pauperism: English Ideas on Poor Relief, 1795–1834* (London: Routledge and Kegan Paul. 1969); David Blaug, 'The Myth of the Old Poor Law and the Making of the New' *Journal of Economic History*, 23: 2 (1963), 151–184; Dorothy Marshal, 'The Old Poor Law, 1662–1795', *English Historical Review*, 8: (1937), 44–5.
75. Cited in Poynter (1969), 330.
76. John T. Fain, *Ruskin and the Economists (*Nashville: Vanderbilt University Press, 1956), 139–41; Willie Henderson, *John Ruskin's Political Economy* (London: Routledge, 2000) 40–43; and see Halévy (1949), 316 f.
77. See Francis O'Gorman, "An Entirely Honest Merchant': The Domestic Context of *Unto This Last*' in *Late Ruskin: New Contexts* (Aldershot: Ashgate, 2001), 16–19.
78. 'Letters on Work and Wages', *Works*, 17: 508.
79. *Works*, 17: 95.
80. *Works*, 17: 95; 16: 144.
81. Cited in David Caute, ed., *Essential Writings of Karl Marx* (London: Panther, 1967), 59.
82. *Works*, 17: 183.
83. *Works*, 17: 95.
84. *Works*: 16, 63–4.
85. *Works*, 17: 25–27.
86. For a discussion of the early development of such ideas, see Milton L. Myers, *The Soul of Modern Economic Man: Ideas of Self-Interest, Thomas Hobbes to Adam Smith* (Chicago: University of Chicago Press, 1983).

87. *Works*, 17: lxiii, xlvi.
88. *Works*, 17: l.
89. *Works*, 17: l–lii.
90. *Works*, 17: liii.
91. *Works*, 17: 147, n. 2.
92. *Works*, 17: 164.
93. *Works*, 17: liv–lvi.
94. *Works*, 17: lxii, 119.
95. *Works*, 17: lxviii, 143.
96. *Works*, 17: lxiii–lxiv.
97. *Works*, 17: lxv–lxvi.
98. *Works*, 17: lxvi, 282–3.
99. H.W. Hausermann, *The Genevese Background* (London: Routledge and Kegan Paul, 1952), 157–66.
100. Hausermann (1952), 164.
101. Ruskin to Norton. *Works*, 36: 433; Ruskin to Gosse, c. Dec. 1863, in Hausermann (1952), 174–5.
102. Ruskin To Gosse, c. Dec. 1863, in Hauserman (1952), 175.
103. *Works*, 17: 217–83.
104. *Works*, 17: 245–49. On the distinction between pre- and modern natural law theories, see Rosenthal (2008), Appendices 1 and 2: 267–306.
105. On Hooker's account of natural law, see Frederick C. Beiser, *The Sovereignty of Reason: The Defence of Rationality in the Early English Enlightenment* (Princeton: Princeton University Press, 1996), Ch. 2; A.P. d'Entrèves, *The Medieval Contribution to Political Thought.* (Oxford: Oxford University Press, 1939), Chapters 5 and 6; Peter Muntz, *The Place of Hooker in the History of Thought* (Westport: Greenwood Press, 1971), 52–4, 82–6, 129–31 and Appendix A; Michael Oakeshott, 'Richard Hooker' in: *What is History? and other essays.* Luke O'Sullivan, ed. London: Imprint Academic, 2004, 207–18, 207–18; Rosenthal (2008), 58–73.
106. *Works*, 17: 236.
107. *Works*, 17: 238.
108. Ibid.
109. *Works*, 17: 237.
110. *Works*, 16: 129–34.
111. *Works*, 16: 129–34.
112. *Works*, 17: 239–41.
113. *Works*, 17: 242–42.
114. David M. Craig, *John Ruskin and the Ethics of Consumption* (Charlottesville: University of Virginia Press, 2006), 203.
115. See Elliott M. Abramson, 'Ruskin's Insights for the Law: A Humanist's Intimations to Techniques', *University of Pittsburgh Law Review*, 43: (1981–82), 403–40.

116. See Francis O'Gorman, "'An Entirely Honest Merchant': the Domestic Context of Unto This Last' in: *Late Ruskin: New Contexts* (Aldershot: Ashgate, 2001), 9–30.
117. It is printed in *Works*, 17: 491–98. Cairnes published his comments in *MacMillan's Magazine*, 9: (1863), 67–9.
118. *Works*, 17: lxxi.
119. Viljoen, Spates, and Henderson all contend that relations between Ruskin and his father were, or became, severely hostile. See the arguments in James L. Spates, *The Imperfect Round: Helen Gill Viljoen's Life of Ruskin.* Foreword by Van Akin Burd. (Geneva, NY: Lulu, 2005); Henderson (2000), 12; Burd, ed., 'Introduction' *Ruskin Family Letters* (1973) Vol. 1: xv–xlvi; Burd, 'Introduction' *John Ruskin and Rose La Touche* (Oxford: Clarendon, 1979), 1–23.
120. Ruskin to Norton, 25 Feb, 1861, in *Letters of John Ruskin to Charles Eliot Norton* (Boston: Houghton Mifflin, 1904), I: 106.
121. Georgiana Burne-Jones, *Memorials of Edward Burne-Jones* (New York: Macmillan, 1904), I: 264–5.
122. *Works*, 17: lxxiv–lxxv; on this episode see Cynthia Gamble, *John Ruskin, Henry James and the Shropshire Lads* (London: New European Publications, 2008), 130–38.
123. See Gamble (2008), 137–8.
124. See James L. Spates, '"Ruskin in Milan, 1862": A Chapter from Dark Star, an unpublished biography of John Ruskin'. www.victorianweb.org/authors/ruskin/spates/viljoen.html
125. One of the revealing aspects of Spate's work on Viljoen is the disclosure of Viljoen's own deep seated family-based hostilities and her apparent effort to work them out through her unending pursuit of Ruskin family history.
126. Walter E. Houghton, *The Victorian Frame of Mind, 1830–1870* (New Haven: Yale University Press, 1957), 83–87; Phyllis Groskurth, *The Woeful Victorian: A Biography of John Addington Symonds* (New York: Holt, Rinehart and Winston, 1964), 42–3.
127. Frederic Harrison, *Autobiographic Memoirs* (London: Macmillan, 1911), I, 205.
128. Ruskin to Burne-Jones, Sept. 8, 1863, in Burne-Jones, *Memorials*, I: 266.
129. Footnote references to Ruskin's writings (unless otherwise stated) are cited as *Works,* and refer to Cook, Edward T. and Wedderburn, Alexander, eds. *The Collected Works of John Ruskin*. London: 1903–1912. 39 v.

Bibliography[129]

Abramson, Elliott M. 1981–82. Ruskin's Insights for the Law: A Humanist's Intimations to Techniques. *University of Pittsburgh Law Review* 43: 403–440.

Altick, Richard D., ed. 1965. *'Introduction', Thomas Carlyle, Past and Present.* New York: New York University Press.

Backstrom, Philip N., Jr. 1963. The Practical Side of Christian Socialism in Victorian England. *Victorian Studies* 6 (4): 305–324.

Baron, Hans. 1938. Franciscan Poverty and Civic Wealth as Factors in the Rise of Humanistic Thought. *Speculum* 13 (1): 1–5.

Beiser, Frederick C. 1996. *The Sovereignty of Reason: The Defence of Rationality in the Early English Enlightenment.* Princeton: Princeton University Press.

Berg, Maxine, ed. 1979. *Technology and Toil in Nineteenth Century Britain.* Atlantic Highlands: Humanities Press.

Bevir, Mark, ed. 2017. *Historicism and the Human Sciences in Victorian Britain.* Cambridge: Cambridge University Press.

Black, E.C., ed. 1969. *British Politics in the Nineteenth Century.* New York: Harper and Row.

Blaug, David. 1963. The Myth of the Old Poor Law and the Making of the New. *Journal of Economic History* 23 (2): 151–184.

Boulding, Kenneth E. 1973. The Shadow of the Stationary State. *Daedalus* 102 (4): 89–101.

Bradley, J.L., ed. 1984. *Ruskin: The Critical Heritage.* London: Routledge and Kegan Paul.

Bradley, J.L., and Ian Ousby, eds. 1987. *The Correspondence of John Ruskin and Charles Elliot Norton.* Cambridge: Cambridge University Press.

Brett, Annabel S. 1997. *Liberty, Right and Nature: Individual Rights in Later Scholastic Thought.* Cambridge: Cambridge University Press.

Burd, Van Akin, ed. 1973. *The Ruskin Family Letters.* Vol. 2. Ithaca: Cornell University Press.

———. 1979. *John Ruskin and Rose La Touche: Her Unpublished Diaries of 1861 and 1867.* Oxford: Clarendon Press.

Burne-Jones, Georgiana. 1904. *Memorials of Edward Burne-Jones.* Vol. 2. New York: Macmillan.

Cate, George Allen, ed. 1982. *The Correspondence of Thomas Carlyle and John Ruskin.* Standford: Stanford University Press.

Caute, David, ed. 1967. *Essential Writings of Karl Marx.* London: Panther.

Ciardi, John, 2003. *The Divine Comedy.* Trans. Dante. New York: New American Library.

Clayton, Peter. 1993. *Octavia Hill.* Wisbech: Wisbech Society and Heritage Trust.

Clubbe, John, ed. 1976. *Carlyle and His Contemporaries.* Durham: Duke University Press.

Collet, C.E. 1946[1943]. Development of Ruskin's Views on Interest. *Economic Journal Supplement* 1: 22–33.

Cooper, Suzanne F. 2010. *Effie: The Passionate Lives of Effie Gray, John Ruskin and John Everett Millais*. New York: St. Martin's Press.

Craig, David M. 2006. *John Ruskin and the Ethics of Consumption*. Charlottesville: University of Virginia Press.

d'Entrèves, A.P. 1939. *The Medieval Contribution to Political Thought*. Oxford: Oxford University Press.

———. 1952. *Dante as a Political Thinker*. Oxford: Clarendon Press.

Dearden, James. 2012. *The Library of John Ruskin*. Oxford: Oxford Bibliographical Society.

Fain, John T. 1956. *Ruskin and the Economists*. Nashville: Vanderbilt University Press.

Friedrich, Carl J. 1963. *The Philosophy of Law in Historical Perspective*. Chicago: University of Chicago Press.

Gamble, Cynthia. 2008. *John Ruskin, Henry James and the Shropshire Lads*. London: New European Publications.

Gash, Norman. 1979. *Aristocracy and People: Britain 1815–1865*. Cambridge: Harvard University Press.

Groskurth, Phyllis. 1964. *The Woeful Victorian: A Biography of John Addington Symonds*. New York: Holt, Rinehart and Winston.

Halévy, Elie. 1949. *The Growth of Philosophic Radicalism*. New York: Augustus M. Kelley.

Harrison, Frederic. 1911. *Autobiographic Memoirs*. Vol. 2. London: Macmillan.

Hausermann, H.W. 1952. *The Genevese Background*. London: Routledge and Kegan Paul.

Hazlitt, William. 1966. *The Spirt of the Age*. London: Oxford University Press.

Henderson, Willie. 2000. *John Ruskin's Political Economy*. London: Routledge.

Hill, William Thomson. 1956. *Octavia Hill: Pioneer of the National Trust and Housing Reformer*. London: Hutchinson.

Hill, W. Speed, ed. 1972. *Studies in Richard Hooker: Essays Preliminary to an Edition of His Works*. Cleveland: Case Western Reserve University.

Hilton, Tim. 1985. *John Ruskin: The Early Years*. New Haven: Yale University Press.

Hobsbawm, E.J. 1952. The Machine Breakers. *Past Present* 1 (1): 57–70.

Houghton, Walter E. 1957. *The Victorian Frame of Mind, 1830–1870*. New Haven: Yale University Press.

Huntington, George P., ed. 1903. *Comments of John Ruskin on the Divina Commedia*. Boston: Houghton, Mifflin.

Jump, J.D. 1948. Ruskin's Reputation in the Eighteen-Fifties: The Evidence of the Three Principal Weeklies. *Publications of the Modern Language Association of America* 6 (2): 678–685.

Landow, George P. 1971. *The Aesthetic and Critical Theories of John Ruskin.* Princeton: Princeton University Press.

Leon, Derrek. 1949. *Ruskin: The Great Victorian.* London: Routledge and Kegan Paul.

Lutyens, Mary. 1965. *Young Mrs. Ruskin in Venice: Her Picture of Society and Life with John Ruskin, 1849–1852.* New York: Vanguard Press.

———. 1968. *Millais and The Ruskins.* New York: Vanguard Press.

MacDonald, Graham A. 2012. The Politics of the Golden River: Ruskin on Environment and the Stationary State. *Environment and History* 18: 125–150.

Marshal, Dorothy. 1937. The Old Poor Law, 1662–1795. *English Historical Review* 8: 44–45.

Masterman, N.C. 1963. *John Malcolm Ludlow: The Builder of Christian Socialism.* Cambridge: Cambridge University Press.

Morrell, Ian. 2003. Exploring the Dark Side: Ruskin and the Problem of Turner's Erotica. *The British Art Journal* 4 (1): 5–46.

Muntz, Peter. 1971. *The Place of Hooker in the History of Thought.* Westport: Greenwood Press.

Myers, Milton L. 1983. *The Soul of Modern Economic Man: Ideas of Self-Interest, Thomas Hobbes to Adam Smith.* Chicago: University of Chicago Press.

Neff, John. 1974. *Carlyle and Mill.* 2nd ed. New York: Octagon.

Norman, Edward. 1987. *The Victorian Christian Socialists.* Cambridge: Cambridge University Press.

Norton, Charles Eliot, ed. 1904. *Letters of John Ruskin to Charles Eliot Norton.* Boston: Houghton Mifflin.

O'Gorman, Francis. 2001. *Late Ruskin: New Contexts.* Aldershot: Ashgate.

———, ed. 2015. *The Cambridge Companion to John Ruskin.* Cambridge: Cambridge University Press.

Oakeshott, Michael. 2004. In *What Is History? And Other Essays*, ed. Luke O'Sullivan. London: Imprint Academic.

Plamenatz, John. 1966. *The English Utilitarians.* Oxford: Basil Blackwell.

Poynter, J.R. 1969. *Society and Pauperism: English Ideas on Poor Relief, 1795–1834.* London: Routledge and Kegan Paul.

Quinton, Anthony. 1973. *Utilitarian Ethics.* New York: St. Martin's Press.

Raphael, D.D. 1985. *Adam Smith.* Oxford: Oxford University Press.

Report of the Poor Law Commissioners. 1840. London: Poor Law Commission Office.

Rosenthal, Alexander S. 2008. *Crown Under Law: Richard Hooker, John Locke and the Ascent of Modern Constitutionalism.* Plymouth: Lexington Press.

Smart, William. 1910. *An Introduction to the Theory of Value on the Lines of Menger, Wieser, and Böhm-Bawerk.* London: Macmillan.

———. 1916. *Second Thoughts of an Economist.* London: Macmillan.

Smith, Adam. 1976. *The Theory of Moral Sentiments.* Indianapolis: Liberty Fund.

Spates, James L. 2005. *The Imperfect Round: Helen Gill Viljoen's Life of Ruskin.* Geneva: Lulu. Foreword by Van Akin Burd.

———. "Ruskin in Milan, 1862": A Chapter from Dark Star, an Unpublished Biography of John Ruskin. www.victorianweb.org/authors/ruskin/spates/viljoen.html

Stanlis, Peter J. 1965. *Edmund Burke and the Natural Law.* Ann Arbor: Michigan State University Press.

Starn, Randolph. 1994. *Ambrogio Lorenzetti: The Palazzo Publico, Siena.* New York: George Braziller.

Tierney, Brian. 1959. *Medieval Poor Law: A Sketch of Canonical Theory and Its Application in England.* Berkeley: University of California Press.

———. 1997. *The Idea of Natural Rights.* Grand Rapids: William B. Eerdmans.

Wallas, Graham. 1940. *Men and Ideas.* London: George Allan and Unwin.

Ward, William C., ed. 1922. *John Ruskin's Letters to William Ward.* Boston: Marshall Jones.

Webb, S., and B. Webb. 1929. *English Local Government.* London: F. Cass.

Wilenski, R., and H. John. 1933. *Ruskin: An Introduction to Further Study of His Life and Work.* London: Faber.

CHAPTER 5

Wealth, Justice and the Medieval Poor Law: 1864–70

I

In mid-November 1863, having put hermit notions aside, Ruskin departed the Alps for England where he then spent much time in the north, making the Winnington Hall School for Girls his headquarters. He was thinking about economics and justice again, and discussed with Burne-Jones the mythological aspects of intended further work for the *Fraser* essays.[1] Such ideas had to be put aside when John James Ruskin died in March 1864. This meant taking on important administrative responsibilities in connection with the family fortune and the need to see to the care of his mother. Larger work suspended, he was content to exchange notes with those who wrote to him, queried him about his previous works, or to submit letters to the press on matters such as work, wages or supply and demand. He also took a greater interest in British foreign policy, particularly with respect to Poland, Italy and Austria. Aside from delivering a few public lectures, he kept close to the family home in London until early 1865 when he gained some relief from his domestic duties. His cousin, Joan Agnew, never daunted by Ruskin's stern mother, came to live at the house, thus commencing a close and warm relationship with Ruskin that would not end until the writer's death and well beyond.[2] Following appointment of estate administrators, Ruskin was soon back into his normal but over-extended work routines.

The next two years saw delivery of some of his most popular addresses, including those published as *Sesame and Lilies* (1865) and *The Crown of*

G. A. MacDonald, *John Ruskin's Politics and Natural Law*,
https://doi.org/10.1007/978-3-319-72281-8_5

Wild Olive (1866). His open public letters on social issues increased and something must now be said about events in the Caribbean, in the course of which Ruskin became embroiled in a major public policy debate in England. It concerned the importance of the rule of law in the Empire and the nation's past involvement in black slavery and emancipation. This was the controversy surrounding the recent actions of the Jamaica Governor, Edward Eyre (1815–1901).

II

In October 1865, a violent disturbance unfolded before the Court House in Morant Bay, Jamaica, instigated apparently by some 40 or so former slave labourers led by Baptist preacher, Paul Bogle (1822–65). It was firmly put down by the resident Governor, Edward Eyre, the explorer and former imperial administrator of good reputation in Australia.[3] In the reprisals meted out in the aftermath there was much loss of life, injury and property destruction. Courts martial were held, followed by summary executions, including that of Bogle and George W. Gordon, a representative in the Jamaica House of Assembly.[4] In England, details remained vague until December when the Secretary for the Colonies, Edward Cardwell, bowing to social pressures, appointed a Royal Commission to investigate the matter. He named as Chairman Sir Henry Storks, current Governor of Malta, but sent to replace Governor Eyre in a temporary capacity in December 1865. A certain cooling down took place until the Royal Commission reported its findings in 1866.[5] The *Report* gave critics of Eyre new ammunition and the incident gradually developed into a *cause célèbre* in England on the matter of justice. The *Report* was both positive and negative from Eyre's point of view, but the negative elements were sufficiently serious that Eyre was recalled from Jamaica and replaced. His career as a civil servant was, in fact, over.[6]

With Eyre's return to England in July 1866, opinion started to polarize more firmly. Unsatisfied with the conclusions of the *Report* as to final accountability, Eyre's accusers gathered around Charles Buxton and J.S. Mill, both instrumental in the formation of a Jamaica Committee which now pressed for Eyre to be brought to trial on criminal charges of murder. This organized advocacy induced a counter-reaction given clear organizational birth in August at a Southampton banquet given in honour of Eyre. In attendance were such staunch imperialists as the Seventh Earl of Cardigan (of Light Brigade fame) and Charles Kingsley, novelist and

Regius Professor of History at Cambridge. Shortly thereafter, the Eyre Defense and Aid Fund was convened with Carlyle nominated to the chair.[7]

Ruskin was not present but he had expressed himself publicly on the matter as early as December 1865 in a letter to the *Daily Telegraph* when his purpose was less to defend Eyre (although he did defend him for imposing order) than to advertise the hypocrisy of undue public concern for slavery in Jamaica, in fact abolished since 1838, when there was so much of what he called industrial 'wage slavery' in England.[8]

Shortly after the first meeting of the Defense and Aid Fund group in the summer of 1866, Carlyle invited Ruskin to join, with a view to having Ruskin relieve him of his administrative duties. Not wanting to displease his aging mentor, Ruskin complied and gave a powerful speech to the committee in September 1866.[9] In a private letter, Carlyle praised 'this right gallant thrust' claiming that 'while the world stands tremulous, shilly-shallying from the gutter, impetuous Ruskin plunges his rapier up to the very hilt in the abominable belly of the vast blockheadism' leaving it 'staring very considerably'.[10] It was vintage Carlyle! The London *Economist* was having none of it, however, and published a strong retort.[11]

Ruskin was modest about his performance, according to his *Diary*. A day before his speech, he recorded that he was 'Doing my duty as well as I can for Governor Eyre'.[12] The phrase 'as well as I can' was telling, for Ruskin had concerns about Eyre's performance and these continued to grow. Having committed to the cause, however, and believing in principles of law and order, he stuck with the pro-Eyre group.[13]

Not all was smooth sailing for those supporting Eyre. Kingsley lost his nerve under the pressure of unexpected public criticism and disappeared from the fray, although not because of any changes in his views.[14] Kingsley's vacillations, however, were indicative of stress in many long-standing friendships.[15] Carlyle, supposedly in charge, was much depressed over the recent death of his wife, Jane Welsh Carlyle. He went off to France in December 1866, leaving Ruskin to co-ordinate committee business. Subscriptions continued to grow, attracting—in addition to military men and imperial administrators—other notables including Tennyson, Dickens, Viscount Melville, geologist Sir Roderick Murchison and scientist John Tyndall. As of November 1866, the list of subscribers supporting Eyre ran to over 1200.

There was no firm breakdown as to who among the prominent or the professions joined which of the two factions, but men of science went heavily towards the Jamaica Committee. It could claim such formidable public intellectuals as Charles Darwin, Sir Charles Lyell and Thomas Huxley, along with radicals and liberals such as Mill, Herbert Spencer, Goldwin Smith and John Bright. Not unexpectedly, many evangelicals and abolitionists were also with the Jamaica Committee. The question divided families and friends. The legal positivist, Frederic Harrison, a Ruskin admirer, opposed Eyre. Darwin, who seldom angered, was greatly irritated when his son questioned the validity of the case against Eyre. Tennyson found himself torn between memories of the India Mutiny, on one side, and his suspicions about Eyre on the other. He was upset when the letter of support he sent to the Eyre Defense and Aid Fund group was only partially printed, thus concealing the strong reservations he had about the events at Morant Bay.[16]

Tennyson was not alone. Ruskin also developed doubts, as he told Carlyle, owing to letters he was given to review from the hand of a colonial engineer, Richard Price. He told Carlyle, as gently as he could, 'how it is that I can't work now so well as I used to do'.[17] A month later, Lady Mary Lyell received a firm opinion from the wife of the Cornish-born Bishop of Natal, William Collenso: 'I am very sorry Mr. Ruskin has given his countenance to Mr. Eyre. He is always led astray by his allegiance to Carlyle, who *of course* would take the line he has done.'[18]

Lawyers of liberal persuasion, such as Harrison, had good reasons to become involved in the case for the timing of the Jamaica incident coincided not only with the termination of the great American struggle of the Civil War but also with the debates and disturbances associated with the pending second Reform Bill. The English were in a bad mood. The trade union movement was in a state of crisis; the harvests had been bad; cholera had reappeared; in May, one of the great banking houses had failed; and the Hyde Park riots of 1866 had issued in damage to public property. All this chaos at home and abroad tended to work in Eyre's favour, implying prudential lessons for the domestic situation. To the nervous citizen, Eyre appeared to be a man trying to do a nasty job on behalf of the public.

The controversy dragged on for several years with the fervour of all parties gradually declining in the face of repeated decisions of the court not to find against Eyre.[19] In 1872, the matter finally closed, with Eyre granted his pension and legal expenses but relieved from further public service. Ruskin had long since tired of the matter, according to William Rossetti, for whatever dutiful images may have been provided by Kingsley or Carlyle, Eyre's performance did not measure up to what Ruskin imagined modern chivalrous conduct should embody.[20]

The Eyre episode was seldom mentioned by Ruskin after 1867. The entire event, in retrospect, was remarkable in terms of what England had already been through in terms of earlier rebellions in Guyana and the elaborate compensation awards made to previous slave owners in the Empire as the cost of abolition.[21] Whatever ambiguous feelings he may have had about events, it did not alter his preference for a strong guiding secular authority as advocated in his post-1850 works. The episode had served to illustrate the growing gap between Carlyle and Ruskin with respect to their respective styles of conservatism and the role of natural law. Carlyle's restless search for authority had taken him along wintry roads towards greater abstraction, unrelieved by useful detail or proposals, all the while alienating old friends. As early as 1850, says one modern critic about Carlyle, 'the bough no longer blossomed' and he 'looked upon literature as a morbid substitute for reality'.[22] It was becoming difficult to recognize the man who earlier in his life had been sufficiently rationalist to toy with the views of the Count de Saint-Simon and even translate his *Nouveau Christianisme* into English.[23]

After 1858, Ruskin started to describe himself as a practitioner of the 'religion of humanity' but it was not a description much akin to the rationalist schemes for a new religion promoted by such as Saint-Simon or Auguste Comte. Frederic Harrison tried to convince him that he shared much with Comte but this was to no avail.[24] Ruskin was moving towards a more traditional and practical conservatism free of modern rationalist cobwebs or the verbal gymnastics of German historicism and idealism. Carlyle, on the contrary, had long been supportive of the work of the ambitious Scottish scholar, James Hutchinson Stirling and his efforts to unravel 'the secret of Hegel' for English readers.[25] This enterprise had no interest for Ruskin. Nor was he attracted to some version of Carlyle's 'strong man' or 'hero' for modern political solutions. It was rather something more familiar upon which, in sociological terms, English reformers should fix their attention. Such a proper direction Ruskin sketched out in his next major work.

III

In 1866 Ruskin entered into correspondence with one Thomas Dixon, a well-informed 'cork cutter' of Sunderland. Of this exchange, 25 letters by Ruskin became the basis of *Time and Tide By Weare and Tyne* published in 1867.[26] Agitation connected with the second great Reform Bill of 1867 had provided the initial context. The letters to Dixon were composed as short reflections on various issues designed to illustrate that English workers obtaining the vote was neither here nor there in terms of good government or in guarantying sound reforms. Some years later, he admitted that he himself had never bothered to cast a vote for a Member of Parliament.[27] The letters went well beyond cautioning workers about rising expectations associated with gaining the vote. He provided a selective commentary on various points raised in *Unto This Last* and *Munera Pulveris.*

Time and Tide set out a very general political economic program that sought to reintroduce, by means of state legislation, concepts favourable to the re-establishment of various 'commons' principles, not just in the area of land, water and air quality, but also in areas of education, the arts, labour rights, local church responsibilities, built-heritage and citizen welfare. There was an egalitarian element but it was expressed in terms of an equality maintained from above with a view to universal access and a right to impartial justice. The role of the state, as an active component, remained minimal, although not absent. In the Preface to *Unto This Last,* he had listed preferred areas for state involvement[28]:

1. Training schools for youth established at government cost.
2. Each child to be taught a trade or calling.
3. Government workshops to be established without monopoly aspirations in which good and exemplary work could be sold.
4. The unemployed to be set to work at the nearest government workshop.
5. Work to be paid at a fixed rate.
6. All who will learn to be taught, and those who won't to be set to penal work.
7. Comfort and home for the old and destitute.

Part of the message to Dixon and his associates was that such a program was a practical one, much of it achievable by direct local action. Any appeal to fixed or abstract ideas was a snare and a delusion. Dangers were associated with unchecked 'enthusiasm' in both religion and politics. Departing from a recent conference in which the reality of the Devil had been the focus of discussion, Ruskin chose to call the Devil 'the deceiving spirit within us' and he related it to the notion that in our mistaken love of God we may convince ourselves that we have managed 'to separate ourselves from our fellows' thereby producing a feeling that 'renders us superior to them'. Before long, 'it takes but one wave of the Devil's hand, and we are burning them alive for taking the liberty of contradicting us'. In a rather dialectical, Hegelian-sounding passage, he suggested that the possibilities for such narrow-minded error may be transferred into a corrupting ideology and then advanced by means of ill-established institutions of education: 'but let the Devil formalise it, and mix the pride of profession with it' and 'get foolish people entrusted with the business of instruction' by 'putting them up in pulpits above a submissive crowd – and you have it instantly corrupted into it's own reverse; you have an alliance against the light'. This situation can result in 'a company of the blind, beseeching those they lead to remain blind also'. Against such arrogant exercises of unified and mobilized conscience, Ruskin cautions the workers to turn their backs on those who contend that the 'heavens and the lights that rule them are untrue' and that 'the laws of creation are treacherous'. Pay no attention to those who claim that they alone 'are true' and that 'light is in us only'. No party man, Ruskin ends this grand secular sermon with the admonition to the workers that the Devil 'is the one to cast your vote against'.[29] No passage in Ruskin, perhaps, more clearly reveals his debt to Hooker and how far removed he was from those 'inner-light' evangelical attitudes which the old Elizabethan had found it necessary to curb.[30] Some years later, Ruskin became exercised over Methodist ideals and identified them with such dissenting attitudes of old.[31]

There was, he told Dixon, a greater need than winning the vote and that was to revive the energies and organization of the existing social classes. Drawing upon what he had learned and taught at the Working Men's College, Ruskin advised Dixon that workers should attempt to organize themselves co-operatively in guilds, as of old, or in other broader organizations. He told him bluntly that the voices of the workers were not worth a 'rat's squeak' until they had well developed opinions. He urged them to converse among themselves and establish their own councils.[32] The following year, in fact, the *Trade Union Congress* was founded at Manchester. Ruskin took an interest in such matters and, in 1868, attended special meetings of the National Association for the Promotion of Social Science gathered to consider matters relating to the 'labour question'.[33] Ruskin's statements before this gathering were in keeping with his arguments made in *Time and Tide* and revealed well the wide gap between his economic and political views and those held by most reform-minded people in the labour movement, which were still well aligned with those of the classical economists.[34]

The road to the future outlined in *Time and Tide* tended to raise eyebrows as its author appeared to be advocating a selective revival of classical and late medieval forms with a strong emphasis on kingship. The first Ruskin utopia was offered as a rather Spartan ideal state, its offices specified in medieval-sounding class and leadership categories. Despite emphasis on justice as a leading virtue, the authoritarian tone of *Time and Tide* and its social control aspirations were not reassuring to those supportive of actions being taken to advance unions, liberties and democratic reform. The journalist and novelist Margaret Oliphant condemned 'this latest lawgiver' for, among other things, his police state tendencies and lack of regard for traditional English liberties. She urged Ruskin to stick with what he knew and to no longer 'bring with him his bachelors and Rosières, his bishops and dukes'.[35] That his proposals were often dressed up colourfully there can be no doubt, but they were harmless enough, in his view, and did little more than suggest helpful modifications of the class system which still prevailed under the present constitution. That system, however much altered by the seventeenth-century civil war and by rapidly changing industrial forms, still seemed to him capable of supporting occasional medieval pageantry in homage to the long traditions of King, Lords and Commons, in league with the traditions of the church.

The shortcomings of current arrangements were, of course, many. In his second letter to Dixon, he lectured the upper classes on their collective failure to set a proper example. He suggested limitations be placed on their own financial needs and promoted the importance of a work ethic for all classes. 'It is the merest insolence of selfishness to preach contentment to a labourer who gets thirty shillings a week, while we suppose an active and plotting covetousness to be meritorious in a man who has three thousand a year'. The man of wealth as a 'pilot of the state' or as a 'captain of industry' in Victorian England, as an ideal character of community leadership, was seldom recognizable when divorced from old ties with the land and its administration. As a social ideal, the contemporary capitalist, as rugged individualist seemed, in the main, the last type to be recommended. In the absence of suitable working economic principles, Ruskin told his countrymen that the 'Captain of Industry' had first to learn that his function was 'to order things well' and to 'administer, not make profits'. In his discussion of 'Mastership', intrinsic value was again stressed: genuine economic activity consisted in learning to distinguish between things worth doing and those not.[36]

Well aware of the political and social abuses associated with the history of European aristocracy, he believed that, beginning in the fifteenth century, the extraction of false rent had become a factor linked with the decline of the nobility in its proper functions. It involved the corruption 'of those who ought to be the rulers and guides' forsaking their tasks in order to 'seek their own pleasure and pre-eminence only.' This degeneration could only be arrested 'by the repentance of that old aristocracy (hardly to be hoped for) or by the stern substitution of another aristocracy worthier than it'. The established classes being in a genuine morass, a new form of aristocracy was called for, the legitimacy of which would be based on its proper designated functions rather than hereditary rents. Aristocrats were to be put on fixed wages and their 'income must in no wise be derived from the rents of land'.[37]

Satisfied that the English people must reform themselves by tried and true constitutional methods, what kinds of offices should government sponsor and how should office holders be selected? His choices reflect the social categories of familiar English history as outlined by the following ranks.

The King Superior Judges Ordinary Judges State
Officers Bishops Officers of War Officers
of Public Institutions

Such chessboard images of *Time and Tide* were considered rather fantastic and some were uneasy with its apparent sanction of more intrusive government. There was certainly room enough for confusion on this point, since Letter Twelve was labelled 'Dictatorship', being Ruskin's exposition of the 'necessity of imperative law to the prosperity of the state'. He made his case using the familiar and mundane example of the crew of a small distressed craft at sea as a model for the generation of laws from a sudden, if temporary, dangerous state of nature, in which case authority had quickly to be established.

Letter Thirteen gives reasons for maintaining a strong link between church and state. In 'Episcopacy and Dukedom' the well-ordered society is a function of an active and official nobility. He reiterated the passage from *The Stones of Venice:* that the 'first duty of a State is to see that every child born therein shall be well housed, clothed, fed and educated, till it attains years of discretion'. The reference is to 'a State' and not to a heroic leader as some singular embodiment of the state.

For purposes of monitoring local conditions of health, conduct and employment, he urged enhanced use of already existing institutions, particularly a revamped hierarchy of Bishoprics and Duchies. His proposals resembled to some degree the system favoured by the Scottish Presbyterian social reformer, Thomas Chalmers (1780–1847), in as much as initial oversight for community welfare would be undertaken at the parish level. The similarity stopped there, however, for Chalmers insisted upon the importance of separating all forms of community assistance and oversight from actions of the state proper.[38] Ruskin, for his part, did not want to encourage randomness in the system, nor any excessive reliance on private charity outside of the church. With proper public funding for the essentials of education, periodic relief and a vigorous pro-work policy, the need for local charity should be kept to a minimum.

His main suggestion was that Bishops and Deacons needed to renew their acquaintance with their flocks and bring wanderers back into the fold. For every 100 or so 'families composing a Christian State' there should be an overseer or Bishop to give good account, with both good and bad being revealed voluntarily to him by adherents. The overseer was to act upon such information and help arrive at remedies. All 'such help and observation' was to be rendered 'without officiousness either of interference or inquisition' the limits of both being determined by National Law. Biographical information would be compiled and kept as a local record in order to provide sources on who should be recognized for merit or office. Despite these obvious theocratic leanings, Ruskin saw 'nothing tending toward espionage in this' or anything particularly 'un-English'. Eventually, such practices would come to be seen as sources of family honour. Above the Bishops there would be other higher regional officers of state, empowered to act upon any general reports submitted from the various overseers, and with a view to advising downwards on specific cases or of reporting to Parliament about possible needed adjustments or innovations in policy.

The model, while seemingly intrusive to us today, is not so far removed from the traditional expectations of adherents to the Scottish Presbyterian Church with its codified 'Book of Discipline' to guide the membership. Periodically elected Elders acted as overseers of the membership, with provisions for upward review of cases of church members indicted of various short-comings. The administrative elements in the Presbyterian system, however, were composed of changing delegates, nominated from the churches, and as a court, therefore, it represented a different philosophy from that prevailing in systems of ancient English Episcopacy. Up until the 1830s, the Scottish state had played a more distant and different role in church affairs from that prevailing in the Church of England. The nomination of ministers who ultimately composed the members sent to higher judicial levels of the Presbyterian Church had, nevertheless, been the subject of local nobility patronage. This situation became a central issue in 1830s Scotland when the evangelical wing of the Presbyterian Church, under the leadership of Thomas Chalmers, mounted a successful, but shattering, effort to reaffirm a purely Scottish form of Presbyterian rule, free of such patronage principles. While Carlyle and Ruskin both admired Chalmers, his essential political ideas, with their heavy reliance on the tools of direct charity and lack of state action, smacked too much of partial solutions as well as a levelling persuasion.[39] *Time and Tide* remained vague as to just how the appointments of his version of local overseers were to be made: they should be by election and for life but 'by what forms of election shall be matter of inquiry'.[40]

For purposes of social cohesion, Ruskin remained as interested in the late 1860s as he had been in the late 1840s in making a case for an episcopacy reflecting a broad national understanding, capable of dealing creatively with domestic issues and absorbing the enterprise of fanatics. In the 1851 'Preface' to *Notes on the Construction of Sheepfolds*, he had singled out for thanks a correspondent who had sent him a pamphlet called 'Sectarianism, the Bane of Religion and the Church'. Two years earlier, his *Diary* revealed the results of his wrestling with Hooker's *Laws*, in search of a proper view of episcopacy: 'Reading today part of Hooker's Seventh Book', he observed 'that the question is very conclusively settled by the two passages quoted from Jerome' whereby it is shown that episcopacy was 'a thing of custom only, but that ancient'.[41] This observation had opened the door for Hooker to suggest that the arrangements in a given country need not be those of another but also that sectarian division within a given country was not desirable. The propagandistic nature of the *Laws* shone through on such a point, for Hooker was making an argument for the new Church of England establishment while also opposing dissenter wishes for their own independent establishments within the realm. Ruskin retained the view that the church was a secular as well as religious establishment.[42] In its worldly form, the church's governing was best done when it recognized the role of talent. It 'could not but seem reasonable that, granting the administration of the Church to be in the hands of Presbyters, yet as in less important affairs bodies of men naturally appoint over themselves for their better regulation one who – either for convenience's sake has a regulative office, as a chairman of a committee, or else, being thought wiser and more prudent and learned than the rest, has a tacit weight, and is asked counsel at, by the rest'. And so it should be 'in the most important matter of Church government: for it is in this manner only that the greatest profit may be reaped from the mind and labours of the better men' those whose authority 'to enlarge' is to provide 'for the well being of the Church and of all'. Sounding like Alexander Pope, Ruskin contended that 'in all things the secret of good success is to place that which works best where it will work most, and to increase the power of the things which have healthiest operation'. Without doubt 'the difficulties are great in the matter of appointment' but it would be well 'if the prime question were first settled: whether or no Episcopacy with good bishops be not a good and desirable thing'.[43]

These views were all supportive of the line he later took in *Time and Tide*. If asked about his views of citizen monitoring and of just how much business government should have in the bedrooms of the nation, then Ruskin's reply was: considerable. He contended that 'the beginning of all sanitary and moral law is in the regulation of marriage' for 'ugly and fatal as is every form and agency of license, no licentiousness is so mortal as licentiousness in marriage'. Subject to 'such modifications in detail as local circumstances and character would render expedient' he provided a list of 'laws such as a prudent nation could institute respecting its marriages'.[44]

Aware that his views would undoubtedly be taken and interpreted as 'mere romance and unrealizable vision' (as they were), he nevertheless took these proposals to be important aspects of a reform program. Against the argument that only so many can benefit from education, he would be the last to deny 'the unconquerable differences in the clay of the human creature'. He insisted, however, that 'enormous difference in bodily and mental capacity had been mainly brought out by differences in occupation and by direct maltreatment'. Here again was the argument advanced in the *Nature of Gothic* about the virtues of a more organic social responsibility and its connection with that individualism which was the birth right of each person. He suggested that 'in a few generations, if the poor were cared for, their marriages looked after, and sanitary law enforced' then a 'beautiful type of face and form, and a high intelligence would become all but universal'. He held that 'in those worst treated children of the English race I yet see the making of gentlemen and gentlewomen – not the making of dog-stealers and gin-drinkers'.[45] The observation was not out of line with things as they stood in England just a few years later in 1870.[46]

> In Manchester 16,000 out of 65,000 children had no schools to which they might go; In Liverpool out of 80,000 children, 40,000 went to government aided schools, 20,000 went to schools which were so low in their standards that they could not qualify for government aid, and 20,000 had no schools at all. In the country as a whole 2,000,000 children out of 4,300,000 of school age were not in school and, of the rest, 1,000,000 were in schools which could not qualify for state aid.

While the range of increased educational opportunity was held to be significant, there would remain a need to undertake a certain amount of servile work. It should not even be above the ruling classes to dirty their hands on occasion. In 1868, he asked: 'If any man will not work, neither should he eat. Does this law apply to all classes of Society?'[47]

Time and Tide explored other possibilities of economic organization and quality control. By means of the 'trade warrant', working-class guilds could become the guardians of quality standards and honest trade practices. He described a related plan for universal education, in keeping with ideas set out in *Mulnera Pulveris,* a plan that included education for education's sake and not merely 'for getting on'.[48] Larger forms of state-supported education should be trans-class and aimed at sorting out all talents. In his *Inaugural Lecture* at Oxford in 1870, he spoke of his hope for 'an ideal of national life' in which the employments of Englishmen, 'though each shall be distinct, none shall be unhappy or ignoble'. His call was to a time when the more formal training of all those distinct classes 'will not be by universities of general knowledge, but by distinct schools'. This included schools for agriculture, forestry, business, management and the merchant marine.[49]

IV

Having established a role for the state in the provision of various forms of welfare, Ruskin had, for some time, noticed that such a role was more keenly appreciated in later medieval Europe, even if unevenly realized in practice. The various ranks of society in England had been more successfully integrated in terms of duties and obligations than was the case in much of the post-1750 world of *laissez-faire*-based urbanizing industrial commerce. The difference was one of attitude towards the value of the person and implied questions about the proper source and nature of human rights.[50]

The medieval church had been the most stable and essential purveyor of social assistance beyond the duties of local feudal landowners. The church had functioned as a state parallel to that of the secular arm, guided by laws of its own.[51] The relevant laws or 'canons' of the pre-Reformation Church had developed in great profusion over the centuries but were finally brought together in coherent form in Gratian's impressive collation of Canon Law, the *Decretum,* of 1140.[52] This work, produced at the University of Bologna, had an important impact on all European churches including those in England.[53] The main doctrine concerning the poor, Tierney observed, was that 'parishioners should pay tithes in full and give to the poor out of the nine parts that remained'. Thus, 'parish priests were instructed to see that their parishioners did not neglect this duty'. Thirteenth-century Bulls given by Popes Gregory X and Nicholas IV were particularly relevant in setting out parish duties to the poor.[54]

It is not certain just when Ruskin became familiar with the *Decretum.* He eventually collected early German copies of both Gratian and the later *Decretals* of Gregory IX, largely for their beauty as illuminated manuscripts. How familiar he was with their literary contents is not clear.[55] He was certainly familiar with Gratian's name through Dante's references to him in the *Paradiso* section of *The Divine Comedy.*[56] The consequences of Ruskin's looking back to the Middle Ages for suitable models for his economic language involved reanimation of terms such as the 'just price' and 'usury' as standard parts of his critical vocabulary. If he had not yet used the word 'usury' in *Unto This Last*, its equivalence is easily recognizable. In the mid-1870s, he started to become somewhat obsessed with the term as promoted in the works of the Sillar brothers.[57] We have already noticed how he referenced Canto Six of the *Inferno* in *Unto This Last* in order to draw attention to fraud and greed as the most destructive of the social vices.[58]

His interest in this famous text involved more than just solving its mysteries. A.P. d'Entrèves observed that Dante's political thought owed much to his refinement of historical understanding and periods and less to 'the drab allegories' and 'insoluble riddles' which were scattered throughout the poem.[59] The literary insights of the late Romantic critics of the new Poor Law of 1834 were steeped in such expanded historical understandings. They did not worship poverty but they also did not despise the poor. Their central objection was that the actual reasons for relief in a Christian society were being replaced by an approach which only thinly disguised the preferences of a privileged industrial leadership to keep wages low. It was this aspect which opened up Southey and Wordsworth to a more positive view of the religiously grounded medieval practices of poor law administration.[60]

In the early thirteen century, much controversy had whirled around the Franciscan Order and its view of poverty. The issue concerned the nature or property ownership and the oath taken by the members. It was contested after 1231 in the time of Pope Gregory IX and as an issue it played out for over a century. At stake were subtle questions about the realities of ownership as opposed to the mere use of goods and property. It was a matter of some importance to a church now rich in land, assets and financial wealth. In 1321, Pope John XXII muddied the waters further by means of a decree which attempted to again undermine the Franciscan position and its oath of poverty. He made it heretical to maintain that Christ and the Apostles did not 'have' anything individually or in common or that they had no 'right of using' the things they did have, or selling, giving or exchanging them. Thus, William of Ockham, one of the most brilliant of the Franciscans, entered into the debate. Drawing upon the now well-organized documents of Canon law, he drew the conclusion that the Pope was preaching heresy. He then proceeded to originate, arguably, an early theory of natural rights.[61]

The legacy of the Franciscan position, for such as Ruskin, was the insight that poverty was a complex issue and that an oath of poverty, while difficult to justify in many logical and practical respects, was not without possibilities or ethical insights. For one thing, it reduced demand for items of no intrinsic value and it opened a path to people prepared to work and serve the community at large. St. Francis himself had stated: 'I have worked with my hands and I choose to work, and I firmly wish that all my brothers should work at some honourable trade. And if they do not know how, let them learn…'[62]

Such statements help explain why Ruskin later made St. Francis one of the patron saints of his Guild of St. George. It was not merely the question of the virtue of work or questions surrounding the ins and outs of property ownership that recommended attention to medieval arrangements. In pre-Reformation times, the granting of charity and hospitality to the poor was recognized to be more than a recurring and inconvenient social issue but an actual Christian duty to do so in a regular and timely manner. Thus, in the English context of the late twelfth century, Bishop Hugh of Lincoln gained Ruskin's notice for his saintly treatment of lepers and his close attention to fulfilling the charitable duties of the Church.[63]

V

Such sources richly inform, directly or indirectly, the works on political economy which Ruskin had completed by 1870. While he knew nothing of the German, Henry Totting of Oyta, (c. 1330–97) how startling to read a passage from his *Tractatus de contractibus* (c. 1388) written at Vienna. Totting's work commenced, as did the third essay of *Unto This Last*, with a reference to the *Book of Wisdom* and the phrase '*Qui Judicatis Terram*'—'ye who judge the earth give diligent love to justice'.[64] A passage from the *Tractatus* which might as easily have been found in Ruskin's essay, denounced the prevailing order so congenial to usury and fraud. In truth, says Totting, 'these evils within the Christian people have grown and gained strength to such an extent' that they 'are reputed just and licit by many' and deniers of these conditions 'colour them with multiple dye, as in various exchanges and contracts which they falsify under the title of just and licit purchase and sale'.[65]

The reasons for the seeming distance of Ruskin's views from the growing liberal currents of his times are thus not far to seek. In the mid-1860s, the works of the Sillar brothers on usury had started to appear. When publishing the first edition of *Munera Pulveris* in 1872, Ruskin admitted that when he was composing the original essays in 1863 he had not yet determined just how central usury was as an economic force, but that he had now come around further to a position closer to that of the Sillar brothers.[66] His condemnation of the principle would become ever more extreme by the mid-1880s. By 1872, he had certainly attracted the negative critical attention of such liberal thinkers as John Morley and Leslie Stephen and of his friend Frederic Harrison. They all took him to task for his extreme impracticality, his lack of appreciation for the presumed upward course of history and his resistance to the compelling reasonableness of many of the Enlightenment's best representatives.[67] Ruskin, however, had a mind susceptible to an appreciation of that romantic form of enlightenment that drew its strength from Rousseau and from Scott's full-blooded accounts of history, beneath which the rational and irrational, the good and the evil, vied for control. Included also are the works of Jean-François Marmontel, which he greatly admired.[68] He was about to be exposed to such forces in his personal life with ever more intensity.

Having been branded an economic heretic, Ruskin had a soft spot for other sorts of heretics, ancient and modern. When, in the mid-1860s, the Bishop of Natal, John Colenso, was being tested for heresy in connection with his radical works of Biblical criticism, Ruskin called him an 'entirely honest man' and had no difficulties with his claims made about the historical qualities of the books of the *Pentateuch*. He then defended him in public.[69] The Colenso family had been in England since 1863 and personal connections soon developed with Ruskin. A daughter, Frances, was in attendance at Winnington Hall and the parents were glad to have Ruskin as a source of friendship and guidance for her and also during her later periods of residence in England.[70] Winnington Hall, however, was taking on a different and much more complex relevance owing to Ruskin's growing preoccupation with Frances's classmate, Rose La Touche. This personal drama continued to unfold throughout the 1860s up to the time when his professional attention was redirected by his appointment to Oxford as the first Slade Professor of Fine Art.

Notes

1. *Works*, 17: lxxvi.
2. For the character of Joan Agnew Severn and her important role in Ruskin's life, see Sheila Birkenhead, *Illustrious Friends* (London: Hamish Hamilton, 1965), Chapters 17 through 38.
3. Geoffrey Dutton, *The hero as murderer: the life of Edward John Eyre, Australian explorer and Governor of Jamaica 1815–1901* (Sydney: Collins, 1967).
4. See Bernard Semmel, *Jamaican Blood and Victorian Conscience* (Cambridge: Houghton Mifflin, 1963), 46–55.
5. *Report of the Jamaica Royal Commission, 1866.* George Edward Eyre and William Spottiswoode (London:HMSO. 1866).
6. The most detailed study of the rebellion is Gad Heuman, *'The Killing Time': The Morant Bay Rebellion in Jamaica* (Knoxville: University of Tennessee Press, 1994).
7. Gillian Workman, 'Thomas Carlyle and the Governor Eyre controversy: An account with some new material' *Victorian Studies*, 18:(1) (1974), 77–102.
8. For Ruskin's letter, see *Works*, 18: 550.
9. *Works*, 18: 551–54.
10. Cited in *Works*, 18: xlvi.
11. 'Mr. Carlyle on Mr. Eyre', *The Economist*, 15 September 1866.
12. *Diary*, Sept. 5, 1866. Cited in *Works*, 18: xlvi.
13. See the comments in David R. Sorensen, 'Ruskin and Carlyle' in Francis O'Gorman, ed. *The Cambridge Companion to John Ruskin* (Cambridge: Cambridge University Press, 2015), 198–99.

14. See Edward Norman, *The Victorian Christian Socialists* (Cambridge: Cambridge University Press, 1987), 56; William H. Scheuerle, 'Henry Kingsley and the Governor Eyre Controversy', *Victorian Newsletter*, 37 (Spring, 1970), 24–27.
15. R.B. Martin, *The Dust of Combat: A Life of Charles Kingsley* (London: Faber, 1959), 259–61.
16. George H. Ford, 'The Governor Eyre Case in England' *University of Toronto Quarterly*, 17 (1947–48), 229–31.
17. Ruskin to Carlyle, Sept. 29, 1866, in Cate, ed., (1982), 120–21.
18. Frances S. Colenso to Lady Mary Lyell, Oct. 25, 1866, in Wyn Rees, ed., *Colenso: Letters from Natal* (Pietermaritzburg: Shuter and Shooter, 1958), 122.
19. Semmel, (1963), Ch. 7.
20. William Rossetti, *Diary*, Feb. 26, 1867. Cited in Leon (1949), 382.
21. On Guyana, see Emilia Viotti da Costa, *Crowns of Glory, Tears of Blood: The Demerara Slave Rebellion of 1823* (New York: Oxford University Press 1994). For the official records of compensation between 1833 and 1851, see British National Archive, Office of Registry of Colonial Slaves and Slave Compensation Commission: Records.
22. John Gross, *The Rise and Fall of the Man of Letters: English Literary Life Since 1800* (London: Penguin, 1991), 37.
23. See K.J. Fielding, 'Carlyle and the Saint-Simonians' in Clubbe, ed. (1976), 35–59; Van den Bossche (1991), 128–30; and Frank E. Manuel, *The New World of Henri Saint-Simon* (Cambridge: Harvard University Press, 1956), 353–63.
24. Harrison, (1907), 91–2; (1911), 1: 231–34.
25. On Carlyle's connections with J.H. Stirling, see Ameila Hutchinson Stirling, *James Hutchinson Stirling: His Life and Work* (London: T. Fisher Unwin, 1912), vi, 48–59, 94–96, 136–40, 206–11.
26. *Works*, 17: 295–482.
27. *Works*, 27: 544.
28. *Works*, 17: 21–23.
29. *Works*, 17: 363–66.
30. For parallel observations to those given here by Ruskin, see Hooker, *Of the Laws of Ecclesiastical Polity*, Book IV.
31. Ruskin's heated exchange in print with 'A Wesleyan Preacher' in 1878 indicts the error of those who claimed inner conscience-driven access to righteousness or salvation. *Works*, 28: 711, 731, 750–1; 29: 28–9.
32. *Works*, 17: 325–26. And see Richard B. Litchfield, *The Beginnings of the Working Men's College* (London: Working Men's College, 1903), 4.
33. *Works*, 17: 538.

34. See Lawrence Goldman, 'John Ruskin and the Working Classes in Mid-Victorian Britain' in Keith Hanley and Brian Maidment, eds. *Persistent Ruskin: Studies in Influence, Assimilation and Effect* (Surrey: Ashgate, 2013), 15–32.
35. Margaret Oliphant 'The Latest Lawgiver', *Blackwood's Magazine*, 103 (June, 1868), 675–91.
36. *Works*, 17: 275.
37. *Works*, 17: 439.
38. See Henry Hunter, ed., *Dr. Chalmers and the Poor Laws: Problems of Poverty* (London: Thoemmes Press, 1995), v–xi.
39. See Hunter, ed. (1995) and Ruskin to Dr. John Brown, Feb. 9, 1848, in John Brown and D.W. Forrest, eds., *Letters of Dr. John Brown* (London: Adam and Charles Black, 1907), 291.
40. *Works*, 17: 381.
41. Ruskin's *Diary*, 18 March 18 1849, in *Works*, 12: lxxiii.
42. For this view, as developed by Hooker, see W.D.J. Carghill Thompson, 'The Philosopher of the "Politic Society": Richard Hooker as a Political Thinker', in W. Speed Hill, ed., *Studies in Richard Hooker* (Cleveland: Case Western Reserve University, 1972), 22–23.
43. Ruskin's *Diary*, 18 March 1849, in *Works*, 12: lxxiii.
44. *Works*, 17: 420–22.
45. *Works*, 18: 405–6.
46. Frederick C. Dietz, *A Political and Social History of England* (New York: Macmillan Co. 1928), 451.
47. Speech at the National Association for the Promotion of Social Science, 4 July 1868, *Works*, 17: 538.
48. This was a central tenet of the Working Men's Collage program. See Litchfield (1903).
49. *Works*, 20: 21–22.
50. Certain aspects of Florentine Law were mentioned favourably. *Works*, 28: 23–42.
51. Brian Tierney, *Medieval Poor Law* (Berkeley: University of California Press, 1959), 5. On the shortcomings of actual execution of such duties, see Leff (1961), 40–41.
52. Gratian, *The Treatise on Laws, with The Ordinary Gloss*. James Gordley, trans. Introduction by Katherine Christensen (Washington: Catholic University of America, 1993).
53. Z.N. Brooke, *The English Church and the Papacy* (Cambridge: Cambridge University Press, 1952), 36–43.
54. Tierney (1959), 96–97; Baron, (1938), 1–37.
55. Dearden (2012), 137, 143; personal communication, Dr. Stella Panayotova. The Fitzwilliam Museum. University of Cambridge. 14 Dec. 2014.

56. Gratian (1993), ix; for Ruskin's detailed knowledge of Dante, see George P. Huntington, comp. *Comments of John Ruskin on the Divina Commedia*, with an Introduction by Charles Eliot Norton. (Boston: Houghton Mifflin, 1903).
57. See *Works*, 17: 220 n.; 28: 121–2, 400–1, 728; 34: 580.
58. See *Works*, 27: 313–14.
59. A.P. d'Entrèves, *Dante as a Political Thinker* (Oxford: The Clarendon Press, 1952), 7.
60. See David M. Craig, *Robert Southey and Romantic Apostasy: Political Argument in Britain, 1780–1840* (Woodbridge: Boydell Press, 2007).
61. See Brian Tierney, *The Idea of Natural Rights* (Grand Rapids: Emory University Press, 1997), Ch. 4; On the complexities of these questions, see Brett (1997), Ch. 1; Rosenthal (2008) 222–25.
62. Cited in Tierney (1959), 11 and 142 n.9.
63. *Works*, 22: 409; 29: 387–9; 35: 482. Ruskin was familiar with J.A. Froude's, 'A Bishop of the Twelfth Century' in *Short Studies on Great Subjects* (London: Longman's Green, 1907), II: 52–86. See also David H. Farmer, *Saint Hugh of Lincoln* (London: Darton, Longman and Todd, 1985), 44–48.
64. *Works*, 17: 62.
65. Translations from the Latin by Annabel Brett in Brett (1997), 32. Compare, Ruskin, *Works*, 17: 56–7.
66. *Works*, 17: 220 n.
67. See Judith Stoddart, 'Conjuring the Necromantic Evidence of History' in her *Ruskin's Culture Wars: Fors Clavigera and the Crisis of Victorian Liberalism* (Charlottesville: University Press of Virginia, 1998), 102–03.
68. *Works*, 5: 67; 18: lxi–lxii, 48; 27: 250–56.
69. *Works*, 17: 521; 36: 424–25, 430, 473.
70. Frances eventually enrolled as a member of the Guild of St. George before her premature death in 1887 from tuberculosis. See Helen G. Viljoen, ed., *The Brantwood Diary of John Ruskin* (New Haven: Yale University Press, 1971), 571–74.
71. Footnote references to Ruskin's writings (unless otherwise stated) are cited as *Works*, and refer to Cook, Edward T. and Wedderburn, Alexander, eds. *The Collected Works of John Ruskin*. London: 1903–1912. 39 v.

Bibliography[71]

Bagehot, Walter. 1866. Mr. Carlyle on Mr. Eyre. *The Economist*, 15th September.
Baron, Hans. 1938. Franciscan Poverty and Civic Wealth as Factors in the Rise of Humanistic Thought. *Speculum* 13 (1): 1–37.
Birkenhead, Sheila. 1965. *Illustrious Friends*. London: Hamish Hamilton.

Bossche, C.R.V. 1991. *Carlyle and the Search for Authority*. Columbus: Ohio State University Press.

Brooke, Z.N. 1952. *The English Church and the Papacy*. Cambridge: Cambridge University Press.

Brown, John, and D.W. Forrest, eds. 1907. *Letters of Dr. John Brown*. London: Adam and Charles Black.

Cate, George Allen, ed. 1982. *The Correspondence of Thomas Carlyle and John Ruskin*. Stanford: Stanford University Press.

Clubbe, John, ed. 1976. *Carlyle and His Contemporaries*. Durham: Duke University Press.

Craig, David M. 2007. *Robert Southey and Romantic Apostasy:Political Argument in Britain, 1780–1840*. Woodbridge: Boydell Press.

d'Entrèves, A.P. 1952. *Dante as a Political Thinker*. Oxford: Clarendon Press.

da Costa, Emilia Viotti. 1994. *Crowns of Glory, Tears of Blood: The Demerara Slave Rebellion of 1823*. New York: Oxford University Press.

Dearden, James. 2012. *The Library of John Ruskin*. Oxford: Oxford Bibliographical Society.

Dietz, Frederick C. 1928. *A Political and Social History of England*. New York: Macmillan.

Dutton, Geoffrey. 1967. *The Hero as Murderer: The Life of Edward John Eyre, Australian Explorer and Governor of Jamaica 1815–1901*. Sydney: Collins.

Farmer, David H. 1985. *Saint Hugh of Lincoln*. London: Darton, Longman and Todd.

Ford, George H. 1947–48. The Governor Eyre Case in England. *University of Toronto Quarterly*, 17: 229–231.

Froude, J.A. 1907. *Short Studies on Great Subjects*. London: Longman's Green.

Gratian. 1993. *The Treatise on Laws, with The Ordinary Gloss*. Trans. James Gordley. Introduction by Katherine Christensen. Washington, DC: Catholic University of America.

Gross, John. 1991. *The Rise and Fall of the Man of Letters: English Literary Life Since 1800*. London: Penguin.

Hanley, Keith, and Brian Maidment, eds. 2013. *Persistent Ruskin: Studies in Influence, Assimilation and Effect*. Surrey: Ashgate.

Harrison, Frederick. 1907. *John Ruskin*. London: Macmillan.

Heuman, Gad. 1994. *'The Killing Time': The Morant Bay Rebellion in Jamaica*. Knoxville: University of Tennessee Press.

Hill, W. Speed, ed. 1972. *Studies in Richard Hooker*. Cleveland: Case Western Reserve University.

Hooker, Richard. 1977–1998. *The Works of Richard Hooker, ed.* W. Speed Hill, Folger Edition. Cambridge, MA: Harvard University Press, 7 v.

Hunter, Henry, ed. 1995. *Dr. Chalmers and the Poor Laws: Problems of Poverty*. London: Thoemmes Press.

Huntington, George P., comp. 1903. *Comments of John Ruskin on the Divina Commedia,* with an Introduction by Charles Eliot Norton. Boston: Houghton Miffllin.

Leon, Derrick. 1949. *Ruskin: The Great Victorian.* London: Routledge and Kegan Paul.

Litchfield, Richard B. 1903. *The Beginnings of the Working Men's College.* London: Working Men's College.

Manuel, Frank E. 1956. *The New World of Henri Saint-Simon.* Cambridge, MA: Harvard University Press.

Martin, R.B. 1959. *The Dust of Combat: A Life of Charles Kingsley.* London: Faber.

Norman, E.R. 1968. *Anti-Catholicism in Victorian England.* London: George Allen and Unwin.

O'Gorman, Francis, ed. 2015. *The Cambridge Companion to John Ruskin.* Cambridge: Cambridge University Press.

Oliphant, Margaret. 1868. The Latest Lawgiver. *Blackwood's Magazine* 103: 675–691.

Rees, Wyn, ed. 1958. *Colenso: Letters from Natal.* Pietermaritzburg: Shuter and Shooter.

Report of the Jamaica Royal Commission. 1866. *George Edward Eyre and William Spottiswoode.* London: HMSO.

Scheuerle, William H. 1970. Henry Kingsley and the Governor Eyre Controversy. *Victorian Newsletter* 37 (1): 24–27.

Semmel, Bernard. 1963. *Jamaican Blood and Victorian Conscience.* Cambridge: Houghton Mifflin.

Stirling, Ameila H. 1912. *James Hutchinson Stirling: His Life and Work.* London: T. Fisher Unwin.

Tierney, Brian. 1959. *Medieval Poor Law.* Berkeley: University of California Press.

———. 1997. *The Idea of Natural Rights.* Grand Rapids: Emory University Press.

Viljoen, Helen G., ed. 1971. *The Brantwood Diary of John Ruskin.* New Haven: Yale University Press.

Workman, Gillian. 1974. Thomas Carlyle and the Governor Eyre Controversy: An Account with Some New Material. *Victorian Studies* 18 (1): 77–102.

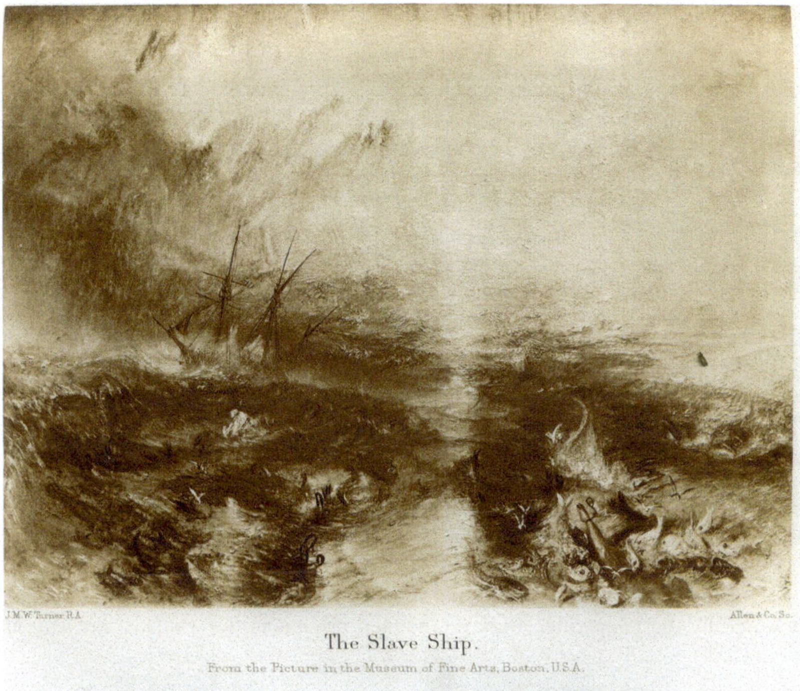

Fig. 5.1 *The Slave Ship* (1840) by Joseph Mallord William Turner (1775–1851). This famous work was given to Ruskin in January, 1844, by his father as a New Year's gift. Ruskin sold it in 1872 and it was shipped to America where eventually it was purchased by the Boston Museum of Fine Arts. Ruskin wrote of the advancing 'shadow of death upon the guilty ship'. Credit: *Cook and Wedderburn, Ruskin's Collected Works*

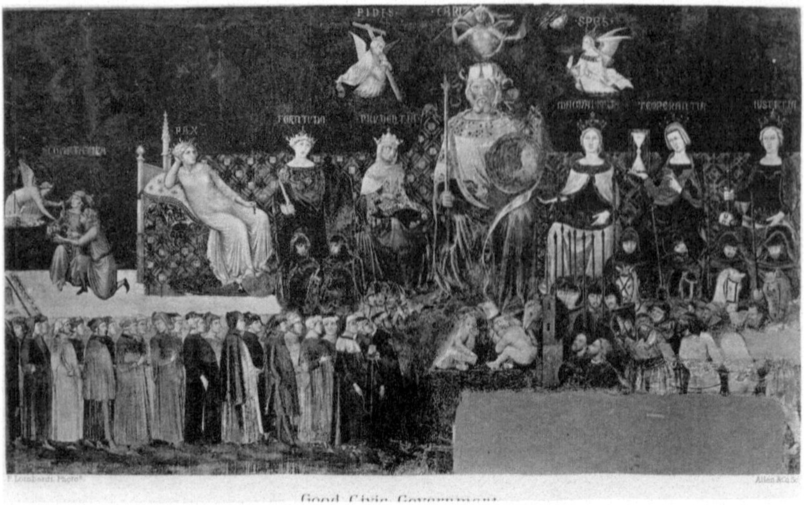

Fig. 5.2 From the Allegory of 'Good Civic Government' by Ambrogio Lorenzetti (c. 1290–1348). This was completed in 1339 in the *Palazzo Pubblico* of Siena. It shows the crowned head of government surrounded by the virtues required by the good ruler. Ruskin remarked upon it in *The Political Economy of Art* (1857). Credit: *Cook and Wedderburn, Ruskin's Collected Works*

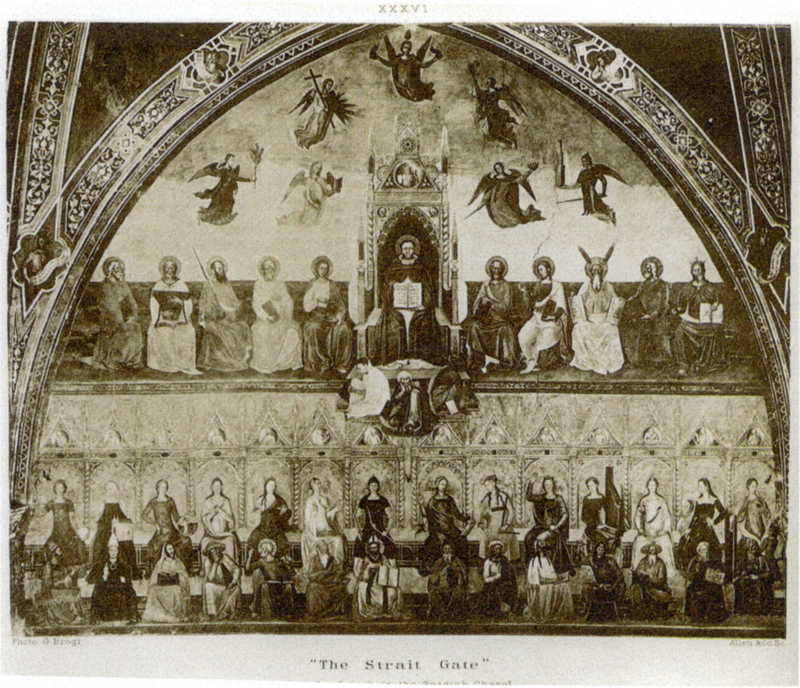

Fig. 5.3 'The Triumph of St. Thomas Aquinas' by Andrea Da Firenza (active 1343–77). This fresco in the *Santa Maria Novella* Church in Florence dates from about 1367 and depicts the well- ordered late medieval world. The cardinal virtues move above St. Thomas while below him are three suppressed heretics: Sabellius, Averroës, and Arius. Ruskin discussed the work as 'The Strait Gait' in his late guide book, 'Mornings in Florence'. Credit. *Cook and Wedderburn, Ruskin's Collected Works*

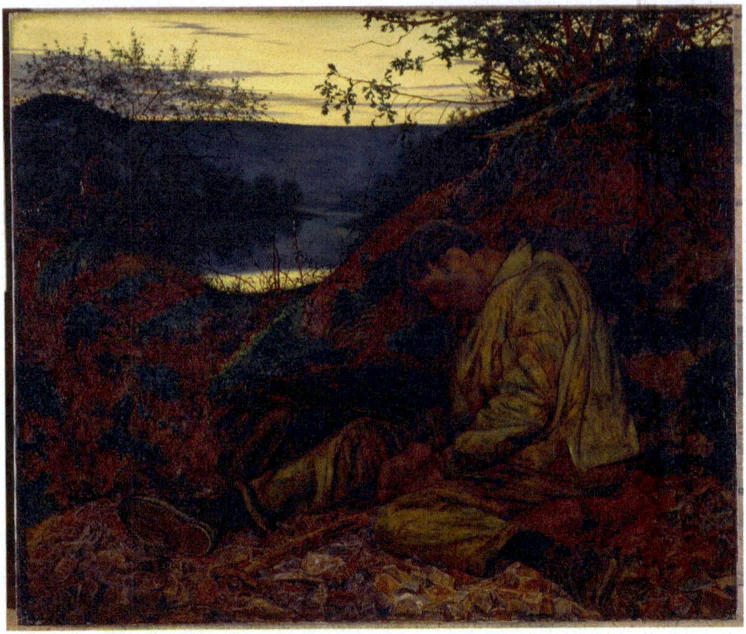

Fig. 5.4 *The Stone Breaker* (1855), by Henry Wallis (1830–1916). This moving work is by one of the lesser-known Pre-Raphaelite painters. In his *Academy Notes* for 1858, Ruskin called it 'The Picture of the Year'. It shows a labourer at dusk, fallen dead at his work. It is an example of what Ruskin denounced as the result of 'industrial slavery'. Credit: Birmingham Museums Trust

CHAPTER 6

Towards Pluralism: Oxford Teaching and Natural Law: 1870–77

I heard his lectures and for some time saw him almost everyday. His mobile lips were not yet covered by a beard, and he always wore his precise costume, with an intensely blue neckcloth. His face was that of a man who had seen, and was to see again, hell, as well as paradise.
– Graham Wallas.
On Ruskin at Corpus Christi College.

I

Ruskin's appointment as the new Slade Professor of Art at Oxford University was secured with the help of friendly Board members such as Henry Acland and Henry Liddell.[1] His duties commenced in 1870, the appointment giving him a place of formal respectability in the community as well as a public pulpit. From his new estate in the Lake District and his rooms at Oxford, he prepared not just lectures but initiated his periodic letters to the working men of England, *Fors Clavigera*.[2] During the period between 1870 and 1884, two distinct paths can be followed. His formal lectures touched on much that was extraneous and fleeting but, in the main, they were concerned with the arts, the history of nations, the importance of forms of work, the character of proper science and the joys of natural history. To read his lectures aloud, said a witness, is to gain insight into his popularity with students of the day, many of whom went on to make a mark in life.[3] A more recent writer contends that 'People did not crowd his lectures to appreciate art but to appreciate Ruskin.'[4] *Fors*

G. A. MacDonald, *John Ruskin's Politics and Natural Law*,
https://doi.org/10.1007/978-3-319-72281-8_6

Clavigera, on the other hand, the same writer described as a 'book of Messianic meanderings and prophetic imprecations' and as the work that amounted to Ruskin's '*Apologia*'.[5] Graham Hough cautions us not to confuse those ringing evangelical sermon tones by which Ruskin habitually linked beauty with morals with the belief that the perception of beauty also involved immediate perceptions of 'right and wrong'. His use of the analogy was more akin to that of the modern anthropologist. It referred to the commonly held understandings by those in a given society about 'character and conduct' and implied that the meaning of beauty is 'not isolated from the rest of human life' nor is it purely 'an affair of the intellect or the senses' but involved emotions keyed to an appreciation of one's way of life and social expectations.[6] All such factors came together in what Ruskin called 'taste'.[7] However that may be, Ruskin's Oxford lecture performances had about them much of the traditional sermon.[8]

The many lapses into extreme asides or matters of seeming little consequence were not just signs of mounting struggles with his mental health, says McClelland, but part of his disguise and a use of irony designed to attract the readers' attention towards 'the conditions of modern life and the hopes and desires of deluded men'.[9] Ruskin acknowledged his own ruse: 'If I took off the Harlequin's mask for a moment you would say I was simply mad.'[10] To be sure, however, symptoms of Ruskin's later serious mental breakdowns were ever more evident in these years. His post-1869 'brain fever' attacks were stimulated by at least two sources.[11] The first was the preoccupation with the mistress of his mind, young Rose La Touche. The second was the death of his mother in 1871. After that date, the proper use of his accumulated wealth came to preoccupy him, even if his domestic obligations were greatly reduced. His first response to his new wealth was to dispose of the London property and relocate to Lake Coniston in the Lake District where he purchased Brantwood, a large hillside home with a grand view. He attempted to redistribute his personal fortune and to live more modestly from the proceeds of his own work, even becoming his own publisher. This self-publishing approach, if questionable at first, appears to have eventually worked in his favour. The approach certainly did not make him less wealthy as many of his books came into strong demand in his later years.[12] It should be noted also that Ruskin never did, by the standards of the time, ever develop a capacity to 'live modestly' although he was certainly generous with his funds to others and did not squander his money on conspicuous unnecessaries.

Evidences of concern for his wealth and what to do with it are found regularly in both the Oxford lectures and in *Fors Clavigera*, where he regularly aired the topic in either a personal or more general way. The concept of 'usury' starts to make an appearance in his vocabulary, steadily taking on an identity as the general source of most social error, as it had for Sir Thomas More in his time. In the early 1870s, Ruskin started to read More's *Utopia* with closer attention.[13] His interest in the now forgotten works of the Sillar brothers on the topic of usury came to dominate much of his late economic thinking and provided the occasion for one of Ruskin's last appearances in print.[14]

Despite many distractions, Ruskin's capacity for work remained enormous in the years after 1869. He was fortunate to be surrounded by family, friends and colleagues who helped him through difficult emotional episodes.[15] Whatever the wide swings of attention and mood in *Fors Clavagira*, some of the other late works were of a very high order in terms of focus and coherence.[16] This can be said of his third book on drawing instruction, *The Laws of Fésole* (1879) and the 1880 prefatory essay to *Rock Honeycomb*, his edition of Sir Philip Sidney's *Psalter*, prepared as a library item for members of the Guild of St. George.[17]

II

It was in such a spirit of advocacy of 'work by all', including aristocrats, and accompanied by a good deal of humour, that in 1871 Ruskin sought to instruct some of his Oxford students in the art of road building. His Hinksey Road project was the target of amused comment by *Punch*, among others, and E.T. Cook reported that Ruskin himself admitted that as a road it was probably 'the worst in the three kingdoms'.[18] The work failed, according to the account of one who was there 'partly because of the soil, partly because of the laziness of the undergraduates' and partly because 'Mr Oscar Wilde would insist on stopping and lecturing upon the beauties of the colour of the soil turned up.'[19] The project did help to open Ruskin's eyes about both the feasibility and limitations of voluntary work in the countryside under current assumptions of political economy.[20]

The new Slade Chair provided Ruskin with an opportunity to reconsider his body of work and qualify past conclusions about the nature, meaning and production of art. In this he was first influenced by his own growing disenchantment with denominational and sectarian religion.

Second, Turner's partial fall from grace in the late 1850s, as previously described, had caused Ruskin to reconsider not just the personality of his hero but his larger contention that the great artist was necessarily a reflection of his society. Finally, there was Ruskin's loss of much of his youthful enchantment with nature in the 1850s, a necessary coming to terms, perhaps, with what was long implicit in his early grasp of the findings of modern science, especially geology, zoology and chemistry.[21]

These three themes of religion, personality and nature would be continuously revisited in the late writings as he simultaneously worked out a practical political theory for the Guild of St. George. For a man who did not have much good to say about public opinion, *Fors Clavigera* was actually a quite remarkable exercise in public consultation. He used the periodical to advance his own opinions but had the good sense to print what others had to say in reply, even if they strongly objected to some of his ideas or proposals. He courted controversy in its pages but seldom refused courtesy to his respondents. A main difficulty was that a subscription to *Fors Clavigera* was too expensive for most of those 'Working men of England' to whom the publication was supposedly directed and its readership remained rather limited.[22]

Having said a good deal about the art and architecture of Venice in his earlier writings, he turned in the Oxford lectures towards medieval and Renaissance Florence, Siena and Padua. Venice still interested him as well, as a logical focus for comparison with the sea-based British Empire.[23] The histories of the land-based Italian city states, on the other hand, illustrated different kinds of civic experience as expressed in their art.[24] In the late Renaissance phases of these cities, he still saw little to recommend them and much to lament. As with his response to English cities, he never warmed up to Florence in its contemporary form. In 1840, says Alexander Bradley, 'he took an almost immediate dislike to Florence and Siena, first voicing that instinctive distrust of all things Renaissance which later grew into harder hostility'.[25] His growing familiarity with Italy after 1845, however, led him to make distinctions and he developed an appreciation for the earlier 'primitive' aspects of Italian Church art in the later medieval period, particularly as realized in the works of Fra Angelico and Giotto.[26] He reviewed aspects of the history of Tuscany in *Val D'Arno*, one of his Oxford lecture series of the 1870s. Such reviews played well into his other developing projects dealing with political economy.

III

His studies of art, early and late, often drew to his attention the importance of those forms of labour organization associated with guilds. The structure of his own latter-day guild reflected his hostility to the modifications of guild practices ushered in by the altering commercial practices of the 'wicked Renaissance'. It was not just his steady reading of Dante which helped him form negative views of fifteenth-century Italy but also the inferences made from his continual reading of Sismondi's great *History of the Italian Republics.*[27] There was much in this work that Ruskin appreciated, including his economic views, many of which came to inform his own, despite Sismondi's 'republican bias'.[28] The virtues of the laws of the early Italian republics had given way, said Ruskin, to the financial and oligarchical corruption of the later periods as reflected by incessant warfare and debased cultural productions.[29] This was a view embraced as early as 1845, but not so firmly as to deny that the city republics represented striking achievements and had developed some sound laws in support of a remarkable vision of participatory citizenship. He communicated his interpretation at some length in a letter to his father.[30] Thus 'Sismondi most truly says that in Florence, where every citizen of common respectability, down to the lowest tradesman' had the chance of 'becoming one of the twelve Anziani, of supreme authority', it was the 'struggle to obtain this position' and the 'faculties developed' that gave great force of character to the nation. This was, however, 'a morbid excitement' for it necessarily involved some 'following reaction and degradation'. Such government 'cannot subsist, it can have no settled principles'. It may be 'an admirable school for the people, but a miserable instrument in its own proper function'. There were distinct geographic and historical realities involved as to why even its admirable aspects had often to fail in relation to 'the scale of the nation' for 'in a city divided into twenty companies it works but well, but it is absurd altogether in a kingdom divided into twenty provinces'. The main difficulty, then, concerned stability: 'Independent cities have some reason in being republican, but it must be at the expense of continual jealousies, wars, and seditions.' He then asserted the position to which he would continue to adhere: 'Peace can only be secured by fixed positions of all ranks and settled government of the whole.'[31]

Here was an early indication of an interest in guild ideas. The actual origins of the idea of reviving a working model of a guild in the world of late Victorian England can be found in his years working at the Working

Men's College through association with one of his students, William Ward. In 1855, they had discussed the idea of a co-operative organization with art as its central basis.[32] This initial idea for a 'Protestant Convent' came to nothing, but its echo was heard in 1857 when he wrote in the *Political Economy of Art* of the need for 're-establishing guilds of every important trade'. He argued that there should be 'a great council or government house for the members of every trade' in towns engaged 'principally in such trade' with minor council-halls elsewhere as required. The concerns of these houses would be akin to those customarily looked to in earlier times by guild bodies.[33] Ruskin also knew something of Southey's literary works and his *Colloquies*, which he had been reading 'with pleasure' as early as 1843.[34] Southey's interest in both poor law reform and in communal villages as a way to restore dignity to the unemployed were likely fruitful sources of influence on him.[35] The guild idea was advanced again in 1858 at a notable lecture given at Cambridge, one listened to with rapt attention by the young Octavia Hill.[36]

Such ideas of guild regeneration had actually been touched upon as early as 1853, we have seen, when Ruskin first made the acquaintance of Hill and her family, the start of a long collaboration in art work and later in small-scale housing projects for the poor of London and its environs.[37] These projects, supported by Ruskin with both money and encouragement, may be considered the first real achievement of his guild approach. Much has been made of the rupture between them in 1877 but this was almost entirely a function of Ruskin's poor mental health. The way in which the situation was handled by Hill was a credit to her common sense.[38]

The guild idea was taken up again by Ruskin in 1867 as a result of the personal conflicts created by his own inheritance of wealth and by his correspondence with Dora Livesy and Thomas Dixon.[39] The advice offered to Dixon and his fellow workers was that in forming their organization they should, in the manner of guilds, make their own constitutional laws and regulations by which to guide member performances.[40] Since his writings on political economy had, to date, not registered with the informed public, perhaps he would take his own advice and try to demonstrate their viability by other means.

IV

There was something else in the air at Oxford that was compatible with Ruskin's desire to re-energize the aristocracy and the Empire along more positive moral lines. When he took up his professorship, a young man was already starting to make his mark in the university, the 23- year old Francis H. Bradley. There is no reason to think the two men ever met. Despite his youth, Bradley was in poor health by 1872. While by no means anti-social, he remained reclusive owing to his fragility and commitment to writing. It is possible, however, that Bradley could have heard Ruskin lecture on some occasion for he was interested in public affairs, had read some of Carlyle, was of a conservative disposition and an opponent of Benthamite utilitarianism.[41] If, for a moment, we can imagine Ruskin having the patience to read any of Bradley's idealist philosophy, we would probably think him in sympathy with aspects of the *Ethical Studies* of 1876. On the surface there is little to distinguish Ruskin's practical social positions from those of Bradley, as rendered in 'My Station and Its Duties'.[42]

There were others about Oxford with a more obvious connection to Ruskinian influence concerning co-operation and social solidarity. About Thomas Hill Green, Lord Lindsay observed that he and his fellow idealists 'had been profoundly influenced by Carlyle', but unlike that gloomy figure, they were also firm democrats who thought social reform would issue best out of a reformed state. Green died in 1882, soon followed to the grave by the promising young economic historian, Arnold Toynbee, another of the Hinksey Road builders.[43] These men were greatly mourned by those in the ranks of late nineteenth-century English reform. They were not, however, the only ones influenced by the art professor. Included were Ruskin's future editors, Alexander Wedderburn and Edward Cook, along with Hardwicke Rawnsley, an important future conservationist in the Lake District. William G. Collingwood must also be mentioned, Ruskin's future secretary and biographer.[44] To these may be added such staunch renewers of the Empire as Cecil Rhodes, Alfred Milner and the Canadian, George R. Parkin. They, with others, formed the crucible of 'Imperial Roundtable' thinking, discussed first in the circle known as 'Milner's Kindergarten'.[45] The driving motives of those around Milner may be briefly summarized. They took the view that the British Empire represented 'the unfolding of a great moral idea' associated with freedom and that imperial unity was an important tool with which to spread such convictions. Furthering education in the interest of imparting a sense of 'duty and obligation' towards state service was an important policy issue, one which should consider members of all classes.[46]

The sources of such aspirational statements can easily be found in Ruskin's Oxford lectures and indeed reflect, to a degree, his chivalric ideals. He would not, however, have espoused any kind of Hegelian inevitability of future imperial achievement or the notion that unqualified economic freedom was a fundamental building block for a good empire. A well-run empire should to be informed by virtuous laws and policies capable of facilitating opportunities for willing hands seeking productive work. It should also be a theatre for testing and expanding sound laws along more pluralistic horizons, appropriate to the requirements of mixed populations.[47] His vision infected a good number in 'Milner's kindergarten' but the results on the ground were highly variable.[48] A certain irony attaches to Gandhi's attraction to the lessons of *Unto This Last* after 1904, which he put to good use in his campaign to drive the English out of India.[49]

V

From a philosophical angle, the late works and lectures demonstrate a shift towards the embrace of natural law ethics consistent with his increasingly bare-bones version of Christianity. As mentioned in Chap. 1, natural law, as a term, has a long history dating back to ancient times. Roman law demonstrated that under the umbrella of the 'law of nature' concrete human laws could be fashioned for use at the local, national and international level; and that such positive laws, correctly formulated, could be looked to with confidence by people of all nations and circumstances, even slaves. The unifying premise was that there is some kind of overarching moral content to natural law, accessible by human reason. The presence of that common element allowed for the formulation of positive laws, locally varied, defective by degree, but capable of amendment in the light of experience and further exercises of reason.

In the medieval reformulation, reasoning man's ability to perceive precepts of 'natural law' were seen to be in conformity with the revealed Law of God, a view which reached a high water mark in the work of St. Thomas Aquinas: natural law is 'nothing else than the rational creature's participation in the eternal law'. A close student of natural law suggests that it 'provides a name for the point of intersection between law and morals'.[50] This hierarchical version of Aquinian law, absorbed by Hooker, was utilized as the grounding for his attempt to redefine the Tudor Church by means of a *via media*, one capable of accommodating the outlooks of moderate Puritans, Calvinists and old Catholics.[51] In considering Hooker's formulation of natural law, Peter Munz appropriately located it within a theological tradition in which human nature 'though weakened' is recognized as not 'entirely corrupted' and still capable 'within the order of nature itself' of recognizing 'through reason' those 'rules of conduct which are known as natural law'. This was the view of human nature, which Ruskin, by and large, endorsed in the second volume of *Modern Painters*.

Against this interpretation was the more severe, Calvinist-inspired outlook of the Puritan (the tradition most directly attacked by Hooker), which suggested that man was born in 'utter depravity' and required a theological vision which rejected the basis of the Aristotelian argument that the human condition was foremost a social condition.[52] The Puritan account of the human condition being one of hopeless isolation was understandably seen by opponents as eccentric and contrary to reason itself.[53] These were, indeed, the poles of debate between which Luther and Erasmus had come to part ways over the issue of free will.[54] The universal qualities claimed for natural law by those in the scholastic tradition were dignified, if also abstract, and adaptable by practitioners of the positive and common law of daily practice. Natural law principles served to help rationalize many a practical or jurisdictional purpose.[55] Just how familiar Ruskin was with the work of Aquinas is not certain. His general importance was recognized through his reading of Dante. While preparing *Mornings in Florence* in the mid-1870s, he would have learned other essentials from the notes prepared for him by the well informed J. Caird. As was the obscure Henry Totting of Oyta, Aquinas was much interested in the *Book of Wisdom*, a detail suggested in the great fresco by Andrea Da Firenze.

In early seventeenth-century western Europe, natural law, as a term, started to split into two streams, one more precisely scientific and one social, a gradual response to the advances made in astronomy since the time of Copernicus. The scientific aspect came to be associated with the empirical evaluation of observable things of the world in their inanimate or developmental sense. The social version of natural law continued to be concerned with the proper understanding of the rules of ethics and human conduct. Throughout that century, the uses of 'reason' were explored but often in the context of a debate between 'ancients and moderns' depending on how much of the 'new learning' was embraced by a given practitioner.[56] Thomas Hobbes increasingly embraced a radical materialist interpretation of the new scientific position in which all phenomena were unified under the heading of 'behaviour', a position refined and recast by Locke and by others throughout the eighteenth century.[57] Law reformer Jeremy Bentham became the strong advocate for the view that the term 'natural law' had quite lost its usefulness as a covering term in social contexts. Benthams' position was taken up in the nineteenth century by those who favoured the dominant value of empirical or 'positive' law in court proceedings; that is, by those who argued that tangible law was always of a statute and analysable kind and that it ultimately originated at a human hand. From this point of view, the sanction of law was not to be found in the mists of time and tradition or by Biblical command. Law was the result of more mundane human trial and error. This involved a considerable begging of the question with respect to foundations and Bentham and his school were appropriately identified as 'philosophical radicals'.[58] Roman Catholics remained the strongest defenders of older accounts of natural law and its social applications.[59]

Reflecting the economic and social changes afoot in early modern Europe, Hugo Grotius and others had, by 1625, put versions of international law more firmly in place, still finding much to draw upon from the older traditions of natural law, Christian and Classical. Their recast and more secular sounding version of natural law eventually employed the idea of reason in the direction of universal natural rights, eventually proclaimed with force in the United States and France and again in the twentieth century in the United Nations Charter and in the International Declaration on Human Rights. Such principles remained fuzzy in practice, as the Nuremburg and Eichmann trials revealed.[60] It may be said, however, that the natural law tradition has never died out but has rather shared the legal stage, to a degree, with modern empirical national versions of law administration.[61]

Romantics such as Wordsworth and Southey had absorbed the Grotian seventeenth-century adjustments to natural law, as did Ruskin. *Time and Tide*, and much in the late writings, display a continuing study of ancient authors and a tendency to draw connections between God's Law and Natural Law. The 'book which has been the accepted guide of the moral intelligence of Europe' also 'enforces certain simple laws of human conduct' which have 'been agreed upon, in every main point, by all the religious and by all the greatest profane writers, of every age and country'. This book enjoined truth, temperance, charity and equity 'and you know that every great Egyptian, Greek, and Indian, enjoins these also'.[62] If

Ruskin maintained a prejudicial view of Italian Renaissance humanists and their preoccupation with recovering old texts, it should be noted that he himself was an enthusiastic participant in the nineteenth-century classical revival in England and made his own contributions to 'recovery' of various texts through his translations from Greek and Latin and from his collecting of medieval manuscripts and art works.[63]

An expanding view of culture was now reflected in his reading of the works of the Oxford linguistics scholar and close student of Asian religion, Frederich Max Müller, along with the works of others engaged in exploring new horizons of culture and prehistory. He was familiar with the efforts to push back the known limits of human history in the work of his 'botanizing' friend, Sir John Lubbock (Lord Avebury) who in 1865 published the first edition of his pioneering work, *Prehistoric Times*. He knew also the new anthropology of E.B. Tylor.[64] This growing appreciation of the antiquity of humanity was revealed in a new preface to *Sesame and Lilies*, where he discussed the problem of the perception of good and evil and made a statement reminiscent of Grotius: 'the only right principle of action here is to consider good and evil as defined by our natural sense of both; and to strive to promote the one, and to conquer the other, with as hearty endeavour as if there were, indeed, no other world than this'.[65]

The claims of the old Christian creed had been reduced in his outlook to something approximating an important historical tradition promoting obligations of right conduct associated with the 'doing' of justice. By 1874, he had adopted a distinctly more pluralist social position on religion, whereby God's Law embraced adherents of Judaism and Islam, even though he understood himself to be primarily addressing citizens of an old Christian culture.[66] Perhaps the surest statement Ruskin that made in attempting to fuse his older notion of the Law of God with a more general kind of Natural Law principle, was given in *Val D'Arno* (1874). Drawing on the poet Horace and his conception of '*pietas*', he stated[67]:

> And you will find... that there is always a quite clear notion of right and wrong in your minds, which you can either obey or disobey, at your pleasure... It is the only source of true cheerfulness, and of true commonsense; and whether you believe the Bible or don't, – or believe the Koran, or don't, – or believe the Vedas, or don't, – it will enable you to believe in God...and be such a part... of the universe as your nature fits you to be...

The point was reinforced by a rather uncharacteristic reference to Kant, via Carlyle, on the idea of 'the moral sense' in human beings. It is a famous Kantian passage which Ruskin could approve in its simplicity: 'Two things strike me dumb: the infinite Starry Heaven; and the Sense of Right and Wrong in Man.'[68]

This understanding of right and wrong was not, however, based on Kant's insistence that we undertake cool and rational interrogation of immediate circumstances in search of a correct universal decision. Ruskin understood, as did certain more historically minded figures of the eighteenth-century Enlightenment, that there is a 'moral sense' ingrained in the human being through early habituation, in somewhat the way argued by Adam Smith, Thomas Reid and Montesquieu, among others.[69] The secret lay in that Aristotelian kind of inherent human capacity which allows and responds to proper training and education producing 'dispositions' to act in one way and not another. It was something to be accounted for as part of the makeup of all individuals as they mature through socialization and practice, including a primary training in religion.[70]

In *Val D'Arno,* a regard for a kind of pluralism arose from a respect for historically conditioned displays of behaviour rather than from any rational analyses by individuals of 'what to do' in contingent circumstances. In the best historical examples of civil association, chivalric principles surface in the ruling classes and infiltrate the consciousness of the wider society. Ruskin praised such principles as portrayed in Kenelm Digby's *Broad Stone of Honour* where 'every phase of nobleness' was illustrated.[71] If in his own time aristocracy was under assault as a principle and the state of the upper classes decayed, he still held that the proper stuff of leadership and creativity was yet to be found in it over against the rising prominence of the powerful men of commerce or the promoters of democracy.[72]

VI

In the early 1880s a Scottish economist, William Smart, became one of the earliest to comment on the influence of Plato on Ruskin's social thought.[73] Ruskin's reading of Plato, particularly of *The Laws*, became more detailed after his appointment to Oxford, selective translation occupying a good deal of his time. His interest in late Plato had been evident in the early 1850s when he drew upon the *Phaedrus* during preparation of *The Stones of Venice.* In one passage, he drew a parallel between Plato and St. Paul with respect to art and the gods. 'It is the testimony of the ancients' says

Ruskin, 'that the madness which is of God is a nobler thing than the wisdom which is of man'.[74] He had been reflecting on the imaginative power of the 'grotesque' as it often comes uncalled by way of dreams to the artist, conquering him, and allowing the true artist to speak as a seer or prophet. This power opens the door to an external source of a transcendent but unknowable moral 'good'. It comes mysteriously in somewhat the same fashion as suggested later by Iris Murdoch, who saw art as an important route towards an acceptable modern understanding of the good.[75]

It may seem strange that one as attached to art as Ruskin should embrace Plato so strongly when the latter is well known for his hostility towards the arts, overly imaginative literature and routine mechanical crafts. Their views on the role of music far better indicates their affinity, for with Plato the early training in harmony was a way to prepare the young for all other serious tasks in life, including the contemplation of justice and the selection of leaders.[76] For Plato, music was less an aspect of the arts and more something to be employed as part of sacred celebration and proper moral education. For Ruskin, all good art was also a celebration and was moral in character. He had simple musical tastes and a leaning towards church music and folk melodies and even did a little composition. Whatever Mendelssohn's importance in reviving the music of Bach, his inflated oratorios were not to Ruskin's taste, nor were the operas of Verdi.[77] The emotionally transcendent nature of music which appeals so much to modern sensibility seemed foreign to Ruskin. He assigned an important role to music in early education but a very selective role.[78]

Plato exercised another kind of appeal for him owing to the former's dialectical dialogue style, traits that R.G. Collingwood noted as features of Ruskin's method of discourse.[79] Considerations of the 'good life' were much more readily perceived by the reader of Plato than by means of the logic-chopping *Ethics* of Aristotle. The latter's approach had much troubled Ruskin in his undergraduate days.[80] He put the dialogue style to use in parts of the *Political Economy of Art*, while some of Plato's general ideas about justice are important in *Unto This Last*.[81]

Since taking 'Pascal's Wager' in the late 1840s, there had opened up in Ruskin a spiritual anxiety not uncharacteristic of many thinkers of his times.[82] Over the next 25 years, he moved about a good deal in theological terms, even dabbling in spiritualism after the death of Rose La Touche in 1875.[83] The 'religion of humanity', conventional religion, spiritualism, eastern religions, none of these had been fully satisfactory. He continued to use the term ‘God’ as the most fitting term for an external reference point and ultimate source of good, but this God was distant, abstract and very different in character from the dark, attentive, punitive overseer of his youth. Late in life he claimed satisfaction with a simple creed, far removed from such overbearing Christianity. The task of a Christian, he now said, was to live with forbearance in the face of adversity and to joyfully embrace the tenets of Biblical instruction concerning proper conduct.[84] With his more intense reading of Plato and his gathering knowledge of non-European mythologies, the concept of law took on the more general aspect of something reflective of the world’s pluralistic perceptions of the divine but about which we could understand little.

From this point of view, Letter 82 of *Fors Clavigera* reveals a shift in Ruskin’s politics. Here he makes a link between the *Book of Psalms* and Plato’s *Republic*. Departing from a passage in *The Laws*, Ruskin contrasted Longfellow’s statement that ‘Life is real, life is earnest’ with Plato’s contention that life, on the contrary, is unreal and not earnest.[85] ‘The gist of it’ says Ruskin, is that ‘the Gods alone are great, and have great things to do’. Man is in fact, ‘a poor little puppet, made to be their play thing’ and the ‘virtue of him’ is to ‘play merrily’ in the little show of his life, ‘so as to please the Gods’. When analysed, says Ruskin, these passages contain ‘three phases of most solemn thought’. The first may be considered an amplification of ‘What is man that thou are mindful of him?’ The second concerned the passage: ‘He walketh in a vain shadow, and disquieteth himself in vain.’ The third, that his real duty is to ‘quiet himself, and live in happy peace and play, all his measure of day’.[86] These lines are quoted with reference to *Psalms* 8:4 and 39:6. The practical outcome is that ‘religious service is to be entirely with rejoicing – that only brightness of heart can please the Gods; and that asceticism and self-discipline are to be practiced only that we may be made capable of such sacred joy’.[87] He drew conclusions from this about one aspect of Plato’s work: ‘The extreme importance of this teaching is in its opposition to the general Greek instinct that “Tragedy” or song in honour of the Gods, should be sad.’ This instinct, he says, has survived to the present day ‘in the degree in which men disbelieve in the Gods themselves and in their love’.[88] The discussion then moves into that previously mentioned approving review of Plato on the role of music in education and its bearing on the choice of proper rulers.[89]

VII

The 'language' of natural law in Ruskin owed much to late medieval and English Renaissance writings which still retained pre-modern understandings of science as knowledge based on a unified view of the social and material worlds.[90] Even such an empiricist as Bacon did not care to divide the world into one of pure motion guiding all belief and behaviour, as would Hobbes. On social matters, Ruskin was inclined to refer to the law of God rather than natural law, but on occasion referred to those 'abiding laws obeyed by all nations'.[91] The great chain of being still held for him as an interpretive device, although there were apparent signs of erosion in some of the links, first perceived by him through geology. For Ruskin to continue to rely on this ancient image of rational order, in spite of his own inner understanding about the weakened state of the chain, was a self-deception, but one adhered to for pragmatic social reasons, not uncharacteristic of positions adopted by many of his fellows.[92] His positon, we have seen, fostered a series of tensions, both inner and professional, and in some cases these tensions marred his contributions to science in the eyes of other practitioners such as T.H. Huxley. The prevalence of 'God talk' in his writings suggests his main defence against the rise of ideas which he considered to be socially disruptive. The frequent references to the Divine, to providence, or to the wisdom of the ages, were seldom made in the interests of any contemporary sectarian religious body or the cause of Christian proselytizing. Such usages were mainly employed as conservative curbs on too easily made claims to a firm knowledge of things which were, in his view, complex or mysterious. Whether he actually believed it or not, he continued to advertise the idea that religion and science were best comprehended with reference to a stable world underwritten by natural laws, as was the case for many in the Classical world.[93]

The main virtue of natural law for Victorian politics was that an argument could be made for a church-state relationship, however firm or however vague, as a sound principle of social continuity. Since the time of Justinian, this attitude had prevailed throughout greater Europe and Russia and parts of the Mediterranean world, even though there was much historical variation within the patterns of conduct followed within that greater unity. It was the achievement of Venice, through its commercial empire, to have accommodated these variations in its civic and commercial relations with considerable skill and with a feel for toleration extended even to Jews. The Reformation had thrown a wrench into Western

Christendom, the worst features of which were minimized in England owing to its physical state of isolation. After centuries of chess-playing between Emperors and Popes for dominant secular authority, it fell to Henry VIII to firmly set the mould for new national dispensations across Europe in which papal secular power was greatly reduced. There were times of religious bloodshed in England, including the Civil War, but nothing nearly as widespread or persistent as the French Wars of Religion or the Thirty Years War in central Europe.

Nothing was quite so symbolic of this sea-change in England as the near-simultaneous deaths of Thomas More, William Tyndale and Desiderius Erasmus. More had remained loyal to the old order of papal dominance and died for it. Indeed, a good number of close students of the history of English law, including Maitland, have seen in More's death the end of a long tradition of natural law principles informing the common law.[94] Maitland observed that in 1535 'the great stream of law reports that had been flowing…since the days of Edward I, become discontinuous and then runs dry'.[95] Tyndale, for his trouble of translating the Bible into English, was kidnapped in Antwerp by agents of Emperor Charles V and, through the stealth of English opponents of Luther and reform, publicly burned. Erasmus, the promoter of a 'via media' between Lutheran Reformers and the old church, died more peacefully and still a Roman Catholic, despite having enemies on all sides. Henry VIII's immediate royal successors reflected the unresolved nature of this turmoil and it was only with the coming to power of Elizabeth I that some stability was achieved through her 'settlement' legislation of 1559, aided by the subsequent need to rally the country against the aggression of Spain and of Catholic resistance in Ireland.[96]

In the later years of her reign, it fell to Hooker, taking his departure from the legacy of Erasmus, to provide a detailed rationalization for the new order. His major work proceeded by means of a search for an acceptable 'via media' between the forces of radical Protestantism and those adherents of the old Church of Rome who might yet be made comfortable in the new Tudor Church. It would be necessary, on the one hand, to make room for some toleration for Free Church forces and, on the other, to 'trim' away Thomas More's stubborn insistence that papal authority should be preserved. Hooker had a distinct advantage in this trimming exercise: in the figure of the Monarch he already had a functioning personage who had replaced the Pope. When he commenced preparation of *The Laws of Ecclesiastical Polity*, a tradition of the new church-state relation had already achieved some stability, Roman Catholic pretenders had been put down, and old church procedures kept as familiar as possible but purged of sacramental abuses and Papal claims.

The approach taken by Hooker in *The Laws* was essentially scriptural and historical. The author made much of the nature of the traditions of the church in their common essences but also of their variability on particulars in keeping with local customs, conditions and geographical circumstances. The Church had been, and should continue to be, flexible on many theological and ritual points where only 'things indifferent' were concerned. A church supported by the state should be a large tent, capable of hosting all of good will, not a small and exclusive meeting hall of the more radical and narrow-chested. He stressed the historical vicissitudes of the concept of 'episcopacy' to demonstrate that the Roman Pope had no scripturally based monopoly on his position as Head of the Church, but was only the accidental beneficiary of geography by virtue of the ancient and dominant role of Rome in early political history.

In providing reasons for the people to accept the new dispensation, Hooker drew on the principles of natural law made reasonable by Thomas Aquinas, but was certainly influenced also by the newer understanding of natural law formulated by Luther and then Calvin in his *Institutes of the Christian Religion*.[97] It is not the purpose here to sort out just how much Hooker owed specifically to these two perspectives, only to acknowledge that the role of reason was important in his assessment of the scriptures, as supportive of a larger frame of natural law at work in the world.[98]

The upshot of Hooker's elaborate justification of the new church is that he is usually considered, despite his death in 1600, as the first of the so-called 'Caroline divines' who came to represent much of the higher church attitude which prevailed during the reign of Charles I and after the Restoration. The Royalist and Erastian attitudes of these 'divines' tended to favour retention of the externals of Roman Church ritual but rejected as false many of the powers said to be possessed by the Pope and priesthood. They tended to embrace a belief in the divine right of Kings and considered the monarch worthy to be head of the church. Attempts by Parliament and Cromwell to uproot their influence failed and their attitudes took on renewed life after the reported conversion of the future James II to Roman Catholicism.[99]

Two aspects of Caroline divination played an important role in Ruskin's outlook on daily religious practice. These were exercised through the influence of men such as Hooker and Jeremy Taylor and through his appreciation of the poetic works of George Herbert whom he started to read in his undergraduate years, as he told his 'college friend' in 1840.[100] Making sufficient room for historical factors in the assessment of society and the English Church was the first of these aspects and the rational objection to the claims of papal infallibility was the second.[101] The historical element was almost second nature to Ruskin from the start, but it became more critical through his reading of Hooker in the 1840s with respect to episcopacy as a phenomenon subject to historical change. His objections to the threat of 'Papal aggression' to the British Constitution and to the claims made by the church concerning their ritualist procedures, we have seen, were expressed with some vigour in his earlier works, but these particular anti-Roman Catholic institutional prejudices modified as his own views about religion moved in an ever more latitudinarian direction. He came to focus on conduct and adopt that calm and existential outlook so well expressed in Herbert.[102]

It is of interest that Ruskin's reading of Herbert's poetry was already underway during his youthful involvement in The Geological Society, a time when he was first feeling a need to somehow reconcile the results of the new science with the importance of religious observance. Herbert, along with many of his contemporaries, such as John Donne, had been alive to the new science of their own times, particularly the astronomical revelations of Copernicus, Kepler and Galileo. The traditional earth-centred universe had given way to something very different and was now being inspected in greater detail and disturbingly documented in its dynamism and vastness. As in the mid-nineteenth century, the new learning was not a source of comfort to those who felt such knowledge as a reinforcement of the idea that the world was winding down.[103] Before Herbert became a man of the cloth, he had been a man of action, much engaged in politics and worldly engagements. His poetry imparts, foremost, a weariness with society and a retreat from its vain enterprises, yet it remained sensible to the requirements of being a gentleman of proper manners.[104] His poetry also speaks to an up-to-date knowledge of what was about him in scientific terms. Ruskin admired his cycle *The Temple*, which contained the poem 'The Agony' which begins:

> Philosophers have measur'd mountains,
> Fathom'd the depths of seas, of states, and kings,
> Walk'd with a staffe to heav'n, and traced fountains:
> But there are two vast, spacious things,

The which to measure it doth more behove:
Yet few there are that sound them; Sinne and Love.

Here is a compressed account of Ruskin's dilemma, illustrative of the course of religious solitude upon which he had long been set. The passage encapsulates his need to resolve, in some satisfactory way, the conflicts which his possession of undeniable new scientific knowledge presented to the moral claims imposed by his domestic evangelical upbringing. The way in which he generally did this was through retention of the general conservative position adopted by the Caroline divines, and that position later characterized in the eighteenth century by Dr. Johnson as appropriate to 'one who adheres to the ancient constitution of the State and the apostolical hierarchy of the Church of England'.[105] The account of natural law implicitly understood by such conservatives would come to be modified under the dissolving rationalist and materialist influences of Hobbes, Locke, Bolingbroke and Hume.[106] Deism became a more satisfactory expression for traditional human needs for an external religious reference point as the eighteenth century unfolded but one eventually countered by the strong reaction of Wesley's warmer evangelical reassertion of the presence of a God concerned with human affairs. Ruskin ignored both of these poles of reference in favour of the rather self-deceptive retention of the great chain of being, a convenient traditional system for explanation of the practical day-to-day operation of the world, an account much in favour in early seventeenth-century England.

His public pronouncements continued to promote the spiritual nature of art as a social principle; but his own understanding of the spiritual, in any conventional Christian sense, had taken on ever darker qualities.[107] His attachment to Sidney, Spenser and Herbert went hand in hand with that practical theological reasoning which issued in a firm attention given to proper conduct as the main focus for the proper religious life. Hooker had provided the base in England for the flowering of Caroline moral theology with its deep debt to the Aquinas version of natural law.[108] It was a view which retained its appeal for Ruskin who disregarded the assault on it made by Hobbes and the confusion of it embodied in the works of Locke.[109]

VIII

It would be an exaggeration to say that what held many of the diverse topics of the late writings together was a conscious quest for a unified theory of natural law within which all human actions, ethical and practical, might be subsumed. It would be more accurate to say that Ruskin made wilful assertions, on many occasions, in favour of such a condition in a less than systematic way. These occasions issued in sometimes less than genteel disagreements with his contemporaries when it came to science.[110] The scientific works of the late period, such as *The Eagle's Nest*, *Deucalion* and *Proserpina* were coherent only to those who were prepared also to side with him in his decidedly pre-Hobbesian account of natural law or his preference for Linnaeus as a pleasing guide to natural history. The moral question for Ruskin was not a matter of being ignorant of what modern geology foretold, or of what Darwin argued or of what Mill claimed. Whatever the merits of these thinkers, their specific kinds of quests for knowledge were seen to be detrimental to the promotion of good citizen lives. These lives would be better guided under the authority of some unified perception of natural law.

There was nothing very evasive in this position as far as Ruskin was concerned, who made no effort to conceal it. A convenient illustration of his position is given in closely linked passages of *Deucalion*, a late work which brought together many of his thoughts on geology.[111] The tension between his possession of up-to-date knowledge and his preference for an older platform of understanding incapable of adequately controlling that knowledge, is illustrated in the frankest terms in the second chapter of the second volume of *Deucalion*.

Having proclaimed his lack of credentials as a philosopher, or his wish to be one, he then demonstrated that he was, in fact, quite well informed about modern developments. 'During the last twenty years, so many baseless semblances of philosophy have announced themselves' and 'the laws of decent thought and rational question…transgressed' that he finds it necessary to now 'put into clear terms the natural philosophy and natural theology' implied in his previous works, those terms 'accepted by the intellect of leaders of all past time.'[112] The universities themselves are much to blame where 'moral philosophy once taught is only remembered as an obscure tradition' and where 'natural science in which they are proud presented only as an impious conjecture'.[113] He goes on to announces his intention to republish volume two of *Modern Painters* for he is generally still satisfied that he expressed there 'with sincere and very deep feeling' a sound view of 'the first and foundational law respecting human contemplation of the natural phenomena under whose influence we exist', which was to say 'a Living Spirit greater than our own'.[114]

The topic has suddenly shifted from minerals to one of moral discourse in which the notions of good and evil are described as universal categories in conduct and cultures. His 'writings on political science', he says, have concerned the 'principles of justice and mercy which are fastened in the hearts of men' and he speaks of the betrayal of both the creative and governing spirit which supposedly emanates from the eternal law by the 'supposed victory, in the present age of the world, of the deceiving spiritual power, which makes the vices of men his leading motives of action, and his follies, its leading methods'.[115] These older myths are a surer guide 'than the Darwinian' or of 'any other conceivable materialistic theory'.[116]

This digression now moves towards social criticism. He cites a French novel of 1865 which he credits with putting into clear form 'the darkness of materialism in its denial of the hope of immortality'.[117] His interpretation of the fate of the protagonist in the novel is subtle, for the final outcome supposedly illustrates the calm openness of a hero who dies without regrets. His death helps further the cause of his family and of the 'religion of humanity', the current creed of nineteenth-century materialism. The point made is that the view is not new or particularly novel. Rather, such selfless behaviour is actually in line with the best traditions of self-sacrifice in most cultural traditions.[118] He repeated one of his fundamental views about religion, the importance of habituation in its genesis and adherence, observing that fine testimonies of the arts, or any other practice, reveal themselves as 'a part of moral education' and are not, for the most part, stimulants of faith and belief, but rather evidences of them.[119] Thus, we come close to the end of the rather brief second volume of *Deucalion*, this chapter appropriately called 'Revision' and dealing more with his personal views about science and religion than with geology.[120] The appended notes suggest more to follow, but there would be no more. Intimations of the excuse offered for his resignation from Oxford in 1884 are found in *Deucalion*, where he accuses many scientists of being part of the cult of modern destructive powers which lead to 'the vivisection room'.[121] He offers a guarded reference to the 'spectres which sometimes haunt the human mind' and suggests that these might be more fruitful lines for scientific enquiry than many of the lines commonly used. This may be a fearful reference to his breakdown of 1878 and of what might still be to come.

If *Fors Clavigera* may be considered Ruskin's 'Apologia' for long-held principles, then the intense recapitulation of his views on science, religion and ethics presented in these few pages of *Deucalion* may be seen as a condensed version of that 'Apologia'. What remains less clear is how Ruskin justified his late views given his longstanding interest in science. Over the years, there is clearly demonstrated a steady shift away from his early acceptance of the directions being taken by the new geology. The enthusiasm of 1837, expressed to his father when reporting the activities of a recent meeting at The Geological Society, when he talked 'long into the night' with Darwin, had given away to some minor discomfort in 1842 in his letters 'to a college friend'. In 1853 he had confessed to Acland that he had no peace owing to the steady sound of 'those dreadful hammers' indicating that, as in religion, he was unable to make up his mind about the evidence before him. The knowledge that the *Bible* was not sustainable as a geological history document was taken only so far as knowledge to be further acted upon. The ambiguity was magnified because Ruskin's own language of geology was distinctly modern. He uses the terms which had come into play in the hands of Saussure and Hutton, Lyell and Agassiz. He employs the proper descriptive language of 'branded and brecciated concretions' and 'denudation' and 'formation' and of 'silicas' and 'chalks' and all the other developing nomenclature of mineralogy and dynamic landforms. He is aware that the great factor in geology is time or history. Be one a 'uniformitarian' or a 'catastrophist' in geology, there was no escaping the role of time and change. These were the great lessons of Hutton and Lyell. Yet, in appended notes to *Deucalion* (probably composed in 1874), he writes about the ancient stability of the Alps and the limited effects of glacial action as though he had never read Lyell or Agassiz, or believed them.[122]

In seems that even the safest kinds of modern evolutionary arguments were being resisted in this case. They are not entirely denied, however, as though a memory of those heady days of 1837 still exercised some sway. Having recently heard Huxley speak on evolution, he does not deny its credibility but insists, in response, that his own writings are those 'of the harmonies and intervals in being of the existent animal creation'. He still speaks of Linnaeus and his 'nobly religious passion' informing his *Systeme Naturea*.[123] This was no adequate response to Huxley and flew in the face of his own early confessed knowledge of the matter. Thus, a life-long tension between knowledge and a fear of public expression of it, had become severe by the time he composed *Deucalion*.

What accounts for this willingness to suspend enquiry at some point, particularly in science, as though curiosity was no longer welcome beyond a certain point? In most matters open to his vision or contemplation, Ruskin was considered a most curious man. Even his severest critics acknowledged that nobody analysed a painting with more skill than Ruskin. The answer seems to revolve around two matters. The first concerned his distrust of theory and the second concerned a fear of looking into questions of origins, the two issues not unrelated.

He referred to 'the happier days of Linnaeus and de Saussure' as men without grand concerns for system and theory, as opposed to 'the wild theories or foul curiosities' of our own times.[124] Ruskin was proud to deal in 'facts' as though 'facts' can have some self-evident meaning free of a theory of language. It hardly needs saying that Linnaeus certainly thought he was constructing a system. For his part, de Saussure was certainly interested in the larger body of geological work to which he contributed including working towards a theory of the earth.[125] In his fast-moving response to Huxley, Ruskin retreated to some of his most comfortable ground: Pope's *Essay on Man* and Herbert's *The Temple*.[126] He then resorted to more familiar figures, Byron, Burns, Goethe and Carlyle, a group he credits with sympathetic views on the limitations of system. These do not believe that the 'mysteries of good and evil are reducible to quite visible Kosmos, as they stand, but that there is another Kosmos, mostly invisible, yet perhaps tangible, and to be felt, if not seen'.[127]

Here is perhaps the crux of Ruskin's predicament. His objection against the scientists is not that they pursued systematic explanations of the world, but their contention that it was possible to detect some great truth about the nature of that system by deeper and deeper human probing and inspection. Be it the search for the source of life through microscopes, or by means of vivisection, or by experimental chemical interactions, all such procedures partook of the same impious fallacy. Nor were the benefits of geology to be found in seeking the deeper meaning of the sources of colour or crystallization (as argued in the final chapter of *Deucalion*). Rather, it was the joy of a 'science of aspects' which should prevail in all of its empirical splendour, achieved by a continuous detailing of hard fact, quite unburdened by theory. How odd to see Ruskin, a good naturalist, suddenly abandon the naturalist's curiosity. He chastised Louis Agassiz for his expenditure of money and time on preparing descriptions and drawings of small life forms, creatures which Ruskin thought 'nasty ugly things' undeserving of names.[128] It is an uncharacteristic departure, for his regular 'green' sounding agricultural arguments and appreciation for the regular interactions of land and life usually showed the way to a respect for all living forms. This reaction to Agassiz was surely the result of a deep-rooted and persisting inner conflict, well beyond the understanding of his fellow scientists, even those who did not particularly like snakes or 'vermin' as immediate companions. Agassiz was doing only what Linnaeus was doing: describing and classifying. The bottom links of the 'great chain' were surely as valid as the top ones, but Ruskin thought Agassiz to be probing too far and with too much insistence.

In what he mistook for a misguided direction of modern scientific curiosity, Ruskin sensed the same Renaissance-born, ego-driven, pride-ridden mentality at work, driven by progressives who preferred to construct ever more elaborate systems and classifications rather than explore nature within the calmer parameters of the great chain of being, a chain which somehow should ignore 'nasty, ugly things' from consideration. It was not then, that Mill, Darwin, Huxley, Spencer and so many others, lacked a vision of a unified natural law: it was that they had opted for the wrong vision of such a unified natural law. Their visions appeared to be products of their evolution-oriented imaginations rather than the hierarchical one imposed in advance on the world to which reverence was due. This interpretation and his arguments did not register with scientists, even friendly ones. Practitioners saw no inconsistency between their articulation of systems and a potential fit of those systems within a broader system of a unified covering law. Indeed, moderns might even argue that they too, embraced a hierarchical view of law, much in accord with the one understood by Hooker and Aquinas, in which room was left for mystery, but mystery which one should not hesitate to explore further.

There was, on Ruskin's part, a longstanding reluctance, to play the game of science to the end, even though it seemed important to him to try to do so. He could enjoy 'botanizing' in the field with Lubbock or Darwin up to the point where they started to go on about their theories when he then parted conversation. To look too deeply into the workings of the natural world was as frightening as scrutinizing some of his own disturbing dreams.[129]

He had tried to make his own peace with the nineteenth century, insisting that any unified version of natural law was one that preserved the scientific and humanistic orders together. There could be no compromise with the materialism of such as Hobbes or with the somewhat confused version of natural law given by Locke.[130] A copy of the anonymous and chaotic *Vestiges of Creation* (1844) was in the Ruskin family library although there are no signs that its fanciful arguments from design and its distinctive arguments for a uniform natural law were ever referenced.[131] Rather, Ruskin's view of natural law shared more with that of the well-regarded but theologically conservative geologist, Adam Sedgwick, who claimed that 'all nature is but the manifestation of a supreme intelligence'.[132]

The road, then, to a proper understanding of such comprehensive natural law lay in the manner by which people were habituated through family, church and state. Where a vision of God as the source of just law was lacking at the civic level, idolatry and tyranny were bound to follow.[133]

Notes

1. R.H. Wilenski, *John Ruskin: An Introduction to Further Study of His Life and Work* (London: Faber, 1933) 99–100; Kenneth Clark, *Ruskin at Oxford: An Inaugural Lecture* (Oxford: Clarendon Press, 1947).
2. The letters appeared monthly or intermittently between 1871 and 1884, and were published in *Works*: Volumes 27 through 29.
3. See G.W. Kitchin, *Ruskin in Oxford and Other Essays* (London: John Murray, 1904), 40.
4. V.A. McClelland, 'Ruskin's Apologia', *Downside Review*, 255: (1961), 134.
5. *Ibid.*, 128–34; *Works*, 18: 392–9.
6. Graham Hough, *The Last Romantics* (London: Gerald Duckworth, 1949), 18.
7. *Works*, 3: 109–10; 16: 144.
8. Judith Stoddart, 'The Formation of the working Classes: John Ruskin's *Fors Clavagira* as a Manual of Cultural Literacy' in Patrick Scott and Pauline Fletcher, eds. *Culture and Education in Victorian England* (Lewisburg: Bucknell University Press, 1990), 43–58; Dinah Birch, Ruskin's Multiple Writing: *Fors Clavigera*' in Birch, ed. (1999), 179.
9. Ibid., 129.
10. *Fors Clavagira*, Letter 62, cited in McClelland (1961), 129.
11. Reflection on Ruskin's mental health commenced well before his death and has not ceased. Wilenski published a chart outlining the pattern of the highs of Ruskin's creative periods and the lows of his acute depressions. See Wilenski (1933), 15–24. Recent commentaries include: P.A. Kempster and J.E. Alty, 'John Ruskin's relapsing encephalopathy', *Brain*, 131 (2008), 2520–25; James L. Spates, 'Ruskin's Dark Night of the Soul: A Reconsideration of His Mental Illness and the Importance of Accurate Diagnosis', *Journal of Pre-Raphaelite Studies*, N.S. 18 (Spring, 2009), 18–58.

12. On Ruskin's publishing ventures, see Mark Frost, *The Lost Companions and John Ruskin's Guild of St George: A Revisionary History* (London: Antham Press, 2014), 63–65.
13. Ruskin to Ellis, July, 1870, in *Works*, 37: 12.
14. See his Introduction to Robert G. Sillar, *Usury, An Allegory: Pernicious Effects on English Agriculture and Commerce.* (London: 1885). See also Collet, (1946), 23–33.
15. On Ruskin's mental health episodes in his later years, see Tim Hilton, *John Ruskin: The Later Years* (New Haven: Yale University Press, 2001), Chapters 23, 31–33.
16. A number of recent writers have sought to find in *Fors Clavagira* coherent trains of thought. See Dinah Birch, 'Ruskin's Multiple Writings: *Fors Clavigera*' in Birch, ed. (1999), 175–87; Francis O'Gorman, 'Do Good Work, Whether You Live or Die' in O'Gorman (2001), 81–95.
17. See *Works*, 15: 333–485 and 31: 105–28. On Ruskin's essay, see J.C.A. Rathmell, 'Explorations and Recoveries–1: Hopkins, Ruskin and the Sidney Psalter' *The London Magazine*, 6 (9): (1959), 51–66.
18. E.T. Cook, ed. *Studies in Ruskin* (London: G. Allen, 1890), 44.
19. Attributed to J.H. Whitehouse, cited in Quentin Bell, *Ruskin* (New York: George Brazziler, 1978), 100; See also Henry W. Traunt, *Matthew Arnold's 'Scholar-Gypsy' and Thyrsis and the Country they Illustrate* (Oxford: Henry W. Traunt, 1910), 84–92.
20. For photographs and commentary on this episode, see Henry W. Traunt, *Matthew Arnold's 'Scholar-Gypsy' and Thyrsis and the Country they Illustrate* (Oxford: Henry W. Traunt, 1910).
21. On his loss of feeling for nature, see Rosenberg (1961), 25–28.,
22. Lawrence Goldman, John Ruskin and the Working Classes in Mid-Victorian Britain' in Keith Hanley and Brian Maidment, eds. (2013), 25.
23. *St. Mark's Rest* was his late historical reverie on Venice. *Works*, 24: 191–400.
24. Alexander Bradley, *Ruskin and Italy* (Ann Arbor: UMI Research Press, 1987), 20–21.
25. Bradley (1987), 13; Ruskin to Carlyle, 26 July, 1874, in Cate, ed. (1982), 207–8.
26. *Works*, 2; 233; 4: 352; 12: 240–43; 12: 213–23; 24: 1–123.
27. *Works*, 4: xx, xxix; Dearden (2012), 318–19; Cooper (2010), 58.
28. *Works*, 23: 43, 63; 34: 353.
29. See '*Pax Vobiscum*', Chapter 5 of *Val D'Arno*, *Works*, 23: On the early guilds of Florence, see Nicholas Rubinstein, 'The Beginnings of Humanism in Florence' in Denys Hay, ed., *The Age of the Renaissance* (New York: McGraw-Hill, 1967), 30–31.
30. Ruskin to J.J. Ruskin, 24. Aug. 1845, in Harold Shapiro, ed., *Ruskin In Italy: Letters to this Parents 1845* (Oxford: Clarendon Press, 1972), 183–86.

31. Ibid. For the complete letter, see Appendix 2 of this study.
32. Ruskin to Ward, 1855, in *Works*, 36: 185–86. For their correspondence, see *John Ruskin's Letters to William Ward: With a Short Biography of William Ward* (Boston: Marshall Jones Company, 1922).
33. *Works*, 16: 97–8.
34. Ruskin, *Diary*, Dec. 4, 1843, in *Works*, 3: 653n; Dearden (2012), 323.
35. See David M. Craig, *Robert Southey and Romantic Apostasy: Political Argument in Britain, 1780–1840*. Woodbridge: Boydell Press, 2007), 181–85; Jonathan Mendilow, *The Romantic Tradition in British Political Thought* (London: Croom Helm, 1986), Ch. 2.
36. *Works*, 16: 172; Hill to Mary Harris, Nov. 1, 1858, in Emily S. Maurice, ed., *Octavia Hill: Early Ideals* (London: George Allen and Unwin, 1928), 140–41.
37. See Peter Clayon, *Octavia Hill* (Wisbech: Wisbech Society and Preservation Trust, 1993), 11–13; William Thomson Hill, *Octavia Hill:Pioneer of the National Trust and Housing Reformer* (London: Hutchinson, 1956), Ch. 4; *Works*, 17: cx; 19: xxiv–v; 27: 175–6.
38. See Maurice, ed. (1928), 115–208. The collection of letters also include several by Hill to Mary Harris containing accounts of Ruskin.
39. See 'Letters to an unnamed correspondent', May 15 and 21, 1867, cited in Wilenski (1933), 88. This was presumably Thomas Dixon. On Livesy see, Olive Wilson, ed., *My Dearest Dora: Letters to Dora Livesey, Her Family and Friends from John Ruskin, 1860–1900* (NP: 1984).
40. *Works*, 17: 328.
41. Biographical details for Bradley are few, for reasons given by the philosopher G.R.G. Mure in his memoir. See his 'F.H. Bradley', *Encounter*, 16 (1): (1961), 28–35. On the strengths and weaknesses of Bradley's anti-utilitarianism, see Anthony Quinton, *Utiltarian Ethics* (New York: St. Martin's Press, 1973), 93–97.
42. F.H. Bradley, 'My Station and Its Duties' in *Ethical Studies: Selected Essays* (New York: Liberal Arts Press, 1951), 98–147.
43. Cook, ed. (1890), 44–6.
44. On Rawnsley and Collingwood, see Vicky A. Jonsson and Fredrik A. Jonsson *Green Victorians: The Simple Life in John Ruskin's Lake District* (Chicago: University of Chicago Press, 2016), Ch. 5.
45. Carroll Quigley, *The Anglo-American Establishment* (San Pedro: GSC Associates, 1981), Ch. 4. See also Alexander May, *The Round Table, 1910–66*. (Oxford: D.Phil. Thesis, 1995), and George R. Parkin, *Imperial Federation: The Problem of National Unity* (London: Macmillan, 1892).
46. Quigley (1981), 10.
47. See 'The Future of England' (1869), a supplement to *The Crown of Wild Olive*. *Works*, 18: 494–514; and 'Inaugural Lectures' (1870), *Works*, 20: 1–179.

48. Ronald Robinson, 'Oxford in Imperial Historiography' in Frederick Madden and D.K. Fieldhouse, eds. *Oxford and the Idea of Commonwealth* (London: Croom Helm, 1982), 30–48.
49. Elizabeth T. McLaughlin, *Ruskin and Gandhi* (Lewisburg: Bucknell University Press, 1974), 23–31, 82–90.
50. A.P. d'Entrèves, *Natural Law: An Introduction to Legal Philosophy.* Rev. ed. (New Brunswick: Transaction Publishers, 1994), 111.
51. See G.R. Elton, *England Under the Tudors* (London: Methuen, 1969), 401, 403, 427.
52. Alexander S. Rosenthal, *Crown Under Law: Richard Hooker, John Locke and the Ascent of Modern Constitutionalism* (Plymouth: Lexington Press, 2008), 113–19; Peter Munz, *The Place of Hooker in the History of Thought* (Westport: Greenwood Press, 1971), Ch. 2.
53. Munz (1971), 87–9.
54. See Cornelis Augustijn, *Erasmus: His Life, Works and Influence* (Toronto: University of Toronto Press, 1991), Ch. 11.
55. See *Works*, 23: 378.
56. Richard F. Jones, *Ancients and Moderns* (Berkeley: University of California Press, 1961).
57. See Norberto Bobbio, *Thomas Hobbes and the Natural Law Tradition.* (Chicago: University of Chicago Press, 1993), Ch. 5; Peter J. Stanlis, *Edmund Burke and the Natural Law* (Ann Arbor: Michigan State University Press, 1965), 16–27.
58. See Elie Halévy, *The Growth of Philosophic Radicalism* (Boston: Beacon Press, 1955).
59. See Jacques Maritain, *Existence and the Existent* (New York: Pantheon, 1948); *The Rights of Man and Natural Law* (New York: Charles Scribner's, 1951).
60. Hannah Arendt, *Eichmann in Jerusalem: A Report on the Banality of Evil.* Rev. ed. (New York: Penguin, 1994), 253–58.
61. See H.A.L. Hart, *The Concept of Law*, 2nd. ed. (Oxford: Clarendon Press, 1994), 193–200.
62. *Works*, 17: 350–51.
63. See Frank M. Turner, *The Greek Heritage in Victorian Britain* (New Haven: Yale University Press, 1981), 17, 41–2.
64. Ruskin was reading Müller by at least 1865. *Works*, 18: 69, 288. On his meeting with Müller and Emerson, see Ruskin to Max Müller, 4 May, 1873, in Bodleian Library, Oxford, Ruskin Papers. Western Manuscripts; On Lubbock, see *Works*, 20: xxxvii–xxxviii. See *Works*, 37: 405, 590–91. On Tylor see *Works*, 28: 613–14.
65. *Works*, 18: 42. On Grotius and his assertion that natural law would have to exist, even if God did not, see d'Entrèves, (1994), 54; see also the

discussion in Brian Tierney, *The Idea of Natural Rights* (Grand Rapids, 2001), 319–24.

66. On this question see Wheeler, *Ruskin's God* (2001), Ch. 9. The point was emphasized again in 1882 in his 'Statement' on the purposes of the Guild. *Works*, 30: 58–9.
67. *Val D'Arno*, in *Works*, 23: 128–33.
68. *Works*, 23: 132. The passage from Kant appears in the conclusion of *The Critique of Practical Reason* (1788).
69. See Jonathan Israel, *A Revolution of the Mind: Radical Enlightenment and the Intellectual Origins of Modern Democracy* (Princeton: Princeton University Press, 2010), Ch. 5.
70. *Works*, 12: 176–79; 11:11; 28: 654.
71. *Works*, 7: 361 and n. 2. On Digby see Mark Girouard, *The Return to Camelot: Chivalry and the English Gentleman* (New Haven: Yale University Press, 1981), Ch. 5.
72. *Works*, 17: 439; 18: 484, 499.
73. See William Smart, *John Ruskin: His Life and Work* (Glasgow: Wilson and McCormick 1880), and *A Disciple of Plato: A Critical Study of John Ruskin* (Glasgow: Wilson and McCormick, 1883).
74. *Works*, 3: 284; 11: 178–9.
75. Iris Murdoch, *The Sovereignty of Good* (London: Routledge, 1970) 58–66, 83–87. See also O'Hear (2009).
76. *Works*, 29: 233–47; Plato, *Republic* 424b–c.
77. For Ruskin on Mendelssohn, see *Works*, 22: xli, 497.
78. *Works*, 17: 368; 19: 176, 344; 29: 230–31.
79. R.G. Collingwood, *Ruskin's Philosophy* (Kendal: Titus Wilson, 1922); Reprinted in Alan Donagan, ed., *Essays in the Philosophy of Art* (Bloomington: University of Illinois Press, 1964), 3–42.
80. *Works*, 1: xxxv–xxxvi; Letters to a College Friend, 418–19; Katherine Gilbert, 'Ruskin's Relation to Aristotle' *Philosophical Review*, 49 (1):, (1940), 52–62.
81. See *Works*, 16: Addenda: 'Fatherly Authority', 105–9; Willie Henderson, *John Ruskin's Political Economy* (London: Routledge, 2000), Ch. 5.
82. See Basil Willey, *More Nineteenth Century Studies: A Group of Honest Doubters* (New York: Columbia University Press 1977); Geoffrey Clive, *The Romantic Enlightenment* (New York: Meridian, 1960).
83. See Hilton (2001), 325–31.
84. His starkest formulation appeared in a letter to *The Scotsman*, 6 May, 1886. *Arrows of the Chase*, *Works*, 34: 594.
85. Plato, *Laws*, vii. 803, 804, cited in *Fors Clavigera*, Letter 82 (1877), *Works*, 29: 233, n. 3.
86. *Works*, 29: 233–4.

87. *Works*, 29: 234.
88. Ibid.
89. *Works*, 29: 230–31, 235–44.
90. See the general discussion in R.S. White, *Natural Law in English Renaissance Literature* (Cambridge: Cambridge University Press, 1996), Ch. 1.
91. *Works*: 28: 30.
92. Owen Chadwick, *The Secularization of the European Mind in the Nineteenth Century* (Cambridge: Cambridge University Press, 1975), 229–32.
93. Shirley Letwin 'Nature, History and Morality' in Peters, ed. (1975), 229–50.
94. John C.H. Wu, 'The Natural Law and Our Common Law' *Fordham Law Review*, 23 (1): (1954), 13–48.
95. Cited in Wu (1954), 24.
96. David B. Quinn, *The Elizabethans and the Irish* (Ithica: Cornell University Press, 1966), Chapters 2 and 10; Brendan Kane, 'Elizabeth on rebellion in Ireland and England: semper eadem?' in Brendan Kane and Valerie McGowan-Doyle, eds. Elizabeth I and Ireland (Cambridge: Cambridge University Press, 2014), 261–85.
97. See W.J. Torrance Kirby, *Richard Hooker's Doctrine of the Royal Supremacy* (Leiden: E.J. Brill, 1990), 41 f.
98. On these questions, see A.J. Joyce, *Richard Hooker and Anglican Moral Theology* (Oxford: Oxford University Press, 2012), 87, 150–58.
99. David B. McIlhiney, 'The Protestantism of the Caroline Divines', *Historical Magazine of the Protestant Episcopal Church*, 44 (2): (1975), 143–154.
100. *Works*, 1: 409; On Ruskin and Taylor see Dearden (2012), 335, and *Works*, 11: 47 n.
101. McIlhiney (1975), 145.
102. See John L. Idol, Jr. Ruskin and Herbert, *George Herbert Journal*, 4(1): (1980), 11–28.
103. See Douglas Bush, *Science and English Poetry: A Historical Sketch, 1590–1950* (New York: Oxford University Press, 1950), Ch. 2.
104. See Michael C. Schoenfeldt, *Prayer and Power: George Herbert and Renaissance Courtship* (Chicago: University of Chicago Press, 1991).
105. Dr. Johnson, cited in Quinton (1982), 9.
106. Quinton (1982), 10.
107. The term 'existential' is understood here in much the way it is expounded in Clive (1960) and Murdoch (1970).
108. See H.R. McAdoo, 'Anglican Moral Theology in the Seventeenth Century: An Anticipation' in Paul Elmen, ed. *The Anglican Moral Choice* (Wilton: Morehouse-Barlow, Inc., 1983), 33–64.

109. See the lucid exploration of the problems posed by Hobbes and Locke for natural law theory and its more recent interpretation, in Rosenthal (2008), 267–306.
110. See the informative discussion in Francis O'Gorman, 'The Eagle and the Whale' in Wheeler, ed. (1996), 45–64.
111. *Deucalion* was published between 1879 and 1883 and is printed in *Works*, 26: 95–370.
112. *Works*, 26: 333–4.
113. *Ibid.*
114. *Ibid.*, 334.
115. *Ibid.*, 334–6.
116. *Ibid.*, 336.
117. *Ibid.*, 336–7. The novel was *Un Cure du Docteur Portalais* by Robert Halt (pen name of Charles Vieu).
118. *Ibid.*, 337–8.
119. *Ibid.*, 338.
120. See also the commentary in Paul Wilson, 'Over Yonder are the Andes' in Wheeler, ed., (1996), 65–84.
121. *Works*, 26: 344.
122. Ibid., 369–70.
123. *Ibid.*, 343.
124. *Ibid.*, 338–9.
125. Douglas W. Freshfield, *The Life of Horace Benedict Saussure* (London: Edward Arnold, 1920), Ch. 17.
126. *Works*, 26: 344.
127. *Ibid.*, 344–5.
128. See Wilson, in Wheeler, ed. (1996), 82.
129. Francis Watson, 'The Devil and Mr. Ruskin', *Encounter*, 38 (6): (1972), 64–70.
130. See Roshenthal (2008) 289–306; Crowe (1977), 237–42.
131. In 1884 the identity of the author was finally revealed as Robert Chambers of Edinburgh. C.C. Gillispie, *Genesis and Geology: The Impact of Scientific Discoveries Upon Religious Beliefs in the Decades Before Darwin* (New York: Harper and Row, 1959), Ch. 6; Dearden (2012), 67.
132. Cited in Henry Ladd, *The Victorian Morality of Art* (New York: Ray Long and Richard R. Smith Inc., 1932), 149–50; and see Gillispie (1959), 112–13; Ruskin, *Works*, 26: 243 n.
133. *Works*, 16: 25; 17: 243.
134. Footnote references to Ruskin's writings (unless otherwise stated) are cited as *Works*, and refer to Cook, Edward T. and Wedderburn, Alexander, eds. *The Collected Works of John Ruskin*. London: 1903–1912. 39 v.

Bibliography[134]

Arendt, Hannah. 1994. *Eichmann in Jerusalem: A Report on the Banality of Evil*. Rev. ed. New York: Penguin,.

Augustijn, Cornelis. 1991. *Erasmus: His Life, Works and Influence*. Toronto: University of Toronto Press.

Bell, Quentin. 1978. *Ruskin*. New York: George Brazziler.

Birch, Dinah, ed. 1999. *Ruskin and the Dawn of the Modern*. Oxford: Oxford University Press.

Bobbio, Norberto. 1993. *Thomas Hobbes and the Natural Law Tradition*. Chicago: University of Chicago Press.

Bradley, Alexander. 1987. *Ruskin and Italy*. Ann Arbor: UMI Research Press.

Bradley, F.H. 1951. *Ethical Studies: Selected Essays*. New York: Liberal Arts Press.

Bush, Douglas. 1950. *Science and English Poetry: A Historical Sketch, 1590–1950*. New York: Oxford University Press.

Cate, George Allen, ed. 1982. *The Correspondence of Thomas Carlyle and John Ruskin*. Stanford: Stanford University Press.

Chadwick, Owen. 1975. *The Secularization of the European Mind in the Nineteenth Century*. Cambridge: Cambridge University Press.

Clark, Kenneth. 1947. *Ruskin at Oxford: An Inaugural Lecture*. Oxford: Clarendon Press.

Clayon, Peter. 1993. *Octavia Hill*. Wisbech: Wisbech Society and Preservation Trust.

Clive, Geoffrey. 1960. *The Romantic Enlightenment: Ambiguity and Paradox in the Western Mind, 1750–1920*. New York: Meridian.

Collet, C. E. 1946. Development of Ruskin's Views on Interest., *Economic Journal Supplement*, 23–33, January.

Collingwood, R.G. 1922. *Ruskin's Philosophy*. Kendal: Titus Wilson.

Cook, E.T., ed. 1890. *Studies in Ruskin*. London: G. Allen.

Cooper, Suzanne F. 2011. *Effie: The Passionate Lives of Effie Gray, John Ruskin and John Everett Millais*. London: St. Martin's Press.

Craig, David M. 2007. *Robert Southey and Romantic Apostasy: Political Argument in Britain, 1780–1840*. Woodbridge: Boydell Press.

Crowe, Michael B. 1977. *The Changing Profile of the Natural Law*. The Hague: Martinus Hijhoff.

Dearden, James. 2012. *The Library of John Ruskin*. Oxford: Oxford Bibliographical Society.

d'Entrèves, A.P. 1994. *Natural Law: An Introduction to Legal Philosophy*, Rev. ed. Introduction by Cary J. Nederman. New Brunswick: Transaction Publishers.

Elmen, Paul, ed. 1983. *The Anglican Moral Choice*. Wilton: Morehouse-Barlow, Inc.

Elton, G.R. 1969. *England Under the Tudors*. London: Methuen.

Freshfield, Douglas W. 1920. *The Life of Horace Benedict Saussure*. London: Edward Arnold.
Frost, Mark. 2014. *The Lost Companions and John Ruskin's Guild of St George: A Revisionary History*. London: Antham Press.
Gilbert, Katherine. 1940. Ruskin's Relation to Aristotle. *Philosophical Review* 49 (1): 52–62.
Gillispie, Charles Coulston. 1959. *Genesis and Geology: The Impact of Scientific Discoveries Upon Religious Beliefs in the Decades Before Darwin*. New York: Harper and Row.
Girouard, Mark. 1981. *The Return to Camelot: Chivalry and the English Gentleman*. New Haven: Yale University Press.
Halévy, Elie. 1955. *The Growth of Philosophic Radicalism*. Trans. Mary Morris,. Boston: Beacon Press,.
Hanley, Keith, and Brian Maidment, eds. 2013. *Persistent Ruskin: Studies in Influence, Assimilation and Effect*. Surrey: Ashgate.
Hart, H.A.L. 1994. *The Concept of Law*. 2nd ed. Oxford: Clarendon Press.
Hay, Denys, ed. 1967. *The Age of the Renaissance*. New York: McGraw-Hill.
Henderson, Willie. 2000. *John Ruskin's Political Economy*. London: Routledge.
Hill, William T. 1956. *Octavia Hill: Pioneer of the National Trust and Housing Reformer*. London: Hutchinson.
Hilton, Tim. 2001. *John Ruskin: The Later Years*. New Haven: Yale University Press.
Hough, Graham. 1949. *The Last Romantics*. London: Gerald Duckworth.
Idol, John L., Jr. 1980. Ruskin and Herbert. *George Herbert Journal* 4 (1): 11–28.
Israel, Jonathan. 2010. *A Revolution of the Mind: Radical Enlightenment and the Intellectual Origins of Modern Democracy*. Princeton: Princeton University Press.
Jones, Richard F. 1961. *Ancients and Moderns*. Berkeley: University of California Press.
Jonsson, Vicky A., and A. Fredrik. 2016. *Green Victorians: The Simple Life in John Ruskin's Lake District*. Chicago: University of Chicago Press.
Joyce, A.J. 2012. *Richard Hooker and Anglican Moral Theology*. Oxford: Oxford University Press.
Kane, Brendan, and Valerie McGowan-Doyle, eds. 2014. *Elizabeth I and Ireland*. Cambridge: Cambridge University Press.
Kempster, P.A., and J.E. Alty. 2008. John Ruskin's Relapsing Encephalopathy. *Brain* 131: 2520–2525.
Kirby, W.J.T. 1990. *Richard Hooker's Doctrine of the Royal Supremacy*. Leiden: E.J. Brill.
Kitchin, G.W. 1904. *Ruskin in Oxford and Other Essays*. London: John Murray.
Ladd, Henry. 1932. *The Victorian Morality of Art*. New York: Ray Long and Richard R. Smith Inc.

Madden, Frederick, and D.K. Fieldhouse, eds. 1982. *Oxford and the Idea of Commonwealth*. London: Croom Helm.

Maritain, Jacques. 1948. *Existence and the Existent*. New York: Pantheon.

———. 1951. *The Rights of Man and Natural Law*. New York: Charles Scribner's.

Maurice, Emily S., ed. 1928. *Octavia Hill: Early Ideals*. London: George Allen and Unwin.

McClelland, V.A. 1961. Ruskin's Apologia. *Downside Review* 79 (255): 128–134.

McLaughlin, Elisabeth T. 1974. *Ruskin and Gandhi*. Lewisburg/London: Bucknell University Press/Associated University Presses.

McIlhiney, David B. 1975. The Protestantism of the Caroline Divines. *Historical Magazine of the Protestant Episcopal Church* 44 (2): 143–154.

Mendilow, Jonathan. 1986. *The Romantic Tradition in British Political Thought*. London: Croom Helm.

Munz, Peter. 1971. *The Place of Hooker in the History of Thought*. Westport: Greenwood Press.

Murdoch, Iris. 1970. *The Sovereignty of Good*. London: Routledge.

Mure, G.R.G. 1961. F.H. Bradley. *Encounters* 16 (1): 28–35.

O'Gorman, Francis. 2001. *Late Ruskin: New Contexts*. Aldershot: Ashgate.

O'Hear, Anthony. 2009. Ruskin and the Distinction Between Aesthesis and Theoria. The Meaning of Ruskin's Theoretic Faculty. Lecture to The Ruskin Society, London, April 7, http://fortnightlyreview.co.uk/2011/04/ruskin-crown/

Parkin, George R. 1892. *Imperial Federation: The Problem of National Unity*. London: Macmillan.

Peters, R.S., ed. 1975. *Nature and Conduct*. London: Macmillan.

Quigley, Carroll. 1981. *The Anglo-American Establishment*. San Pedro: GSC Associates.

Quinn, David B. 1966. *The Elizabethans and the Irish*. Ithica: Cornell University Press.

Quinton, Anthony. 1973. *Utilitarian Ethics*. New York: St. Martin's Press.

Rathmell, J.C.A. 1959. Explorations and Recoveries–1: Hopkins, Ruskin and the Sidney Psalter. *The London Magazine* 6 (9): 51–66.

Rosenberg, John D. 1961. *The Darkening Glass*. New York: Columbia University Press.

Rosenthal, Alexander S. 2008. *Crown Under Law: Richard Hooker, John Locke and the Ascent of Modern Constitutionalism*. Plymouth: Lexington Press.

Scott, Patrick, and Pauline Fletcher, eds. 1990. *Culture and Education in Victorian England*. Lewisburg: Bucknell University Press.

Shapiro, Harold, ed. 1972. *Ruskin in Italy: Letters to this Parents 1845*. Oxford: Clarendon Press.

Schoenfeldt, Michael C. 1991. *Prayer and Power: George Herbert and Renaissance Courtship*. Chicago: University of Chicago Press.

Sillar, Robert G. 1885. *Usury, an Allegory: Pernicious Effects on English Agriculture and Commerce*. London: A. Southey.
Smart, William. 1883. *A Disciple of Plato: A Critical Study of John Ruskin*. Glasgow: Wilson and McCormick.
———. 1880. *John Ruskin: His Life and Work*. Glasgow: Wilson and McCormick.
Spates, James L. 2009. Ruskin's Dark Night of the Soul: A Reconsideration of His Mental Illness and the Importance of Accurate Diagnosis. *Journal of Pre-Raphaelite Studies* 18 (Spring): 18–58.
Stanlis, Peter J. 1965. *Edmund Burke and the Natural Law*. Ann Arbor: Michigan State University Press.
Traunt, Henry W. 1910. *Matthew Arnold's 'Scholar-Gypsy' and Thyrsis and the Country they Illustrate*. Oxford: Henry W. Traunt.
Tierney, Brian. 1997. *The Idea of Natural Rights*. Grand Rapids: William B. Eerdman's.
Turner, Frank M. 1981. *The Greek Heritage in Victorian Britain*. New Haven: Yale University Press.
Watson, Francis. 1972. The Devil and Mr. Ruskin. *Encounters* 38 (6): 64–70.
Wheeler, Michael. 1999. *Ruskin's God*. Cambridge: Cambridge University Press.
———, ed. 1996. *Time and Tide: Ruskin and Science*. London: Pilkington.
White, R.S. 1996. *Natural Law in English Renaissance Literature*. Cambridge: Cambridge University Press.
Wilenski, R.H. 1933. *John Ruskin: An Introduction to Further Study of His Life and Work*. London: Faber.
Willey, Basil. 1977. *More Nineteenth Century Studies: A Group of Honest Doubters*. New York: Columbia University Press.
Wilson, Olive, ed. 1984. *My Dearest Dora: Letters to Dora Livesey, Her Family and Friends from John Ruskin, 1860–1900*. NP.
Wu, John C.H. 1954. The Natural Law and Our Common Law. *Fordham Law Review* 23 (1): 13–48.

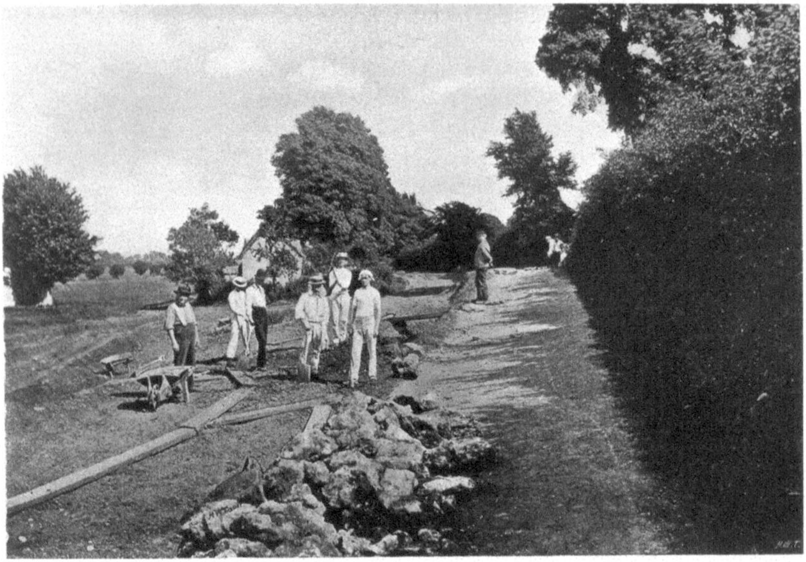

Fig. 6.1 The Hinksey Road Workers in 1874. Ruskin initiated a real work project for some of his students aimed at improving a stretch of the Hinksey Road near Oxford. A source of humour for *Punch Magazine*, it nevertheless appealed to some of his brightest students, including Oscar Wilde and Arnold Toynbee. Credit: Henry W. Taunt. Matthew Arnold's 'Scholar Gypsy' and 'Thyrsis' and the Country they Illustrate. Oxford: Henry W. Taunt and Co. 1900

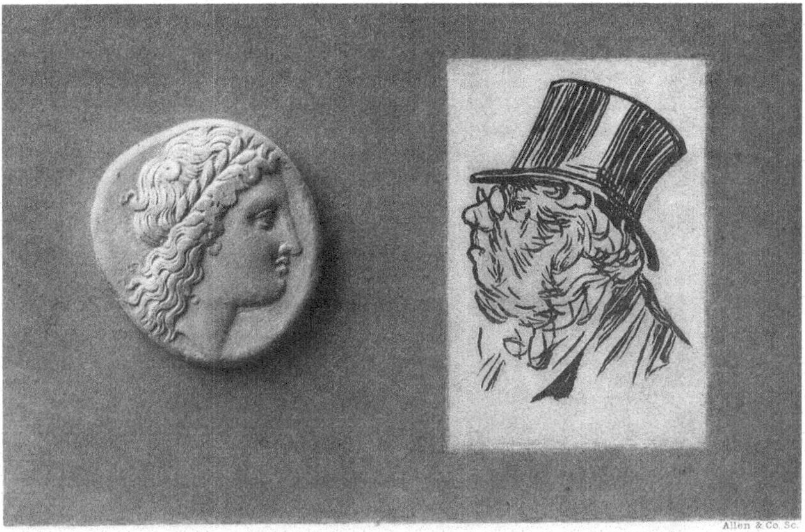

Fig. 6.2 The Apollo of Syracuse and the Self-Made Man. Ruskin contrasted this coin image of Apollo (actually of Croton, not Syracuse) with a *Punch* Cartoon by Charles Keene called 'A Capital Answer'. A 'self-made' man was to Ruskin a contradiction in terms, there being no such thing. Credit: *Cook and Wedderburn ed. Ruskin's Works.* 1903–12

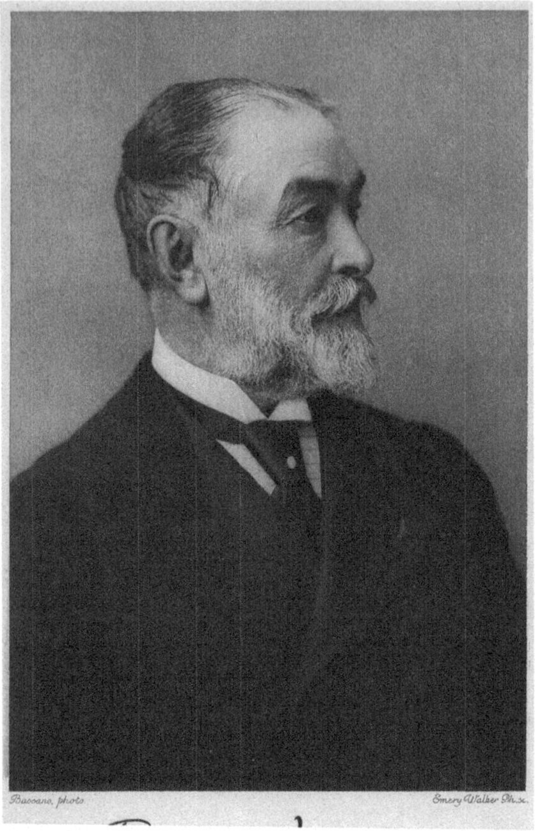

Fig. 6.3 Frederick Harrison (1831–1923). An exponent of the 'positivist philosophy' of August Compte, Harrison admired Ruskin's assault on the Utilitarian system. They worked together at Maurice's Working Men's College. A legal reformer, he and Ruskin found themselves in opposing camps during the Eyre controversy of 1865. In 1907, Harrison published a biography of Ruskin. Credit: Frederick Harrison, Autobiographic Memoirs. London: Macmillan, 1911

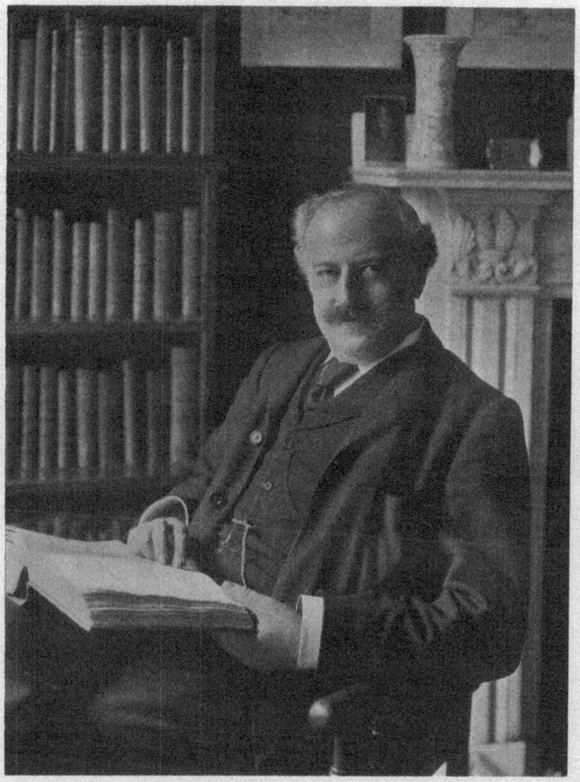

Fig. 6.4 Edward Tyas Cook (1857–1919). One of the editors of the collected works edition, Cook's interest in Ruskin began at Oxford in the later 1870s where he carefully recorded details of his lectures. Close to Alfred Milner, Cook became an important figure in the Round Table Movement, aimed at reconfiguring the British Empire along commonwealth lines. Credit: J. Saxon Mills, Sir Edward Cook. London: Constable, 1921

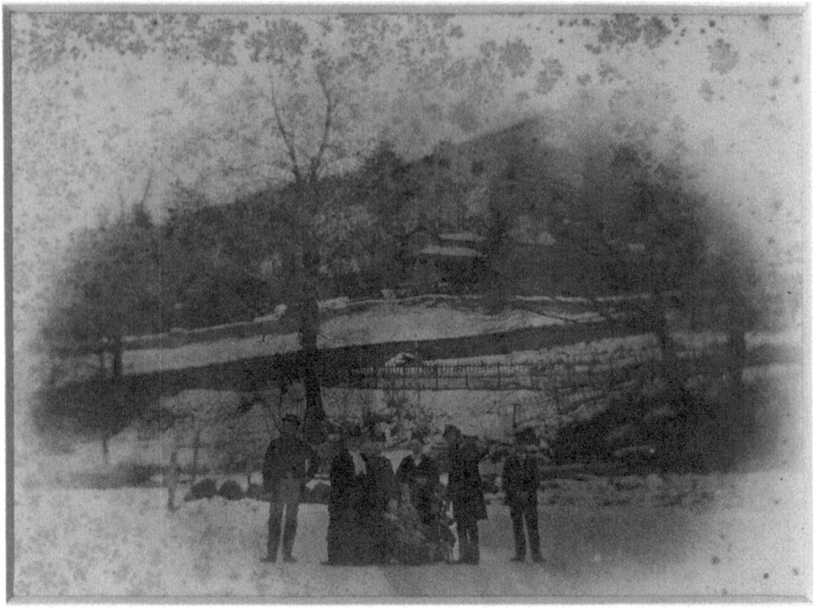

Fig. 6.5 Fanny Talbot (1824–1917). This north England nurse contributed land and buildings at Barmouth, Wales, to Ruskin's Guild of St. George in 1874. She is seen here in 1879 standing centre with Ruskin next to her leaning on a cane. The photo was taken on the ice of Coniston Lake below Ruskin's estate of Brantwood. Credit: Ruskin Foundation (Ruskin Library, Lancaster University)

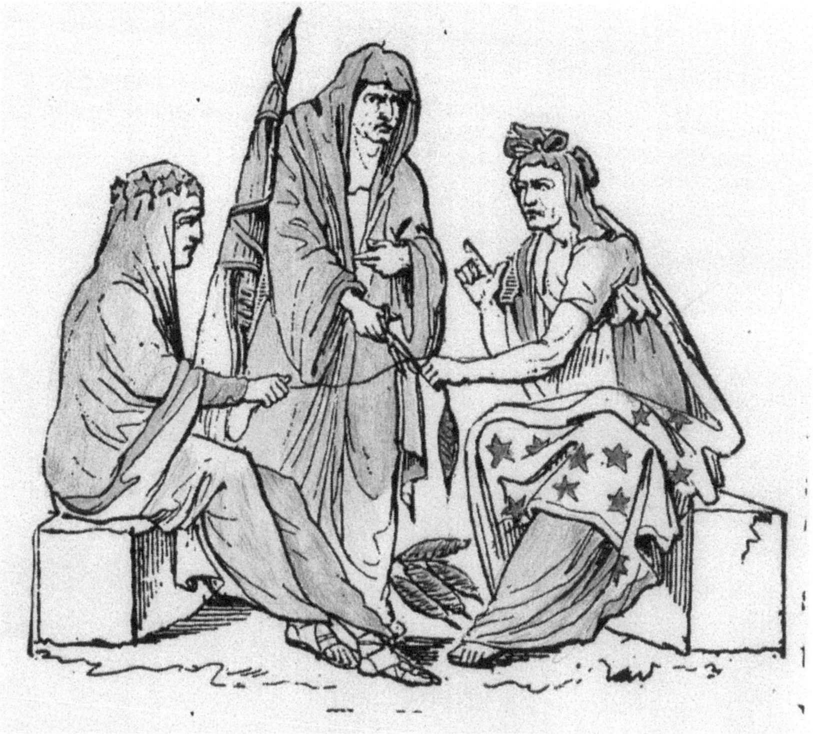

Fig. 6.6 *Atropos*. She was one of the three *Moirae*, the Greek goddesses of fate and destiny. Being the oldest of them, she determined the death of mortals by cutting the thread of life with her shears. In *Munera Pulveris*, Ruskin cited her as the force which ends the formal life of a nation trapped in unresolved anarchy. Credit: Alexander S. Murray. Manual of Mythology: Greek and Roman Norse and Old German, Hindoo and Egyptian Mythology. Philadelphia: Henry Altamus, 1898

CHAPTER 7

Easing Towards 'A Vast Policy': Establishing the Guild of St. George

I

In the last chapter it was noticed how, after 1870, Ruskin's theological position continued its retreat from the sectarian and broadened into a latitudinarian ethical creed more distinctly informed by natural law. Coupled with this was a marked scepticism about the directions being taken by the states of modern Europe and its outliers with their improving technical capacities for warfare associated with ever-greater concentrations of financial power. The situation he illustrated to his students by the sardonic contrast of the Apollo of Syracuse with a self-made man of the day. In turning his attention towards more practical questions of political and social reform, he found much to draw upon in the writings of some of these English Renaissance writers in whom principles of natural law were well ingrained. While Ruskin did not think himself involved in utopian thinking, the suggestion is difficult to avoid in his social writings.

The utopian tradition of writing in England has been rich and varied and Ruskin received due notice from his contemporaries and later writers for his distinctive contribution.[1] He was, himself, wary of the term 'utopia' and it does not appear in his works very often, usually in a rather disparaging way. He first broached the word in a lecture on architecture given in Edinburgh in November, 1853, referring to it as 'another of the devil's pet words', his main objection being that as a term it was not very useful, usually indicating a misguided preoccupation with some abstract pursuit of perfection. At the more practical level, he argued that certain things

G. A. MacDonald, *John Ruskin's Politics and Natural Law*,
https://doi.org/10.1007/978-3-319-72281-8_7

were merely possible or they were not.[2] This was all observed in passing as the lecture, and its three companions, did not focus on social reform, although in the fourth, he did elaborate further on his pamphlet 'Pre-Raphaelitism' of 1851 and the achievements of those artists who belonged to the Pre-Raphaelite Brotherhood. He supported this new artistic movement in England with its emphasis on the spiritual and on the bold use of colour. The lecture also provided him opportunity to again advance his hostile views of the Italian Renaissance period.[3]

A more distinct reference to utopianism came in 1856 in volume three of *Modern Painters* while discussing 'the moral of landscape'. In the two previous chapters, he had contrasted the art of medieval landscape with that of modern. The chapter on the modern contains some of Ruskin's most disciplined and coherent writing distinguishing the Renaissance and Enlightenment worlds of art and culture from that of the Medieval and why he found the works of both Walter Scott and Turner to be so important as moderns.[4] In then turning to the 'moral of landscape', he starts to promote themes which will be taken up with great determination in the future. Whatever the virtues of many modern advances, they are not the real stuff of human happiness in comparison with what may be freely taken by those living good lives: 'all real and wholesome enjoyments possible to man have been just as possible to him, since first he was made of the earth, as they are now'.[5] Perhaps thinking of Holy Roman Emperor Charles V in 1555 and his suddenly adopted cloistered life, Ruskin mused that now and then 'a wearied king, or a tormented slave, found out where the true kingdoms of the world were', which is to say, in a life of simplicity. He added that 'I am Utopian and enthusiastic enough to believe that the time will come when the world will discover this.'[6] In the mid-1870s, however, he suggested that utopian pursuits often smacked of an evangelical scheme for the provision of 'carriages for all'.[7] In 1884 he contended that the utopian imaginary of his time still thought the world best 'stubbed by steam' and that 'human arms and legs' should be left 'eternally idle'.[8] This was all corruption of the old religion and of that Biblical 'wisdom literature' which stressed just dealings and spiritual leadership as the best part of utopianism.[9]

The modern utopian tended towards a certain character, one who harboured views in league with 'the Parisian notion of Communism'. The allusion was to recent efforts by the Communards to burn the Tuileries and the Louvre Art Gallery during the brief Paris Commune period after the Franco-Prussian War of 1871. A century after the French Revolution, there remained no very satisfactory residue of the efforts of the *philosophes* to soften punishment policies and erode class boundaries in the name of equality.[10] Rather, Ruskin saw ever-increasing mass warfare posing a threat to all manifestations of higher culture and sensibility. This was so of modern Paris especially where recently 'her own forts' had been 'raining ruin on her palaces' but the people 'without faith enough in heaven to imagine the reverse of this'. Thus, 'Utopia and its benedictions are probable and simple things compared to the Kakotopia and its curse which we had seen actually fulfilled.'[11] While confessing that he himself was 'a Communist of the old school – reddest also of the red'—he thought himself to be to one side of these 'new' communists. Being of the old school, he understood that 'our property belongs to everybody, and everybody's property to us'.[12] His mood, indeed, was much in keeping with the writings of the historian and fictional writer Marmontel. Ruskin keenly admired his detailing of the best of French rural life in the years before the Revolution, exercising an effect upon him similar to that of Gothelf.[13]

Promotion of a comprehensive social condition on the authoritarian Platonic republican model was not foremost in his mind when he set about establishing his Guild. He knew well enough the value, but also the limitations of what earlier writers such as Francis Bacon and Thomas More had suggested about ideal communities. When he turned to Francis Bacon, he valued the focus on education and science in *The New Atlantis* and other writings.[14]

In More's *Utopia* (1516), he found views on economic organization and practice in line with his own previously published advocacy, particularly concerning principles of intrinsic value and the suggestion that members of all classes should work regularly.[15] (See Appendix 4) While Ruskin probably did not read *Utopia* before 1870 when he received a copy from F.S. Ellis, he certainly knew something of More's dramatic biography and about his controversies with Protestant reformers.[16] The reasons for his interest in this work are not far to seek. Book I shows Sir Thomas displaying a lively interest in current west European trade expansion facilitated by the new Cape of Good Hope route and particularly through the fantastic observations attending the New World discoveries.[17] It is in the New World that he locates Utopia with its wisely governed citizens. The details are revealed through a three-way conversation between More, his Antwerp friend, Peter Gilis, and a much travelled fictional character called Raphael. The recently published *Voyages* of the explorer, Amerigo Vespucci, provided the factual background for Raphael's accounts of life in Utopia.

These accounts are a vehicle for comparison of the relative merits or shortcomings of Utopian and English domestic practices in political economy and social justice.

Of primary interest to More were the cumulative effects of the land enclosures which had become widespread in rural England, in favour of sheep and wool production controlled by a relatively few landed magnates and investors. These practices expelled peasant families from their traditional holdings and in turn fostered the decline of smaller rural towns with their associated craftsmen and functionaries. The overall result was a rise in petty thievery which then led to judicial executions. A host of craftsmen and labourers, including returned soldiers or sailors, found employment increasingly difficult to obtain, and harsh penalties attended even petty theft, including the gallows. Says Raphael: 'no penalty on earth will stop people from stealing if it's their only way of getting food'.[18] Meanwhile, the forms of theft multiplied as the concentration of wealth and property in fewer hands became greater, facilitated by usurious practices.[19]

This combination of an economy stacked in favour of oligopolists entrenched in the landholding classes, an increasing use of the gallows and outward-bound privateers as vanguards of empire, does not provide a pleasing picture of More's England, but for Ruskin it provided an all too familiar one in its essentials. It is an account parallel to the one he gave in *Unto This Last*. More's countryside has lost its essential source of strength and continuity, a setting where the medieval poor laws are no longer functioning with any reliability. Ruskin's countryside is one long beset by the disruptive policies of a regularly revised series of Elizabethan poor laws, replaced after 1834 by an ever-more questionable series of regulations sponsored by rationalist utilitarian reformers. The cities had become Dickensian nests of slums, filth and want, the citizens grown accustomed to what Ruskin often called conditions of 'wage slavery'.

Much in Book II of *Utopia* Ruskin found congenial, conforming well with his own observations. There were similarities between the policies and programs of the 'Utopians' and of the Guild. Book II is a more freewheeling affair than Book I, as it was written first, according to Erasmus. Later scholars have raised questions about this contention but, however it may be, Ruskin took both as he found them.[20] The second book contains less dialogue and more monologue from the mouth of the fictional Raphael, who throws out a good number of contrasting ideas and arguments to his silent companions.[21] Many straw men are set up, only to be knocked down. Much of this was of a philosophical and speculative nature, a good bit of which Ruskin no doubt found windy or to one side. The points made about warfare, however, were to his liking, for More spoke of the great attending waste of energy, resources and life. In keeping with such criticism of warfare, there is a good deal of indirect reference to the work of Machiavelli, less to the prudential pragmatism of *The Prince*, but rather to passages concerning the inadvisability of the use of mercenaries by governments.[22] The suggestion is that the seeds of indiscriminate citizen warfare were being sown in the sixteenth century, years of urban expansion and growth of European nation states. One discerns in More a lament for the final fading of any traces of an older chivalry at work in this changing Europe, whatever the anachronistic festive and seasonal rituals maintained in the Court of Henry VIII.[23]

There was much to applaud in Book II of a more concrete nature. Ideas abound concerning the proper routines of education for men and women, about modesty in dress and diet, marriage arrangements and suitable forms of recreation.[24] A role for government in public health and protection of waters and woodlands finds its way into *Utopia* as does a general condemnation of pomp and glory, either by rulers or by the well to do.[25] Ruskin could also agree with much of what More had to say about slaves and prisoners. As More did, he wished to see far fewer people confined for minor crimes in Victorian England, reserving harder time and forms of labour for those who resisted their own reform.[26] Striking is the accord between the two men on the importance of habituation as the main vehicle for reconciling citizens to their work and as the source of the reduction of sinful behaviour. Says Ruskin, 'the character of men depends more on their occupations than on any teaching we can give them, or principles with which we can imbue them'.[27] The austerity of life on the Isle of Utopia is severe, however, as in Plato's *Republic*, and many suggestions in More go well beyond those which would eventually come to regulate the Guild of St. George.

One of the recurring questions about More concerns his view of communism and the related question of his attitude towards private property.[28] Various interpretations continue to circulate. Many are satisfied that More held positive views about communism and about common community of goods as an ideal, but that these views were also qualified in the light of practical social experience.[29] J.H. Hexter concluded that there was no mistaking the radical nature of the work.[30] More may be said to be in the tradition of St. Francis of Assisi in wanting to stress the spiritual value of those prepared to actually live, as orders, according to a 'community of goods' doctrine and to do work appropriate to the welfare of all, both within the immediate community and outside of it. His opposition to the doctrines of Luther were much caught up in this issue. He saw Luther as one prepared to unleash the wanton ways of secular forces and greed and to dissolve important relations between church and state.[31]

Ruskin did not give clear expressions about his views on More's communism. To the extent that he actually thought More a genuine communist and hostile to private property, he would be in disagreement. He may have understood, as have others, that More was playing the spokesman for many different views in *Utopia*. Ruskin, too, had a double identity, elusively calling himself a 'communist of the old school' but also a Tory defender of private property. That he was such a defender there is no doubt, even if he saw the holding of such property as limited under law and conditional as to its extent and uses. His statement about private property also being the 'property of all' would suggest agreement with the natural law principles espoused by the Decretalists and endorsed in those medieval poor law tennets which contended that people in need had a claim to a share of property controlled by others.[32] He certainly believed, that, in the case of England and Europe, private property arose out of longstanding legal conventions and traditions, providing the basis of the local leadership exercised by the nobility. Such leadership, however debased in Victorian times, was more reliable than untested democracy.

Ruskin's initial reaction to *Utopia* was fairly typical of many later commentaries, noting its ambiguities. To Ellis, he wrote: 'What an infinitely wise – infinitely foolish book it is! Right in all it asks – insane in venturing to ask it, all at once.'[33] The sentence suggests that, if he was not quite certain which were More's views in the *Utopia*, on the whole, he found More to be generally 'under sanction always of the higher authority of which of late the English nation has wholly set its strength to defy – the founder of its religion'.[34]

Ruskin acknowledged debts to More but in the 1870s, as noticed in Chap. 6, he turned with renewed attention to Plato, and particularly to the latter's last major dialogue, *The Laws*, for an improved understanding of justice. A number of translations of passages issued from his pen in which he departed in certain particulars from the recent versions prepared by Benjamin Jowett.[35] The emphasis of *The Laws* is more practical than *The Republic*, evidence of the assisting hand of Aristotle in the production of that work.[36] The actors are no longer young men, as in *The Republic*, but older men of experience, designing laws for a new colony for Crete, an enterprise not foreign to the tasks confronting contemporary administrators of the British Empire.

The editors of his works observed that 'the forms into which Ruskin threw his reconstruction of society belong to the sphere of utopian suggestion'.[37]Having acknowledged that the rule for St. George's Guild took much inspiration from Thomas More, Francis Bacon and Plato, there were yet other sources. These included writers as obscure as St. Anthony of Padua (1195–1231), Giovanni Villani (1226–1348) and Jeremias Gotthelf (1797–1854).[38] St. Anthony was identified as a proponent of sound land management and named Patron of the Guild. From the historian Villani, he took information on the laws of fourteenth-century Florence. Gotthelf's fictional stories of rural Swiss life he had known since youth. Their contents gradually meshed with his memories of his early tours of Europe and the observations published in his first book of substance, *The Poetry of Architecture* of 1838.[39] In the later 1870s, Ruskin sponsored a translation from the German of *Ulric The Farm Servant*, which was published by 1888. Cook and Wedderburn credit Ruskin for introducing Gothhelf to English readers, the stories being, they claimed, 'the literary forerunners of Auerbach, Tourgenieff and Tolstoy'.[40] What appealed to Ruskin in these works (which he thought comparable to those of Scott), was the way in which they imparted the character of the 'sweet, quiet, half-wild, kindly and calmly inhabited Bernese lowlands'.[41] He remarked on the qualities which made this Swiss landscape, before the arrival of railways, worthy of inspiration. It was a place of proper social conduct in which traditions had been maintained and rapid urban economic change and excessive commerce resisted. It was a land in which domestic practices reminiscent of those endorsed in Xenophon's *Economist* were evident.[42]

There were other aspects of conventional utopian thinking which, in the main, Ruskin resisted: an inclination towards the urban and the frequent promotion of machine technology improvements, positively endorsed as aids to profitable work. These two elements were linked by Lewis Mumford. He argued that the earliest cities were in fact the first realizations of the utopian ideal; second, that such realization was linked to the discovery of the machine, which in the earliest ceremonial cities involved the authoritarian organization of humans into co-ordinated work units for pursuit of official substantive purposes. Compulsively co-ordinated humans, then, were the first true machine.[43] Ruskin's reform ideas tended to be anti-urban and anti-technological in this sense, oriented to a rural commune way of life, of which Xenophon was the exemplar rather than Plato.[44] These two aspects were reinforced in the years after 1861 through the mounting recognition that the modern nation state and its cities were becoming theatres for expanding technical capacities in warfare, rendering small-scale civilian life dangerous and impossible. The American Civil War and the Franco-Prussian War, along with the negative experiences associated with the Eyre affair, caused Ruskin to reassess the entire connection between the morality of soldier warfare and civic virtue, a message he delivered very bluntly in 1865 to the young military men in training at Woolwich.[45] Pacifism, on the other hand, was never viewed by him as realistic. The best he could do, beyond promoting the cause of wise leadership, was to promote the life of one honourable soldier known to him. Thus, as recommended reading for the Guild membership, he edited an edition of the life of Herbert Edwardes, a military man with a talent for resolving local imperial conflicts without resorting always to military action.[46]

What was to be gleaned from this and older accounts that might speak to the modern condition? First, having drawn attention to the differences in circumstance which separated classical and late medieval times from those of contemporary England, he stated: 'the reader is to observe that the teaching of St. George differs by extension from that of Plato, in so far as the Greek never imagined that the blessings of education could be extended to servants as well as to masters'.[47] Human beings were in no way equal in talents or prospects but they did deserve equity of treatment and opportunity under law. A good society will assist people to find their proper station in life.[48] It was feasible to extend comprehensive education across established class and gender lines owing to the modern possibilities of material abundance, although this abundance was still imperfectly realized in terms of rational production, distribution and consumption.[49]

Second, having determined that the first duty of a state was, in part, the provision of daily necessities and housing to the young, he noticed, that such a duty was more keenly appreciated in the late medieval realms of Europe, even if unevenly realized in practice. The various ranks of society had been more successfully integrated along co-operative lines and in terms of social duty than was the case in the developing modern culture of *laissez-faire* based commerce.[50]

Third, the number of daily choices made per family about consumption in past times was much smaller than in the industrial age. Invented wants and entertainments had proliferated. National policies structured around recognition of the intrinsic value of goods and services, as urged in *Unto This Last*, were admittedly difficult to implement under conditions of modern industry and international trade, but he had made a useful distinction between 'wealth' and 'illth'.[51] This 'green' sounding economic policy involved distinguishing things worth having, and actions worth doing, from those not. J.A. Hobson, A.R. Orage, and the founders of the 'social credit' movement, noted his emphasis on an economics of intrinsic value and improved distribution as an element missing from much conventional economic thought.[52] Were there historical examples suitable as guides for setting such priorities? Small-scale, domestic agriculture was an essential first consideration. Xenophon's *Economist* provided a useful guide for the local co-operative labour of all classes and against which could be contrasted modern economies and their increasing range of useless invented wants and military expenditures.[53]

If the desirable social condition was one supported by appropriate agricultural and industrial production of useful articles, a further consideration was posed, springing from Ruskin's contemplation of European art, architecture and commerce: that of the conservation of older non-polluting technologies and handcraft traditions. Appropriate tools were an important element with respect to the happiness of the worker and the possibilities for great art. Ruskin's attitude reflected what Mumford later observed about *techné* as a conception. Mumford posed an identity of tools with acquired skill and dexterity, as opposed to mere machines of mass production.[54] In 'The Nature of Gothic', Ruskin had written: 'You must either make a tool of the creature or a man of him. You cannot make both.' For men 'were not intended to work with the accuracy of tools, to be precise and perfect in all actions'.[55]

'Utopia' appears, in the end, to be not a place but a set of attitudes. The identification of the Swiss Bernese as a place of functioning utopian principles found early expression in one of his most successful books, a youthful children's morality tale, *The King of the Golden River*, written for his future wife and ever in print.[56] The tale is set in a valley in the Alps. When all has finally been put right and covetous villains given their come-uppance, it 'became a garden again, and the inheritance which had been lost by cruelty was regained by love' a place where 'the poor were never driven from the door'.[57] In this delightful tale, we can find foreshadowed much of his later 'green' thinking about the properly ordered society.[58]

II

In the wide-ranging *Fors Clavigera*, Ruskin regularly gave space to his plans for a projected social experiment, The Guild of St. George. Owing to increasingly poor mental health, however, the project took shape only slowly. As an organization it eventually achieved legal status in 1878, just when Ruskin was on the verge of his worst mental collapse.[59] There was a reason for Ruskin's taking up the guild idea after entering upon his Oxford professorship. The connection between war and chivalry had long been on his mind and, as with many people over the centuries, his attitude to war remained ambiguous. The military virtues were, on one hand, ancient, bold and a source of disciplined intelligence. On the other, much had changed in the European context between the field carnage of the Napoleonic Wars and the urban devastation of the Franco-Prussian War, recently concluded. In between, the Crimean War was somewhat farcical in some of its chivalrous pretentions but it spelled the end of a certain kind of older style of localized open-field warfare in favour of more modern and co-ordinated mechanized techniques. The air bombardment of Venice in 1849 had marked a similar shift in the direction of new technological capabilities on the horizon although still rather chaotic in execution. The idea of indiscriminate warfare on civilian populations was evident in many places and certainly came to fruition during the American Civil War with the mass mobilization of citizen soldiers, the burning of Atlanta and the retribution march through Georgia. The Franco-Prussian War brought the possibilities of such indiscriminate methods home to Ruskin as never before. Had Oliphant perused the essays of *The Crown Of Wild Olive* as closely as she did *Time and Tide*, she might have found less reason to think Ruskin interested in promoting centralized statecraft. *Time and Tide* had, in fact, argued that more swords should be beaten into ploughshares than forged, and that improved local forms of civil association were required as a counter to enhanced state powers.

The guild tradition was an old and complex one in both England and Europe. By the time of Richard III's reign in 1483, it is estimated that there were 40,000 religious and trade guilds in England.[60] By various degrees, guild bodies came to acknowledge that skilled work should have defined standards. They became a source of group protection and mutual assistance and the means of fostering group legitimacy as a fundamental component of sound civil association.[61] Guild practices in England were influenced by those on the continent but there was a domestic resilience to them which gradually produced a general acceptance of guild bodies by all elements of English society, including by the office of the King.[62]

The legitimacy of guilds, defended in law, encouraged the conditional admission of selected European guilds into England. Such admissions contributed not only to Royal revenues but also imparted to English merchants and artisans some of the business acumen of their European counterparts.[63] Guild traditions persisted in England until the last years of the reign of Henry VIII, whose centralizing policies destroyed not only the monasteries but also much of the fabric of the guilds.[64] The centralizing of state functions was continued by Elizabeth I with passage of the Act of Apprentices in 1562, which sought to bar persons from participating in any trade, craft or ministry without first serving a seven-year apprenticeship.[65] This was just one sign of the enhanced powers of the English Crown, an element related to the beginnings of its sea-borne empire. Francis Bacon noticed the increased powers of the monarch in his times relative to those of the prominent nobility: 'So as the Kings of this realm, finding long since that kind of commandment in the noblemen unsafe unto their crown' they thought it appropriate to 'restrain the same by provision of laws' and with the aid of the statute of retainers 'men now depend upon the prince and the laws, and upon no other'.[66] The Tudor poor laws reflected this centralizing tendency which often worked to restrict labour mobility and stigmatize poverty. Such traits persisted for several centuries and were still evident at the time of the poor law reforms of 1834.[67]

The presumed manner by which guild traditions, as they developed in the later medieval city states of Italy, became the seedbed of a future secular and democratic style of politics, generated much academic discussion in the later twentieth century. This new 'democratic' style, it was argued, culminated in the thought of James Harrington and later blossomed into the republican traditions of America.[68] That there coexisted alongside these new proposals other forms of citizen participation and other accounts of civil association, quite stable and reliable, formed the substance of many counter-arguments to the wisdom of these levelling trends. These counter-arguments acknowledged the place of various classical and medieval communitarian practices, opposing them to any supposed virtue of an increase in the regularity of democratic voting exercises advocated by such as Harrington.[69] Such counter-arguments noted the persistence of the daily practices of the guild and the traditional role of the church in support of orderly conduct and poor relief, along with upper-class resistance. These were all institutional counterweights curbing the supposed all-pervasive appeal of the new republican model. In many instances, the church had itself been the sponsor of specialized guilds or had been supportive of them.[70]

The force of these traditional communitarian elements had been particularly strong in England where, owing to the relative isolation of England from Europe, versions of mixed government pre-dated the Norman invasion and remained more or less continuous thereafter.[71] The King, reflecting a striking and ancient political and theological idea, had 'two bodies', one natural and one which transcended the historical contingencies of his own life, giving continuity to the English view that governments were 'mixed' in composition.[72] The myth of King, Lords and Commons in England had, indeed, long and vital roots, the signing of *Magna Carta* being merely one of its more striking symbolic moments but one with distant antecedents in both England and Europe.[73]

In the wake of the bloodshed and imperial outreach bred by the French Revolution, the corporatist historical traditions of England became ever more agreeable to the Romantic writers of the Lake District and later to the young Ruskin who read them so avidly. Despite the alleged balance of powers displayed by the American constitution, he, like his father's Ultra-Tory guests at table, took on a dislike of American political and commercial practices.[74] In 1857, he complained of American instability and linked it to democratic excesses.[75] He complained regularly to Charles Norton that the civil war was the great confirmation of such weakness.[76] Mixed government gave greater play to conventional classes and associations, those important guarantors of orderly life, over against the divisive forces of an untrammelled individualism which he believed had first taken root in Renaissance Italian cities.[77]

III

The reasons for taking the name of St. George for the guild were partly associated with that Saint's long association with Venice and also with a desire to readapt the notion of a 'White Company' associated with the fourteenth-century soldier and mercenary, Sir John Hawkwood.[78] In the end, Saint George proved a more suitable candidate from the standpoint of chivalry.[79] He had played a symbolic role in English life since Edward III's re-establishment of the chapel in Westminster Castle, originally founded by Henry III in 1240, dedicated to Edward the Confessor. In

1348, fresh from victories at Crécy and Calais, Edward III organized the 'Most Noble Order of the Garter' as a society of Knights, 26 in number. The Sovereign himself was declared a statutory member of this Order whose members were committed to 'show fidelity and friendliness' towards one another. The King, by wearing the blue garter, was thereby linked to his knights 'in amity and peace'. It is an appealing tale, but it was just one of many historically deceptive, late-medieval exercises in the calling-up of chivalrous ideals, as of a 'heroic dream', said Huizinga, more reflective of an imagined feudal past than of its reality.[80] It had, however, its practical uses. Within a year of the establishment of the Order of the Garter, Edward re-dedicated the chapel in the names of the Virgin Mary, St. George and St. Edward, complete with a unit of clergy charged with chanting and praying for the safety of the Royal family and all faithful souls. It was a Royal establishment of a most unusual kind, for in 1351 the Pope granted exemption to it from the jurisdictions of both the Archbishop of Canterbury and the Bishop of Salisbury, Windsor Castle being in the diocese of the latter. Statutes of 1352 outlined the details of all these arrangements.[81] Thereafter, the well-travelled Saint's reputation for good and heroic work turned him into a national patron. Ruskin, much attracted by the dragon legend, saw him a worthy namesake for his guild, much promoted after 1871.[82]

It took several years for the Guild's legal work to be completed and when achieved, in 1878, the hoped-for tithing membership did not materialize in any number. When Carlyle first heard of the project, William Allingham reported that he thought it 'an absurdity' and gave nothing to it.[83] What was striking about the founding documents is that the austere and state oriented qualities of *Time and Tide*, reminiscent of Plato's *Republic*, were largely absent, replaced by a countryside paternalism, more inspired by Xenophon's *Economist*. Even here, the patriarchal aspect was muted when compared with the authoritarian aspects of Plato's vision. Indeed, while Ruskin was prepared to underwrite much of the costs of the Guild, he understandably showed no inclination to administer actual sites, preferring to delegate the responsibly to those whom he trusted. The practical management decisions he left to what he hoped were competent 'companions'.[84] The constitution even conceded that the 'Master' might be voted out of office, thus allowing to enter a democratic confidence quite foreign to Plato and Xenophon.[85]

When the Guild commenced its mainly agricultural work on the ground the medieval trappings were soon enough dropped, although there was no harm in naming St. Francis of Assisi as Patron of St. George's Bank, odd as that may sound.[86] The main objects of the Guild were stated to be[87]:

> To determine and institute in practice the wholesome laws of labour (especially agricultural life and economy) and to instruct first the agricultural and as opportunity may serve other labourers and craftsmen in such Science, Art, Literature as are conducive to good husbandry and craftsmanship.

Suggestions such as a special currency and for distinctive Guild clothing quickly fell to one side. Other appeals to medievalism were of a comparative and symbolic nature, meant to stimulate appreciation for ideal social and co-operative principles.[88] At the start, he had assured one of his Trustees, Lord Cowper-Temple, that the Guild was 'not to be communism' but, on the contrary, 'the old Feudal system applied to do good instead of evil – to save life instead of destroy…as the system gets power, I hope to see it alter laws all over England.'[89]

The Guild, then, was conceived as an inspirational model, an example of one way to ease towards specific reforms. Others interested in making similar guild initiatives could re-adapt the model along different lines. To be sure, Ruskin himself did not have overly high expectations: 'This St. George's Company of ours is mere raft-making amidst irrevocable wreck – the best we can do, to be done bravely and cheerfully, come of it what may.'[90] Still, he held out some greater hope. In October, 1875, he told his readers that he believed 'there be yet honesty and sense enough left in England to nourish the effort' and that 'from its narrow source there will soon develop itself a vast Policy'.[91] Its conservative and non-threatening qualities were suggested by Edith Hope Scott, an early member of the Guild, as well as its historian: 'St. George's Guild is the first Utopia – so far as I know – to be passed and confirmed by any Board of Trade.'[92]

IV

What was the character of this working experiment and from what sources did it draw? We have noticed in the previous chapter many of the connections he made with earlier 'utopian' thought. Following Plato, Ruskin held that just rulers sprang from citizens trained into satisfactory habits of work and moral conduct. Musical training in youth was fundamental. Education was no longer just for the few, as Plato believed inevitable, but was now for the many. Armed with ancient accounts of the good life premised upon restraint and work, his model community allowed small groups of people to combine and limit their material demands while pursuing healthful and necessary work and worthy pastimes. Members were to take responsibility for what was immediately under their control and 'tithe' to the purposes of the Guild as a sign of commitment.

The initial idea was that improvement was to be pursued incrementally by means of an unlimited number of acts of agricultural land reclamation and industrial rediscovery of older craft traditions. It was an inherently conservative program for these acts were to take appropriate notice, under proper instruction, of not just English historical achievements but also of past European experience. Through a gathering centripetal instructional force, they would provide positive sources for national legislative reform. Acts of land reclamation would deal mainly with the revival of marginal lands through sound, non-steam driven, agricultural practices and by local craft traditions. All Guild activities were to be premised on ethical principles of conduct and political economy. For example, the 'trade warrant' to be issued assured that guild members would themselves become the guardians of quality standards and honest trade practices. The Guild would also promote vital education, cheerful and healthful local ceremonies and entertainments, and provide necessary welfare procedures to the sick and aged. The emphasis was on local control.

In seeking inspiration beyond guild theory itself, we have seen that Ruskin drew upon diverse sources. He had also found instructive the portrayals of political virtues and vices by Lorenzetti and Giotto in Siena, Florence and Padua.[93] The sources of such virtues and vices in art had roots in Patristic period literature and in the centuries when the legacy of Rome was gradually modified by its official adoption of Christianity after Constantine. Past visions of a Christian commonwealth defended by pious, scholarly and chivalric individuals such as St. Jerome, St. Martin of Tours or St. Hugh of Lincoln, greatly appealed to Ruskin. The library (or the *Biblioteca Pastorum*) that he compiled for his guild members was rich in titles displaying the ideals of such dedicated lives.[94] Towards the establishment of this library, he sometimes engaged his Oxford students. Alexander Wedderburn and William Collingwood, for example, were commissioned to prepare a new translation of Xenophon's *Economist* for publication and use in the guild library.[95]

V

The long pursuit of legal precision for the description of the Guild produced a model legal form in 1878, executed under the Companies Act (1867), issued to the Guild by the Board of Trade.[96] This document was somewhat path-breaking with respect to future non-profit group efforts to conserve parklands, heritage districts and other special landscapes, by means of the attachment of conservation caveats to specific parcels of land. Documents of this kind have since become the stock and trade of such bodies as The National Trust, the Nature Conservancy and a host of other conservation-minded organizations outside of England.[97] It is a reason why some credit must be given to Ruskin as a facilitator of The National Trust, along with Octavia Hill and Canon Hardwicke Rawnsley.[98]

The Constitution for the Guild did not provide an outline for an ideal state. It outlined procedures for one of many possible local associations as might be variously developed under the British Constitution. A passage from the Creed of the Guild affirms its law-abiding qualities:

> I will obey all the laws of my country faithfully; and the orders of its monarch, and of all persons appointed to be in authority under its monarch, so far as such laws or commands are consistent with what I suppose to be the law of God; and when they are not, or seem to be in anywise in need of change, I will oppose them loyally and deliberately, not with malicious, concealed or disorderly violence.

The touch of pacifist separatism helps explain, perhaps, the popularity of Ruskin's Guild with many Quakers in the Birmingham area.[99] Similarly, informed in 1874 that a group of English Cistercians at St. Bernard's Monastery in Leicestershire were already working land on St. George's principles, he replied that it was all very well, but getting Monks to work cooperatively was one thing, and getting a representative group of the English to do so, quite another.[100]

The chequered history of the achievements of the Guild has been related on a number of occasions and only a brief description need be given here.[101] In 1876, before the letters patent for the Guild were actually issued, Ruskin purchased land at Totley, near Sheffield. His hopes for these 13 acres, what he called his 'first essay of St. George's work', were expressed more in terms of political theology. His Sheffield workers were to be 'Life Guards of a New Life…more in the spirit of body of monks gathered for missionary service, than of a body of tradesmen gathered for the promotion even of the honestest and usefullest trade'.[102] The farm was established and, after a shaky start, it persisted under stable arrangements until 1929. It was just one of many efforts at agricultural, commercial or educational initiatives in line with the creed and code of the Guild. Here is where he hoped the first 'companions' of St. George might become established in a spiritual society. His close friends, the Cowper-Temples, were unnerved about the apocalyptic nature of Ruskin's conversations at this time, much of it brought on by his worsening mental health.[103] Lacking confidence in Ruskin's judgement and because the land purchase at Sheffield was considered premature, his two main trustees both resigned in 1879.[104]

Ruskin's hasty establishment of a museum on the outskirts of Sheffield was also controversial, although more successful in the long term.[105] Up until 1891, a number of other landholdings were either purchased or donated in the Birmingham and Liverpool areas, and elsewhere.[106] While his bouts of illness meant that Ruskin had soon to withdraw from all practical involvements with the Guild, he could, in 1881, take some satisfaction with the Laxey Woollen Mill, Isle of Man: 'the most important step hitherto taken in furtherance of our objects'.[107]

Until Ruskin's death, the Guild's success was limited in terms of membership and enduring enterprise. It did survive in altered form, aided by Ruskin Societies and other offshoots although its post-1900 achievements have been mainly educational rather than economic.[108] Such communitarian models did not prove to be very workable in twentieth-century England, its colonies, or in America.[109] If the essential message of *Unto This Last* did gradually win applause from many who agreed that there 'was no wealth but life' and that there was an important ethical content to economics, his various proposals for renewed political organization fell to one side.[110] The state-oriented ethic of 'discipline and interference' urged in 1857 as the basis of renewal had certain emotional appeal for labour advocates in the 1880s and had some resolution in the reforms brought in by William Beveridge after 1908; but, as such, these reforms issued more out of utilitarian principles than Ruskin would have approved.[111]

His relative lack of interest in accommodating the economic practices and industrial forms prevalent in most English cities explains in part the failure of his program. He differed from William Morris in not believing that modern technological practices could be modified along craft lines. Even to the extent that Ruskin was primarily interested in rural reconstruction of small unit holders, his vision fell down over what C.F.G. Masterman referred to as the Master's 'extraordinary over-estimate of the possibilities of agriculture in this dismal, wind-swept northern isle of ours'.[112]

While one finds the details of the Guild first articulated in the post-1870 letters of *Fors Clavigera*, those details were themselves a reflection of much that had already been proposed and achieved since the days of his Working Men's College collaboration. While his interest was in education, rural rehabilitation and commercial craft revival, there was no anti-urban bias in principle. The co-operative ethic and the idea that day-to-day management should be in the hands of the participants rather than in those of distant or hidden investing or financing agents, had been well tested by Octavia Hill at the London Marylebone houses and elsewhere. This 'small is beautiful' approach, with its 'green' overtones, suggests that there remains to be considered the larger context of his thought. To what degree did his authoritarian-sounding, state-oriented proposals for legislated reform action actually assume the formal pursuit of substantive purposes by means of the instrumentality of the state? John Gunnell observed that it is usually 'the problem of actualization, the problem of how to transform social behaviour and its institutions in the image of a new vision of order that haunts political theory'.[113] Such was both Ruskin's predicament and preoccupation in the 1870s.

Notes

1. See W.H.G. Armytage, *Heavens Below: Utopian Experiments in England, 1560–1960* (Toronto: University of Toronto Press, 1961), 289–304; Michael H. Lang, *Designing Utopia: John Ruskin's Urban Vision for Britain and America* (Montreal: Black Rose Books, 1993); W. F. Brundage, *A Socialist Utopia in the New South: The Ruskin Colonies in Tennessee and Georgia, 1894–1901* (Urbana: University of Illinois Press, 1996).
2. *Works*, 12: 56.
3. On the context of the 1851 pamphlet and its original text, see *Works*, 12: xlix–lvii; 319–96; for the 1853 lecture, see *Works*, 12: 134–64.
4. *Works*, 5: 340–53.
5. *Works*, 5: 382.
6. *Works*, 5: 382–3.
7. *Works*, 28: 259.
8. *Works*, 29: 498.
9. See Wheeler, (1999), 158–61.
10. See Franco Venturi, *Utopia and Reform in the Enlightenment* (Cambridge: Cambridge University Press, 1971), 114–16.

11. *Works*, 27: 144. 'Kakotopia' stands for the modern term 'dystopia'.
12. *Works*, 27: 115–16.
13. *Works*, 18: lxi–lxiii, 47–8; 27: 250–566.
14. *Works*, 5: 353, 387; 17: 148; 18: 514; 20: 290; 28: 23; 29: 242.
15. *Works*, 27: 113, 117.
16. *Works*, 22: 534; 27:113 n.1; 37: 37:12. See also Dearden (2012), 232; Frederic Seebohn, *The Oxford Reformers* (London: J.M. Dent, 1929), 219–20.
17. In the early days of the New World discovery, just how far-fetched many of these claims were is well reviewed in Lewis Hanke, *Aristotle and the American Indians* (Chicago: Henry Regnery, 1959), Ch. 1.
18. Thomas More, *Utopia*. Translated with an Introduction by Paul Turner (London: Penguin, 1965), 44.
19. Ibid., 42–49.
20. For a close consideration of this issue, see J.H. Hexter, *More's Utopia: The Biography of an Idea* (Princeton: Princeton University Press, 1952), Part 1.
21. Ibid.,
22. More (1965), 108–18; Machiavelli, *The Prince*, Quentin Skinner and Russell Price, eds. (Cambridge: Cambridge University Press, 1988), Ch. 12–14. See also William Urban, *Medieval Mercenaries: The Business of War* (London: Greenhill, 2006), Ch. 12.
23. See Arthur B. Ferguson, *The Indian Summer of English Chivalry* (Durham: Duke University Press, 1960) 169–73.
24. See Appendix 4 of this study, where many of these items are noticed in Ruskin's translation from More.
25. See More (1965), 86–89.
26. More (1965), 101–2; Ruskin, 'Notes on the General Principles of Employment for the Destitute and Criminal Classes' in *Works*, 17: 541–6.
27. *Works*, 17: 541; cf. More (1965), 74–80.
28. See Hexter (1952) and Edward L. Surtz, 'Thomas More and Communism' *PMLA* 64 (3) (1949), 549–564.
29. Alistar Fox, *Thomas More: History and Providence* (New Haven: Yale University Press, 1983), 55–6.
30. J.H. Hexter, *The Vision of Politics on the Eve of the Reformation: More, Machiavelli, Seysse* (New York: Basic Books, 1973), 134.
31. Stutz (1949), 550.
32. *Works*, 27: 115–16; Tierney (1997), 67–73.
33. Ruskin to Ellis, July, 1870, in *Works*, 37:12.
34. *Works*, 28: 23.
35. Benjamin Jowett, *The Dialogues of Plato: Vol. 5. The Laws and Index*. 2nd. ed. (Oxford: Clarendon Press, 1875); For examples of Ruskin's translations see *Fors Clavigera*, Letter 82 (Oct. 1877) in *Works*, 29: 232–46.

36. See Ernest Barker, ed. *The Politics of Aristotle* (Oxford: Oxford University Press, 1958), xiii–xiv.
37. *Works*, 27: lix.
38. *Works*, 27: 328, 482 and 32: xxxii–xxxv. Ruskin drew heavily on Villani's *History of Florence* in *Val D'Arno. Works*, 11 On Gotthelf, see *Works*, 6: 172 and 32: xxxii, 345 f. Gotthelf was a pen name used by the Swiss author, Albert Bitzius.
39. *Works*, 28: 132.
40. The translation was prepared by Julia Firth of Ambleside, a member of the Guild of St. George. *Works*, 32: xxxv.
41. Ibid., xxxii.
42. *Works*, 32: 345.
43. Lewis Mumford, 'Utopia: The City and the Machine' in Frank E. Manuel, ed., *Utopias and Utopian Thought* (Boston: Houghton Mifflin, 1966), 3–24.
44. *Works*, 31: 26–29.
45. See 'War' in The Crown of Wild Olive in *Works*, 18: 459–93.
46. See *A Knight's Faith*, in *Works*, 31: 375–510. Sir Herbert Edwardes (1819–1868) served in India.
47. *Works*, 29: 230.
48. For an informative discussion of the question of the person of special talent and that person's relation to good governance, as understood by Plato and Socrates, see Janet Coleman, *A History of Political Thought* (Oxford: Blackwell, 2000), 1: 102–7. See also *Works*, 18: 499–502.
49. See the detailed discussion in Sherburne (1972), Ch. 6; on Ruskin's views on education for women see Jan Marsh, 'On Sesame and Lilies: Education in a Humane Society' in Deborah E Nord, ed., *Sesame and Lilies: John Ruskin* (New Haven: Yale University Press, 2002), 142–64.
50. Certain aspects of old Florentine Law refer. *Works*, 28: 23–42.
51. *Works*, 17: 89, 168, 499.
52. *Works*, 17: 262–83; J.A. Hobson, *John Ruskin: Social Reformer.* London: James Nisbit and Co. 1898; *Confessions of an Economic Heretic* (Hassocks: Harvester Press, 1976), 38–42; Michael Coyle, 'A Profounder Didacticism: Ruskin, Orage and Pound's Perception of Social Credit', *Paideuma* 17(1) (1988), 7–28; John L. Finlay, *Social Credit: The English Origins* (Montreal: McGill-Queen's Press, 1972), 28–34, 41–43, 78–9.
53. 'War' in the *Crown of Wild Olive*, (1866). *Works*, 18: 459–93.
54. Lewis Mumford, 'Utopia: The City and the Machine' in Manuel, ed. (1966), 3–5.
55. *Works*, 10: 192.
56. See *Works*, 1: It was written in 1841 but not published until 1851.
57. *Works*, 1: 347.

58. See Graham A. MacDonald, 'The Politics of the Golden River: Ruskin on Environment and the Stationary State', *Environment and History*, 18 (2012), 125–50; James S. Dearden, 'The King of the Golden River: A Bio-Bibliographical Study', in Rhodes and Janik (eds.) (1982), 32–59.
59. See Watson (1972), 64–70; *Works*, 30: 5–12; Hilton (2001), Ch. 23.
60. Patrick Armitage, *The Old Guilds of England* (London: Weare and Co. 1918), 98.
61. Antony Black, *Guilds and Civil Society in European Political Thought from the Twelfth Century to the Present* (Ithica: Cornell University Press, 1984), Ch. 6; Armitage, (1918); Gervase Rosser, *The Art of Solidarity in the Middle Ages: Guilds in England, 1250–1550* (Oxford: Oxford University Press, 2015).
62. Armitage (1918), Chs. 2–3.
63. Ibid., 40–42.
64. Ibid., 52, 154.
65. Ibid., 120.
66. Francis Bacon, *Works*, II, 232, cited in J.H. Hexter, 'Storm over the Gentry' in *Reappraisals in History* (Evanston: Northwestern University Press, 1961), 144. See also J.P. Cooper, *Land, Men and Beliefs: Studies in Early-Modern History* (London: Hambledon Press, 1983), Ch. 4.
67. See David Blaug, 'The Myth of the Old Poor Law and the Making of the New', *Journal of Economic History*, 23 (2) (1963), 151–84; J.R. Poynter, *Society and Pauperism: English Ideas on Poor Relief, 1795–1834* (London: R. and K. Paul. 1969).
68. A widely discussed contribution to this literature appeared in 1975. See J.G.A. Pocock, *The Machiavellian Moment: Florentine Political Thought and the Atlantic Republican Tradition.* With a new Afterword. (Princeton: Princeton University Press, 2003); see also Cesare Vasoli, 'The Machiavellian Moment: A Grand Ideological Synthesis' *The Journal of Modern History, (*49) 4 (1977), 661–70; J.H. Hexter, *On Historians* (Cambridge: Harvard University Press, 1979), Ch. 6.
69. Black (1984), 39–40, 81; Brian Tierney, *Religion, Law and the Growth of Constitutional Thought, 1150–1650* (Cambridge: Cambridge University Press, 1982), 87–88; Cary J. Nederman, *Lineages of European Political Thought: Explorations along the Medieval/Modern Divide from John of Salisbury to Hegel* (Washington DC: Catholic University Press of America, 2009), Ch. 12; Shelley Burtt, *Virtue Transformed: Political Argument in England, 1688–1740* (Cambridge: Cambridge University Press, 1992).
70. Armitage (1918), Ch. 2; Black (1984), 58–65; Rosser (2015), 71–78.
71. Tryggvi J. Oleson, *The Witengamot in the Reign of Edward the Confessor* (Toronto: University of Toronto Press, 1955), 110–13; Frank Stenton, *Anglo-Saxon England*, Third ed. (Oxford: Clarendon Press, 1971), 545–55.

72. Ernst Kantorowicz, *The King's Two Bodies: A Study in Medieval Political Theology* (Princeton: Princeton University Press, 1957), 3–6; R. L. Schuyler, and C. C. Weston, eds., *Cardinal Documents in British History* (New York: Van Nostrand, 1961), 78–81.
73. See J.C. Holt, *Magna Carta*, 2d ed. (Cambridge: Cambridge University Press, 1992), Ch.4.
74. Robert Hewison, 'Notes on the Construction of the Stones of Venice', in Rhodes and Jenik, eds., (1982), 138–40.
75. *Works*, 16: 137; 17: 346, 432; 27: 248.
76. Ruskin to Norton, Feb. 10, 1863, in Charles Eliot Norton, ed. *Letters of John Ruskin to Charles Eliot Norton* (Boston: Houghton Mifflin, 1904), I: 134–37.
77. *Works*, 6: 449; 10: 359, 400–1; 11: 129–31; and see Pocock (2003), 66–80, 550–51.
78. *Works*, 23: 112, 157; 27: 15–18, 267–70, 295–6.
79. On Hawkwood, see Christopher Starr, *Medieval Mercenary: Sir John Hawkwood of Essex* (Essex: Essex Record Office 2007).
80. Johann Huizinga, *The Autumn of the Middle Ages* (Chicago: University of Chicago Press, 1996), Ch. 3.
81. See Shelagh Bond, *St. George's Chapel: Windsor Castle* (London: Pitkin Pictorials, 1973), 3; P.J. Begent and H. Chesshyre, T*he Most Noble Order of the Garter: 650 Years* (Spink and Son Ltd. 1999).
82. See also Jonathan Good, *The Cult of Saint George in Medieval England* (Woodbridge, Suffolk: The Boydell Press 2009).
83. William Allingham's *Diary*, March 6, 1876, (Fontwell: Centaur Press, 1967), 245.
84. Just how chaotically this often turned out has been well documented in Mark Frost. *The Lost Companions and John Ruskin's Guild of St George: A Revisionary History*. London: Anthem Press, 2014).
85. 'Abstract of the Objects and Constitution of St.George's Guild' (1877), Clause 4. *Works*, 30: 4.
86. *Works*, 27: 328, 482; 35: 391–2.
87. Cited in Edith Hope Scott, *Ruskin's Guild of St. George* (London: Methuen, 1931), 3; and see *Works*, 30: 3–12, 58–9.
88. *Works*, 27: 328, 482; 35: 391–2. Details of suggested Guild procedures and the first members are described in Catherine W. Morley, *John Ruskin: Late Work, 1870–1890* (New York: Garland, 1984), and see Scott, (1931).
89. Ruskin to Cowper, 4 Aug. 1871, in Bradley, ed. (1964), 314.
90. *Works*, 28: 263–4.
91. *Works*, 28: 436–7
92. Scott (1931), 3.
93. These same artworks have come under scrutiny by a few twentieth-century commentators. See Quentin Skinner, *Ambrogio Lorenzetti: The*

Artist as Political Philosopher (London: The British Academy, 1985); Nicolai Rubinstein, 'Political Ideas in Sienese Art', *Journal of the Warburg and Courtauld Institute*, 21(1958), 197–207; Judith N. Shklar, *The Faces of Injustice* (New Haven: Yale University Press, 1990), 45–47, 102–6.

94. Ruskin knew Froude's recent study of St. Hugh of Lincoln published in *Fraser's Magazine* in 1870 as 'A Bishop of the Twelfth Century'. This was reprinted in the second volume of Froude's *Short Studies on Great Subjects* (London: Longman's Green, 1907).
95. *Works*, 31: xvii, xix, 30. Both men came to serve Ruskin over his remaining years, Wedderburn as one of his main editors and Collingwood as secretary and biographer. On Collingwood, see Vicky Albritton, and Fredrik A. Jonsson, *Green Victorians: The Simple Life in John Ruskin's Lake District* (Chicago: University of Chicago Press, 2016), Ch. 6.
96. It became a last-minute necessity to substitute the word 'Guild' for 'Company' because, under the act, an organization which was not capable of declaring a dividend could not be called a company.
97. Gill Chity, '"A great entail": the historic environment', in Wheeler, ed. (1995), 102–22. See also Phillip Hoose, *Building an ark: Tools for the preservation of natural diversity through land protection* (Washington DC: Island Press, 1981).
98. On Guild of St. George land at Barmouth, Wales and its designation in 1895 as the first holding of the National Trust, *Dinas Oleu*, see www.ipcvision.com/page01/page14/natt-01.htm; On Ruskin and the National Trust, see *Works*, 30: xxx–xxxi; H.D. Rawnsley, *Ruskin and the English Lakes* (Glasgow: James MacLehose, 1902), Ch. 5; E.T. Cook, *The Life of Ruskin* (London: George Allen and Unwin), 2: 575–6; Chitty, (1995), 113–22.
99. Peter Wardle and Cedric Quayle, *Ruskin and Bewdley* (St. Albands: Brentham Press, 1989), 3–11; Stuart Eagles, *After Ruskin: The Social and Political Legacies of a Victorian Prophet, 1870–1920* (Oxford: Oxford University Press, 2011), 232–261.
100. *Works*, 28: 45–6; and see W.H.G. Armytage, *Heavens Below: Utopian Experiments in England, 1560–1960.* (London: Routledge and Kegan Paul, 1961), 289–304.
101. For recent commentaries, see Eagles, (2011), Ch. 4, and Frost (2014).
102. Cited in Armytage (1961), 293.
103. Armytage (1961), 290.
104. Frost (2014), 142–45.
105. Robert Hewison, *Art and Society: Ruskin in Sheffield, 1876* (London: Brentham Press, 1979), 19–22; Janet Barnes, *Ruskin in Sheffield* (Sheffield: Sheffield Art Department, 1985), 5.
106. Frost (2014), 97.

107. Cited in Armytage (1961), 301; Works, 30: 330–35. See also Sue King, *A Weaver's Tale: The Life and Times of the Laxey Woollen Industry, 1860–2010* (Laxey: St. George's Woollen Mills Ltd. 2010), 28–33.
108. See Anthony Harris, *Why Have our Our Little Girls Large Shoes? Ruskin and the Guild of St. George* (London: Brentham Press, 1985); Eagles, (2011), Ch. 4.
109. Brundage, (1996); Isaac Broome, *The Last Days of the Ruskin Cooperative Association* (Chicago: Charles H. Kerr, 1902).
110. Charles A. Beard, 'Ruskin and the Babble of Tongues', *The New Republic* (Aug. 5, 1936), 369–71.
111. E.F. Hennock, *The Origins of the Welfare State in England and Germany, 1850–1914* (Cambridge: Cambridge University Press, 2007), Chs. 11, 12, 16; José Harris, *William Beveridge: A Biography* (Oxford: Clarendon Press, 1977), 471–2.
112. G.F.G. Masterman, 'Ruskin the Prophet' in J.H. Whitehouse, ed. *Ruskin the Prophet: and Other Centenary Studies* (London: Allen and Unwin, 1920), 52–3.
113. John G. Gunnell, *Political Theory: Tradition and Interpretation* (Cambridge: Winthrop Publishers, 1979), 149.
114. Footnote references to Ruskin's writings (unless otherwise stated) are cited as *Works,* and refer to Cook, Edward T. and Wedderburn, Alexander, eds. *The Collected Works of John Ruskin.* London: 1903–1912. 39 v.

Bibliography[114]

Albritton, Vicky, and Fredrik A. Jonsson. 2016. *Green Victorians: The Simple Life in John Ruskin's Lake District.* Chicago: University of Chicago Press.

Allingham, William. 1967. *Diary.* Fontwell: Centaur Press.

Armitage, Patrick. 1918. *The Old Guilds of England.* London: Weare and Co.

Armytage, W.H.G. 1961. *Heavens Below: Utopian Experiments in England, 1560–1960.* Toronto: University of Toronto Press.

Barker, Ernest, ed. 1958. *The Politics of Aristotle.* Oxford: Oxford University Press.

Barnes, Janet. 1985. *Ruskin in Sheffield.* Sheffield: Sheffield Art Department.

Beard, Charles A. 1936. Ruskin and the Babble of Tongues. *The New Republic,* 369–71, August 5.

Begent, P.J., and H. Chesshyre. 1999. *The Most Noble Order of the Garter: 650 Years.* London: Spink and Son Ltd.

Black, Antony. 1984. *Guilds and Civil Society in European Political Thought from the Twelfth Century to the Present.* Ithica: Cornell University Press.

Blaug, David. 1963. The Myth of the Old Poor Law and the Making of the New. *Journal of Economic History* 23 (2): 151–184.

Bond, Shelagh. 1973. *St. George's Chapel: Windsor Castle.* London: Pitkin Pictorials.

Bradley, J.L., ed. 1964a. *The Letters of John Ruskin to Lord and Lady Mount-Temple*. Columbus: Ohio State University Press.

———., ed. 1964b. *Ruskin: The Critical Heritage*. London: R and K. Paul.

Broome, Isaac. 1902. *The Last Days of the Ruskin Cooperative Association*. Chicago: Charles H. Kerr.

Brundage, W.F. 1996. *A Socialist Utopia in the New South: The Ruskin Colonies in Tennessee and Georgia, 1894–1901*. Urbana: University of Illinois Press.

Burtt, Shelley. 1992. *Virtue Transformed: Political Argument in England, 1688–1740*. Cambridge: Cambridge University Press.

Coleman, Janet. 2000. *A History of Political Thought*. 2 vols. Oxford: Blackwell.

Cook, Edward T. 1911. *The Life of Ruskin*. 2 vols. London: George Allen and Unwin.

Coyle, Michael. 1988. A Profounder Didacticism: Ruskin, Orage and Pound's Perception of Social Credit. *Paideuma* 17 (1): 7–28.

Dearden, James. 2012. *The Library of John Ruskin*. Oxford: Oxford Bibliographical Society.

Eagles, Stuart. 2011. *After Ruskin: The Social and Political Legacies of a Victorian Prophet, 1870–1920*. Oxford: Oxford University Press.

Ferguson, Arthur B. 1960. *The Indian Summer of English Chivalry*. Durham: Duke University Press.

Finlay, John L. 1972. *Social Credit: The English Origins*. Montreal: McGill-Queen's Press.

Fox, Alistar. 1983. *Thomas More: History and Providence*. New Haven: Yale University Press.

Frost, Mark. 2014. *The Lost Companions and John Ruskin's Guild of St George: A Revisionary History*. London: Anthem Press.

Froude, James A. 1907. *Short Studies on Great Subjects*. 5 vols. London: Longman's Green.

Good, Jonathan. 2009. *The Cult of Saint George in Medieval England*. Woodbridge: The Boydell Press.

Gunnell, John G. 1979. *Political Theory: Tradition and Interpretation*. Cambridge: Winthrop Publishers.

Hanke, Lewis. 1959. *Aristotle and the American Indians*. Chicago: Henry Regnery.

Harris, José. 1977. *William Beveridge: A Biography*. Oxford: Clarendon Press.

Harris, Anthony. 1985. *Why Have Our Little Girls Large Shoes? Ruskin and the Guild of St. George*. London: Brentham Press.

Hennock, E.F. 2007. *The Origins of the Welfare State in England and Germany, 1850–1914*. Cambridge: Cambridge University Press.

Hewison, Robert. 1979. *Art and Society: Ruskin in Sheffield, 1876*. London: Brentham Press.

Hexter, J.H. 1952. *More's Utopia: The Biography of an Idea*. Princeton: Princeton University Press.

———. 1961. *Reappraisals in History*. Evanston: Northwestern University Press.
———. 1973. *The Vision of Politics on the Eve of the Reformation: More, Machiavelli, Seysse*. New York: Basic Books.
———. 1979. *On Historians*. Cambridge, MA: Harvard University Press.
Hilton, Tim. 2001. *John Ruskin: The Later Years*. New Haven: Yale University Press.
Hobson, J.A. 1898. *John Ruskin: Social Reformer*. London: James Nisbit and Co.
———. 1976. *Confessions of an Economic Heretic*. Hassocks: Harvester Press.
Holt, J.C. 1992. *Magna Carta*. 2d ed. Cambridge: Cambridge University Press.
Hoose, Phillip. 1981. *Building an Ark: Tools for the Preservation of Natural Diversity Through Land Protection*. Washington, DC: Island Press.
Huizinga, Johann. 1996. *The Autumn of the Middle Ages*. Chicago: University of Chicago Press.
Jowett, Benjamin. 1875. *The Dialogues of Plato: Vol. 5. The Laws and Index*. 2nd ed. Oxford: Clarendon Press.
Kantorowicz, Ernst. 1957. *The King's Two Bodies: A Study in Medieval Political Theology*. Princeton: Princeton University Press.
King, Sue. 2010. *A Weaver's Tale: The Life and Times of the Laxey Woollen Industry, 1860–2010*. Laxey: St. George's Woollen Mills Ltd.
Lang, Michael H. 1993. *Designing Utopia: John Ruskin's Urban Vision for Britain and America*. Montreal: Black Rose Books.
MacDonald, Graham A. 2012. The Politics of the Golden River: Ruskin on Environment and the Stationary State. *Environment and History* 18: 125–150.
Machiavelli, Niccolo. 1988. In *The Prince*, ed. Quentin Skinner and Russell Price. Cambridge: Cambridge University Press.
Manuel, Frank E., ed. 1966. *Utopias and Utopian Thought*. Boton: Houghton Mifflin.
More, Thomas. 1965. *Utopia*. Trans. Paul Turner. London: Penguin.
Morley, Catherine W. 1984. *John Ruskin: Late Work, 1870–1890*. New York: Garland.
Nederman, Cary J. 2009. *Lineages of European Political Thought: Explorations Along the Medieval/Modern Divide from John of Salisbury to Hegel*. Washington, DC: Catholic University Press of America.
Nord, Deborah E., ed. 2002. *Sesame and Lilies: John Ruskin*. New Haven: Yale University Press.
Norton, Charles Eliot, ed. 1904. *Letters of John Ruskin to Charles Eliot Norton*. 2 vols. Boston: Houghton Mifflin.
Oleson, Tryggvi J. 1955. *The Witengamot in the Reign of Edward the Confessor*. Toronto: University of Toronto Press.
Pocock, J.G.A. 2003. *The Machiavellian Moment: Florentine Political Thought and the Atlantic Republican Tradition*. With a New Afterword. Princeton: Princeton University Press.

Poynter, J.R. 1969. *Society and Pauperism: English Ideas on Poor Relief, 1795–1834.* London: R. and K. Paul.
Rawnsley, H.D. 1902. *Ruskin and the English Lakes.* Glasgow: James MacLehose.
Rhodes, Robin E., and Del I. Jenik, eds. 1982. *Studies in Ruskin: Essays in Honour of Van Akin Burd.* Athens: Ohio University Press.
Rosser, Gervase. 2015. *The Art of Solidarity in the Middle Ages: Guilds in England, 1250–1550.* Oxford: Oxford University Press.
Rubinstein, Nicolai. 1958. Political Ideas in Sienese Art. *Journal of the Warburg and Courtauld Institute* 21: 197–207.
Schuyler, R.L., and C.C. Weston, eds. 1961. *Cardinal Documents in British History.* New York: Van Nostrand.
Scott, Edith Hope. 1931. *Ruskin's Guild of St. George.* Introduction by Michael Sadler. London: Methuen.
Seebohn, Frederic. 1929. *The Oxford Reformers.* London: J.M. Dent.
Sherburne, James Clark. 1972. *John Ruskin and the Ambiguities of Abundance: A Study in Social and Economic Criticism.* Cambridge, MA: Harvard University Press.
Shklar, Judith N. 1990. *The Faces of Injustice.* New Haven: Yale University Press.
Skinner, Quentin. 1985. *Ambrogio Lorenzetti: The Artist as Political Philosopher.* London: The British Academy.
Starr, Christopher. 2007. *Medieval Mercenary: Sir John Hawkwood of Essex.* Essex, Essex Record Office.
Stenton, Frank. 1971. *Anglo-Saxon England.* 3rd ed. Oxford: Clarendon Press.
Surtz, Edward L. 1949. Thomas More and Communism. *PMLA* 64 (3): 549.
Tierney, Brian. 1982. *Religion, Law and the Growth of Constitutional Thought, 1150–1650.* Cambridge: Cambridge University Press.
———. 1997. *The Idea of Natural Rights.* Grand Rapids: William B. Eerdman's.
Urban, William. 2006. *Medieval Mercenaries: The Business of War.* London: Greenhill.
Vasoli, Cesare. 1977. The Machiavellian Moment: A Grand Ideological Synthesis. *The Journal of Modern History* 49 (4): 661–670.
Venturi, Franco. 1971. *Utopia and Reform in the Enlightenment.* Cambridge: Cambridge University Press.
Wardle, Peter, and Cedric Quayle. 1989. *Ruskin and Bewdley.* St. Albands: Brentham Press.
Watson, Francis. 1972. The Devil and Mr. Ruskin. *Encounters* 38 (6): 64–70.
Wheeler, Michael, ed. 1995. *Ruskin and Environment: The Storm Cloud of the Nineteenth Century.* Manchester: Manchester University Press.
———. 1999. *Ruskin's God.* Cambridge: Cambridge University Press.
Whitehouse, J.H., ed. 1920. *Ruskin the Prophet: And Other Centenary Studies.* London: Allen and Unwin.

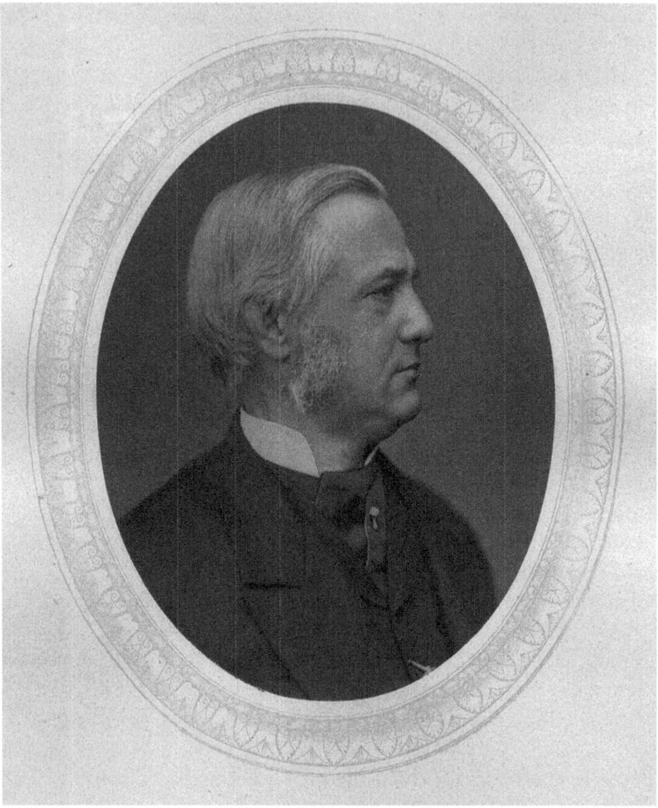

Fig. 7.1 Friedrich Max Müller (1823–1900). Born in Germany and trained as a linguist, Müller came to England in 1846. From the collections of the East India Company, he made translations of the great Indian Classics. He and Ruskin met at Oxford and became friends, Müller doing much to expand Ruskin's cultural horizons. Credit: Woodbury Process photograph by Samuel Lock and George Whitfield. 1878

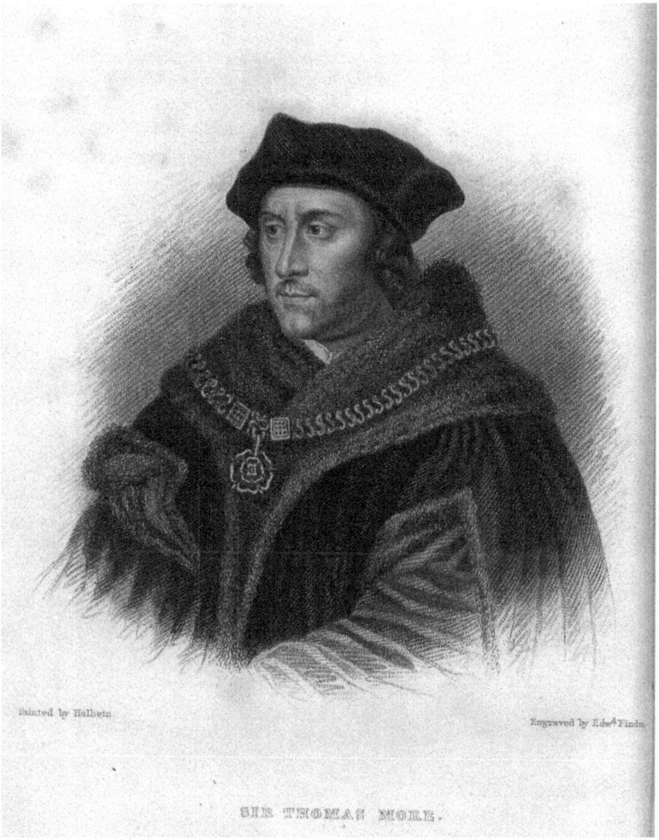

Fig. 7.2 Sir Thomas More (1478–1535). This famous Roman Catholic and Humanist scholar refused to acknowledge Henry VIII as the rightful head of the Church in England and was beheaded for treason. He authored many works, including *Utopia*, that influenced the political thought of many, including Robert Southey and Ruskin. Credit: Robert Southey, Sir Thomas More. London: John Murray, 1831

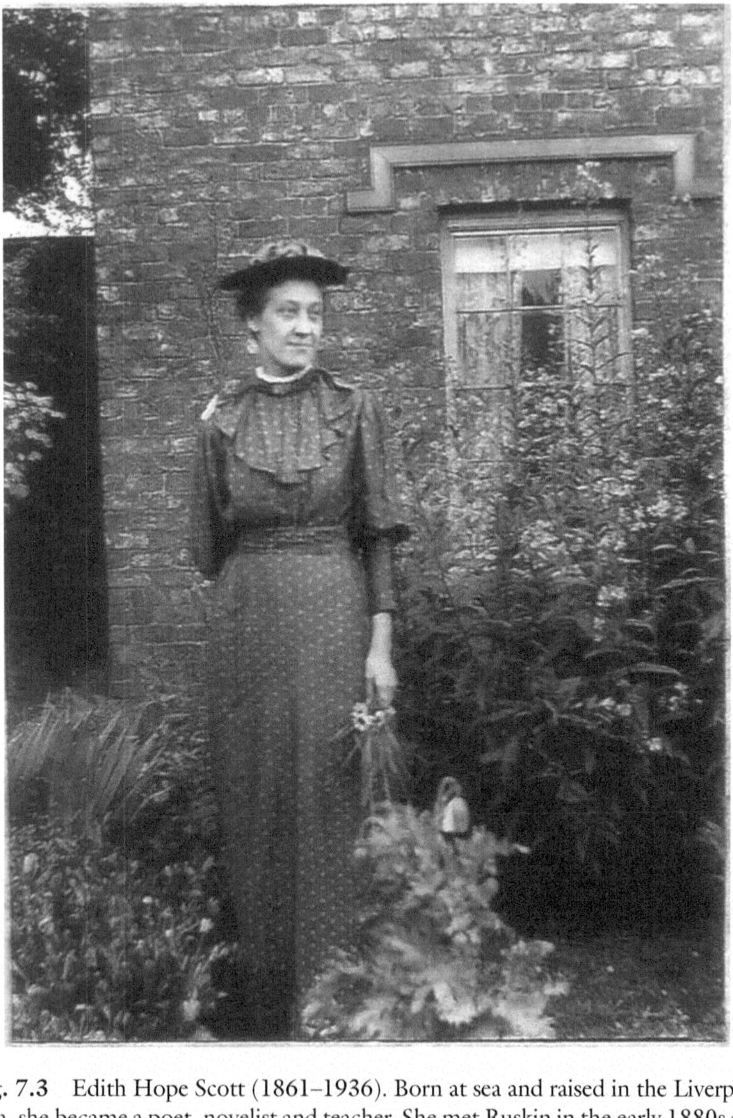

Fig. 7.3 Edith Hope Scott (1861–1936). Born at sea and raised in the Liverpool area, she became a poet, novelist and teacher. She met Ruskin in the early 1880s and became one of the early members of the Guild of St. George. She published *Ruskin's Guild of St. George* in 1931. Credit: Courtesy: Thomas Stapledon, Liverpool, UK

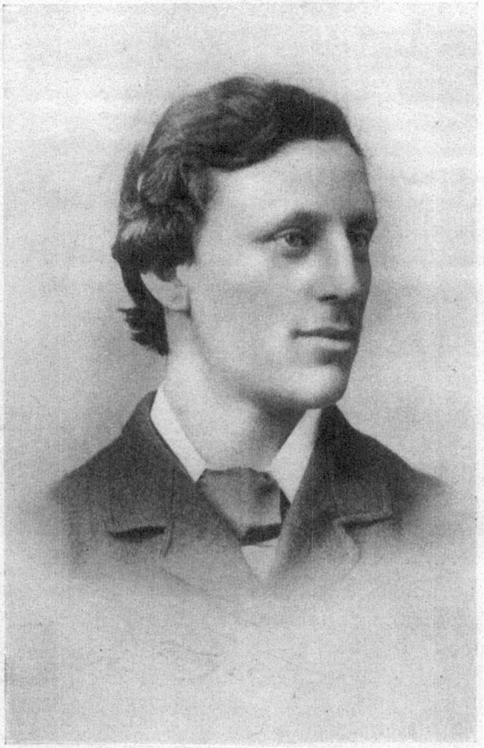

Fig. 7.4 Arnold Toynbee (1852–83). One of the Hinksey road-diggers, Toynbee bore a striking resemblance to his famous uncle, historian Arnold J. Toynbee. His contributions to English history and political life were cut short but survive at Toynbee Hall, founded in East London in his honour in 1884. Ruskin's letters to him and to his father reveal the great regard in which he was held. Credit: Gertrude Toynbee, Reminiscences and Letters of Joseph and Arnold Toynbee. London: Henry J. Glaisher, 1900

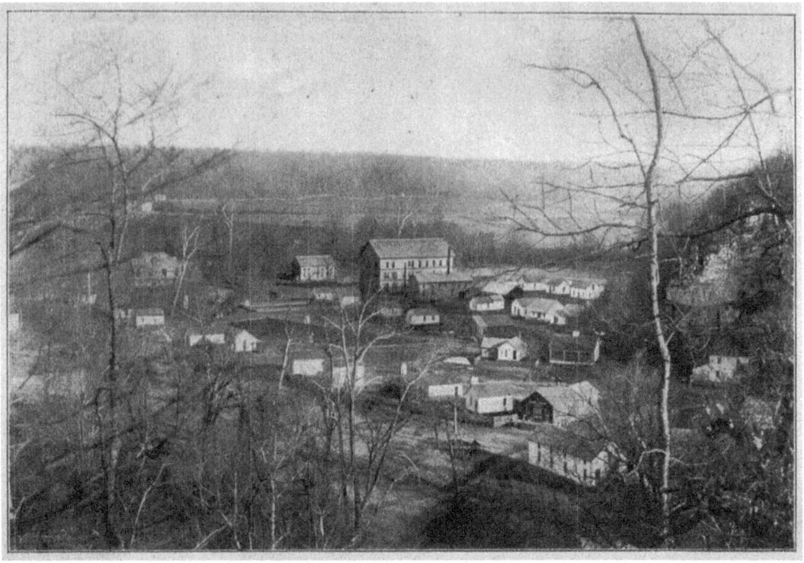

Fig. 7.5 The last of Ruskin, Tennessee. c. 1898. Most of the experimental communities in North America founded in Ruskin's name were short lived, including the Ruskin Cooperative Association in Tennessee, which lasted only between 1894 and 1899. Credit: Isaac Broome, The Last Days of the Ruskin Cooperative Association. Chicago: Charles H. Kerr and Company. 1902

CHAPTER 8

The Condition of Political Virtue: Co-operative Individualism and Civil Association

The best Party is but a kind of a Conspiracy against the rest of the Nation.
—George Seville, Marquess of Halifax Maxims (1700)

I

The modes of human experience of main interest to Ruskin concerned art, literature, history, religion, science, and political economy. The regular outcomes of these practices he measured by means of practical and moral yardsticks. From a philosophical point of view, Ruskin considered all knowledge to be, in part, moral knowledge and this view was first given systematic expression in his writings on art. For critical readers of his time, this moral quality was not always the most admirable or convincing feature of his work but his style appealed to just as many who found in regular sermons and religious 'tracts' satisfactory moral guidance.[1] The more precise degrees of understanding and knowledge sought by philosophy were of little importance to him as opposed to the improvement of human conduct achieved by regular attention paid to the moral content of these various modes of experience. The extent to which philosophy was important at all was a result of its practical accessibility and he claimed that he found all he needed in Sydney Smith's lectures on moral philosophy.[2] The constant punctuation of his writings with apposite Biblical quotations were by way of practical moral illustrations rather than invocations to seek salvation or endorsements of sectarian preference. They were appeals to a 'wisdom

G. A. MacDonald, *John Ruskin's Politics and Natural Law*,
https://doi.org/10.1007/978-3-319-72281-8_8

literature' of uncommon power.[3] In his debate with Maurice in the early 1850s, Ruskin contended that distinctions between the 'visible' and 'invisible' church were of no great substance if what was of real concern was a person's steady conduct as measure of faith.[4]

A lack of interest in philosophical precision set him apart from Carlyle, despite the warmth of the personal relationship. Carlyle's interest in German metaphysics and in the work of James Hutchison Stirling, the great importer of Hegel into England, found no echo in Ruskin beyond those detected submerged in his descriptive methods by R.G. Collingwood.[5] The road to improved human conduct was not through excessive ratiocination or by the pursuit of world historical schemes. It was found through adherence to the inherited routines and steady self-improvement fostered by work and study, faithfully exercised in a context of legal norms. The good life was one of balanced actions and pursuits in a local situation, undisturbed by dreams of social mobility and restless preoccupation with 'getting on'. In looking about mid-Victorian England, he did not see much that endorsed this vision, but rather much excess wealth in too few hands, unhealthy cities and widespread poverty and shortages of essentials.[6] In one of his most caustic images of the attitudes of the more prosperous members of the commercial class, he reminded his readers of the passage in Matthew about the importance of each 'bearing the cross' when it comes to charity. This idea has been '*exactly* reversed by modern Protestantism, which sees in the cross, not a furca to which it is to be nailed; but a raft on which it, and all its valuable properties are to be floated into Paradise'.[7]

By the 1870s, Ruskin had come to the view that the conditions of political virtue were recognizable and achievable, in the first instance, by local organizations committed to an appreciation of the moral content of all human activity and the beauty of that which was near at hand. To say that was not to say that such a condition was easily achieved. Informed in 1874 that a group of English Cistercians at St. Bernard's Monastery in Leicestershire were working land on St. George's principles, he replied that it was all very well, but getting some Monks to work co-operatively was one thing, but getting a representative group of the English to do so, quite another.[8]

The first requirement for active political virtue, then, was that of a satisfactory co-operative local condition, sanctioned in a specified number of ways by charter and oath. The St. George program was considered conducive to the flourishing of good lives. It was a vehicle for the cultivation of healthy, but not virtuosic, individualism. While a certain amount of attention might be paid to community of goods, the primary condition of political virtue was not an inherently communistic condition as might be realized in the more rigorous procedures of religious orders or sects such as the *Unitas Fratrum* or a Hutterite community. The Guild was rather more an extension of the classical family estate of Xenophon than of a religious order. 'The Guild' Stuart Eagles observed, 'defined itself against the terms of contemporary political discourse, existing as a society within society'.[9] It was not inherently separatist, however, for its terms acknowledged the need to participate at a second level of political virtue: that imposed by the regular legislative terms of the existing commonwealth. There was to be a ready, if not overly eager, interaction between the membership and the larger economic and political community, but on terms considered acceptable to the Guild and in accord with its charter. This was to be its method of fostering improved political virtue in the terms of current British civil association. To 'alter the laws of England', it was necessary for 'companions' to engage with the larger society and to act as mediators of modernity with respect to its major heads: labour, science, art, religion and political economy.

Arguing for the structure of a medieval-sounding guild may appear both romantic and anachronistic as an approach to political and economic reform of the modern world. The practical realities of his times had been, however, much on his mind since 1857. What, then, may be concluded about the larger context of Ruskin's political thought and the route taken to his final position?

In previous chapters, it has been noticed that his ideas were associated with three main traditions in England: (1) that of Christianized natural law as the basis of an ethical and political system; (2) that of an historically recognized tradition of 'mixed' government; and (3) that of the guild tradition as the ideal basis of local industrial or professional organization. In the first case, he owed much to the pre-Enlightenment Judeo-Christian tradition; in the second and third, he owed more to post-1066 English models of law and guild practice than he did to post-1660 European reform texts concerned with theories of rights and sovereignty.

His embrace of domestic strands of law and organization endorsed two points. The first allowed for a view of individualism much in accord with Classical and Christian Canon law tenets which asserted the dignity of the person. The second stressed those economic and social practices which encouraged co-operation. Through this combination, a more comprehensive view of individualism was entertained by Ruskin, distinct from the Hobbesian competitive striver for personal advantage at the core of the abstract economic man of the orthodox political economists. These more co-operative principles shaped central aspects of life in England before the industrial revolution. Whatever the historical merits of this view, and of the guild as an appropriate vehicle of political virtue, the claims of the legally constituted state of modern England had also to be considered. What were the ways in which Ruskin's guild approach sought to 'alter laws all over England'?

II

The underlying platform of his political and religious outlook was built upon natural law assumptions. Rumours of the passing of natural law as a basis of public ethics and politics have often been heard but just as regularly denied, even by essentially secular theorists of law.[10] Unlike the detailed enquiries of modern philosophers into the existence or non-existence of natural law as a viable doctrine, Ruskin acknowledged the term in a straightforward way. Natural law was something shaped by the larger and incomprehensible workings of the Divine Wisdom.[11] The principle was self-evidently at work in both social and scientific spheres and it amounted to a given in the underpinnings of all worlds of experience. To acknowledge the reality of natural law was to acknowledge the persistence of a universal ordering of things in the midst of perpetual states of change, of that 'being and passing away' so well understood by many of the ancients.[12] If the ultimate nature of this order remained mysterious, the acknowledgement of some kind of external reference point, be it named 'law' or 'God' or 'nature' was essential to the smooth running of any society. On social matters, Ruskin was inclined to refer to the law of God rather than natural law, but on occasion referred to those 'abiding laws obeyed by all nations'.[13]

It followed from this position that terms such as justice, faith, hope and charity represented important ethical elements of the classical and medieval worlds and he argued they should continue to inform the political vocabulary of England. His neglect of Italian Renaissance humanist texts was borne with a good deal of inconsistency given his lively interest in English Renaissance letters and his youthful understanding of the rapid advances in geological and other scientific knowledge. To remain committed to a 'great chain of being' vision of science required considerable feats of mental gymnastics or outright and wilful self-deception. If his position was exaggerated, there was probably no less inconsistency in his position than adhered to other doubters who found it agreeable to remain nominal Christians and who would not have denied the importance of virtue as a social concept.

Despite a lack of interest in systematic philosophy as such, Ruskin's views were somewhat in line with those of the late twentieth-century philosopher, Alasdair MacIntyre, who, in continuing to acknowledge principles of virtue, contended that to speak of morality is either to speak of historical displays of a practice or else of nothing at all: 'Moral philosophies are, before they are anything else, the explicit articulations of the claims of particular moralities to rational allegiance.'[14] The unavoidable daily recognition of diverse moralities in play in contingent situations made the question of public ethics significant for Ruskin. To a professor at his graduation, he had sheepishly confessed his neglect of the scriptures while at Oxford but came away puzzled by the glib response. The professor told him he should not worry about it, for it was no longer a very important matter. Such was the nature of the apathy respecting the importance of traditional public religion in educated England in the 1840s.[15]

Yet, the political organization of that same England still legally reflected the reforms of the Elizabethan and later periods with their theological conventions. Despite political adjustments made in seventeenth century, England's political constitution retained much of the church-state relation in place since the time of Elizabeth. The Crown was still the nominal head of the church. Hooker, as the main spokesman for those reforms, remained a highly valued source of national wisdom. That such an important figure in the Oxford Movement as John Keble should have brought out a new edition of Hooker's *Laws of Ecclesiastical Polity* speaks to how deeply the Tudor traditions still ran.[16]

In the 1840s Ruskin's views also started to become informed by an amalgam of seventeenth-century elements, including Cambridge Platonism, Christian poetic symbolism, and the latitudinarian religious views of certain prominent figures such as Edward Hyde, the Earl of Clarendon, whose works were in the Ruskin family library.[17] Hyde was among those broadening minds accustomed to gather for conversation at Great Tew.[18] The poets of Ruskin's preference from this period spoke a language steeped in images of virtue, providing continuities with what he saw embedded in late medieval art.

In 1857, remarking upon the virtues illustrated in the 'Good Civic Government' murals in the *Palazzo Pubblico* of Siena, he detected the persisting importance of the conventional virtues mediating a world of perpetual change. These virtues represented the principles of the natural law underlying the contingent events which animated the practices and educational elements of daily late-medieval life. The frescoes of Lorenzetti did not illustrate the emergent abstract 'civic virtue' of the commercially ambitious cities of the later Italian Renaissance but instead older conventional virtues, illustrating the day-to-day fulfilment of obligations required to maintain the organic interstices of a Christian society. Visualized at Siena were the lives of active labourers, of a viable rural-urban symbiosis, and the components of proper moral civil association. Conversely, the frescoes also illustrated the ingredients of social breakdown, when 'bad civic government' prevailed.[19] Ruskin acknowledged Siena and its public art as a reflection of its considerable stability and its constitution under 'the nine', which if not as durable as that of sea-protected Venice, with its aristocratic oligarchy, yet remained impressive.[20] In 1871, Ruskin returned to an analysis of the virtues portrayed in frescos by Giotto in the Arena Chapel in Padua.[21]

The lives and works of many pre-Reformation saints of the church were of interest to Ruskin in his later years, none more so than St. Francis of Assisi. While preparing *The Bible of Amiens* (1885), he consulted illuminated manuscripts and made visits to European sites associated with saintly work. He had already become familiar with the monastery of St. Francis and taken periods of retreat there.[22] In the lectures entitled *Val d'Arno*, ethical statements took the form of natural law utterances rather than sectarian or secular ones. If he made no direct references to John of Salisbury (1120–80), Ruskin's espousal of a more organic, community-based view of social organization was much in keeping with those of Salisbury and of others, such as St. Benedict and St. Bernard of Clairvaux. John of Salisbury's work has been described as partaking of a functional approach to liberty rather than one based on some nascent version of civic liberal individualism.[23] The essence of this 'functional' approach, outlined in his *Policraticus* (c. 1159), combined a recognition of the dignity of the individual and his liberty of conscience with the political claims of the group into which one had been born. Salisbury's effort 'to allow for meaningful individual choice' within a larger context favouring 'a high degree of political cooperation' was, says Nederman, 'perhaps the most striking feature of his argument'.[24]

All three of these directions appealed to Ruskin. The duty of government was to safeguard the doing of justice to the whole population, the members represented by a 'mixed government' of King, Lord and Commons, not the representatives of competing individuals or commercial corporate interests. The crown, or some legitimate ruling authority, was central to such mixed government and Ruskin, as did John of Salisbury, understood that the 'moment government ceases to be the practical enforcement of Divine law, it is tyranny.'[25] Unlike Salisbury, however, Ruskin's creed for the Guild of St. George, did not concede any right of revolution.[26] Years earlier, he had described that crisis moment of anarchy associated with the total breakdown of government and the onset of civil war. All principles of proper civil association are suspended and fate, in the form of the Goddess Atropos, has 'her way with it' by cutting the thread of life.[27] A state of civil war becomes the occasion for a necessary (not always successful) redefinition of the social contract.[28]

> …and when…the corruption and profanity are in the higher instead of the lower orders there arises, first helpless confusion; then, if the lower classes deserve power, ensues swift revolution, and they get it; but if neither the populace nor their rulers deserve it, there follows mere darkness and dissolution, till, out of the putrid elements, some new capacity of order arises, like grass on a grave; if not, there is no more hope, nor shadow of turning, for that nation.

This kind of passage is suggestive with respect to what has been mentioned earlier about Ruskin's view of history and its Vico-like aspects concerning cycles and phases. One of the Hinksey Road diggers was Arnold Toynbee (1852–83). His promise as an historian was cut short but his isolation of the 'Industrial Revolution' as a period concept was indicative of his talent. He had been inspired by Ruskin's attempt to breathe morality back into economics and Toynbee's influence on his peers was considerable.[29] It is curious to notice that Ruskin's occasional articulation of a historical process of 'rise and fall' in the fate of nations bears a resemblance to the more sophisticated version of such a theory employed by Toynbee's famous nephew, Arnold J. Toynbee (1889–1975). His use of the term 'challenge and respose' was an important feature of his large study of global history.[30]

III

For the English, 'good government' has customarily meant forms of 'mixed' government, the components acting in some degree of concert in the genesis of law.[31] This view of a long, if uneven, succession of mixed governments stretching back to Anglo-Saxon times, came under review in the years leading up to the English Civil War and during the following Republican period. King Charles I had, somewhat inadvertently (and certainly ironically), been the first to actually articulate the idea of 'mixed monarchy' as a principle of English government. This came about through what Corinne Weston called his 'vastly influential Answer to the Nineteen Propositions of June, 1642'. If Charles I came to this conclusion only reluctantly, a 'mixed' element had long been a popular and mythical understanding of English history.[32] In his pre-1642 claims to divine right, Charles had made rather too much of his own position. It was not done smoothly, noted Ruskin, for the 'sharp *amusia*' of King Charles and his cavaliers had been 'in grasping at more than the established laws gave them', while Cromwell and his roundheads had been no better.[33]

The re-emergent and visible symbols of the traditions of 'mixed government' gained momentum after the restoration of 1660, although not without much hesitation, violence and a redefinition of its character.[34] The Cromwell period did have lasting effects, England strengthening its growing commercial and imperial ambitions, particularly in Ireland.[35] The continuing alienation of Ireland notwithstanding, the early eighteenth century did see a more pleasing accommodation with Scotland through the 1707 union.

The values of a balanced constitution and limited monarchy found a champion in Lord Bolingbroke, who managed to wed a version of historical 'country' republican virtue to a mythical version of a Patriot King. Like Halifax, he opposed the rise of the influence of Whig party faction around the Court Party.[36] Bolingbroke's position steadily became that of a minority after the death of Queen Anne in 1714. The Whig party came to ever-greater dominance, the vehicle of urban interests and imperial enterprise. There was also an increased rationalism in the air generated from France and Scotland. Sympathetically, the Church of England absorbed some of these moderating influences through its latitudinarianism and inclinations towards social utility.[37] If high and low churchmen had their differences after 1688, their views were close enough for both to find what they needed in Hooker as the continuing justifier of a national church.[38]

There was rather little that attracted Ruskin to eighteenth-century literature outside of certain writings in the Christian tradition, the works of a few favoured authors, such as Pope, Swift and Dr. Johnson, and some relevant works about art.[39] As had Bolingbroke, Ruskin appreciated the attachment to the 'great chain of being' extolled in Pope's *Essay on Man*.[40] With the exception of Dugald Stewart, perhaps, he had not pursued the main works of the philosophers in Scotland. Stewart was a late figure in the Scottish Enlightenment and an important translator of Adam Smith to Victorian England. Ruskin studied his work as an Oxford undergraduate and displayed a certain knowledge of his philosophy in *Modern Painters*. He disagreed with Stewart's view of the imagination and certainly would not have agreed with his liberal optimism about the current direction of European society, of which Stewart took the French Revolution to be an important and positive harbinger. Such as he had helped infect nineteenth-century political economy in those ways to which he objected, for they had made arguments linking wealth with virtue and they contemplated history with a cool and calculating eye.[41] Gibbon, as well, remained something of an acquired taste for Ruskin. The great historian's rational scepticism did not appeal in the first instance although it is clear that Ruskin consulted Gibbon a good deal.[42] It was rather through Homer and Walter Scott that he found persuasive illustrations of the historical interplay of virtue and vice. While he does not appear to have known anything of Vico, his attitude towards history is much in accord with the obscure Neapolitan in his appreciation of large cycles and the importance of a persisting coherence of group moral sensibility in the workings of history.[43] These provided quite different perspectives from those promoted by Enlightenment marchers of mind who tended to see only the need to conquer the folly of the past.[44]

That a society, in its politics, might be characterized as virtuous in some general or secular way, had been argued at great length during the Enlightenment until the idea came tumbling to the ground during the course of the French Revolution and its aftermath. A reprieve for older versions of natural-law-based ethics was granted in the wake of the conservative reaction symbolized by the accomplishments of the Congress of Vienna.[45] If natural law underwent a long secular 'subjective' upgrade by means of the birth of democratic republicanism and the scepticism brought on by new schools of scientific thought, older traditions of natural law still continued to exercise influence well into the late eighteenth century. They re-emerged invigorated, in various forms, after the defeat of Napoleon and the success of Metternich's Congress system and associated pacts sanctioning the 'Holy Alliance'.[46] Lord Castlereagh, the British foreign secretary, thought the Holy Alliance 'a piece of sublime mysticism and nonsense'.[47] The remnants of the national border agreements made under the Congress System were seriously challenged in 1848, but the shadow of 1815 still lurked until the end of Crimean War.[48] The post-1815 conservative reaction to the defeat of Napoleon informed the literature of later romantics such as Southey, now warm to the pragmatic values of tradition and religion as guides to the virtuous life. An Enlightenment legacy of a different order remained, however, in the form of a philosophically radical version of utilitarian ethics and liberal political economy.[49] The tension between these two attitudes continued throughout Victorian times, informing debate, its divisive qualities having been noticed.

In the later twentieth century, arguments were made that the civic arrangements of many cities of Renaissance Italy were the first to reflect a more abstract approach to virtue in ways that were particularly 'republican'.[50] There were no interests which were not public interests and these were best safeguarded by regular citizen 'participation' in politics.[51] Others differed and argued that there had also been continuing attachment to older ideas of virtue developed by means of established forms of social inculcation. Civic virtue issued from individuals trained in the arts of correct behaviour and not in the habits of making regular, allegedly rational, political choices at the polls.[52] Accordingly, by this second account, modern republicanism, born in the midst of an alleged 'Machiavellian moment' by which civic virtue came of age, did not by any means cancel the influence of other versions that carried on under the cloak of aristocratic or more centralized and hierarchical regimes.

In England, Parliament had become a more independent force in law-making by the early nineteenth century, dominated by newer party factions rather than by the old corporate interests of Lords, Commons and the Monarchy, now 'limited'.[53] In Ruskin's eyes, 'mixed government' had suffered in the process after the parliamentary 'winning of the initiative' in the eighteenth century, its effectiveness as a law-making body now reduced, having become a mouthpiece for much self-interested commercial talk.[54] Most evangelical reformers, in the House of Commons or outside of it, he thought cut from the same mistaken *laissez-faire* cloth.[55] The extent to which Parliament remained useful was a reflection of the actual number of members of independent opinion. Despite his many complaints in print against J.S. Mill, Ruskin supported his candidacy for the House, simply because Mill was 'a man of independent opinion'.[56] If he left just what the advantages of electing men of 'independent opinion' somewhat vague, his view resembled Burke's argument that Honourable Members owed virtual representation to all their constituents and not to selected interests. Members were to consult their best judgements on issues before the House and look to the general welfare of the nation.[57]

Persons who grew up influenced by those accustomed to governing and to the art of legislating were better equipped for such positions themselves. Despite current shortcomings, the British aristocratic classes still had much to offer in terms of governing experience. In his correspondence with Thomas Dixon in the 1860s, Ruskin told him that the workers had to develop a capacity for informed opinion before their voices would be worth anything in the House and that this was best done by learning such skills within the walls of their own enterprise associations, governed by their own by-laws, all operating within the scope of the larger laws of the land.[58] The Guild of St. George was established on such premises and despite its operation under a 'Master', the Guild endorsed principles of worker administration and leadership.[59]

By playing down the primacy of Parliament in the political life of the nation in favour of regenerated classes, Ruskin was recalling the imagined organic arrangements of distant medieval communal life. At the heart of such arrangements, suggests Cary Nederman, was 'the claim that the community is…composed neither of individuals nor of citizens, but, rather, of functional groupings or parts, arranged according to the nature of their contribution to the community as a whole'.[60] This appeal in the direction of the medieval was far from perfect, for the workings of Parliament were much different in the twelfth century. Just as certainly, however, Ruskin's embrace of the 'organic' does not really lean in the direction of early twentieth-century versions developed by syndicalists or by proponents of the Italian corporate state.[61] Such recent efforts, limited as they have been, suggest that specified group interests should be represented by blocks within the larger ruling chamber of the nation. These blocks endorsed egalitarian and socialistic principles and might be seen as variations of those sectoral interests or 'party factions' proclaimed by Ruskin to be not the strength but the essential disease afflicting the House of Commons. Social classes were inevitable in Ruskin's mind, but economic groups, politically represented as such, were not the key to the promotion of good lives.

When Ruskin told Lord Cowper-Temple that he hoped to see the Guild of St. George 'change laws all over England', what then was meant? Whatever else, it certainly meant legal change in the long term after an interim flourishing of other similar guilds across the land. The existence of localities in which modest self-sufficiency, healthy entertainments and useful education were achieved would presumably be the source of a new independence of mind in Parliament, minds brought up to distinguish between the abundant and the redundant. Such persons would then champion passage of the kinds of enabling and preventative legislation advocated in *Munera Pulveris* and *Time and Tide*.

Despite being raised in a home of anti-republican views, especially that of the American kind, Ruskin did not have hard preferences about the formal designations of governments. The conventional 'forms' first articulated and analysed by Aristotle (kingship, aristocracy and democracy, along with their corrupted counterparts) were satisfactory as definitions, as far as they went, but were not to be seen as forms with hard boundaries in the psychological sense.[62] Whatever the formal designation, there remained in any well-developed polity an authority endowed with the right to exercise power, a minority endowed with the ability to advise or legislate, and the wider democratic element from which consent, at least in the long term, had to be derived, as a daily support to the established authority.[63]

The post-1688 revised constitutional monarchy of England was the outcome of a history in which ancient principles of mixed government were acknowledged and now revived once again after the failure of Cromwell's republican experiment. This failure was not total, for the republican period had its lasting influences.[64] These were absorbed within the greater cumulative tendency of British national history, with all its violence and variations, perceived to be one favouring monarchy, class stability and a freedom from *ultra montagne* Roman Catholic influence. Historical experience favoured the wisdom of a mixed government capable of digesting the occasionally over-enthusiastic enterprise of rulers or of zealots and their followers.[65]

The question of Ireland and British policy provides a good example of where Ruskin saw the limits to mixed government. His views on Ireland separate him from Carlyle once again. The latter had a high opinion of Cromwell and a low opinion of Ireland, even during the famine.[66] As in Cromwell's time, that debased nation still required, he claimed, ever more draconian measures and certainly no abandonment by England. His contact with 'Young Ireland' was sympathetic only but hardly supportive. For Daniel O'Connell, he had only contempt.[67]

If no great supporter of McConnell's methods, Ruskin was yet in agreement with him that the two Union Acts of 1800 should be cancelled. Ireland was too culturally distinct in its ways and religion to be successfully accommodated in the British House of Commons and under the British Constitution.[68] Ending union would help reduce the need for Catholic revival in England and restore the constitution of both countries to a more viable church-state relation. The cumulative history of bitterness precluded any on-going political bond. From the British point of view, if there had been concerns in the late eighteenth century about the potential threat posed by an Ireland allied with France, this was now greatly diminished.[69] In the 1860s, Ruskin found himself in agreement with J.S. Mill on the Irish land question and reform, enough to say: 'Mill Right at Last'.[70] By the 1880s, however, the situation over land was still not resolved and the long series of Irish coercion acts passed by Parliament since 1801 reached new heights in 1881 with passage of Gladstone's 'Protection of Person and Property Act', an act aimed at curbing actions of the Irish Land League and other reformers.[71]

IV

In Ruskin's crisp little side essay on republicanism sent to his father in 1845 (see Appendix 2), he landed on a point of departure for much that has been considered more recently regarding the role of Italian civic humanism in the development of political practice in Europe and the Americas.[72] Many voices have contributed to this discussion about the purported emergence of secular republican virtue in the modern world.[73] The appearance of a 'subjective' version of civic virtue in the Italian city states was, some have argued, a generalized abstract virtue that flowed out of an ethic favourable towards regular citizen participation in selecting political leaders. This new ethic appeared in the context of what, it has been noticed, Pocock called 'the Machiavellian moment'. This shift in public morals surfaced first in the early Italian Renaissance states by a secularizing of the older Classical-Christian version of human rights of the person into a claim of natural rights of a more abstract and subjective nature. These rights now resided existentially in the individual and were not sourced in older conventions of natural law. Such claims provided the basis for a turn towards arguments favourable to a more regular popular confirmation of the official representatives of the urban civic order, a confirmation bestowed by voting individuals who saw themselves as living vehicles of independent will and choice. The political possibilities were sensed by Machiavelli and these were taken to an extreme form in the work of Hobbes, who attempted to redefine human nature along scientific and behaviourist lines of will and artifice. This new way of thinking, Pocock suggested, was modified in the works of Harrington and Locke, among others, and eventually helped shape a wider form of republican thought which was to have momentous consequences in the United States and France through expanded citizen participation in government.[74] If questions surrounding the emergence of a new ethic of citizen 'participation' in politics and of versions of 'subjective' human rights have made for lively discussion in recent times, others noted the persistence of older notions grounded in natural law and which, by degree, continued to inform governments, including those of the Italian city republics of the fifteenth century.[75]

Ever sceptical of what Renaissance times had to offer by way of social lessons, Ruskin turned away from the direction of its rationalist legacy as manifested in the writings of the eighteenth-century Enlightenment project. Nature's realm remained mysterious and unknowable in its final details, and was ever-changing at the surface, as the early Greek philosophers had contended. There remained only the mysteries of law, the stability underlying all festering historical change.[76]

V

Edward Norman noted that Ruskin was not much interested in contemporary party politics and, indeed, had made no secret of it.[77] After 1854, however, his involvement with Maurice and the 'Christian Socialists' at the Working Men's College went far to convince him that issues of social policy should become his main concern in life. If Ruskin was not always at one with Maurice, or with the more evangelical traits of Christian Socialism, the class-co-operative model of the college and its promotion of education for personal enjoyment, rather than for merely 'getting on', were principles he continued to stress. The term 'socialism' here did not imply an impulse towards state ownership or control, but rather 'socializing' or 'solidarity' between members of different classes in a way appropriate to Christian fellowship.

This has not always been recognized by later commentators. G.B. Shaw, we have seen, interpreted his later political writings as tending towards modern totalitarianism of the Bolshevik variety, in as much as he understood them to favour the centralized political authority of an elite. Shaw certainly appreciated Ruskin's wider cultural contributions but here he may have been attributing to him some of his own Fabian inclinations favouring elite leadership.[78] After World War I, Charles Masterman, a liberal English politician, appears to have agreed with much of Shaw's interpretation.[79] There is nothing, however, to find in Ruskin that would suggest the desirability of a classless society run by a segregated elite dictatorship supposedly drawn from an alleged classless population. Ruskin's local reform model was clearly conceived without prejudice towards the monarchy, a revived aristocracy, or a reactivated Church with Bishops and Clergy hard at work in their regions.[80] In addition, a commercial managerial elite was not to fade away but to remain active, but on a scale of wages, a scale not supplemented by excessive rents. The Soviet model is even less credible in light of the degree to which public religion persisted in Ruskin's thought, despite his own doubts and shifts in belief.[81] This persistence was quite evident throughout his works generally and in the documents guiding the Guild of St. George. No atheists qualified for membership, even though Ruskin regretted imposing such a stricture.[82]

Enhancing or establishing local bodies, such as guilds or special purpose associations, rather than large federated trade unions, was the proper way to advance working-class interests, a process which would help workers develop distinctive voices and opinions.[83] While Parliament was historically important, he saw its deliberative value much diminished under current party domination, each preoccupied with special commercial claims or the protectionist needs of the landed class. Lesser bodies, organized for co-operation, as he had told Dixon, could eventually provide well-informed counterweights to such factionalism. When much of the talk in the mid-1860s was in favour of expanding the franchise, he supported independent-minded people such as J.S. Mill, in their bid to become members of the House of Commons.

This view of Parliament sheds light on his particular view of individualism. Distinct personal identities issue from our birth-right qualities tempered by local forces of habituation within a larger political-economic context of shared values. Religion and ethics were best understood as practices rather than creeds. The regular habit led to such perfection in behaviour as was possible. To be recognized as an individual is to be acknowledged as one who willingly participates in an on-going system of co-operative norms. 'Independence you had better cease to talk of' for you are not only dependent on 'every act of people whom you never heard of' but also on 'every past act of what has been dust for a thousand years'.[84] 'The Nature of Gothic' has long been recognized as an expression of what might be called 'cooperative individualism'.[85] This form of individualism corresponds well with the one described by Antony Black for the late Middle Ages: 'In towns and guilds, the individual asserted his rights against outsiders by his very membership, which gave him "liberty" and defined his social position'.[86] John of Viterbo (c. 1250), suggested that '*civitas* means the citizens liberty, the inhabitants' immunity'.[87] Its antithesis was found in those Renaissance traits which Ruskin and Norton felt had spawned egoistical tendencies encouraging the artist to aspire to the status of virtuoso instead of craftsman, or the citizen to look only to his own perceived self-interests. Therein lay the origins of modern atheism and anti-social political views.[88] Ruskin's view contrasts somewhat with Burke, who, in Jesse Norman's account, leaned more strongly towards a position of 'liberal individualism'.[89]

VI

After Ruskin's appointment to the Slade Professorship, his earlier analysis of social ills was reinforced by environmental stewardship considerations. In 1871, he informed the press that 'the first thing the king of any country has to do is to manage the streams of it'.[90] Passages from his main treatise on science, *The Eagle's Nest* (1872), have a distinctly twentieth-century ring.[91]

> ...the misuse we made of our discoveries will be remembered against us in eternal history; our ingenuity in the vindication or denial of species will be disregarded in the face of the fact that we destroyed, in civilized Europe, every rare bird and secluded flower; our chemistry of agriculture will be haunted with the memories of irremediable famine; and our mechanical contrivance will only make the age of the *mitrailleuse* more abhorred than that of the *guillotine*.

His late treatise on geology echoed this passage, although, somewhat implausibly, he stated that in 'all of his earlier writings on the origin of sculpture and mountain form' he had connected such efforts 'with the practical hope of arousing the attention of the Swiss and Italian mountain peasantry to an intelligent administration of the natural treasures of their woods and streams.'[92] It is unlikely that any of Ruskin's past geological writings were known to any of the 'peasantry' of this quarter.

The theme of 'stewardship' as a public virtue had, however, found its way into the economic writings by his reflections on the proper nature of human consumption. Europeans were, in his view, expending far too much labour and energy in the pursuit of non-economic objectives, particularly in the case of war industries.[93] Desirable environmental values, as objects of policy, could be stated plainly: 'Pure Air, Water and Earth' are three of the six 'chiefly useful things to be got by political economy'.[94] With much classical reference, he informed his fellow citizens that they had transformed 'the Mother Earth, *Demeter* into the Avenger Earth, *Tisiphone*,' by turning 'every river of England into a common sewer, so that you cannot so much as baptize an English baby but with filth'.[95]

The post-1860 writings proved inspirational to progressive urban planners, conservationists and architects such as Patrick Geddes, Ebenezer Howard and Frank Lloyd Wright. All saw connections with their own advocacy of greenbelt cities and improved stewardship of public and private lands.[96] A general concern for social stability rather than for the promotion of undisciplined economic growth links these diverse consumption schools of thought. From this point of view, there may be noticed the rather unexpected affinity of some of Ruskin's views with those of John Stuart Mill. The men overlapped considerably with respect to what Mill termed 'the stationary state' and on history, education and the reform of electoral representation in Parliament. The brief outline of 'the Stationary State' given in Mill's *Principles of Political Economy* (1848) asks: to 'what ultimate point is society tending by its industrial progress?'[97] Mill was sure that previous economists understood that economic growth cannot be endless and that a point of stability must be reached. To the extent that economists grasped this point, they nevertheless found it an 'unpleasing and discouraging prospect' for they continued to endorse only principles of the progressive state, by which Mill meant an expansionist economy.[98] The gloomiest version of this 'prospect' had been rendered by the Rev. Thomas Malthus in his now famous reflections on population and the notion that certain natural 'checks' would periodically keep human numbers stable, notably famine, warfare and disease. Despite later adjustments, his work remained rooted in a nervous Calvinist outlook that life in society was dark.[99] Other economists took a marginally brighter view, that population was best controlled by utilitarian policies administered through institutions such as the Workhouse and by emigration.[100] Such policies, we have seen, were criticized by Southey and Wordsworth as seriously misguided and neglectful of the traditions of Christian morality and duty.[101]

Much of the back-to-the-land impulse in Ruskin is to be explained by the strong anti-urban bias marking his work. He had come to politics for reasons directly connected with his Dickensian reading of nineteenth-century social conditions. In *Fors Clavigera*, he protested that Europeans were busy assaulting fresh air 'so as to bring such a pestilence on the globe as would end all of you'. Indeed, the 'horrible nests, which you call towns' are but 'laboratories for the distillation into heaven of venomous smokes and smells, mixed with effluvia from decaying animal matter and infectious miasmata from purulent disease'.[102] Against this modern inferno, he urged revival of the guild traditions of old rural parish England rather than the civic communes of Italy and Germany. His encounter with the world of the industrial revolution was essentially negative, although his guild did have a presence in London, Sheffield and Laxey on the Isle of Man. Rural reconstruction, however, remained the main objective. W.G. Masterman later attributed much of the guild's failure to Ruskin's 'extraordinary over-estimate of the possibilities of agriculture in this dismal, wind-swept northern isle of ours'.[103] It is not surprising, perhaps, that people living in the wider spaces of the new world proved more amendable to the rural character of his ideas, if with only short-lived success.[104]

The anti-urban bias notwithstanding, his emphasis on a scaled-down approach to consumption and on raising questions of quality of life, pointed to later twentieth-century concerns with the viability of an ever-expanding economy and the associated idea of 'limits to growth' and steady-state economics.[105] The close student of urban history, Lewis Mumford, contended that Ruskin was 'the first economist to express the realities of energy income and living standards in relation to production' and that his 'grasp of consummatory and creative functions, neglected by the monetary economists, makes him – despite frequent solecisms – the fundamental economist of the biotechnic order'.[106]

VII

The role of co-operation in the reform of society was often touched upon by Ruskin after 1848. An example of his hopes for the Guild's influence on practical industry was realized through the actions of George Thompson, who registered his woollen factory at Huddersfield under the Friendly Societies Act and then 'introduced welfare, pension and profit-sharing schemes for his workers'. Ruskin wrote to him about the 'momentous and absolutely foundational step taken by you in all that is just and wise, in the establishment of these relations with your workmen'.[107] Thompson became the third Master of the Guild of St. George in 1909 and during his tenure maintained a somewhat Ruskinian policy towards worker relations and projects.[108]

The guild's influence on the later Guild Socialism movement was limited, for the impulse behind the latter was syndicalist and oriented to worker control over a given industry, accompanied by nationalization of resources. Such tendencies would have been too levelling and egalitarian for Ruskin to endorse, little in keeping with his views on the need for the independence of industry and retention of the control of property in private hands, except in special circumstances.[109] Nor was his guild totally in line with the objectives of the 'cooperative movement' in England, although there were certain points of contact such as the idea of local groups producing their own food.[110] The Guild of St. George, like Robert Owen's model of community, aimed at promoting a localized road to the good life in which co-operation was the broad guiding principle. The co-operative movement in England was, on the other hand, more utilitarian in its concern with lowering consumer prices and improved ways of distribution at local and national levels but less concerned with the nature of the products themselves, their quality, or the terms of production. In short, the Guild of St. George was about the promotion of a comprehensive local social condition in which the individual found a satisfying place among kindred spirits of differing talents and capacities. They were united by a disposition to value things and persons in their proper place. It was composed of persons voluntarily participating in a legally constituted enterprise association functioning within a larger system of national legislation. Its political economic practices, however, contrasted strongly with that self-regarding 'possessive individualism' which supposedly had come to animate much of the larger social and economic life of England after the time of Hobbes, a way of life to which the party-oriented legislators in Parliament were, in Ruskin's estimate, vastly over-committed.[111] The 'cooperative individual' then, was a unique, full-blooded and contented personality, not the restless and Faustian individual identified with the persona of the 'economic man' posed by the promoters of Victorian political economy and whose spokesmen were well represented in Victorian parliaments.[112]

VIII

Ruskin did not use the term 'distributive justice' in his works but the idea was clearly implicit in many statements, beginning with that concerning 'the first duty of a state' and also the well-known Biblical phrase used as a title: '*Unto This Last*'. Necessary resources, facilities and cultural opportunities were to be made available to all, if not in equal amounts, at least in adequate amounts. Owing to his aristocratic conservatism and hostility to *laissez-faire* economic theory, Ruskin's influence on the emergence of the twentieth-century British welfare state was often recognized as relevant but rather limited in scope.[113] His condemnations of the legal conventions which guided the actions of 'the conventional plutonomy' (as Frederic Harrison phrased it) were better appreciated by 1900, for by then *Unto This Last* had sold in the tens of thousand, unlike the slow sales of the early 1860s.[114] His practical proposals, however, remained distinctly out of keeping with current reform tendencies. José Harris has observed that William Beveridge, in advancing the cause of the welfare state in England, had actually thought more in terms of 'the social service state' and that such a citizen-participatory model bore certain Ruskinian traits.[115] The distinction is a subtle one, perhaps, from the vantage point of the twenty-first century, but the difference between the well-organized centralized bureaucratic welfare state and alternative ways of providing 'services' will be kept in mind here when considering Ruskin's proposals.

In 1857, reflecting on the experience of revolutionary France, Ruskin did not object to the solidarity claims made on behalf of universal 'fraternity' but insisted on preserving room for the other implied elements of this image: 'paternity' and, by implication, 'maternity'.[116] Thus, he spoke of the importance of introducing the 'paternal' element into the laws of the land and of allowing for 'preventative' and 'enabling' measures as checks upon the customary *laissez-faire* measures so much favoured by parliamentarians.[117] This family-oriented language allowed him to speak a good deal about obedience as a virtue of personal conduct. In his ill-advised efforts to manage his guild he frequently demonstrated, in his dealings with individuals, the shortcomings of his obsession with obedience.[118] It is clear, however, that his local 'authoritarianism' found its pedigree in forms of conduct more common to the Middle Ages or the classical world of Xenophon.

While Ruskin often gave reason enough for readers to call into question his dogmatic pronouncements about who should do what, where and why, there is, in fact, little to find in his more general principles notions which were not in line with British law and traditional practices. First, his understanding of authority reflects those conservative precepts which acknowledge that the power of present rulers and officers of government have been authoritatively sanctioned and acknowledged by citizen subscribers from day to day. The forms of government may have altered over time, but government remained 'authoritative' if recognized to be so by the general consent demonstrated by daily behaviour.[119] The periodic labour restlessness in England in the first half of the nineteenth century demonstrated the inherently conservative quality of most English radical movements, an indication of how normative English attitudes remained, across all class lines, with respect to the legitimacy of the home government.[120]

Ruskin's appeal to medievalism was not a search for a vanished way of life but a call to reanimate well-established medieval group principles which still informed the constitution: King, Lords, Church and Commons. In calling for a strengthening of the underlying class components, he opposed them to the representation in Parliament by party-oriented commercial interests. The late guild experiment was a demonstration that 'small' was not only 'beautiful' but also 'traditional'. The local procedures and social composition of the parish provided a more suitable matrix for reform than the centralizing procedures of 1834, so insisted upon by their designers.[121] 'Sir,', said Chadwick to Playfair, 'the devil himself was expelled from paradise for opposing centralization.'[122] Fifty years later, the ancient local forms of administration came under even firmer attack with passage of the Local Government Act of 1888. Another contrarian of the day lamented the situation, if with much less interest in the 'medieval' as such. England was 'drifting towards a type of government associated with terrible events – a single Assembly armed with full power over the constitution'.[123]

When asked about the source of traditional authority in politics, Ruskin's response was that it was to be found in the larger ground representing all that customarily goes on in societies. To be an 'authoritarian' was merely to be one who acknowledges the legitimacy of the authority exercised under current rules and ruler-ship, those rules a reflection of the daily conduct of society as a whole.[124] Authority existed through the repeating recognition of the bonds of an obligatory moral relationship between citizens and those who govern on their behalf. When this implicit co-operation of consent between governors and governed erodes, a state of nascent anarchy was said to be unfolding.[125] Those signing the Creed of the Guild of St. George were not to claim, therefore, a right to revolt by violent means when confronted by serious injustice but rather to commit themselves to resist such error by firm but peaceful means.

Proper civic behaviour, like religious behaviour, was learned behaviour, not the result of some individualized recourse to ratiocination arbitrated by an innate 'moral sense'.[126] Politics was 'doing' as was religion. It was the 'practice' and not the 'proclamation' which led to social stability and the understanding of the recurring requirements of justice. Following Plato, he held that early education and the training in harmony were the essential requirements of the citizen gaining an appreciation for the importance of justice in all dealings.[127] In considering the heavenly circle of Venus in the 'Paradiso' section of *The Divine Comedy*, Gervase Rosser summarizes for us how Dante and his late friend, Charles Martel, converse over the question of citizenship, its character and importance. 'Now say, would it be worse for man on earth were he no citizen?' asks Martel. Dante replies in the affirmative. The two are surrounded by the well-co-ordinated dancing spirits of the 'Amorous', not the ones of the previously lustful, but those who were motivated by true *caritas*. In their dancing, they now represent the image of the well-functioning society. The related Aristotelian idea is that citizens are to be active in their given roles according to their diverse capacities, each helping compose a community under recognized law.[128] The community is the guardian of individuals of differing capacities who all have a claim to be safeguarded by the law, not a claim to be allowed to develop an untrammelled individuality which goes its own way. Hence, as we have seen, was the importance for Ruskin of music in fundamental education and citizenship.[129] The image of justice, derived from the 'Wisdom of Solomon', Ruskin had also borrowed from the 'Paradiso' for his own purposes in *Unto This Last*: '*Diligite Iustitiam, Qui Judicatis Terram*'—'Love righteousness ye that are judges of the earth.' The geographical unit of the parish, rather than the long-reach of some anonymous central office of state, seemed a more likely place for the provision and continuity of appropriate education and of any needed substantive social services. Here was the proper crucible for the generation of good lives and that sense of individualism which flourishes through co-operative action. 'Some muscular bonding through dance and song' was, says McNeill, 'an important cement for human communities in times past'. Ruskin, if romantically, urged renewed attention to such daily details.[130]

What remains, then, of the instrumental Ruskinian state announced with some force in *The Political Economy of Art* and *Time and Tide*? The claim, in *The Stones of Venice*, that there was a 'first duty of government' to provide for certain substantive conditions of the population and for the healthy maintenance of its national environment, was made largely with reference to the importance of the enacting of sound enabling and preventative legislation at the national level. While there are passages in Ruskin which support the idea of direct government action by bureaucratic entities, there is little said in detail about them and little about their desirability except in the last resort. He does describe circumstances when such should be brought into play. The thrust of his late works is mainly towards amending local arrangements for provision of most essential functions outside of defence, although there remained a local role for defence. Schools, public works or health and welfare facilities, provided from the centre, might, be required in special circumstances of remoteness or a lack of viable alternatives. Formal state-sponsored organizations seem to be emergency organs of least preference in Ruskin, as opposed to his expectations of what should be better undertaken at the local level and by co-operative means. At the time of his death, however, English conservatives, liberal and labourites, alike, were on a much different track, even if many now read him with renewed interest.

What was that track? In the late 1950s, Noel Annan asked about 'the curious strength of positivism in English political thought' in the nineteenth century.[131] He linked this persistence to the admiration for 'scientific method' endorsed by so many. Frederick Harrison was a fine example of such a person as was John Stuart Mill, all promoting a version of Comptian progress or the virtues of individualism. A few economists, such as William Smart or Alfred Marshall, as well as the young Hegelians at Oxford, such as Bradley, T.H. Green and the young Toynbee, stood out as contrarian harbingers for a new historical sociology which in the early twentieth century started to dismantle positivist assumptions.[132] Ruskin, although not interested in such labels, was yet a stimulant to such broader historical sociological thought, and certainly was an early source for that higher idealist philosophy of the twentieth century that survived the famous attack made upon it by Bertrand Russell and G.E. Moore.[133] One hears an echo of Ruskin in Marshall's caution that once essential goods have been provided to all, any subsequent preoccupation with the steady provision of other less necessary items or pursuits risks becoming the enemy of good distribution and a source of social erosion.[134] That most exotic of the Hinksey Road builders, Oscar Wilde, characteristically, put it more wittily in *The Soul of Man Under Socialism*: 'Property not merely has duties, but has so many duties that its possession to any large extent is a bore.'[135] Ruskin was beyond hearing those words from 1891 and certainly could do nothing to help his ill-starred student, who died in the same year as his Master. He probably would have agreed with the general tone of Wilde's remarks, adding that there was, in fact, a pleasure attending those duties associated with the use and preservation of things which properly belonged to all, things which 'availed towards life'. Part of that duty involved the selection of leaders, and that was ultimately a task enjoining the joyous cultivation of sacred music among the population, for there lay the start of the road leading towards good rulers capable of warding off the scissoring actions of *Atropos.*

Notes

1. For critical reactions to Ruskin's works, see Bradley, ed. (1984), 34–195. On the importance of sermons and tracts in Victorian England, see George P. Landow, *The Aesthetic and Critical Theories of John Ruskin* (Princeton: Princeton University Press. 1971) Ch. 4; Dinah Birch, 'Ruskin's Multiple Writing: *Fors Clavigera*' in Birch, ed. (1999), 179.
2. *Works*, 34: 565; and see Sydney Smith, *Elementary Sketches of Moral Philosophy* (New York: Harper and Bros. 1850).
3. See Michael Wheeler, *Ruskin's God* (Cambridge: Cambridge University Press, 1999).
4. *Works*, 12: 529–32.
5. R.G. Collingwood, *Ruskin's Philosophy* (Kendal: Titus Wilson, 1922).
6. See Ruskin's essay 'Traffic' in *The Crown of Wild Olive*. *Works*, 18: 433–58.
7. *The Bible of Amiens* (1885), *Works*, 33: 112.
8. *Works*, 27: 45–46.
9. Stuart Eagles, *After Ruskin: The Social and Political Legacies of a Victorian Prophet, 1870–1920* (New York: Oxford University Press, 2011), 53.
10. See H.A.L. Hart, *The Concept of Law* (Oxford: Oxford University Press, 1961), 193–200, and the supplementary essays in A.P. d'Entrèves, *Natural Law: An Introduction to Legal Philosophy*. (New Brunswick: Transaction Publishers, 1994); and Michael B. Crowe, *The Changing Profile of the Natural Law* (The Hague: Martinus Hijhoff, 1977), 275–77.
11. *Works*, 8: 71.

12. Aristotle credited Zeno with this important insight of stability in the midst of change. See Shirley Letwin, 'Nature, History and Morality' in R.S. Peters, ed., *Nature and Conduct* (London: Macmillan, 1975), 230.
13. *Works*: 28:30.
14. Alasdair MacIntyre, *After Virtue*, 3rd ed. (Notre Dame: Notre Dame University Press, 2007), 268.
15. *Works*, 11: 133. On the question of apathy, see Edward Alexander, *Matthew Arnold, John Ruskin and the Modern Temper* (Columbus: Ohio State University Press, 1973), Ch. 3.
16. On the uses of Hooker in England, see Lee W. Gibbs, 'Richard Hooker's *Via Media* Doctrine of Scripture and Tradition', *Harvard Theological Review*, 95 (2) (2002), 40–70.
17. James Dearden, *The Library of John Ruskin* (Oxford: Oxford Bibliographical Society, 2012), 73.
18. On 'Great Tew', see H.R. Trevor-Roper, 'The Great Tew Circle', in his *Catholics, Anglicans and Puritans: 17th Century Essays* (London: Secker and Warburg, 1987), 166–230.
19. *Works*, 16: 54–56; see the detailed discussions of these frescoes in Rubinstein (1958), 179–207, Skinner (1985), and Starn (1994).
20. See William M. Bowsky, *A Medieval Commune: Siena under the Nine, 1287–1355* (Berkeley: University of California Press, 1981).
21. *Works*, 27: 79–198. See also section six of *Mornings in Florence*, for Ruskin's treatment of Giotto and the virtues portrayal in the Shepherd's Tower in Florence. *Works*, 23: 409–35.
22. See *Works*, 23: xlvii; 26, 225; 33: xxii.
23. Cary J. Nederman, 'Freedom, Community and Function: Communitarian Lessons of Medieval Political Theory', *American Political Science Review*, 86 (4) (1992), 977–86.
24. *Ibid*., 980.
25. *Works*, 16:105.
26. See Cary J. Nederman, 'A Duty to Kill: John of Salisbury's Theory of Tyrannicide', *Review of Politics*, 51 (1988), 365–89; see Appendix 3 of this study for the text of the Creed of the Guild of St. George.
27. *Works*, 17: 235. Ruskin drew attention to Hesiod's account of the three cloth-weaving sisters of fate, Clotho, Lachesis and Atropos, in the last volume of *Modern Painters*. *Works*, 7: 394.
28. *Works*, 17: 235; and see Michael Oakeshott, *On Human Conduct* (Oxford: Oxford University Press, 1975), 146–7.
29. Francis C. Montague, *Arnold Toynbee* (Baltimore: John Hopkins University, 1889), 14; E.T.Cook, *The Life of Ruskin* (London: George Allen and Unwin, 1911), II: 191.

30. See H. F. Kearney, 'Arnold Toynbee: Challenge and Response', *University Review*, 1 (4) (1955), 33–41; William H. McNeill, *Arnold J. Toynbee* (New York: Oxford University Press, 1989), 286–88.
31. Frederick W. Maitland, *The Constitutional History of England* (Cambridge: Cambridge University Press, 1913), 6; Tryggvi J. Oleson, *The Witengemot in the Reign of Edward the Confessor* (Toronto: University of Toronto Press, 1955), 110–13; J.G.A. Pocock, *The Ancient Constitution and the Feudal Law*, 2nd ed. (Cambridge: Cambridge University Press, 1987), Ch. 2.
32. Corine C. Weston, *Subjects and Sovereigns: The Grand Controversy over Sovereignty in Stuart England* (Cambridge: Cambridge University Press, 1981), 3; and R.L. Schuyler and Corine C. Weston, *Cardinal Documents in British History* (New York: Van Nostrand, 1961), 78–81.
33. *Works*, 29: 263.
34. Robert S. Bosher, *The Making of the Restoration Settlement: The Influence of the Laudians, 1649–1662* (London: Dacre Press, 1957); Doreen J. Milne, 'The Results of the Rye House Plot and Their Influence upon the Revolution of 1688', *Transactions of the Royal Historical Society* 5th Series, 1 (1951), 91–108.
35. See Philip P. McKeiver, *A New History of Cromwell's Irish Campaign* (Manchester: Advance Press, 2007).
36. See Shelley Burtt, *Virtue Transformed: Political Argument in England, 1688–1740* (Cambridge: Cambridge University Press, 1992), 87–98; Isaac Kramnick, *Bolingbroke and His Circle: The Politics of Nostalgia in the Age of Walpole* (Cambridge: Harvard University Press, 1968), 30–36; Quinton (1978), 41–44.
37. Aspects of this rationalizing element are well explored in Basil Willey, *The Eighteenth Century Background* (London: Chatto and Windus, 1940). See also Creed and Boys-Smith, (1934).
38. George Every, *The High Church Party, 1680–1718* (London: S.P.C.K. 1956), Ch. 1.
39. *Works*, 27: 586 n; 35: 61,151. For reviews of Ruskin's knowledge of eighteenth-century texts and art, see Henry Ladd, *The Victorian Morality of Art* (New York: Ray Long and Richard R. Smith Inc. 1932), Ch. 4, and Landow (1971), 98–105.
40. Kramnick (1968), 222; *Works*, 16: 446–7.
41. See the essays in, Istvan Hont and Michael Ignatieff, eds., *Wealth and Virtue: The Shaping of Political Economy in the Scottish Enlightenment* (Cambridge: Cambridge University Press, 1986).
42. Particularly when writing *The Bible of Amiens* and *Our Fathers Have Told Us*. See *Works*, 33, and Dearden (2012), 129.

43. See the essay on Vico by Isaiah Berlin in *The Crooked Timber of Humanity* (London: Fontana Press, 1991), 49–69.
44. The influence of Scott on Ruskin was significant. Of many uncompleted works, a biography of Scott was one, towards which he had accumulated much material. See *Works*, 13: 446; 34: 305; 27: 531, 561–621. On the nature of the tension in eighteenth-century Enlightenment thought, see Jonathan Israel, *A Revolution of the Mind: Radical Enlightenment and the Intellectual Origins of Modern Democracy* (Princeton: Princeton University Press 2010), Chapters 5 to 7.
45. See Harold Nicolson, *The Congress of Vienna* (London: Constable, 1948), 276–77.
46. Peter Stanlis, *Edmund Burke and the Natural Law* (Ann Arbor: Michigan State University Press, 1965), Ch. 3.
47. Mark Jarrett, *The Congress of Vienna and its Legacy: War and Great Power Diplomacy after Napoleon* (London: I. B. Tauris, 2013), 173.
48. René Albrecht-Carrié, *A Diplomatic History of Europe since the Congress of Vienna* (New York: Harper, 1958), 65–68, 84–106.
49. See John Plamenatz, *The English Utilitarians* (Oxford: Basil Blackwell, 1966), Chaps. 4–8; Elie Halévy, *The Growth of Philosophic Radicalism* (Boston: Beacon Press, 1955), 313–72.
50. J.G.A. Pocock, *The Machiavellian Moment: Florentine Political Thought and the Atlantic Republican Tradition.* With a new Afterword. (Princeton: Princeton University Press, 2003); Hans Baron, 'The Florentine Revival of the Philosophy of the Active Political Life' in: *In Search of Florentine Humanism: Essays in the Transition from Medieval to Modern Thought* (Princeton: Princeton University Press, 1988), 134–57.
51. Pocock (2003), 383–400, and Antony Black, *Guilds and Civil Society in European Political Thought from the Twelfth Century to the Present* (Ithica: Cornell University Press, 1984), 147–50.
52. Alisdair MacIntyre, (2007), Ch. 15; Ruskin, *Works*, 16: 55–57. See Appendix 2 of this study.
53. Richard Pares, *Limited Monarchy in Great Britain in the Eighteenth Century* (London: The Historical Association, London, 1971).
54. *Works*, 17: 327, 331; 34: 159. See Wallace Notestein, 'The Wining of the Initiative by the House of Commons' in Lucy S. Sutherland, ed., *Studies in History* (London Oxford University Press, 1966), 145–203.
55. *Works*, 17: 404; 23: 353; 27: 649. On the affinity of much evangelical opinion with laissez-faire economic thought in the first half of the nineteenth century, see A.M.C. Waterman, *Revolution, Economics and Religion: Christian Political Economy, 1798–1833* (Cambridge: Cambridge University Press, 1991), Chapters. 5, 6; Boyd Hilton, *The Age of Atonement: The Influence of Evangelicalism on Social and Economic*

Thought, 1785–1865 (Oxford: Clarendon Press, 1986), Ch. 2; Richard Brent, 'God's Providence: Liberal Political Economy as Natural Theology at Oxford, 1825–1862', in Bentley, ed. (1993), 85–107.

56. *Works*, 18: 550.
57. See Edmund Burke, 'Speech to the Electors of Bristol' 3 Nov. 1774. *Works of Edmund Burke*, (Boston, Wm. Estes, 1889) 1:446–48. It is not clear whether Ruskin ever read Burke's speech.
58. *Works*, 17: 325–26.
59. See *Works*, 29: 137; 30: xxxiii, 8–9. That Ruskin did not always adhere to his own principles in this regard has been made clear in Mark Frost, *The Lost Companions and Ruskin's Guild of St. George* (London: Antham Press, 2014).
60. Nederman, (1992), 978.
61. See Charles Gide and Charles Rist, *A History of Economic Doctrines* (Boston: D.C. Heath, 1915), 479–83, 641–2; Rudolf Rocker, Anarcho-Syndicalism (London: Pluto Press, 1989), Ch. 3; Bob Holton, *British Syndicalism, 1900–14: Myths and Realities* (London: Pluto Press, 1976).
62. On Aristotle's initial classifications, see Barker, ed., *The Politics of Aristotle* (London: Oxford University Press, 1958), 11.
63. See his early reflections on such principles in Ruskin to J.J. Ruskin, 1845, *Works*, 36: 55–57, reproduced in Appendix 2 of this study. See also *Works*, 12: 550–54.
64. See Bosher (1957).
65. *Works*, 12: xxiii, 527n; 28: 469.
66. See J. A. Froude, *Carlyle's Life in London* (New York: Charles Scribner's 1884), I: 338–43.
67. See Thomas Carlyle, *My Irish Journey in 1849.* J.A. Froude, ed. (New York: Harper Bros. 1882). This work was not published in Carlyle's lifetime but was brought together by Froude from Carlyle's original notes. See also Fred Kaplan, *Thomas Carlyle: A Biography* (Ithaca: Cornell University Press, 1983), Ch. 13; Julie M. Dugger, Black Ireland's Race: Thomas Carlyle and the Young Ireland Movement' *Victorian Studies*, 48 (3) (2006), 461–85.
68. For Ruskin's views on Ireland, see *Works*; 8: 267–69; 9: 423–24; 18: 173–74; 29: 403–4; and see Sherburne (1972), 204–5.
69. On the motives of those who promoted the Union Acts of 1800, see Alan J. Ward, *The Irish Constitutional Tradition: Responsible Government and Modern Ireland, 1782–1992* (Dublin: Irish Academic Press, 1994), 20–29; on Anglo-French relations after 1830, see Norman Gash, *Aristocracy and People:Britain, 1815–1865* (Cambridge: Harvard University Press, 1979), 292–3.

70. *Works*, 17: 443–45. Ruskin was referring to Mill's pamphlet *England and Ireland* (1867).
71. See Philip Bull, *Land, Politics and Nationalism: A Study of the Irish Land Question* (Dublin: Gill and Macmillan, 1996), 54–93.
72. See Appendix 2 of this study.
73. Cf. Baron (1988); Quentin Skinner, *The Foundations of Modern Political Thought: Volume One: The Renaissance* (Cambridge: Cambridge University Press, 1978); Pocock (2003).
74. Pocock (2003), 392–95.
75. Black (1984), 81–83; Tierney (1997), Ch. 13; Nederman (2009), 52–3.
76. See Letwin, (1975), 230.
77. E.R. Norman, *The Victorian Christian Socialists* (Cambridge: Cambridge University Press, 1987), 134; *Works*, 27: 14–15; 29: 337.
78. On Fabian interest in Ruskin, see Edith J. Morley, *John Ruskin and Social Ethics*. Fabian Tract No. 179. (London: Fabian Society, 1917).
79. C.F.G. Masterman, 'Ruskin the Prophet' in W.H. Whitehouse, ed. *Ruskin the Prophet*. (London: George Allen and Unwin, 1920), 51; Lucy Masterman, *C.F.G. Masterman* (London: Nicolson and Watson, 1939), 314–15.
80. *Works*, 18: 381.
81. Norman (1987), 124–25. The author, however, underestimates the importance that Ruskin gave to a revived national church as a factor in public policy.
82. *Works*, 28: 420n.
83. 'John Ruskin and the Working Classes in Mid-Victorian Britain', in Keith Hanley, and Brian Maidment, eds. *Persistent Ruskin: Studies in Influence, Assimilation and Effect*. Surrey: Ashgate, 2013), 15–32.
84. *Works*, 27: 50.
85. This suggested expression contrasts with what C.B. MacPherson described as 'possessive individualism' recognized as the fundamental social ethic of the post-Hobbesian world in England. See MacPherson (1962).
86. Antony Black, 'The Individual and Society' in J.H. Burns, ed., *The Cambridge History of Medieval Political Thought, c. 350-c.1450* (Cambridge: Cambridge University Press, 1988), 591.
87. John of Viterbo, *De Regimene Civitatum*, cited in Black (1988), 591.
88. Ruskin to Norton, 27 Dec., 1872, and Norton to Ruskin, 29 Dec.,1872, in J.L. Bradley, and Ian Ousby, eds. *The Correspondence of John Ruskin and Charles Elliot Norton* (Cambridge: Cambridge University Press, 1987), 270–72.
89. Jesse Norman, *Edmund Burke: The First Conservative* (New York: Basic Books, 2013), Ch. 9.

90. 'Roman Inundations' *The Daily Telegraph*, 12 Jan., 1871, in *Works*, 17: 547.
91. *Works*, 22: 147.
92. *Deucalion*, II in *Works*, 26: 339.
93. See Joan Abse, *John Ruskin: The Passionate Moralist* (New York: Alfred A. Knopf, 1980) 200–01.
94. *Works*, 27: 90–91.
95. *Works*, 27: 92–3.
96. On Geddes, see Francis O'Gorman, 'Ruskin's Science of the 1870s: Science, Education and the Nation', in Dinah Birch, ed., *Ruskin and the Dawn of the Modern* (Oxford: Oxford University Press, 1999), 45–6; Ebenezer Howard, *Garden Cities of Tomorrow* [1904] (Cambridge MA: M.I.T. Press 1965); Meryle Secrest, *Frank Lloyd Wright: A Biography* (New York: Knopf, 1992), 127–30; Rosenberg (1961), 71–76.
97. John Stuart Mill, *Principles of Political Economy: Book IV,* Ch. 6. (Toronto: University of Toronto Press, 1965), 752–57; MacDonald (2012), 125–50; Jonsson (2017), 186–210.
98. *Ibid.*, 752.
99. See Frederick A. Jonsson, 'Island, nation, planet: Malthus in the Enlightenment' in Robert J. Meyhew, ed., *New Perspectives on Malthus* (Cambridge: Cambridge University Press, 2016), 128–152.
100. Mark Blaug, 'The Myth of the Old Poor Law and the Making of the New', *The Journal of Economic History*, 23 (2) (1963), 151–184.
101. Mendilow (1986), Chapters 1 and 2; Craig (2007), Ch 8.
102. *Works*, 27: 91.
103. G.F.G. Masterman, 'Ruskin the Prophet' in Whitehouse, ed. (1920), 52–3.
104. See Isaac Broome, *The Last Days of the Ruskin Cooperative Association* (Chicago: Charles H. Kerr, 1902); W. F. Brundage, *A Socialist Utopia in the New South: The Ruskin Colonies in Tennessee and Georgia, 1894–1901*(Urbana: University of Illinois Press, 1992); Fred Braches, *Charles Whetham: A Remarkable Resident of Ruskin. Whonnock Notes* No. 18. (Whannock, BC: 2012).
105. E.J. Mishan, *The Costs of Economic Growth* (Harmondsworth: Penguin Books Ltd., 1969); Donella H. Meadows, *The Limits to growth: A report for the Club of Rome's Project on the Predicament of Mankind* (New York: Universe Books, 1972); Herman E. Daly, *Steady State Economics*, 2d. ed. (Washington DC: Island Press, 1991).
106. Lewis Mumford, *The Culture of Cities* (Boston: Harcourt, Brace and Co., 1938), 269–72, 542.
107. Spence (1957), 200.
108. Scott (1931), 109–10.

109. *Works,* 17: 438; 29: 494; Margaret Cole, *Beatrice Webb* (New York: Harcourt and Brace, 1946), 132–33.
110. Differences in approach between the independent guild of Ruskin, and others, and the co-operative movement proper, are outlined in, Cole (1946), Ch. 4.
111. As argued in MacPherson (1962); and see *Works,* 17: 285.
112. Examples of such 'cooperative individuals' are described in Peter Wardle and Cedric Quayle, *Ruskin and Bewdley* (St. Albans: Brentham Press, 1989), and in Edith Hope Scott, *Ruskin's Guild of St. George* (London: Methuen, 1931).
113. José Harris, 'Ruskin and Social Reform' in Birch, ed. (1999), 8.
114. See Laurence Goldman, 'Ruskin, Oxford and the British Labour Movement, 1880–1914', in Birch, ed. (1999), 57–8; Alan Lee, 'Ruskin and Political Economy', in Hewison, ed. (1981), 83.
115. Harris (1999) in Birch, ed. (1999), 29–30.
116. *Works,* 16: 22–23.
117. *Works,* 16: 25–26.
118. Frost, (2014).
119. This psychological element is stressed in A.L. Goodhart, *English Law and the Moral Law.* The Hamlyn Lectures, Fourth Series. (London: A. Stevens, 1953), 22–23.
120. See Malcolm I. Thomis and Peter Hold, *Threats of Revolution in Britain, 1789–1848* (Hamdon: Archon Books, 1977), Ch. 1.
121. On the wide range of services provided locally in traditional England, see Tate (1969).
122. Lyon Playfair, *Memoirs and Correspondence* (London: Cassell, 1899), 64.
123. Fitzjames Stephen to Lytton, 6 May, 1880, cited in Donald Southgate, *The Passing of the Whigs, 1832–1886* (London: Macmillan, 1965), xvi.
124. *Works,* 17: 231–33. Cf. the account provided in 'The Authority of the State' in, Michael Oakeshott, *Religion, Politics and the Moral Life,* Timothy Fuller, ed. (New Haven: Yale University Press, 1993), 74–90.
125. *Works,* 17: 75;18: 359, 478.
126. *Works,* 12: 178.
127. *Works,* 17: 75;18: 359, 478; 29: 234–41.
128. Gervase Rosser, *The Art of Solidarity in the Middle Ages: Guilds in England, 1250–1550* (Oxford: Oxford University Press, 2015), 187.
129. For a thoughtful exploration of this theme in more global terms, see William H. McNeill, *Keeping Together in Time: Dance and Drill in Human History* (Cambridge: Harvard University Press, 1995).
130. *Ibid.,* 152.
131. Noel Annan, *The Curious Strength of Positivism in English Political Thought* (London: Oxford University Press, 1959).

132. *Ibid.*, 10–14; F. C. Montague, *Arnold Toynbee* (Baltimore: Johns Hopkins University, 1889), 11–14, 35–45.
133. Annan (1959), 10, and see William M. Johnston, *The Formative Years of R.G. Collingwood* (The Hague: Marinus Nijhoff, 1967), 17–30.
134. Annan (1959), 13.
135. Oscar Wilde, *The Soul of Man Under Socialism* (New York: Humboldt, 1891), 7.
136. Footnote references to Ruskin's writings (unless otherwise stated) are cited as *Works,* and refer to Cook, Edward T. and Wedderburn, Alexander, eds. *The Collected Works of John Ruskin*. London: 1903–1912. 39 v.

Bibliography[136]

Abse, Joan. 1980. *John Ruskin: The Passionate Moralist.* New York: Alfred A. Knopf.

Albrecht-Carrié, René. 1958. *A Diplomatic History of Europe Since the Congress of Vienna*. New York: Harper.

Alexander, Edward. 1973. *Matthew Arnold, John Ruskin and the Modern Temper.* Columbus: Ohio State University Press.

Annan, Noel. 1959. *The Curious Strength of Positivism in English Political Thought.* London: Oxford University Press.

Barker, Ernest, ed. 1958. *The Politics of Aristotle.* London: Oxford University Press.

Baron, Hans. 1988. *In Search of Florentine Humanism: Essays in the Transition from Medieval to Modern Thought.* Princeton: Princeton University Press.

Bentley, Michael, ed. 1993. *Public and Private Doctrine: Essays in British History Presented to Maurice Cowling.* Cambridge: Cambridge University Press.

Berlin, Isaiah. 1991. *The Crooked Timber of Humanity.* London: Fontana.

Bevir, Mark, ed. 2017. *Historicism and the Human Sciences in Victorian Britain.* Cambridge: Cambridge University Press.

Birch, Dinah, ed. 1999. *Ruskin and the Dawn of the Modern.* Oxford: Oxford University Press.

Black, Antony. 1984. *Guilds and Civil Society in European Political Thought from the Twelfth Century to the Present.* Ithica: Cornell University Press.

———. 1988. The Individual and Society. In *The Cambridge History of Medieval Political Thought, c. 350–c.1450*, ed. J.H. Burns, 588–606. Cambridge: Cambridge University Press.

Blaug, Mark. 1963. The Myth of the Old Poor Law and the Making of the New. *The Journal of Economic History* 23 (2): 151–184.

Bosher, Robert S. 1957. *The Making of the Restoration Settlement: The Influence of the Laudians, 1649–1662.* London: Dacre Press.

Bowsky, William M. 1981. *A Medieval Commune: Siena Under the Nine, 1287–1355*. Berkeley: University of California Press.

Braches, Fred. 2012. *Charles Whetham: A Remarkable Resident of Ruskin*, Whonnock Notes No. 18. Whannock: Whonnock Community Association.

Bradley, J.L., and Ian Ousby, eds. 1987. *The Correspondence of John Ruskin and Charles Elliot Norton*. Cambridge: Cambridge University Press.

Broome, Isaac. 1902. *The Last Days of the Ruskin Cooperative Association*. Chicago: Charles H. Kerr.

Brundage, W.F. 1992. *A Socialist Utopia in the New South: The Ruskin Colonies in Tennessee and Georgia, 1894–1901*. Urbana: University of Illinois Press.

Bull, Philip. 1996. *Land, Politics and Nationalism: A Study of the Irish Land Question*. Dublin: Gill and Macmillan.

Burke, Edmund. 1889. *Works of Edmund Burke*. Boston: Wm. Estes.

Burns, J.H., ed. 1988. *The Cambridge History of Medieval Political Thought, c. 350–c.1450*. Cambridge: Cambridge University Press.

Burtt, Shelley. 1992. *Virtue Transformed: Political Argument in England, 1688–1740*. Cambridge: Cambridge University Press.

Carlyle, Thomas. 1882. In *My Irish Journey in 1849*, ed. J.A. Froude. New York: Harper Bros.

Cole, Margaret. 1946. *Beatrice Webb*. New York: Harcourt and Brace.

Collingwood, R.G. 1922. *Ruskin's Philosophy*. Titus Wilson: Kendal.

Craig, David M. 2007. *Robert Southey and Romantic Apostasy: Political Argument in Britain, 1780–1840*. Woodbridge: Boydell Press.

Creed, J.M., and J.S. Boys-Smith. 1934. *Religious Thought in the Eighteenth Century, Illustrated from Writers of the Period*. Cambridge: Cambridge University Press.

Crowe, Michael B. 1977. *The Changing Profile of the Natural Law*. The Hague: Martinus Hijhoff.

d'Entrèves, A.P. 1994. Introduction by Cary J. Nederman. *Natural Law: An Introduction to Legal Philosophy* (Rev. ed.). New Brunswick: Transaction Publishers.

Daly, Herman E. 1991. *Steady State Economics*. 2nd ed. Washington, DC: Island Press.

Dearden, James S. 2012. *The Library of John Ruskin*. Oxford: Oxford Bibliographical Society.

Dugger, Julie M. 2006. Black Ireland's Race: Thomas Carlyle and the Young Ireland Movement. *Victorian Studies* 48 (3): 461–485.

Eagles, Stuart. 2011. *After Ruskin: The Social and Political Legacies of a Victorian Prophet, 1870–1920*. New York: Oxford University Press.

Every, George. 1956. *The High Church Party, 1680–1718*. London: S.P.C.K.

Frost, Mark. 2014. *The Lost Companions and Ruskin's Guild of St. George*. London: Antham Press.

Froude, J.A. 1884. *Carlyle's Life in London*. New York: Charles Scribner's.
Gash, Norman. 1979. *Aristocracy and People: Britain, 1815–1865*. Cambridge, MA: Harvard University Press.
Gibbs, Lee W. 2002. Richard Hooker's *Via Media* Doctrine of Scripture and Tradition. *Harvard Theological Review* 95 (2): 40–70.
Gide, Charles, and Charles Rist. 1915. *A History of Economic Doctrines*. Boston: D.C. Heath.
Goodhart, A.L. 1953. *English Law and the Moral Law*, The Hamlyn Lectures, Fourth Series. London: A. Stevens.
Halévy, Elie. 1955. *The Growth of Philosophic Radicalism*. Trans. Mary Morris. Boston: Beacon Press.
Hanley, Keith, and Brian Maidment, eds. 2013. *Persistent Ruskin: Studies in Influence, Assimilation and Effect*. Surrey: Ashgate.
Harris, José. 1999. Ruskin and Social Reform. In *Ruskin and the Dawn of the Modern*, ed. Dinah Birch, 7–34. Oxford: Oxford University Press.
Hart, H.A.L. 1961. *The Concept of Law*. Oxford: Oxford University Press.
Hewison, Robert, ed. 1981. *New Approaches to Ruskin: Thirteen Essays*. London: Routlege & Keegan Paul.
Hilton, Boyd. 1986. *The Age of Atonement: The Influence of Evangelicalism on Social and Economic Thought, 1785–1865*. Oxford: Clarendon Press.
Holton, Bob. 1976. *British Syndicalism, 1900–14: Myths and Realities*. London: Pluto Press.
Hont, Istvan, and Michael Ignatieff, eds. 1986. *Wealth and Virtue: The Shaping of Political Economy in the Scottish Enlightenment*. Cambridge: Cambridge University Press.
Howard, Ebenezer. 1965. *Garden Cities of Tomorrow [1904]*. Cambridge, MA: M.I.T. Press.
Israel, Jonathan. 2010. *A Revolution of the Mind: Radical Enlightenment and the Intellectual Origins of Modern Democracy*. Princeton: Princeton University Press.
Jarrett, Mark. 2013. *The Congress of Vienna and Its Legacy: War and Great Power Diplomacy After Napoleon*. London: I. B. Tauris.
Jonsson, Frederick A. 2016. Island, nation, planet: Malthus in the Enlightenment'. In *New Perspectives on Malthus*, ed. Robert J. Meyhew, 128–152. Cambridge: Cambridge University Press.
Jonsson, Frederick A. 2017. Political Economy. In *Historicism and the Human Sciences in Victorian Britain*, ed. Mark Bevir, 186–210. Cambridge: Cambridge University Press.
Johnston, William M. 1967. *The Formative Years of R.G. Collingwood*. The Hague: Marinus Nijhoff.
Kaplan, Fred. 1983. *Thomas Carlyle: A Biography*. Ithaca: Cornell University Press.

Kramnick, Isaac. 1968. *Bolingbroke and His Circle: The Politics of Nostalgia in the Age of Walpole*. Cambridge, MA: Harvard University Press.
Ladd, Henry. 1932. *The Victorian Morality of Art*. New York: Ray Long and Richard R. Smith Inc.
Landow, George P. 1971. *The Aesthetic and Critical Theories of John Ruskin*. Princeton: Princeton University Press.
Letwin, Shirley. 1975. Nature, History and Morality. In *Nature and Conduct*, ed. R.S. Peters, 229–250. London: Macmillan.
MacDonald, Graham A. 2012. The Politics of the Golden River: Ruskin on Environment and the Stationary State. *Environment and History* 18 (1): 125–150.
MacIntyre, Alasdair. 2007. *After Virtue*. 3rd ed. Notre Dame: Notre Dame University Press.
MacPherson, C.B. 1962. *The Political Theory of Possessive Individualism*. Oxford: Clarendon Press.
Maitland, Frederick W. 1913. *The Constitutional History of England*. Cambridge: Cambridge University Press.
Masterman, Lucy. 1939. *C.F.G. Masterman*. London: Nicolson and Watson.
McKeiver, Philip P. 2007. *A New History of Cromwell's Irish Campaign*. Manchester: Advance Press.
McNeill, William H. 1989. *Arnold J. Toynbee*. New York: Oxford University Press.
———. 1995. *Keeping Together in Time: Dance and Drill in Human History*. Cambridge, MA: Harvard University Press.
Meadows, Donella H. 1972. *The Limits to Growth: A Report for the Club of Rome's Project on the Predicament of Mankind*. New York: Universe Books.
Mendilow, Jonathan. 1986. *The Romantic Tradition in British Political Thought*. London: Croom Helm.
Meyhew, Robert J., ed. 2016. *New Perspectives on Malthus*. Cambridge: Cambridge University Press.
Mill, John Stuart. 1965. *Principles of Political Economy: Book IV*. Toronto: University of Toronto Press.
Milne, Doreen J. 1951. The Results of the Rye House Plot and Their Influence upon the Revolution of 1688. *Transactions of the Royal Historical Society 5th Series* 1: 91–108.
Mishan, E.J. 1969. *The Costs of Economic Growth*. Harmondsworth: Penguin Books Ltd.
Montague, F.C. 1889. *Arnold Toynbee*. Baltimore: Johns Hopkins University.
Morley, Edith J. 1917. *John Ruskin and Social Ethics*, Fabian Tract No. 179. London: Fabian Society.
Mumford, Lewis. 1938. *The Culture of Cities*. Boston: Harcourt, Brace and Co.
Nederman, Cary J. 1988. A Duty to Kill: John of Salisbury's Theory of Tyrannicide. *Review of Politics* 51: 365–389.

———. 1992. Freedom, Community and Function: Communitarian Lessons of Medieval Political Theory. *American Political Science Review* 86 (4): 977–986.
———. 2009. *Lineages of European Political Thought: Explorations Along the Medieval/Modern Divide from John of Salisbury to Hegel.* Washington, DC: Catholic University Press of America.
Nicolson, Harold. 1948. *The Congress of Vienna.* London: Constable.
Norman, E.R. 1987. *The Victorian Christian Socialists.* Cambridge: Cambridge University Press.
Norman, Jesse. 2013. *Edmund Burke: The First Conservative.* New York: Basic Books.
Oakeshott, Michael. 1975. *On Human Conduct.* Oxford: Oxford University Press.
———. 1993. In *Religion, Politics and the Moral Life*, ed. Timothy Fuller. New Haven: Yale University Press.
Oleson, Tryggvi J. 1955. *The Witengemot in the Reign of Edward the Confessor.* Toronto: University of Toronto Press.
Pares, Richard. 1971. *Limited Monarchy in Great Britain in the Eighteenth Century.* London: The Historical Association.
Peters, R.S., ed. 1975. *Nature and Conduct.* London: Macmillan.
Plamenatz, John. 1966. *The English Utilitarians.* Oxford: Basil Blackwell.
Playfair, Lyon. 1899. *Memoirs and Correspondence.* London: Cassell.
Pocock, J.G.A. 1987. *The Ancient Constitution and the Feudal Law.* 2nd ed. Cambridge: Cambridge University Press.
———. 2003. With a New Afterword. In *The Machiavellian Moment: Florentine Political Thought and the Atlantic Republican Tradition.* Princeton: Princeton University Press.
Quinton, Anthony. 1978. *The Politics of Imperfection.* London: Faber and Faber.
Rocker, Rudolf. 1989. *Anarcho-Syndicalism.* London: Pluto Press.
Rosenberg, John D. 1961. *The Darkening Glass.* New York: Columbia University Press.
Rosser, Gervase. 2015. *The Art of Solidarity in the Middle Ages: Guilds in England, 1250–1550.* Oxford: Oxford University Press.
Rubinstein, Nicolai. 1958. Political Ideas in Sienese Art. *Journal of the Warburg and Courtauld Institute* 21: 197–207.
Schuyler, R.L., and Corine C. Weston. 1961. *Cardinal Documents in British History.* New York: Van Nostrand.
Scott, Edith Hope. 1931. *Ruskin's Guild of St. George.* London: Methuen.
Secrest, Meryle. 1992. *Frank Lloyd Wright: A Biography.* New York: Knopf.
Sherburne, James Clark. 1972. *John Ruskin and the Ambiguities of Abundance: A Study in Social and Economic Criticism.* Cambridge, MA: Harvard University Press.

Skinner, Quentin. 1978. *The Foundations of Modern Political Thought: Volume One: The Renaissance*. Cambridge: Cambridge University Press.

———. 1985. *Ambrogio Lorenzetti: The Artist as Political Philosopher*. London: The British Academy.

Smith, Sydney. 1850. *Elementary Sketches of Moral Philosophy*. New York: Harper and Bros.

Southgate, Donald. 1965. *The Passing of the Whigs, 1832–1886*. London: Macmillan.

Spence, Margaret E. 1957. *The Guild of St. George*. Manchester: Manchester University Press.

Stanlis, Peter. 1965. *Edmund Burke and the Natural Law*. Ann Arbor: Michigan State University Press.

Starn, Randolph. 1994. *Ambrogio Lorenzetti: The Palazzo Pubblico, Siena*. New York: George Brazillier.

Starr, Christopher. 2007. *Medieval Mercenary: Sir John Hawkwood of Essex*. Essex: Essex Record Office.

Sutherland, Lucy S., ed. 1966. *Studies in History*. London: Oxford University Press.

Tate, W.E. 1969. *The Parish Chest: A Study of the Records of Parochial Administration in England*. 3rd ed. Cambridge: Cambridge University Press.

Thomis, Malcolm I., and Peter Hold. 1977. *Threats of Revolution in Britain, 1789–1848*. Hamdon: Archon Books.

Tierney, Brian. 1997. *The Idea of Natural Rights*. Grand Rapids: William B. Eerdman's.

Trevor-Roper, H.R. 1987. *Catholics, Anglicans and Puritans: 17th Century Essays*. London: Secker and Warburg.

Ward, Alan J. 1994. *The Irish Constitutional Tradition: Responsible Government and Modern Ireland, 1782–1992*. Dublin: Irish Academic Press.

Wardle, Peter, and Cedric Quayle. 1989. *Ruskin and Bewdley*. St. Albans: Brentham Press.

Waterman, A.M.C. 1991. *Revolution, Economics and Religion: Christian Political Economy, 1798–1833*. Cambridge: Cambridge University Press.

Weston, Corine C. 1981. *Subjects and Sovereigns: The Grand Controversy Over Sovereignty in Stuart England*. Cambridge: Cambridge University Press.

Wheeler, Michael. 1999. *Ruskin's God*. Cambridge: Cambridge University Press.

Whitehouse, W.H., ed. 1920. *Ruskin the Prophet*. London: George Allen and Unwin.

Wilde, Oscar. 1891. *The Soul of Man Under Socialism*. London: Humboldt.

Willey, Basil. 1940. *The Eighteenth Century Background*. London: Chatto and Windus.

Erratum to: John Ruskin's Politics and Natural Law

Graham A. MacDonald

G. A. MacDonald, *John Ruskin's Politics and Natural Law*,
https://doi.org/10.1007/978-3-319-72281-8

DOI 10.1007/978-3-319-72281-8

The figure illustration credits were missing in the original publication which is now updated.

The updated original online version if this book can be found at https://doi.org/10.1007/978-3-319-72281-8

G. A. MacDonald, *John Ruskin's Politics and Natural Law*,
https://doi.org/10.1007/978-3-319-72281-8_9

Appendix 1: Ruskin on Republicanism

This text is an abridged version of a letter from Ruskin to his Father, 24 Aug. 1845, sent from Baveno, Italy. It concerns his wide reading interests at that time and his conclusions about republicanism.[1]

My Dearest Father.

... I have been looking over the extracts you sent me from Arnold which are very full of sound sense[2]...That respecting the incomprehensibleness of English gentlemen to Messrs. Guizot & Sismondi is very good also, & yet as the servant says of Coriolanus, there is more in Sismondi than I could think – he is a good deal in the right in several points. His great theory is the necessity of giving men at some period of their life a high & ungoverned position, in order that the preparation for it & the expectation of it may give the utmost dignity & energy to the individual character – and of this there can indeed be no dispute, that men become new creatures altogether according to the responsibilities entrusted to them, & forces and faculties are developed in them of which they themselves were before altogether unconscious. Sismondi most truly says that in Florence, where every citizen of common respectability down to the lowest tradesman, had the chance, the probable chance, of becoming one of the twelve Anziani of supreme authority, the struggle to obtain this position, to make themselves fit for it, and the faculties developed in the possession of it, gave to the whole nation

G. A. MacDonald, *John Ruskin's Politics and Natural Law*,
https://doi.org/10.1007/978-3-319-72281-8

such force of character, for a time, as no other ever exhibited. But I conceive it to be a morbid excitement, & one essentially involving the necessity of following reaction & degradation. Such a government cannot subsist, it can have no settled principles, it is an admirable school for the people, but a miserable instrument in its own proper function – besides, even in the former end it must fail, more or less, according to the scale of the nation – in a city divided into twenty companies, it works well, but it is absurd altogether in a Kingdom of twenty provinces. Independent cities have some reason in being republican, but it must be at the expense of continual jealousies, wars, & seditions. Peace can only be secured by fixed positions of all ranks, and settled government of the whole. I want to study the English people under Elizabeth, for the development of intellect was then great under an absolute monarchy, & the King's love of Shakespeare is very glorious, but with that exception, there is nothing that the world has ever *shown* that can stand, intellectually, beside the power of mind thrown out by the fighting, falling, insane republicanism of Florence – in Giotto, Orcagna, & Dante, alone, its first fruits, with all the clusters of mighty ones their satellites... and gathering all into one great flash to expire under the Medicis in M. Angelo – nothing can be set beside this I say, except the parallel republicanism of fighting & falling Athens, giving us Aeschylus & Phidias & Aristophanes & Thucydides. But then there are such wide differences in republicanism. That of Florence is more opposed to that of America than our monarchy to the spirit of the French Revolution. The government of Florence was one of the most tyrannical in Italy – while it lasted – sweeping everything away that opposed it, banishing, executing, raising houses of rebellious families to the ground on the slightest provocation, and that with so strong a military arm that the people could not have the slightest power over it, it's popularity consisting solely in this, that every citizen had his two months turn at it, but no popular movement, no sedition, no clamour could affect in any way – it was iron bound and rock built, & nothing could overthrow it internally – when it fell, it fell by the loss of a battle equivalent to the annihilation of the state, though it is to be observed that this battle was brought up on the rashness of two of the popular members of the council. But surely there is something widely different between this Kingly & Authoritative republicanism and the "liberty" of America, where the nation is too vast to let its members have any share in the government, & therefore they have none at all.

I cannot conceive anything finer, as a school, than the Florentine system. Suppose you yourself knew that in a certain time you would be, during two months, one of twelve persons, who without any appeal or restriction, in a secret council, without the nation even knowing the object of their deliberations, could make or unmake laws & execute every measure they chose to adopt on the instant – would not this give you other views & thoughts than you have, & make you in every respect a greater man – while on the members of the government there was always the check of knowing that in two months, they were to sink again into entire... obedience to be subjected without appeal to the laws they...had made and the authority they had exercised with the remembrance of the good or evil they have done attached to their name. This is very different again, even from the popular assembly of Athens – a government of mob entirely, liable to be led by every demagogue, incomparably weaker & wilder than that of Florence, but developing intellect in the same way, owing to the minds of the people being all brought practically to bear on political matters. Both these governments in their brilliant instability, one may oppose to that of Venice, where we have the tyrannical government of Florence made hereditary – the moment it is so, the formation of an aristocracy makes it consistent, stable and powerful, but with the stability and power, ceases the development of intellect. Venice leaves no writers, and in art she leaves us a school entirely devoted to the musical part of it, not to the intellectual – of *art* per se she is mistress, but of art as a medium of mind, she...knows nothing. The stable monarchy-forms of Austria and Sardina seem nearly parallel cases. England leaves more appeal to the people, & draws more brains, but even she produces nothing great except in war-time.

Nothing can come of nothing – the French revolution brought out all the little intellect they had, and it was all froth & fury. Egypt, in old times is a curious instance of a people of enormous powers of mind kept entirely dormant in a fixed condition by unchangeableness of ranks & and authoritative monarchy & priesthood – we shall soon see in Bavaria, the utmost result of mind that can be obtained by the fostering power of monarchy without inherent energy of the people....

Appendix 2: Proposed Rules for Marriage Given in *Time and Tide* (1867)

1. Permission to marry should be the reward held in sight of its youth during the entire latter part of the course of their education.
2. It should be granted as the national attestation that the first portion of their lives had been rightly fulfilled.
3. It should not be attainable without earnest and consistent effort, though put within reach of all who were willing to make such effort.
4. The granting of it should be a public testimony to the fact that the youth or maid to whom it was given had lived within their proper sphere, a modest and virtuous life, and had attained such skill in their proper handicraft, and in arts of household economy as might give well-founded expectations of their being able honourably to maintain and teach their children.
5. No girl should receive her permission to marry before her seventeenth birthday, nor any youth before his twenty-first.
6. It should be a point of somewhat distinguished honour with both sexes to gain their permission of in the eighteenth and twenty-second years; and a recognized disgrace not to have gained it at least before the close of their twenty-first and twenty-fourth. I do not mean that they should in anywise hasten actual marriage; but only that they hold it a point of honour to have the right to marry.
7. In every year there should be two festivals, one in the first of May and one at the feast of harvest home, in each district at which… permissions to marry should be given publicly.

G. A. MacDonald, *John Ruskin's Politics and Natural Law*,
https://doi.org/10.1007/978-3-319-72281-8

8. Every bachelor and rosiere should be entitled to claim, if they needed it, according to their position in life a fixed income from the state, for seven ears from the day of their marriage, for the setting up of their homes; and however rich they might be by inheritance, their income should not be permitted to exceed a given sum, proportional to their rank, for the seven years following…but should accumulate in the trust of the state until that seventh year in which they should be put (on certain conditions) finally in possession of their property.
9. The men, thus necessarily not before their twenty-eighth nor usually later than their thirty-first year, become eligible to offices of state.

Appendix 3: Oath of the Guild of St. George[3]

I. I trust in the Living God, Father Almighty, Maker of heaven and earth and of all things and creatures, visible and invisible.

I trust in the kindness of his law, and the goodness of his work. And I will strive to love Him, and keep His law and see His work, while I live.

II. I trust in the nobleness of human nature, in the majesty of its faculties, the fulness of its mercy, and the joy of its love.

III. I will labour, with such strength and opportunity as God gives me, for my own daily bread; and all that my hand finds to do, I will do with my might.

IV. I will not deceive, or cause to be deceived, any human being for my gain or pleasure; nor hurt or cause to be hurt, any human being for my gain or pleasure.

V. I will not kill or hurt any living creature needlessly, nor destroy any beautiful thing, but will strive to save and comfort all gentle life, and guard and perfect all natural beauty upon the earth.

VI. I will strive to raise by own body and soul daily into higher powers of duty and happiness; not in rivalship or contention with others, but for the help, delight and honour of others, and for the joy and peace of my own life.

G. A. MacDonald, *John Ruskin's Politics and Natural Law*,
https://doi.org/10.1007/978-3-319-72281-8

VII. I will obey all the laws of my country faithfully; and the orders of its monarch, and of all persons appointed to be in authority under its monarch, so far as such laws or commands are consistent with what I suppose to be the law of God; and when they are not, or seem to be in anywise in need of change, I will oppose them loyally and deliberately, not with malicious, concealed or disorderly violence.

VIII. And with the same faithfulness, and under the limits of the same obedience, which I render to the laws of my country, and the commands of its rulers, I will obey the laws of the Society called of St. George, into which I am this day received; and the orders of its masters, and of all persons appointed to be in authority under its masters, so long as I remain a Companion, called of St. George.

Appendix 4: Ruskin's Translation from More's Utopia

The following is Ruskin's own translation from the Latin of a section of Book II of Thomas More's *Utopia* that he found instructive. It appeared in Letter No. 7 of *Fors Clavigera* (July, 1871), when commencing his ideas for the Guild of St. George. Reproduced from *Works*, 27: 118. Ruskin worked from Arber's 1869 edition, which in turn drew upon the 1556 edition of *Utopia*.

'The chief, and almost the only business of the government, is to take care that no man may live idle, but that every one may follow his trade diligently: yet they do not wear themselves out with perpetual toil from morning to night, as if they were beasts of burden, which, as it is indeed a heavy slavery, so it is everywhere the common course of life amongst all mechanics except the Utopians; but they, dividing the day and night into twenty-four hours, appoint six of these for work, three of which are before dinner three after; the then sup, and, at eight o'clock, counting from noon, go to bed and sleep eight hours: the rest of their time, besides that taken up in work, eating and sleeping, is left to every man's discretion; yet they are not to abuse that interval to luxury and idleness, but must employ it in some proper exercise, according to their virtuous inclinations, which is, for the most part, reading.

But the time appointed for labour is to be narrowly examined, otherwise, you may imagine that, since there are only six hours appointed for work, they

G. A. MacDonald, *John Ruskin's Politics and Natural Law*,
https://doi.org/10.1007/978-3-319-72281-8

may fall under a scarcity of necessary provisions: but it is so far from being true that this time is not sufficient for supplying them with plenty of all things, either necessary or convenient that it is rather too much and this you will easily apprehend, if you consider how great a part of all other nations is quite idle. First, women generally do little, who the half of mankind; and if some few women are diligent, their husbands are idle: then consider the great company of idle priests, and of those that are called religious men; add to these, all rich men, chiefly those that have estates in land, who are called noblemen and gentlemen, together with their families, made up of idle persons, that are kept more for show than use; add to these, all those strong and lusty beggars that go about, pretending some disease in excuse for their begging; and upon the whole account, you will find that the number of those by whose labours mankind is supplied is much less than you, perhaps, imagined: then, consider how few of those that work are employed in labours that are of real service! for we, who measure all things by money, give rise to many trades that are both vain and superfluous, and serve only to support riot and luxury: for if those who work were employed in such things as the conveniences of life require, there would be such an abundance of them, *that the prices of them would so sink that tradesmen could not be maintained by their gains.* if all those who labour about useless things were set to more profitable employments, and if all that languish out their lives in sloth and idleness (every one of whom consumes as much as any two of the men that are at work) were forced to labour, you may easily imagine that a small proportion of time would serve for doing all that is either necessary, profitable, or pleasant to mankind, especially while pleasure is kept within its due bounds: this appears very plainly in Utopia; for there, in a great city, and in all the territory that lies round it, you can scarce find five hundred, either men or women, by their age and strength capable of labour, that are not engaged in it! Even the heads of government, though excused by the law, yet do not excuse themselves, but work, that, by their examples, they may excite the industry of the rest of the people.

Notes

1. The letter is printed in *Works*, 36: 55–57 and also, in a more complete form and with comments, in Harold I. Shapiro, ed., *Ruskin in Italy:Letters To His Parents, 1845* (Oxford: Clarendon Press, 1972), 183–86.
2. The reference is to A.P. Stanley's *Life and Correspondence of Thomas Arnold* (1844).
3. *Works*, 28: 419–20.

Index[1]

A

B

[1]Note: Page numbers followed by 'n' refer to notes

G. A. MacDonald, *John Ruskin's Politics and Natural Law*,
https://doi.org/10.1007/978-3-319-72281-8

The manufacturer's authorised representative in the EU is Springer Nature Customer Service Centre GmbH, Europaplatz 3, 69115 Heidelberg, Germany. If you have any concerns regarding our products, please contact ProductSafety@springernature.com

Printed and bound by CPI Group (UK) Ltd, Croydon, CR0 4YY
05/10/2026
02228134-0001